Privatization Surprises in Transition Economies

Privatization Surprises in Transition Economies

Employee-Ownership in Central and Eastern Europe

Edited by

Milica Uvalic
Associate Professor of Economic Policy and Director of the Institute
of Economic Studies, University of Perugia, Italy

and

Daniel Vaughan-Whitehead
Senior Adviser, Central and Eastern European Team,
International Labour Office, Hungary

Edward Elgar
Cheltenham, UK • Lyme, US

Published by
Edward Elgar Publishing Limited
8 Lansdown Place
Cheltenham
Glos GL50 2HU
UK

Edward Elgar Publishing, Inc.
1 Pinnacle Hill Road
Lyme
NH 03768
US

A catalogue record for this book is available from the British Library

Library of Congress Cataloguing-in-Publication Data
Privatization surprises in transition economies : employee-ownership
   in Central and Eastern Europe / edited by Milica Uvalic and Daniel
   Vaughan-Whitehead.
       Includes index.
       1. Employee ownership—Europe, Eastern. 2. Privatization—Europe,
   Eastern. 3. Employee ownership—Europe, Central. 4. Privatization—
   Europe, Central. I. Uvalic, Milica. II. Vaughan-Whitehead,
   Daniel.
       HD5660.E915P75 1997
       331.2'164—dc21   96-52677
                                                                        CIP

ISBN 1 85898 621 4

Printed and bound in Great Britain by Hartnolls Limited, Bodmin, Cornwall

Contents

List of Tables and Figures

Tables

Figures

Foreword

The important question of management restructuring or what might be called 'corporate governance restructuring' has recently become the focus of debates on the transition in Central and Eastern Europe. A closely related aspect which has potentially massive implications and which has received remarkably less analytical attention is the development of employee share-ownership. The aim of this book is to investigate the extent and likely impact of employee ownership on the transition process under way in Central and Eastern Europe, and to identify its particular strengths and deficiencies as a privatization strategy.

At the beginning of the transition, the literature on economic reform was critical of the potential role of employee ownership in enterprise restructuring. Numerous external experts advised governments in the region to avoid this type of privatization, as likely to lead to a tremendous increase in wages and inflationary pressures, a deterioration in economic performance, considerable delays in restructuring, labour hoarding and a low propensity to carry out the necessary investment.

Paradoxically, despite this critical – and often ideologically oriented – starting position, employee ownership has rapidly become a predominant property form in much of Central and Eastern Europe. The Czech and Slovak Republics aside, the vast majority of countries in the region have promoted employee ownership through specific policies and legislative frameworks, bringing Central and Eastern Europe to the forefront in this respect. Enterprises with majority employee-owned enterprises are found to be particularly prevalent for instance in Russia, Romania, Poland, Hungary and Slovenia. In addition, the transfer of minority shares to employees is another common feature of nearly all privatization programmes in Central and Eastern Europe. This book tries to explain the different motivations behind this large-scale development, while describing how the resulting institutional arrangements vary between countries.

At a time when most countries of the region are still entrenched in the privatization process, ILO-CEET decided to carry out a comparative project on this topic in order to provide the different governments with more empirical evidence on the privatization process and to help them to make predictions concerning some aspects of the behaviour of firms privatized to their employees. The contributors to this volume have tried to address the problem of the lack of empirical evidence on the economic and social effects of this property form through a series of surveys and enterprise case studies which are presented here for the first time.

The practical results are much more encouraging than the theory predicted. Despite its possible drawbacks compared with other property forms, employee ownership in certain conditions can contribute to the development of a market economy. The contributors also emphasize that enabling workers and management to purchase ownership can in many cases lead to more productive and efficient behaviour. Employee ownership is presented in some chapters as superior in some situations to many other property options, and certainly better than the status quo in which state-owned enterprises predominate. Another aspect often neglected in the current debates on transition, and one to which we would like to attract attention, is the role of privatization in providing social motivation and in preventing social upheaval. In a context of growth of income inequalities, falling real wages – when they are paid at all – and increasing poverty, employee ownership could play an important role in partly compensating the costs that the reforms have entailed for a large proportion of employees, and more generally in promoting economic democracy and creating a new basis for redistributive justice.

The present volume does not favour one form of privatization over another, and this comparative study should be seen as part of a series of studies on the different types of privatized enterprise currently being carried out by the ILO within a vast privatization framework programme. Indeed, one of the main conclusions of this book is that governments should try systematically to follow various privatization paths, several company examples presented in this book indicating for instance that a combination of property forms could be promising in the transition process. It is hoped that it will encourage others to probe more deeply into some of the issues discussed here.

In the preparation of this volume the ILO has been particularly fortunate to be able to count on the contribution of highly knowledgeable experts involved in this field in a wide number of countries of the region. We also had kind assistance from colleagues in Budapest and elsewhere. In particular, we would like to thank Katalin Hárskuti of ILO-CEET for her unfailing assistance, and James Patterson who performed both the copyediting and the typesetting.

Oscar de Vries Reilingh
Director ILO-CEET

List of Contributors

Mark Klinedinst, Associate Professor at the University of Southern Mississippi, USA. Received his doctorate from Cornell University in 1987. Currently he serves on the Board of Directors of the International Association for the Economics of Participation and on the Indian Springs Farmers Co-operative. His research interests include: labour and management decision-making, transition policies in Eastern Europe – especially in Bulgaria – co-operatives, credit unions, employee ownership, union strategies and econometrics.

Josef Kotrba, Senior Researcher at the Economic Institute of the Academy of Sciences of the Czech Republic and Assistant Professor at CERGE of the Charles University, Prague. He is also a member of the board of the Czech Economic Association and a research affiliate of the Centre for Economic Policy Reform, London. His main fields of research are industrial organization, privatization, and economic transformation in Central and Eastern Europe.

György Lajtai, Research Manager at the GKI Economic Research Institute, Budapest. Between 1992 and 1994 he was the Director of Economics at the State Property Agency, responsible for the development of new preferential schemes in privatization. Before this he was also the head of ETOSZ, a consulting firm providing privatization services for employees and trade unions.

Bogdan Lissovolik is a Russian economist with the Moscow Office of the IMF. He obtained his MA and PhD degrees in economics from the European University Institute, Florence. His main field of research is the economics of transition with particular emphasis on the macroeconomic aspects of economic reform in the Russian economy.

Costea Munteanu, Professor of International Economics at the Academy of Economy Studies, Bucharest. Former secretary of state at the Department for Economic Reform. Founding member of the Romanian Economic Society (SOREC) and the European Association for Comparative Economic Studies (EACES).

Niels Mygind is Associate Professor at the Copenhagen Business School and Director of the Centre for East European Studies. His research interests include the effects of different ownership structures and he is currently researching the transition in Central and Eastern Europe.

Domenico Mario Nuti, Professor of Comparative Economic Systems at Rome University and Visiting Professor at the London Business School. Formerly he was an economic adviser to the European Commission on transition economies, and for the last two years he has been an economic adviser to the Government of Poland.

Charles Rock, Professor of Economics at Rollins College, USA. He has worked on the theoretical and practical problems of financing democratic enterprises for several years, and more specifically on co-operatives, forms of workers' participation and comparative economic performance.

Milica Uvalic, Associate Professor of Economic Policy at the University of Perugia. Formerly she worked at the European University Institute in Florence on the socialist economies (particularly former Yugoslavia) and on workers' participation in Western Europe. She has recently been involved in the preparation of a privatization project in the Federal Republic of Yugoslavia.

Daniel Vaughan-Whitehead, Senior Wage Adviser for the ILO's Central and Eastern European Team in Budapest. Before joining the ILO he worked for the European Commission. He has been advising governments from the European Union and Central and Eastern Europe for several years on wages and incomes policy, and forms of privatization, including employee ownership.

1. Introduction: Creating Employee Capitalism in Central and Eastern Europe

Milica Uvalic and Daniel Vaughan-Whitehead

1 INTRODUCTION

For the past two decades, at the heart of capitalism, advanced Western economies have had to cope with a sustained economic crisis. This has led them increasingly to adopt forms of economic democracy, involving employee participation in enterprise results (through profit-sharing, employee share-ownership, or both). Growing interest in these arrangements has been observed not only within academic circles, but also among politicians and governments, trade union organizations, employers' and other associations. The theoretical debate on the potential benefits of employee participation in enterprise results, together with the desire to introduce greater flexibility in payments systems and the commitment to a property-owning democracy (or what the British Labour Party calls a 'stakeholders' society'), have led governments in a number of Western countries to adopt measures actively stimulating their diffusion, which in turn has contributed to the growth of such arrangements.

Employee participation in enterprise results also became one of the priority objectives of the European Commission in the implementation of the *Social Charter for Basic Social Rights of Workers* (European Commission, 1989).[1] A Recommendation was proposed by the Commission, adopted in July 1992 by the European Council, inviting member states to promote the spread of such arrangements (Council of the European Communities, 1992). Among the main reasons for active EU support is the conviction that such schemes are

---

[1] This initiative led to the preparation of the 'PEPPER Report' – 'PEPPER' standing for the Promotion of Employee Participation in Profits and Enterprise Results – in which the experience with these schemes in the single EU countries in the past decade was reviewed (Uvalic, 1991).

1

likely to have beneficial effects on workers' productivity, and so enhance European competitiveness, particularly with regard to its two main competitors, the USA and Japan, which have promoted profit-sharing and employee ownership schemes on a more substantial scale than EU countries.

Strong new interest in employee ownership recently emerged also in the transition economies of Central and Eastern Europe. Following the radical political and economic changes in these countries in 1989, which initiated the transition to multi-party democracies and mixed market economies, employee ownership became highly relevant within the privatization process. In many countries it turned out to be a very important, sometimes even dominant, channel of ownership transformation.

Nevertheless, the impact of this property form on restructuring, economic performance and industrial relations has not been much investigated. This is not surprising, considering that privatization in Central and Eastern Europe is relatively recent and is still an ongoing process, even in the most advanced transition economies. Due to the short period since privatization in Central and Eastern Europe started, evidence on the relationship between various methods of ownership transformation and enterprise performance is scarce. In particular, it is still unclear what employee ownership implies for enterprise performance, and judgements on its impact are only just beginning to emerge. This is the main reason why the present volume focuses on employee ownership in Central and East European transition economies, including both management and worker ownership. Its first objective is to provide a comprehensive review of employee ownership experiences in the region, and to explain how they have been implemented within the privatization process. Its second aim is to present new empirical evidence concerning the social and economic effects of employee ownership as a privatization method, with a view to identifying under what conditions and with what complementary elements employee ownership could become more successful and achieve its expected objectives, including the introduction of democracy to the privatization process as a whole. Of particular concern is the impact on the restructuring process (employment, wages, investment). On the basis of these findings, we identify some policy options that could be followed by governments, and also closely analyse the important role that trade unions and employers' organizations could play in this regard.

2 DIFFERENT PRIVATIZATION ROUTES

Different privatization routes have been pursued in Central and Eastern Europe, usually based on a combination of various methods and techniques. First, the restitution of state assets nationalized after the War to their original owners. Second, 'small privatization', which consists in the sale of small items of state property, such as houses, catering establishments, shops or small plots of land. Third, so-called 'mass privatization' understood as the disposal of a large proportion of state assets to the whole population; almost everywhere it has taken the form of distribution of privatization vouchers – free of charge or subject to a registration fee – to all citizens, either directly or through mutual funds. Fourth, the lease-back of the firm's assets to its management and workers, in which the enterprise remains the property of the state but is leased to the workers and managers before being totally converted into non-state enterprises.[2] Fifth, a part of state property is offered for sale, using a variety of methods, to domestic and foreign private owners. Finally, the privileged sale of part or the whole of state enterprises to their employees and/or managers.

Whereas initially the primary aim of privatization in Central and Eastern Europe – to transform existing state-owned firms into private enterprises – seemed fairly simple, with the passage of time it has become clear that privatization was the easy part, since improved enterprise performance depends, in addition to ownership changes, on a number of other elements. In fact, the transfer of enterprise assets from the state to private owners has in many cases not been sufficient to improve overall enterprise performance and to introduce an effective system of corporate governance. The differences in enterprise behaviour have crucially been determined by the privatization methods chosen, which in turn have led to very different ownership structures – majority ownership by insiders (workers and managers), majority ownership by domestic outside owners (most frequently individual voucher holders, or institutional owners such as investment funds), and majority ownership by outside foreign owners. These alternative ownership structures are expected to lead to different enterprise behaviour, since the objectives of employees, managers and outside investors usually vary considerably.

In Central and Eastern Europe, however, the choice of privatization methods, and therefore the emerging ownership structures, have been seriously constrained by a number of specific features of transition economies. The traditional method of sale used in privatizations in Western market economies could not be extensively used in transition economies because of limited private savings, highly underdeveloped capital markets, and the limited interest of foreign investors. Sales to private owners, even when adopted as a priority privatization method, have faced enormous problems. While a number of countries – including Hungary, Estonia, Romania and Poland – have tried to sell at least some state-owned enterprises

---

[2] This property form is thus a temporary measure, the enterprise then being converted into another property form, generally a joint-stock company.

to either foreign or domestic outside owners, only Hungary and Estonia have managed to privatize a significant share of their state enterprises through direct sales (World Bank, 1996), and only Hungary has been able to sell a substantial share of assets to foreigners. Consequently, in practically all Central and East European countries most enterprise assets privatized so far have ended up being transferred (or sold on favourable terms) to insiders, or have been distributed to citizens through mass privatization programmes.

3 DISILLUSION WITH MASS PRIVATIZATION

One of the most striking features of the privatization process in Central and Eastern Europe has been the widespread reliance on mass privatization (Nuti, 1995a). This innovative method has been promoted, usually using the voucher option, with the aim of privatizing very quickly most state-owned assets.

The Czech-Slovak programmes primarily used the voucher system. Individual citizens could acquire vouchers for a nominal fee (in the former Czechoslovakia) and use them to purchase shares in enterprises. Citizens could also entrust their vouchers to one or more of the newly-established investment funds. Russia also developed the voucher system, where one of the options ensured substantial worker and management ownership. In Romania 30 per cent of state-owned enterprise assets have been distributed to citizens through mutual funds.

A voucher scheme was also implemented in Ukraine. Poland is now (1996) implementing its mass privatization plan after a lengthy preparatory process. The long-awaited mass privatization in Poland will transfer the shares of 514 companies to fifteen National Investment funds the certificates of which will be given to investors in exchange for subsidized vouchers (Nuti, Chapter 6). Such a programme was also launched in Albania in early 1996, while Bulgaria is presently launching its own version.

Mass privatization through vouchers was expected to have a number of advantages. Perhaps its principal advantage is that it involves all citizens in the privatization process without favouring specific population groups, and so is considered to be highly equitable. The creation of 'large-scale capitalism' in this manner is particularly important with regard to the social consequences of the transition. Moreover, mass privatization was considered the fastest possible privatization method since it ensures an almost instant transfer of property rights to private owners. Thus it was expected that it would also lead to the rapid fulfilment of other important transition objectives, such as well functioning commercial and financial markets, rapid enterprise restructuring and an increase in profitability.

It became clear after the first few years of reform, however, that the advantages of mass privatization had been overestimated, as various difficulties began to appear which had not been anticipated.

This approach has shown how difficult it is to allocate equal shares in all enterprises to the entire population: in most cases the state distributed to each citizen a certificate equivalent to a certain number of equity shares to be used for bidding for shares in any state-owned enterprise. The general public could not obtain sufficient information about individual enterprises, however, as a consequence of which bids were registered effectively only for a few well-known or well-advertised firms. As a result, these enterprises have been overvalued, while the shares of other enterprises became undervalued, or there were no buyers for them at all, leaving them in the hands of the state.

Another major disadvantage of these schemes is the loss of potential revenues for the government, since they do not bring any cash to the state from the privatization process. Nor does it provide for the firms themselves the resources necessary for restructuring (Estrin, 1996). It also became clear that the population would have to pay for this hand-out either in higher taxes or lower public expenditure, or a combination of both, so increasing the social costs of transition. According to Stiglitz (1995, p. 185), the give-away of the nation's capital to private individuals can be viewed as negative lump-sum transfers which will necessitate the imposition of higher, distortionary taxes in the future.

The speed of mass privatization has also not corresponded to overoptimistic initial expectations. Technical implementation periods have turned out to be longer than anticipated. In the Czech Republic, the whole process of voucher privatization took more than two years (Kotrba, Chapter 4). Numerous obstacles contributed to slowing down the process, with 'endless opportunities for mistakes, delays, diversions, reversals, almost at every step' (Nuti, 1995a). The most spectacular delay has occurred in Poland. By mid–1994 – four years after the first Act on Privatization (June 1990) was passed by the Polish Parliament, which was supposed to pave the way for mass privatization – not a single state enterprise had been privatized through this method (Chapter 6).

Voucher schemes were also found to lead to a high dispersion of shareholders, so that no individual is able or willing to engage in effective control over the enterprise. The resulting ownership pattern is likely to be extremely diffuse, significantly weakening corporate governance during the crucial transition period; dispersed shareholders also have difficulty in monitoring management performance. In the Czech Republic, the new holders of shares and fund certificates do not seem in a position to exercise effective control over resource allocation in the joint-stock companies of which they are ultimate owners. For the same reason, it is very difficult to convert or to transfer this property form, for example to a foreign or domestic individual investor or investor group, who would have to identify citizens with vouchers who are interested in pursuing a given transaction (Bogetic and Conte, 1992).

The Polish scheme is specifically designed to prevent the emergence of highly dispersed ownership, and the Czech and Slovak investment funds allowed some concentration of ownership to emerge spontaneously. But it is not yet clear whether mass privatizations can offer either effective owners, or allow the newly privatized firms to obtain additional financial resources through capital markets (Estrin, 1996, p.11).

The distribution of vouchers through mutual funds is one way of avoiding some of these problems. With mutual funds, the information requirements are much reduced, since individuals need to learn only about the performance of a few mutual funds. Mutual funds are also more capable of gathering information than most citizens, and are better able to engage in enterprise monitoring and management control. Mutual funds have also led to a series of problems, however, as they have a tendency to seek immediate returns to protect the share value of the fund itself. This might induce mutual funds to avoid massive restructuring aimed at rendering the enterprise profitable in the long run, a course usually incompatible with expectations of high short-term investment returns. For the same reason, they have a tendency to get involved only in the restructuring of the most efficient enterprises. Moreover, at least until recently, mutual funds have been reluctant to intervene in corporate governance. If the markets for shares develop, investment funds paradoxically may not be interested in monitoring and restructuring individual enterprises, as they may simply invest in the market index, like funds in developed market economies (Aoki, 1995, p. 13). When outside control is significant – as in the Czech Republic – the current institutional relationships (between investment funds, banks and firms, for example) have weakened efficiency (EBRD, 1995, p.128). The close and reciprocal ownership ties between the investment funds and banks raise concerns about the governance and performance of funds; in fact, in the Czech Republic, the main investment funds are themselves indirectly owned by the major banks (EBRD, 1995, p.136), which are still owned by the state. Also, a privatized firm with dispersed outside ownership in the hands of individual voucher holders does not have the same governance structure as a firm with a core outside owner (e.g. a foreign investor). Dispersed individual voucher holders will typically have only a limited ability to introduce deep restructuring policies. Investment funds, even when they are core owners, may lack the access to finance and expertise, and even the internal governance structure, to implement the appropriate restructuring policies within the enterprises they own (EBRD, 1995, p.129). In this regard, some have argued that the ceilings sometimes imposed on mutual funds – as in the Czech Republic where the legislation imposed a 20 per cent ceiling on a single investment fund's ownership – would be a major drawback since they may retard the resale of shares to investment funds and so delay restructuring. This restriction is also held to constitute a problem for effective supervision, in that a 20 per cent shareholder will have less incentive to monitor the firm than a 50 per cent shareholder (EBRD, 1995, p.130). Of course, in order for funds to diversify, or to better manage the companies, they must be very large. However, this approach neglects the high risks related to high capital concentration.

In fact, this is one of the other main criticisms of mass privatization through the intervention of mutual funds: extremely large concentrations of wealth and decision-making power which are not easy to monitor, not only for citizens, but also for the state. These large-scale operations can lead in some cases to corruption and inefficiency. In particular, there are fears that they would lead in some cases to enterprise control by foreigners, through their management of mutual funds. There have been complaints of such a concentration process in the Czech Republic. In practice, banks with government acquiescence ended up acquiring holdings which were fairly large. In Poland, National Investment Funds have been set up by the government which, because of the recognized lack of domestic expertise, will be managed by foreign management groups approved by the government (Nuti, Chapter 6). Excessive weight seems to have been attached to these financial intermediaries also in other countries. In Romania, for instance, holders of certificates of the Private Ownership Funds have had very little opportunity to influence the administration and so the performance of the fund.

It was expected that the issue of vouchers would lead to further growth in stock exchange volumes, and would help to consolidate ownership and control – often via investment funds – in newly privatized enterprises. Earlier hopes that voucher privatization would create a vast and liquid share market in a short period of time seem to have been overly optimistic, however. Markets in most countries are still illiquid, while the lack of company information is limiting the entry of foreign institutional investors.

In countries where vouchers/shares were tradable, a substantial number of citizens immediately sold them to boost their declining real wages and spent the additional income on consumer goods, so boosting inflation, while contributing to a plunge in the prices of the shares (Kornai, 1990). This underlined the need to prepare carefully any free distribution of vouchers and to explain the process to the population, so that they feel at ease with the whole privatization process and consider their vouchers as a form of savings. It also emphasized in some cases the advantages of the non-transferability of the vouchers or shares distributed to the population.

That mass privatization may not produce the best owners in the short run is today recognized even by the World Bank, which favoured this privatization form in the early years of transition.[3]

---

[3] Although it is still expected to 'lead to better corporate governance in the long run', if it promotes the development of capital markets (and subsequent rearrangements of ownership) and of intermediary monitoring institutions for the economy as a whole (World Bank, 1996, p.52).

Because of the problems associated with vouchers, the Slovak Republic has decided to focus more on trade sales and insider privatization in the context of its second privatization wave. Hungary has also reversed its direction by cancelling its Small Shareholders' Programme which envisaged voucher distribution in the second half of 1994, opting for direct trade sales and worker and management share-ownership (Lajtai, Chapter 5).

Russia has implemented a mass privatization programme, and so has Slovenia, but in both countries a clear preference was given to insiders (Lissovolik, Chapter 8, and Uvalic, Chapter 10). Other countries have rejected mass privatization (Macedonia, Serbia) or have introduced it only at a later stage and on a limited scale, because sales had brought disappointing results (Montenegro, Croatia). These trends have led to the diffusion of alternative methods, among which the sale of assets to employees has turned out to be dominant.

4 PRIVATIZATION BY DEFAULT

When the transition to a mixed market economy started in Central and Eastern Europe, governments (with very few exceptions) did not intend actively to stimulate substantial employee ownership, although in most privatization laws the sale of shares on privileged terms to insiders was included among the possible methods (*Table 1.1*). In fact, the last thing that the new post-communist leaders wished to promote was the emergence of significant forms of employee ownership, reminiscent of co-operatives and Yugoslav self-management, which they firmly rejected. One of the main policy prescriptions given at the beginning of the transition was that ownership and control of privatizing firms in the region ought to be vested in external shareholders.[4] Yet employee ownership emerged almost everywhere, and insiders – workers and managers – have frequently become significant, sometimes majority shareholders in their firms. In all the other countries of the region – with the exception of the former Czechoslovakia and to some extent Hungary – privatization has led to substantial ownership by insiders. Hungary is an exception because of the significant amount of foreign investment, although insider ownership has dominated in most other privatized firms (Estrin, 1996, p.13). In addition to majority employee ownership, the transfer of minority stakes to workers has been a common feature of most privatization programmes. Thus the overwhelming preponderance of insider privatization in the region is clear (Estrin, 1996, p.15).

---

[4] See more in Acs and FitzRoy (1994); the authors provide a good critique of such views and propose instead a model of employee ownership.

A specific form of privileged sales to employees are leveraged employee–management buy-outs, which became an alternative to mass privatization through vouchers in Central and Eastern Europe in terms of speed and political acceptability. Two main forms of employee ownership emerged: those in which management and employees acquire the majority holding of a firm and become its dominant owners, possibly in conjunction with other owners; and acquisitions of a minority of shares by employees, with the result that they do not acquire company control.

All or part of enterprise shares can be transferred free to the workers, following an egalitarian distribution system – the same number of shares for all employees – or according to seniority, wage rates or a combination of both. In most Central and East European countries, however, the government has sold shares to employees on preferential terms. An alternative to free transfer of ownership or sale on favourable terms is the employee leveraged buy-out, through mechanisms similar to Employee Stock Ownership Plans (ESOPs). The financing of these ESOP schemes may come from a variety of sources – such as private banks or the government – with repayment from future profits. With this system, employees are sure to have control of their enterprise. They appoint the manager and are involved in all strategic decisions. Employee share ownership has been implemented in a differentiated way. Russian plans have provided more gift equity to employees (25 per cent of shares in a corporatized enterprise), as well as greater opportunities to purchase stock at reduced prices (10 per cent of shares), and concessions to managers (allowed to buy a further 5 per cent). Alternatively, employees have the possibility to purchase a controlling interest in the enterprise (up to 51 per cent of shares). Shares have also been offered to workers in the privatization process in Hungary (up to 10 per cent of the capital), so that they represent 32 per cent of all transactions. In Poland, employees receive 20 per cent of capital privatized through trade sales and 15 per cent in companies in the mass privatization programme. Management and employee buy-outs are also the dominant method in Romanian privatization, and in Belarus, Georgia and Latvia (more than 95 per cent, 75 per cent and 70 per cent of all transactions respectively). They also play an important role in Estonian and Bulgarian sales (33 per cent of all transactions in both countries). Employees in Bulgaria can also buy a certain amount of shares at a 20 per cent discount (30 per cent in already transformed corporate state enterprises). In Lithuania at the end of 1995 employees controlled an average of 17 per cent of privatized equity. In Ukraine shares can be bought by workers using their privatization certificates directly placed on their bank accounts during mass privatization. A certain number of additional shares could also be bought in cash by employees for a nominal sum not exceeding 50 per cent of the nominal value of the vouchers (*Table 1.1*).

Table 1.1 Legislation on employee ownership in transition economies

Country	Relevant Law	Year of Adoption	Concession/ Discounts	General terms on	
				Deferred Payment	Limits
Bulgaria	Conversion & privatization law	1992	Prefer. sales 50% (large) 30% (small)	Not explicit	Up to 1 annual salary per employee; 20% of total;
	Amendments	1994		6 yrs	raised to 2 annual salaries per employee
	Mass privat. law	1995	Employees can exchange coupons for enterprise shares		
Croatia	Act on transform. of social firms & amendments	1991	Prefer. sales 20–60% linked to seniority	5 yrs	20,000 DM per employee, 50% of total.
	New privatization law	1996	Pref. sales: Free distribution to refugees, invalids, etc.	20 yrs	DM 7,000– 20,000
Czech Republic	Large-scale privat. law Commercial Code	1991 1991	Up to 10% of shares could be transformed into employee shares and sold for a lower price lowered to 5%		
Estonia	Small-scale privat. law Amendments	Dec. 1990 May 1992	Preemptive rights, variable discounts Preferences for insiders removed		20% of shares
Hungary	Transform. law Privat. law	1989 1992	Self-privat, preferential loans Preferential sales 50% In special cases/ Workers' shares 90%	3 yrs	10–15% of total 15% of equity up to 10% of equity
	ESOP law	1992	Subsidized credit for 15 years for 98% of price	Corporate tax benefits	No limits
	Privat. law	1995	Promotes both EMBOs and ESOPs Only 50% of share price can be financed through loans		

Table 1.1 cont.

Country	Relevant Law	Year of Adoption	Concessions/ Discounts	General Terms on	
				Deferred Payment	Limits
Latvia	Large privat. Decree	March 1991	Preferential price		No limits
	Small privat. law	Nov. 1991	Preemption rights		No limits
	New privat. law	March 1994			
Lithuania	Various laws	1990	Transfers of shares in leased firms to employees & preferential sales, paid partly by vouchers		10% of total
	LIPSP privat. law	1991	Variable discounts paid by vouchers		Limit increased to 30% (1992) & to 50% (1993) of which 20% without voting rights
	Amendments	1993	Preferential treatment of employees abolished		
Macedonia	Act on transform. of social firms	1993	30-70% linked to seniority	5 yrs	25,000 DM per employee, 30% of total
Montenegro	Act on property transform.	1992	30-70% linked to seniority	5 yrs	10,000 ECU per employee, 30% of total
	Amendments	1994	Pref. sales extended to 10 yrs Free distribution: up to 3,000 ECU per employee		10% of total
Poland	Privat. law Art. 37	1990	50%	Preferential interest rates Payments can be postponed for 2 years	1 annual wage, 20% of total; later lowered to 10% free, then raised to 15%
	Mass privat. law 114	1995	15% of capital reserved for employees (also farmers, fishermen)		

Privatization Surprises in Transition Economies

Table 1.1 cont.

Country	Relevant Law	Year of Adoption	Concessions/ Discounts	General Terms on	
				Deferred Payment	Limits
Romania	Privat. law no. 58	1991	10% lower than the highest bid		10% of total
	Law no. 114	1992	Ownership certificates can be exchanged for shares, but up to 30% of equity		
	Act on MEBOs no. 77	1994	In cash (subsidized credit), or in exchange for ownership certificates	5 yrs	
Russia	Mass privat.		Option 1: Employees get 25% of non-voting shares free, and can buy another 10% at a 30% discount; all payments in vouchers		5% for managers
			Option 2: Employees buy 51% of equity half of which can be paid in vouchers		
			Option 3: 1-year lease contract with an option to buy 20% of equity at a 30% discount		
Serbia	Act on transform. of social firms	1991	20–60% linked to seniority	5 yrs	20,000–30,000 DM per employee, 30-50% of total
Slovenia	Act on transform. of firms & amendments	1992	Sales at a 50% discount Free distribution	5 yrs	Up to 40% of equity and an additional 20% free
Ukraine	Act on privatization	1992	Possibility to convert vouchers into enterprise shares	3 yrs	Up to the value of the vouchers (Krbs 30,000)
	Act on privatization certificates	1992	Additional shares for cash		5% for managers

Source: Compiled by the editors.

Table 1.2 shows the extent of employee ownership in 1995. Empirical evidence presented in this volume confirms the large diffusion of employee ownership in most Central and East European countries.[5] In Russia, more than 15,000 enterprises had developed workers' and management share-ownership in the mass privatization programme. In addition, more than 5,000 enterprises were leased to workers' collectives, and most of these collectives are exercising their option to buy their enterprise. In Russia, Option 2 of the mass privatization programme (envisaging the purchase of up to 51 per cent of voting shares by insiders) was by far the most popular option; this option was used in more than 80 per cent of privatizations, and, on average, insiders have obtained 60–70 per cent of equity (Ash and Hare, 1994; Nuti, 1995b).[6] In Poland, insider buy-outs have represented the fastest privatization track so far, with about 1,500 buy-outs by mid-1994. At the end of 1995, employee buy-outs in the 'privatization through liquidation' programme, plus standard sales to management and employees, accounted for more than two-thirds of privatized companies.

In the Polish mass privatization programme vouchers will be converted exclusively into fund certificates, although employees in the enterprises taking part in the scheme are to acquire free of charge 15 per cent of the shares (Nuti, Chapter 6). In Romania, out of more than 1,400 commercial companies privatized by December 1995, 98 per cent have undergone privatization by the management–employee buy-out method (Munteanu, Chapter 7). In Hungary, by September 1994, there were already 184 cases of privatization through Employee Stock Ownership Plans (ESOPs) in which at least 40 per cent of employees were involved; in addition, 43 per cent of cases of self-privatization have been estimated to have resulted in dominant employee stakes (Nuti, 1995b). More than 2,700 enterprises had been privatized with more than 50 per cent of the enterprise voting equity belonging to workers and management. Management and employee buy-outs in Hungary – as in Estonia – often took place in the context of open tenders for company shares. In Lithuania, nearly all enterprises privatized so far have had an element of employee ownership (Mygind, Chapter 2), and the situation is similar in Ukraine (Vaughan-Whitehead, Chapter 9). In Bulgaria, after revision of the

---

[5] For a cross-country summary of the evidence, see Ellerman (1993), Earle and Estrin (1996), Nuti (1995a) and (1995b).

[6] Option 1 was the concession of 25 per cent of free shares, non-voting unless sold, plus an option of a further percentage of voting shares (10 per cent for workers and 5 per cent for administrative officers). Option 3 was the concession of 20 per cent of voting shares at book value for a group of workers and managers undertaking to restructure the enterprise within a year according to a plan; if successful, all workers and managers could acquire a further 20 per cent of the shares at a highly favourable rate. With all three options the rest of the shares were to be sold at public auctions to domestic and foreign investors.

Table 1.2 Extent of privatization methods in large privatization (by number of enterprises), Central and Eastern Europe, 1995

Country	Total no. of state-owned enterprises[1]	Trade sales (tenders, direct sales, auctions)		Mass privatization		Manag. and workers' share ownership		Public offering/ Capital markets	
		+ 50 per cent of enterprise voting equity	– 50 per cent of enterprise voting equity	+ 50 per cent of enterprise voting equity	– 50 per cent of enterprise voting equity	+ 50 per cent of enterprise voting equity	– 50 per cent of enterprise voting equity	+ 50 per cent of enterprise voting equity	– 50 per cent of enterprise voting equity
Bulgaria	3 500	286	–	–	–	109	–	–	–
Czech Republic	4 319	3 898	–	1 622	165	–	–	–	383
Estonia	500	357	–	–	2	120	–	–	–
Hungary	1 848	866	58	2	–	2 787	219	–	55
Latvia	650	45	–	–	39	200	–	–	3
Lithuania	4 800	62	1	2 920	–	–	1 500	–	–
Poland	8 200	142	12	–	–	806	–	22	–
Romania	7 100	10	–	–	–	981	–	9	96
Russia	31 000	40	–	4 400	11 520	11 520	4 480	–	–
Slovak Republic	1 265	361	–	392	111	–	–	–	–
Ukraine	3 500	1	–	49	–	3 500	–	–	–

1. Total number of state enterprises as estimated by the OECD at the starting point of privatization. During the privatization process many of these enterprises will be divided into smaller enterprises, and some will be wound up.

2. For comparative coupons.

Source: OECD estimates; OECD-CCET (1995), *Trends and Policies in Privatization, Annex 1*, pp. 61–62. See OECD report for information on other transition countries.

legislation in 1994, the purchase of shares on preferential terms by employees has been the most popular method in the privatization of small firms (see Rock and Klinedinst, Chapter 3). In former Yugoslavia, since both the 1989–90 Federal law on social capital, and the privatization laws adopted in the meantime by the governments of its successor states, envisage highly preferential conditions primarily for insiders, subscription of shares by employees has been the prevalent method so far in all countries (see Uvalic, Chapter 10).

According to the August 1995 regulations for mass privatization in Bulgaria, employees will be offered 20 per cent of their firm's shares at a reduced price (see Rock and Klinedinst, Chapter 3). By contrast, in the Czech Republic, although out of 1,688 companies privatized as joint-stock companies, 480 proposed (and received approval) to privatize part of their capital through the issue of employee shares, only a minority of firms (around 10 per cent) eventually exercised this option; thus after the first and second waves of privatization, employee shares represented only 3 per cent of the total number of shares in all joint-stock companies privatized by mid-1995 (see Kotrba, Chapter 4). As a result, employee-owned firms are rather rare in the Czech Republic. Among the few known cases is the machinery producer ZPS Zlin which explicitly encouraged its employees to invest in the company's shares; its employees, retired employees and citizens have formed an association of shareholders, which plays an important role as one of the largest local employers. Although a number of newspaper publishing companies were initially transformed into dominant employee-owned firms, due to economic difficulties all of these firms were later sold to foreign publishing groups. Many banks have also used employee ownership to improve motivation, but since in the meantime the price of shares has fallen, bank employees, instead of gaining, have actually incurred losses (Chapter 4).

This development was partly the result of public policy measures forced on the new governments by the need to implement a rapid and smooth transition; partly it happened by default. Employee ownership has emerged as an important privatization channel for a variety of reasons.

One of the most important is the political argument. At the beginning of the transition it was necessary to reach a social and political consensus on privatization. 'Political realities cannot be ignored. Where insiders are strong enough to block participation by outsiders, privatization to insiders is still better than keeping the assets under state ownership, especially in the case of small firms, where competition can quite easily force subsequent restructuring and ownership reshuffling' (World Bank, 1996, p.58). Had employee ownership not been included among the available options, this could have blocked the property transformation process. Some scholars justify the Russian privatization policy not in economic, but in purely political terms, noting that all other plans would have been politically unfeasible (Roland, 1995).

This policy was motivated also by social reasons, in order to obtain wide support for privatization among the working classes and to win employee support for the transition. This method could partly compensate for some of the negative consequences of the present economic reforms, such as the fall in real wages and mass unemployment.

Employee ownership was particularly important in countries with a long tradition of self-management (not only former Yugoslavia, but also Poland and, to a lesser extent, Hungary), in order to compensate for the employees' surrender of their previous self-management rights. Employee ownership was also introduced on a large scale in the transformation of former co-operatives in several countries.

In many cases, the low and often negative value of some state enterprises meant that there would not have been takers other than their employees; this seems to have been the case in Ukraine, but also in most other countries.

Given the general shortage of domestic capital and future uncertainty about profitability in most Central and East European economies, employees were usually in a better position than other domestic buyers. This was not because they had more capital, but simply because they had a better chance than would have been the case if domestic capital was more abundant among outsiders, since they possessed important inside information about their enterprise, and since external buyers felt more uncertainty about the possibility of transforming state-owned firms into dynamic well-performing enterprises.

Insufficient foreign direct investment has also greatly contributed to the frequent use of employee ownership as a privatization method. Since it is through private capital that the state can receive most substantial returns from the privatization process,[7] most Central and East European governments have tried to attract private and more particularly foreign companies by offering generous tax concessions. Joint ventures with foreign partners were also seen as a way of introducing new management techniques, new technologies and access to international markets. However, although the current growth in joint ventures is impressive in some countries, foreign investment has been mainly located in Hungary, Poland and the Czech Republic. The growth of foreign investment has so far been limited, mainly due to political and economic uncertainties. In 1995, some 20 per cent of enterprises sold in Estonia had been privatized with foreign investment, 14 per cent in Hungary, 10 per cent

---

[7] The reduction of the state deficit is a major objective of the privatization process in several countries. In Hungary, for instance, the government has asserted on several occasions that it intends to use revenues obtained from the sale of state property to service the country's internal and external debts.

Table 1.3 Foreign participation in privatization, Central and Eastern Europe, 1995

Country	Number of companies privatized with foreign participation	
	+50 per cent	−50 per cent
Bulgaria	14	–
Czech Republic	125	–
Hungary	102	23
Lithuania	46	-
Poland	60	10
Russia	28	–
Slovak Republic	–	–

Source: OECD estimates; OECD-CCET (1995), Annex 1, p. 64.

in Bulgaria, and less than 2 per cent in Lithuania. Russia has had very limited foreign investment with only 28 companies sold internationally through tenders (*Table 1.3*). Foreign investment could thus only complement other privatization forms.

In many cases, therefore, employees turned out to be the only potential buyers of enterprise shares, the only realistic option for subscribing capital and running the firm, the buyers of last resort (Ellerman, 1993). By becoming shareholders, they hoped to be able to prevent their firm from going bankrupt and so preserve their jobs; they also had most to lose if no change occurred in the current economic situation.

Another form of privatization – the lease-back of the firm's assets to its management and workers, which is generally a temporary property form, the enterprise then being converted into yet another property form – was also found to constitute a first step towards employee-owned enterprises. This happened on a wide scale primarily in Poland, in nearly 70 per cent of directly privatized enterprises (see Nuti, Chapter 6). In Russia and Ukraine, the employees of a few thousand leasehold enterprises are converting them into employee-owned enterprises.

5 POTENTIAL ADVANTAGES

Compared to voucher privatization employee ownership appears to have certain advantages.

First, employee share-ownership brings some cash to the state, even if shares are sold at preferential prices. From the employees' point of view, this option is clearly preferable to the voucher option, often placed in companies of whose past and potential performance they know nothing. Even if workers have to pay for the acquisition of shares, mainly through lower wages dedicated to paying off the capital, this could be regarded as an 'internal cost of transition' asked of the workers of each company, which can be more easily channelled towards higher productivity than the 'external costs of transition' that the mass privatization process seems to represent, and which may become a delusion for the whole population. In this regard, employee-owners who must repay the cost of purchasing their enterprise tend to behave more responsibly than employees who receive their enterprise gratuitously or on extremely favourable terms (Ben-Ner, 1992).

Employee ownership schemes also have the advantage over the voucher system of not leading to a wide dispersion of owners. These schemes allow for the rapid creation of majority owners who can monitor management at relatively low cost and without recreating a national financial elite. They might be better for corporate governance if insiders have better access than outsiders to the information needed to monitor managers, which is likely to be the case.

With regard to the redistribution strategy, however, the employee share-ownership system only considers equity questions for employees, and ignores the claims of non-employee groups, such as the unemployed. In contrast, the voucher option entails redistribution across all classes of citizens. In the case of the Czech Republic, however, the great concentration of voucher points in the hands of a few investment funds may generate a political backlash when people realize that an important part of the economy had been given almost free of charge to a very small number of people (Roland, 1995, p. 39).

In comparison with alternative privatization options, and contrary to initial expectations, employee ownership may also have net advantages in terms of speed. Employee–management buy-outs turned out to be relatively fast and easy to implement, both politically and technically. In Russia, where the authorities deliberately chose from the beginning to implement large-scale privatization to insiders (managers and employees of the individual enterprises), 'the results so far of the privatization programme have been impressive' (World Bank, 1994, p. 6), and most observers agree that 'the most widely noted features of Russian privatization have been its scale and remarkable speed' (Earle, Estrin and Leshchenko, 1995). This rapid pace of privatization was largely due to buy-outs where employees received 51 per cent of the shares of enterprises, partly payable in vouchers. By 1995, less than 3 years after the programme's inception, more than 11,000 enterprises had been privatized with managers and workers owning more than 50 per cent of enterprise voting rights (*Table 1.2*). Simple procedures for the transfer of assets to employees have also speeded up the small privatization process which is approaching completion in a number of countries (OECD, 1995). As recently noted by Aoki (1995), the generic tendency towards insider control in transition economies is an evolutionary outcome of communist legacies, and thus may be the fastest solution to ownership transformation. The mechanical application of the neo-classical model of stockholder sovereignty for corporate governance in the transition will not be effective,[8] since a range of complementary institutions of a particular kind, such as competitive capital and labour markets, and hierarchical work organizations, are missing; worse, the application of this model may even prolong the transition process (Aoki, 1995, pp. 3–5).

Employee ownership is also to be preferred to the mass transfer of enterprise shares to government-owned funds, if demand for such shares in subsequent public offers is expected to be limited, since in this case there is a risk that the transferred capital will remain state property for a long time (with very negative implications for incentives). This has happened in Croatia; consequently, the new privatization law adopted in March 1996 envisages a number of additional incentives for the acquisition of shares by 'small' shareholders (mainly employees), including further discounts and the repayment of subscribed shares within a 20 year period. If employee ownership is used in combination with some other method – such as commercial sales to foreigners – it will represent a welcome alternative to the sale of the entire enterprise at a low price. The combination of methods can have further advantages: it is probable that workers who initially were not interested in purchasing enterprise shares will change their attitude if in the meantime a successful foreign firm becomes a shareholder and invests in the modernization of the firm.

Some of the traditional economic arguments in favour of employee ownership are also particularly relevant for current problems in Central and Eastern Europe. In the first place, employee ownership is often considered to be a means of improving motivation and productivity: workers who obtain shares in their enterprise are expected to be much more committed to its results, leading to lower absenteeism and labour turnover, and to increased investment in firm-specific human capital. By eliminating the distinction between employees and owners, it also tends to reduce social conflicts. Such schemes are also likely to enhance team-work and a co-operative spirit, thereby facilitating improvements in work organization and the adaptation of the labour force to new technologies. According to theorists, the incentive

---

[8] In the orthodox stockholder sovereignty model, the problems of management slack, incompetence, and moral hazard are corrected by outside stockholders through an efficient capital market for corporate valuation and control, as well as institutions such as competitive labour markets for managers and for workers' labour services (see Aoki, 1995; or Nuti, 1995b).

effects of worker ownership are much greater when they are accompanied by greater participation in decision-making. A wide-ranging body of evidence for such a positive association between employee share-ownership and productivity gains has been accumulated in the advanced industrialized countries. This strong consensus, which is most unusual in empirical research, is well presented by Weitzman and Kruse (1990). Studies on EU countries, recently surveyed in the PEPPER report (Uvalic, 1991) also agree in pointing to a positive association between financial participation and productivity. Employee share-ownership also proved to enhance workers' motivation and productivity in the USA and Japan, and to have positive motivational effects in some Central and East European countries.[9]

In some Western countries, financial participation schemes were also found to promote greater wage flexibility and to help avoid lay-offs, so leading to a certain employment stability.[10] The employment effect of employee ownership could also be extremely important for the majority of Central and East European countries today, considering the low level of productivity in many industries and very high unemployment rates, in many cases exceeding the highest rate in the European Union.[11] A related argument concerns wage moderation: if employees become shareholders in their enterprise, they may, in principle, be willing to accept lower wages in order to preserve employment. We seek to ascertain in this volume whether employee share-ownership does result in fewer lay-offs in the restructuring process. This is again particularly important for Central and East European countries today, considering their need for restructuring, high unemployment rates, and monetary constraints on wage increases. Some scholars have discussed the lost opportunities and policy mistakes following the reunification of Germany, suggesting that rapid wage increases to near-Western levels in East Germany could have been avoided if workers there had been given minority ownership shares in exchange for a medium-term wage freeze (Acs and FitzRoy, 1994, p. 88). At the same time, however, employee share-ownership would help ensure that workers begin to be fairly remunerated when enterprises become profitable, so contributing to the progressive increase of living standards.

Finally, some political leaders have also suggested that in a context of lack of domestic capital, employee ownership would represent a means of

---

9 For the USA, see Conte and Svejnar (1990); for Japan, see Jones and Kato (1993). For Central and Eastern Europe, see Vaughan-Whitehead et al. (1995).

10 Such effects have been observed in the USA and in France – see Kruse (1991) and Vaughan-Whitehead (1992). See also Spineewyn and Svejnar (1990).

11 As recently stressed by Weitzman (1995, p. 2), productivity and employment are two of the most important issues facing any economy, and a system change promising even the hint of an improvement, if not a panacea, should merit careful attention.

anchoring the ownership of firms in their country of operation since the majority of shares remain with employees.

6 THE EXPECTED RISKS

Many scholars have also stressed that widespread ownership by insiders entails a number of problems, most of which are well known from the theoretical literature on labour-managed firms (LMF), with particular reference to the Western co-operative and the Yugoslav self-managed enterprise.[12]

The literature emphasizes that enterprises where workers have full or majority control tend to follow policy decisions aimed at maximizing income per worker. Consequently, employees in such firms are automatically expected to distribute excessive wages, maintain above-optimal employment, and underinvest. In the context of privatizations in Central and Eastern Europe, these problems will in turn create obstacles to efficient restructuring, impede access to outside risk capital, and discourage foreign investors and the inflow of fresh capital (see for example, Blanchard et al, 1991).

On the employment side, they tend to maintain above-optimal employment levels because of the reluctance to lay off workers. Their rigid response to changes in product prices, technology, and capital rental could also lead to an inefficient allocation of labour (Ward, 1958; Vanek, 1970; Nuti, 1988).

Medium- and long-term inefficiencies linked to the use of capital are also expected, workers managing the company being reluctant to reinvest net income in the enterprise (cf. the underinvestment or the Furubotn-Pejovich effect, first proposed by Pejovich, 1969).

Because of their short time-horizon, workers tend to favour projects which pay off quickly, and distribute as much as possible of retained earnings in the form of current wages, to the detriment of enterprise reinvestment.

Financial problems are also expected. Capital needed by the labour-managed company will exceed the combined liquid wealth of the workers. The company will thus have to borrow funds on the capital market, which is likely to lead to a high dependence on external financial resources. This in turn may give rise to two sets of interrelated problems: the principal–agent problem, that is, conflict between the owner of capital and its user; and the moral hazard problem, arising from the risk associated with debt financing. The employee-owned firm may also lack the incentive to operate successfully if in risky situations a substantial part of the losses can be avoided by bankruptcy, and

---

[12] For a survey of the LMF theoretical and empirical literature, see Bonin and Putterman (1987), Bonin, Jones and Putterman (1993), or Bartlett and Uvalic (1986).

so lending to a co-operative may involve a higher degree of risk (Nuti, 1988). Consequently, this type of enterprise will be unsuitable outside labour-intensive sectors and for risky ventures.

Finally, it has been argued that majority employee ownership could prevent foreign investment by giving rise to a conflict with a potential foreign investor who wants majority ownership. According to Lipton and Sachs (1990) from the Polish experience, they deter foreign investment, although other studies have presented several enterprise examples where employee share-ownership has been efficiently combined with foreign capital.[13]

These expected adverse effects from traditional labour-managed firms will not necessarily occur in enterprises with employee share-ownership in Central and Eastern Europe, which seem to be confronted with different economic and social conditions. The Central and East European privatizing enterprise seems to differ from labour-managed firms – not only the Western co-operative, but even more from the labour-managed firm in former communist regimes[14] – in several important respects.

First, enterprises in most Central and East European countries have been privatized only partially through insider ownership, among other reasons because most laws imposed a limit on employee acquisition on preferential terms.[15] Second, not all employees participated in such privatizations, since subscriptions were usually voluntary. Third, employee ownership has not always entailed their full control over enterprise decisions; for instance, the practice in some countries has sometimes been to give employees non-voting shares or shares with limited voting rights (see Mygind, Chapter 2, on Estonia). In Russia, employees have frequently ended up owning the majority of shares, but the active owners are managers with often less than one-fifth of the shares (Sutela, 1995). These considerations imply that the privatizing enterprise in Central and Eastern Europe, rather than being fully controlled and owned by all its employees (as is usually the case with the Western co-operative), will more frequently be characterized by less than 100 per cent insider ownership and control.

At this point, whether and to what extent these adverse effects will turn out to be present in the privatization of Central and East European enterprises will depend on a number of additional elements which are frequently not considered. There is a great variety of possibilities regarding insider ownership,

---

[13] For enterprise examples in Chile, see Bogetic and Conte (1992).

[14] It is important to distinguish between the Western co-operative and the Yugoslav-type enterprise, since workers of the Yugoslav LMF had much more limited property rights than worker-members of the Western co-operative.

[15] While the limit should not, in principle, prevent employees from buying additional shares under conditions offered to other (external) buyers, in practice employees have usually limited their acquisitions to shares offered at privileged terms, since they could not afford to buy additional shares.

each of which will have very different implications for enterprise behaviour and efficiency. In order to illustrate the full complexity of these different cases, we will point to some of the essential elements.

1) Insider ownership versus control. The problems mentioned do not depend primarily on whether insiders have acquired a majority stake, but on whether they hold a controlling interest. Insiders can have control without majority ownership, especially if ownership of the remaining shares is dispersed among outside shareholders (Earle and Estrin, 1996). Insiders can also have majority ownership, but without effective control;[16] whether employee ownership actually ensures control over the most important enterprise decisions will depend on concrete circumstances and existing institutional arrangements. Apathy on the part of outside shareholders may allow insiders to control enterprise activities even with substantially less than a 50 per cent holding, whereas employee shareholder apathy may make a 60 per cent shareholding by employees insufficient to exercise a controlling interest.

2) Insider controlling interest and inefficiency. If insiders do obtain a controlling interest, the insider-controlled enterprise may be faced with unique incentive problems, though this may not always be the case. Among the factors crucial for determining enterprise behaviour are, for instance, (a) the individual employee's share in enterprise equity as compared with his share in the firm's wage bill; (b) the ratio between the number of insider shareholders and non-shareholders; and (c) the distribution of ownership and control between various categories of insiders.

    a) Nuti (1995b) has convincingly argued that an employee's short-term interests as a wage-earner are likely to prevail over his longer-term interests as a shareholder only if he has a lower share of company equity than of labour input supply. Nevertheless, this theoretical trade-off might well be modified by the present economic and social conditions in enterprises of the region. In the context of a sharp fall in real wages, and often even the non-payment of wages, workers will undoubtedly prefer immediate cash payments to delayed hypothetical – even if potentially higher – dividends. Moreover, the increased risk of unemployment will shorten the workers' time horizon, who will prefer to secure additional wage increases in the short term.

---

[16] As mentioned earlier, this has in fact frequently been the case in Russian privatized firms.

b)   Within such a framework, an element which could also be important for the balance between insiders' short-term and longer-term
interests is the proportion between the number of employee
shareholders and employee non-shareholders. In general terms, for
a given proportion of equity in the hands of insiders, the less
numerous employee shareholders are, the higher their individual
holdings will be, and the more likely it is that their longer-term
interests will prevail.

c)   A corollary of these arguments is that we must distinguish between
different categories of insider – namely employees and managers –
because of the importance of the distribution of ownership and
control among them. When enterprise shares are mainly bought by
managers – as has recently happened in Estonia and Hungary –
there is no reason (at least in theory) why they should not act in the
interest of other (external) shareholders (Sutela, 1995). In Western
economies, managers are frequently given performance-related
bonuses in the form of enterprise shares (or share options) precisely
in order to ensure that they do act in the interest of other
shareholders.[17] Moreover, the general principle of the market for
corporate control in the West is that if management is not 'efficient'
(in the sense of present value maximization), there is a tendency for
control of the firm to change hands (Chilosi, 1995). However,
given that today in Central and Eastern Europe some important
institutions are still non-existent (including developed capital
markets, a competitive market for managers, and laws protecting
minority shareholders), it is quite possible that managers may not
act in the interest of external shareholders.[18]

[17] For instance in the UK at the beginning of the 1990s, around 60 per cent of existing
arrangements on employee ownership and profit-sharing were in fact discretionary share option
schemes reserved for executives (see Uvalic, 1991).

[18] In Russia, for example, there have been cases when insider managers and their outside
political allies have prevented foreign external owners from attending the general meeting of an
enterprise, precisely in order to minimize their influence, since securities laws do not adequately
protect minority shareholders. This sometimes happens in Japan also, so there may be reasons
(incentives, or lack of regulation) why managers may not behave in the interest of other
shareholders.

7 EMPIRICAL EVIDENCE

7.1 Restructuring and Employment

In general, the theoretical argument that employee-owned enterprises would systematically encourage labour hoarding does not seem to be much confirmed by empirical evidence – unfortunately still very limited – accumulated on this issue. The enterprise survey in Ukraine shows for instance that employee-managed enterprises have reduced employment (by more than 10 per cent in 1994–95) although with a considerable delay, as they had tried to carry out other restructuring alternative measures – product rationalization, workers' mobility, cuts in working hours, etc. – before this last resort (see Chapter 9). Enterprise survey results on 447 MEBO enterprises in Romania also show that these enterprises considerably reduce the number of employees when necessary (see Munteanu, Chapter 7). They would try, however, to carry out other restructuring measures at a first stage. Results on Estonia and Lithuania tend to show that majority employee-owned enterprises have a tendency to avoid employment cuts, while enterprises with minority employee-ownership seem to implement lay-offs like other enterprises. Employee-owned enterprises in Latvia were found to cut employment more than state-owned enterprises. Similarly in Poland, employment was found to be more flexible than in state firms and other privatized enterprises.

Similar behaviour is described by other empirical studies. A survey of Russian enterprises, carried out by the World Bank in 1995, led to some interesting results concerning the differentiated ability of enterprises with different property forms to implement restructuring. After comparing worker-owned enterprises and manager-owned enterprises to state- and outsider-owned enterprises and new private firms, the authors conclude that, contrary to theoretical expectations, worker-owned enterprises do not behave differently in terms of investment, reduction of labour costs and employment. They were found to implement a substantial restructuring strategy with the aim of increasing the efficiency of input use and investments, and to attach significant weight to employment reduction (Earle, Estrin and Leshchenko, 1995). An econometric analysis of employment by the same authors confirmed the absence of significant differences between insider and outsider privatization with regard to employment. Worker-owned enterprises also carried out lay-offs. Their capacity utilization (which is a useful indicator of long-term restructuring) was not found to be smaller, and their investment strategy turned out to be similar to the private group. They were found, for instance, to place a similar emphasis on seeking foreign investors and reducing bank borrowing. Surprisingly, enterprises owned by the workers were found to have the least ties to the state. Not only were they found to have a lower probability of receiving state support, they also received a smaller percentage of their revenue from the state. Insider privatization thus acts to break the links with the state, though more markedly in worker-owned than managerial-owned firms. The authors of the study concluded that, although Russian privatization has created an economy primarily comprising majority worker-owned firms, the effects on behaviour and restructuring are far from negative, and managerial control seems to be assured in these enterprises.

These results probably reflect 'the distinct features of the employee-owned enterprise and of the co-operative or self-managed enterprise, where members are not full co-owners but only share the right to use enterprise capital and to appropriate net value added' (see Nuti, Chapter 6, Section 3).This is the reason why employee-owned enterprises, unlike co-operatives or self-managed firms, would not have an incentive to restrict employment or to exhibit a bias in favour of labour-saving projects (Nuti, Chapter 6).

7.2 Wages and Incomes

The situation concerning wages and other sources of remuneration was also found to be more complex than the traditional theoretical predictions would lead us to expect. The economic and social context seems to have a determining influence in this regard, not only on wage levels but also on the structure of wages and incomes. In the crisis context of Ukraine for instance, employee-owned enterprises were found to have greater problems in paying wages. They were also found to pay relatively lower wages, but to partly compensate by offering employees substantial other benefits. A similar trend was also observed in Russia. Greater preservation of social benefits in employee-owned enterprises was also observed in Poland (Earle and Estrin, 1996, p. 56).

The survey results on Ukraine presented in Chapter 9 show that nearly 80 per cent of employee-owned enterprises operated some form of profit-sharing, a similar trend being observed in Russia and to a lesser extent in Bulgaria (see the company example presented in Chapter 3). Wage differentials in Ukraine were also found to be smaller in employee-owned enterprises, perhaps a sign of the 'wage solidarity' principle which tends to prevail in employee-owned enterprises.

In Estonia, employee-owned firms were found to be characterized by a high downward flexibility of wages, suggesting that lower wages have been traded off for job security. This does not seem to have been the case in Lithuania, where wage levels were in general higher in employee- and management-owned firms, but where labour productivity seems to have been high enough to permit these relatively high wages. In Hungary, wage policies in employee ownership privatized firms have been rather balanced: although wage growth in these firms has been above the industrial average, in most cases it was not above the consumer price index, implying no growth in real terms, nor above productivity growth, so implying no growth of unit labour costs (Lajtai, Chapter 5).

Workers in worker-owned enterprises thus seem temporarily to accept wage cuts in order to promote enterprise profitability and avoid employment reductions. At the same time, other enterprise examples presented in this volume tend to show that workers in enterprises with substantial employee ownership also tend to pay higher wages as soon as their enterprise can register higher productivity and profitability rates. Workers thus seek to promote more decent wage increases and to compensate past wage cuts as soon as enterprise performance improves.

This was also confirmed by the World Bank enterprise survey in Russia. Contrary to initial expectations, wages were found to be the lowest in worker-owned enterprises, while the highest were registered in the new private firms (Earle, Estrin and Leshchenko, 1995). There is therefore no clear evidence that Russian managers and workers are taking advantage of their position to pay themselves higher wages. On the contrary, workers in these enterprises are more likely to accept temporary wage reductions in order to help their enterprise to recover profitability. From the survey, however, they stressed that one objective would be to progressively increase wages, and to establish a more efficient internal wage structure. The different chapters of the present volume thus seem to confirm the search for balanced enterprise development in these enterprises in terms of wages and employment: although employment preservation is among their main priorities, workers carry out lay-offs when necessary for enterprise restructuring. Accordingly, they are also ready to accept low wages although their objective is also to ensure better pay and living standards to the workers in accordance with improved enterprise performance. This self-discipline and the ability to take a long-term view shown by both managers and workers confirm their ability to manage newly privatized enterprises in a responsible and efficiency-oriented way.

7.3 Productivity and Economic Performance

Much of the evidence on employee ownership in Western market economies is supportive of a positive link between employee ownership and productivity. Moreover, the fact that employee ownership has been promoted by a number of Western governments through specific tax incentives, and since 1992 also by the European Union, clearly points to the widespread conviction that its positive effects are likely to outweigh the negative ones. In Central and Eastern Europe, it is difficult to identify the effect of employee ownership on performance, since there is the possibility that employee-owned enterprises were already the best companies before privatization occurred. This seems to be the case in Poland where the best companies were selected by employees (see Nuti, Chapter 6). Moreover, the effects of employee ownership clearly depend on the distribution of shares between the managers and the workers which is unfortunately rarely identifiable.[19] Only a few studies have been carried out on the impact of employee share-ownership in Central and Eastern Europe. However, they all seem to converge on emphasizing some positive effects on productivity and economic performance. The present volume describes some successful examples. In Ukraine, productivity rates appeared to be highest in employee-owned enterprises, which were also found to be less affected by forms of labour inefficiency, such as low work intensity or low quality of work, and the high labour turnover observed in state-owned enterprises. Employee-owned enterprises, however, seem to suffer from lack of demand and falls in sales. Difficulties in finding markets for exports contributed to worsen their sales performance (see Vaughan-Whitehead, Chapter 9).

In Bulgaria, there have been cases in which employees ownership has led to substantial positive changes in an enterprise, and other enterprises in which even majority control by employees has yet to have perceptible effects on work and effectiveness. Nevertheless, a 1992 survey of over 4,000 manufacturing workers in Bulgaria revealed that the majority of workers expected positive effects from employee ownership. Workers agreed that employee ownership would make them work harder (53 per cent of respondents), would not permit laziness (54 per cent), and would ensure quality output (nearly 70 per cent) (Rock and Klinedinst, Chapter 3). This is what has happened for instance in the *CSA* auto service company, described in Chapter 3. Productivity rates might be particularly high when share ownership is associated with substantive participation in decision-making (see Rock and Klinedinst, Chapter 3). Earle and Estrin (1996, pp. 51–6) presenting evidence on Poland, confirm the view that 'employee-owned firms perform well in comparison not only with state-owned enterprises but also with privately-owned and outsider-owned enterprises.' In the three Baltic states, despite some variation in the results, there is no indication that employee ownership entails worse economic performance than in the case of comparable enterprises in the private sector, since productivity and profitability often seems better than for most other enterprises. This indicates that employee-owned enterprises have been restructured at least as much as other types of enterprise. Interestingly, productivity rates also seem to increase even further following an increase in employee ownership, as shown in the cases of Estonia and Lithuania. Moreover, the proposition that the

---

[19] For a good discussion of the advantages and disadvantages of workers' ownership and management ownership respectively, see Earle and Estrin (1996).

slower reduction in the labour force could end up in lower productivity in employee-owned firms was not confirmed by the evidence. Although in Estonia the productivity of employee-owned firms was around the average, in Lithuania the results on labour productivity show a high level in both employee- and management-dominated firms, as well as in minority insider-owned firms. In Lithuania profitability (measured in operating profits on turnover and by net profits on total assets) was relatively high. These positive effects seem stronger than the negative effect from the more sluggish reduction of the labour force (see Mygind, Chapter 2). In Romania, in a sample of 240 companies privatized through the MEBO method, as many as 232 companies increased their turnover and profits by between 15 and 120 per cent, in six companies the increase was between 1 and 15 per cent, and in only two companies was there a decrease; thus these companies succeeded in improving their economic performance in an extremely short period (Munteanu, Chapter 7). IPCT (Bucharest), the first Romanian company to become private through an MEBO, is in dominant employee ownership, but has very much increased its activities since privatization (Chapter 7). Similarly, according to the Hungarian ESOP Foundation (MRP in Hungarian), on the basis of a survey among 169 ESOPs, this type of enterprise would have performed better than the national average (MRP, 1994). This is confirmed by the high ESOP performance presented in Chapter 5. Some Serbian enterprises, among the first to be privatized through employee ownership, have performed rather well in the post-privatization period; for example, Metalac from Gornji Milanovac has undertaken product diversification, set up a quality control system, and implemented a programme for the retraining of its workers (Uvalic, Chapter 10). Similarly, in Slovenia, a number of successful firms were purchased by insiders, and these firms have generally continued to perform rather well. Some banks and newspaper companies in the Czech Republic have also used minority employee-ownership in order to improve staff motivation (see Kotrba, Chapter 4).

The World Bank survey in Russia also led to interesting results on the impact of different majority ownership forms on various elements of company performance, including sales, profits and exports. Worker-owned enterprises were found to perform relatively well in terms of sales growth and also profit rates. They were even found to export more than other ownership types, a feature which is particularly important in the context of falling production and collapse of internal markets in the region (Earle, Estrin and Leshchenko, 1995).

7.4 Industrial Relations and Collective Agreements

1) Employee share-ownership and participation in decision-making

Interviews conducted at several Bulgarian enterprises during 1991–95 support the idea that when substantive employee participation in decision-making is combined with compensation based on economic results, enterprise efficiency is usually enhanced; in one case, labour productivity has increased by a factor of three in nearly 18 months, while in another it has doubled over two years (Rock and Klinedinst, Chapter 3). Nevertheless, in general there is no large measured difference in enterprise performance (for example, value added) according to the amount of perceived influence of workers on decisions; much more important were the market share and incentive compensation schemes (Chapter 3). In the Czech Republic, the Act on State-owned Enterprises has reduced the extent of labour participation in management to 50 per cent representation on Supervisory Boards (the other 50 per cent is nominated by the founding ministry).

2) Employee ownership and collective bargaining

Employee share-ownership, by involving employees more closely in the growth of their enterprise, was also found to facilitate the decentralization trend particularly necessary in post-communist Europe. One important result discussed in some chapters of this volume is that employee share-ownership does not seem to lower trade union influence nor to limit collective bargaining, and the signature of collective agreements confirms the continuation of trade union action in this field. Workers in Bulgaria were frequently able to exert influence on decisions through trade union action (Chapter 3), suggesting the important role trade unions may play in increasing the say of workers in major enterprise decisions. In Hungary, it is reported that there was no ESOP company where employee ownership has weakened the trade union position within the firm (see Lajtai, Chapter 5). Moreover, traditional channels of collective negotiations seem to be functioning smoothly in ESOP firms. Trade unions and employers have thus an important role to play in this regard: trade unions by participating in the promotion, introduction and follow-up of this participatory process and by defending the interests of workers in the elaboration of workers' ownership schemes; employers by developing these forms of economic democracy in enterprises and by making sure that they are oriented towards productivity enhancement instead of short-term interests which can be pursued by all or specific categories of workers. Chapter 9 on Ukraine describes how trade unions were actively involved in the privatization process, and often helped the workers to become owners of their enterprises. Most employee-owned enterprises also reported the conclusion of a collective agreement at the enterprise level (85 per cent in 1994). One other major result from the Ukrainian enterprise survey is the much smaller number of collective agreements in private enterprises, and this for most collective bargaining issues. This is clearly a sign of less intensive collective bargaining in these enterprises.

7.5 Investment Policy and New Technologies

In theory, there is no reason to suppose that employee shareholders in Central and Eastern Europe should prove more short-sighted and have shorter time-horizons than external owners. Many external private owners were found to squeeze cash out of the firm – frequently not reinvesting in it – to maximize short-term returns to themselves and the principal partners. In the Central and East European context of high uncertainty, while workers may try to appropriate retained earnings for private benefits (for example, to build houses or buy cars), the external owner may equally try to appropriate retained earnings to reinvest elsewhere (perhaps in a country where a more favourable economic and institutional framework is likely to assure higher returns). The problem is a general one as it also applies to other (external) shareholders, both domestic and foreign.

In a survey of more than 4,000 manufacturing workers in Bulgaria, undertaken in mid-1992, the responses revealed that about 25 per cent of workers were willing to invest variable amounts in their enterprise. As much as 9 per cent of workers were willing to invest, through deferred wages, more than 5,000 leva (which at that time was more than five times the gross monthly wage of a typical worker). Considering that mid-1992 was almost the worst point of the economic transition in Bulgaria (in terms of the fall in real wages and output), the survey suggests a relatively positive attitude of workers towards investment in their own enterprise. In the case of CSA, a small auto-servicing centre in Bulgaria privatized through an employee–management buy-out, employees have been willing to make additional investments in better equipment; and recently the company invested in an Italian-made automatic car wash machine (Chapter 3). The company Metalac from Gornji Milanovac in Serbia, privatized through employee share-ownership, has undertaken a number of measures which have improved its economic performance, including substantial investment (only recently it invested some DM 40 million; Uvalic, Chapter 10). Results on Ukraine in this volume show the high propensity of majority employee-owned enterprises to introduce new technologies, make some change in work organization, and implement training programmes, often with the objective of carrying out efficient restructuring without reducing employment. This volume presents examples of employee-owned enterprises which have made the necessary investments. This seems to be the case for instance in the Bulgarian company CSA and the Romanian MEBO IPCT Bucharest. More specifically, although there is a possibility of reverse causality as shown by Nuti, data on Poland presented by Earle and Estrin (1996) seem to indicate that 'employee-owned enterprises have the best financial health of any of the organizations. Their profit margins are higher, they are never classified by banks as "uncreditworthy", they are seldom refused bank credit, and they have the newest capital stock.' This observation is further confirmed by higher profitability rates for Polish MEBOs presented in Chapter 6.

It also appears, however, that employee buy-outs often have to face the problem of lack of financial capital. In Estonia and Latvia deep restructuring in the form of new investment in employee-owned enterprises is around the average, but here employee-owned enterprises in particular have faced major problems of lack of bank finance; in Lithuania, preliminary results point in the direction of lower investment in both management- and employee-dominated enterprises (see Mygind, Chapter 2). In Hungary, in employee share ownership privatized firms investment has not increased since privatization, possibly primarily because of increasing indebtedness (Chapter 5). Investment in some Polish MEBOs was also lower than in similar enterprises, mainly due to the burden of lease payments (Chapter 6).

These possible drawbacks on the financial side led many experts to advise the promotion of employee ownership in the privatization of loss-making enterprises only (Earle and Estrin, 1996, pp. 2, 33). Examples from Russia and Ukraine, for instance, confirm that employee ownership effectively accelerates the privatization of non-profitable enterprises when there are no other external buyers, and should thus be encouraged in those sectors. However, given the empirical evidence presented in this volume and elsewhere showing that employees run enterprises, even the most profitable, in an efficient way, and often implement the necessary investment and restructuring measures, we may ask why employees are discriminated against in the privatization process and not allowed to participate in the capital of profit-making enterprises.

In this regard it is important to note that lower investment levels in employee-owned enterprises are often not the result of employee decisions but due to the behaviour of banks which expect a greater lending risk from enterprises controlled by insiders and consequently limit their access to credit. Such behaviour was observed, for instance, in Poland and the Baltic countries. There is no doubt that governments intended to promote forms of employee ownership in the privatization process; at the same time, the necessary steps should be taken to ensure that this type of enterprise is not discriminated against as regards access to capital and financial markets.

7.6 Combination of Employee Ownership with Other Property Forms

It has also been argued that majority employee ownership should be avoided because it will prevent foreign direct investment (or any investment) by giving rise to a conflict with the potential (foreign) investor who wants majority ownership.

Further empirical evidence presented in this volume shows that some foreign investors may actually be keen to have minority insider ownership of the remaining equity in order to get managers and workers to behave as co-owners, not as employees. Employee ownership could thus represent an attraction, rather than a disincentive to foreign investment (Ellerman, 1993, p. 23). In fact, in Bulgaria several foreign companies have provided funding for minority employee ownership.[20] In at least one case the foreign buyers actually created a mechanism in order to allow the employees to buy some of their own enterprise's stock, the majority share being bought by the foreign partners (Chapter 3). In contrast to Estonia, where there were a number of cases of a combination of foreign investment and employee ownership, in Hungary employee ownership (in the form of ESOPs) has been accompanied with foreign ownership only exceptionally, since outside investors seem to distrust ESOPs; if the ESOP is not fully owned by its employees, the usual co-owners are the management or the state. In one of the rare companies with an ESOP and foreign ownership in Hungary, employees fought intensively to get as many shares as possible; when they managed to get 20 per cent at a preferential price and after they were sure that the foreign owner would not dismiss them, they sold their shares to the foreign co-owner in order to realize a relatively large profit (Chapter 5). One promising solution might be to encourage joint ventures with equal equity shares (50 per cent to the employees and 50 per cent to the foreign investor).

The example of the enterprise Vesna in Ukraine suggests that the combination of these two methods has led to an increase in workers' motivation, ensuring at the same time the inflow of fresh capital and the introduction of new technology (Chapter 9). Employee ownership also seems to be effectively combined in some enterprises in Slovenia, for instance IBP Zalec (see Uvalic, Chapter 10).

The World Bank survey in Russia also confirms that enterprises owned by the workers place a substantial emphasis on attracting foreign investors. The study also indicates that foreign participation in worker-owned enterprises would help them to solve their anticipated problems of investment and access to external capital markets. As expected, foreign-owned enterprises were found

---

[20] A Dutch company recently investing in a Bulgarian brewing company financed minority employee shareholding; it is reported that this was not the only case in Bulgaria.

to place more stress on technology, product quality and investment. They were also found to pay higher wages, while worker-owned enterprises paid the lowest. Such a combination could therefore allow worker-owned enterprises with foreign participation to ensure progressively better living standards to the workers and wages more in accordance with productivity objectives.

8 POLICY CONSIDERATIONS: TOWARDS A MORE BALANCED AND MIXED APPROACH

8.1 Transferable versus Non-transferable Shares

As we have seen in a number of different countries, the transferability of the shares distributed or sold to workers and management can be immediate, as in the case of Russia. Share tradability has the potential advantage of leading to the immediate establishment and development of a stock exchange, an important instrument for disciplining managers and essential for the attainment of the efficiency expected from private ownership. Many experts have advised governments to carefully plan privatization to employees to include a guarantee that shares are freely tradable (EBRD, 1995; World Bank, 1996; Earle and Estrin, 1996). The main motivation is to lead to the development of secondary markets and to make sure that employee-owned enterprises could evolve in the transition process into other organizational forms. Non-tradability would prevent outsiders from entering while impeding the concentration of shares among insiders. On the one hand, this flexibility of the ownership structure – with the participation of outsiders and a concentration of capital among insiders – is expected to lead to better corporate governance and flexibility in decision-making. On the other hand, it could lower the incentive for the workers to increase their efforts or to carry out new firm-specific investments because of their fear of expropriation (Earle and Estrin, 1996, p. 20). This might be the case, particularly when transferability would lead to a concentration of capital in the hands of one or a few external private investors or in the hands of the management. This risk is particularly prevalent in countries where real wages have been falling most seriously, such as Russia or Ukraine (where they fell by more than 70 per cent and 50 per cent respectively between 1991 and 1995), and where employees will have an immediate tendency to sell their shares in order to compensate for their declining living standards. In this case, the transferability of shares could strangle at birth the whole project of promoting economic democracy in the workplace, although it could have other potential advantages.

A number of chapters of the present volume show the tendency for shares which are immediately tradable to be rapidly concentrated in the hands of a few managers, a phenomenon observed for instance in the Baltic countries and Croatia. In Hungary, managers have been the main beneficiaries of ESOPs. Concerning Russia World Bank experts report that some managers have tried, illegally, either to block participation by employees or outsiders, or to transfer assets or profits to firms they control (World Bank, 1996, p. 55). These developments may be strongly demotivating for the workers. Share tradability restrictions in ESOPs were implemented in Hungary. Tradability might also lead to foreign capital rapidly taking over an enterprise's shares. As already mentioned, all important newspapers in the Czech Republic were owned by their employees but were progressively sold to foreign publishing groups. By 1990, none of the national dailies remained in the hands of their employees. It is also to be noted that voucher transferability – but also of shares if distributed on a very large scale – could lead (since the distribution of vouchers or shares is equivalent to the distribution of cash) to inflationary pressures, as shown by the example of Russia, where the rouble rate of exchange plummeted on the day voucher distribution began (1 October 1992).

A critical determinant of the longer-run success of privatization is the extent to which ownership rights can change and eventually evolve into more efficient forms, which in turn depends on whether there are restrictions on the sale of shares (World Bank, 1996; EBRD, 1995, p.136). Some explain that their tradability would not necessarily lead to substantial sales of shares. 'Unless constrained to do so because of liquidity problems, no small worker–shareholder will find it profitable to sell his shares to an outside investor before the restructuring process brought about by outside privatization has been completed, because it is the restructuring itself which is likely to increase the value of the firm. Workers may also be reluctant to sell their shares to an outsider if they expect they might lose their jobs as a result of restructuring' (EBRD, 1995, p. 136). In the absence of co-ordinated decisions by insiders, however, bids by outsiders are unlikely to be blocked effectively. Moreover, the above argument tends to overlook the dramatic situation into which most employees have been plunged in the first years of reform and their desperate need for cash (Vaughan-Whitehead, 1995).

A possible solution might be to oblige employees to hold their shares for a certain period – for instance two or three years – which might be sufficient to create a 'small shareholder's mentality' among them without impeding the long-term development of capital markets. If the transfer of shares is allowed only after a few years it is likely that it will take place in a better economic and social context, in which the fall in real wages will have hopefully ceased and employees will not be obliged to sell their shares in order to make up for their insufficient basic income. This option is supported by the current difficult context of restructuring and mass unemployment, which will continue to ensure that workers maximize enterprise profits instead of their short-term interests.

8.2 Voting versus Non-voting Shares

Empirical evidence accumulated in Western countries suggests that financial participation schemes – including employee share-ownership – succeed more often when they are combined with some form of worker participation in decision-making. The experiences of employee share-ownership presented in this volume tend to underline that in a few countries the promotion of this property form in the privatization process does not always entail worker involvement in the enterprise decision-making process, especially in the strategic decisions taken at the management level. This is a complex matter. On the one hand, some of these countries have a tradition of co-operatives and self-management (in particular, Poland and former Yugoslavia), which has resulted in a general tendency for employers and trade unions to promote employee share-ownership alongside worker involvement in decision-making. On the other hand, privatization in these countries constitutes a major change in the property regime, towards private and other mixed forms of ownership, which clearly implies a lower level of involvement of workers in the decision-making process. Legislative changes for instance in former Yugoslavia and in Poland are aimed at limiting workers' self-management rights and replacing the collective responsibility of workers by the individual responsibility of managers and new capital owners.

Vouchers and employee ownership in privatization in the Czech Republic did not lead to increased worker participation in decision-making. In the first place, this is because employees who acquire shares are not authorized to vote on matters for which a two-thirds majority is required, which contributed to a lack of interest on the part of workers in taking up share offers. In the second place, this is due to the way in which voucher privatization led to a high dispersion of capital, making it difficult to constitute a group of shareholders composed of employees and local citizens who could influence enterprise decisions. Nevertheless, some initiatives to create 'entrepreneurs' clubs' have emerged at the local level, for instance in Ostrava, with the aim of forming groups of citizens, employees, and shareholders in selected enterprises in order to participate actively in management decisions. In other countries, limits have been imposed on shareholders' rights, namely dividends and voting rights. Romanian holders of privatization fund certificates receive no dividends for the first three years and have no voting rights for five years (Ben-Ner and Montias, 1994). Employee share-ownership in Bulgaria was developed without giving them any right to participate in enterprise decision-making. In Russia, the first privatization option led to the free distribution of shares, but without voting rights; by contrast Options 2 and 3 introduced the possibility of distributing to the workers a majority of voting shares. In Lithuania, non-voting shares were transformed into voting shares.

Labour–management buy-outs are probably the only way for employees to continue to be involved in the decision-making process on a significant scale.

Although the distribution of non-voting shares can be understood as a direct way of limiting workers' rights as regards the management of the company, it is difficult to envisage the development of such involvement in the capital of the company without other forms of worker participation. If workers bear risks of remuneration and dividend losses through ownership of the capital of their enterprise, it seems logical to give them a voice in how that capital is used.

Ownership changes should be accompanied by the additional institutional changes required to establish corporate control over managerial discretion, whether through actual or potential control over company equity or through other means. Employee control can be exercised in various ways, either individually by employee owners with proportional voting on the basis of the number of shares owned, or in a more democratic way on the basis of one worker-one vote. Criticisms have been formulated against collective modes of decision-making, mainly on the basis of egalitarian voting arrangements which dominated in Yugoslav self-managed enterprises. These criticisms often neglect the productivity benefits that could be associated with greater worker solidarity in egalitarian decision-making systems. Nevertheless, decision-making rights in this last case would be associated much more with employment than with the holding of shares, a system which might be difficult to implement in the specific context of privatization in Central and Eastern Europe, in which not only are several different property forms combined, but workers and managers own a very different proportion of shares.

8.3 Controlling Interest versus Wider Diversification

The Western experience with employee ownership suggests that possible inefficiencies are caused not by insider ownership *per se*, but by workers' controlling interest in enterprise activities (as in worker co-operatives). As already mentioned, a controlling interest can be obtained by employees on the basis of very different share allocations: over 50 per cent of the votes may not be enough if the vote is dispersed among disinterested holders, while less than 50 per cent may be sufficient to exercise control when the rest of the votes are dispersed or disinterested (see Nuti, Chapter 6). In many countries of Central and Eastern Europe shares do not always lead to voting rights, so that majority employee ownership is not always converted into control. One important conclusion of the present volume is that specific problems seem to occur more often when workers have a controlling or majority interest. In Bulgaria for instance economic performance was found to be much worse in enterprises fully owned by the employees (see Rock and Klinedinst, Chapter 3). We saw that in many countries of the region legislation and promotion of these schemes generally led to minority and not majority employee share-ownership. Moreover, we saw that, even if the enterprise is controlled by its insiders, the alleged problems will again be conditional on a number of specific issues. These different cases of employee ownership must be clearly distinguished because of their very different implications. Remedies also exist, such as stipulating a maximum capital stake for insiders, reducing the votes that insiders can exercise individually or collectively, or giving them non-voting shares (as is the case in some countries of the region). In some cases, the enterprise in dominant employee ownership may be only a transitory form, as such firms are likely, for a variety of reasons, to evolve into more traditional types of enterprise; and in case they do survive, this will only be a sign of their viability.

The other solution could be to give workers the right to participate in the capital and management of the enterprise without vesting them with full ownership. This would provide them with strong incentives while limiting some of the possible risks expected from employee-controlled firms. This solution could lead to shared governance, with a wider diversity of property forms in each enterprise. This would not only provide complementary resources (labour and workers' motivation from workers, capital from private owners, and so on), but would also ensure a 'mutual' or 'peer' monitoring process, in which each member of the group monitors his fellows (Stiglitz, 1995). It would also have the advantage of leading to governance structures that involve multiple participants and often non-hierarchical relations. FitzRoy and Kraft (1987) also showed that a horizontal process could help to avoid free-rider problems. This is the case in modern corporations, where shareholders, lenders, suppliers, customers and workers are all shareholders and all exercise some influence over the decisions taken by the firm.

Another solution, recently proposed by Aoki (1995) for the insider-controlled firm, is an external monitoring mechanism, performed by a lead bank, which may work even if insiders are the dominant stockholders. The model shows that sound banking institutions can be designed to play an effective monitoring role in the corporate governance structure of insider-controlled firms. In case of non-performance, the control rights would shift automatically from the insider to the outsider (the lead bank of a consortium).[21] Apart from the means of control, the threat of withdrawing

---

[21] Aoki is fully aware of some of the difficulties in applying this model to transitional economies: the role of banks may be limited because of their undercapitalization, low level of monitoring capacity, and the legacy of soft-budget constraints. But he also offers concrete proposals on how these problems could be resolved.

credit might also be an effective discipline device, the banks withdrawing their funds if they believe the firm is 'misbehaving'. It would provide an important check on the abuse of managerial prerogatives, should the management and workers not take the proper investment decisions for long-term enterprise profitability. In such a system the most delicate task would be to find the right balance of monitoring power for the banks. This balance should not, for example, hinder the ability of the management to take advantage of profitable opportunities, considering the importance of asymmetric information, with insiders having more knowledge concerning internal functioning and the real value of enterprise assets. It is also important that the banks are not provided with an opportunity to abuse their power.

8.4 Mass Unemployment versus a Wage–Employment Trade-off

More generally, various property forms can also lead to different restructuring methods. It is therefore important to identify whether employee share-ownership would help or prevent restructuring, and to define what the role of employee ownership could be in a strategic restructuring policy, with regard to employment, wages and productivity.

Too often in the region, wrong macro- and microeconomic priorities have been placed on the government agenda, and too often under the direct advice of external experts. For example, in order to help enterprises to attain profitability rapidly, massive employment reduction has often been given priority. In an insider-controlled firm, we saw that there can be a strong tendency to maintain existing employment levels and not to lay workers off, which would be sub-optimal because it prevents efficient restructuring, the dismissal of excess labour and the liquidation of obsolete plants. But extensive liquidation of large state-owned firms and massive lay-offs in the immediate future are clearly politically unfeasible (Acs and FitzRoy, 1994). The very heavy social costs of mass unemployment, as can be attested by rapidly growing unemployment rates in the region, also show that this policy is highly unacceptable from both the social and the economic point of view. While it is still important to reduce overemployment where it tends to dominate (for instance, in large overemployed and unprofitable state enterprises), there is an urgent need to develop other restructuring alternatives to mass unemployment (for example, labour redeployment and training programmes), as should have been done from the start of the reform process.

The main alternative seems to be to increase workers' motivation and involvement, leading to internal rationalization and to internal flexibility measures, such as workers' mobility, training, work-sharing, etc. As Acs and FitzRoy (1994) have stressed, since the outcome of a rapid collapse of employment in large state-owned enterprises is incalculable, the overriding policy priority must be primarily to motivate employees to maximum effort. Since the traditional competitive-capitalist 'stick' of immediate plant closure and dismissal is neither feasible nor credible for the largest units whose future is most uncertain, it makes eminent economic sense to give employees the 'carrot' of explicit residual ownership (Acs and FitzRoy, 1994, p. 90). Moreover, a number of authors in this volume show that employee share-ownership can efficiently contribute to this objective of enhanced performance, since it can encourage workers to increase productivity in order to avoid lay-offs. This search for higher profitability in the context of a high risk of unemployment reverses the theoretically expected tendency towards wage maximization. In most cases presented in this volume, far from imposing higher wages to the detriment of the company's long-term investment opportunities (as predicted in the literature), workers in employee-owned enterprises were found to have a tendency to restrain wage growth in order to preserve enterprise viability: wage growth appeared, even in a context of falling real wages, as a secondary objective behind employment stability.

The fact that this theoretical argument was not confirmed is probably due to the peculiar context of the current transition in Central and Eastern Europe. This is dominated by restructuring and mass unemployment, which clearly motivates workers and managers to give priority to the viability of the enterprise before such short-term interests as higher wages and incomes, despite falling living standards. In other words, because of the difficult economic context, workers have an interest in making sure that the enterprise maximizes profits and preserves employment in the long run.

At the same time, other enterprise examples presented in this volume tend to show that workers in employee-owned enterprises, while controlling excessive wage growth, tend to pay higher wages as soon as the situation allows it. This form of worker involvement through employee share-ownership will therefore ensure that the enterprise will promote more decent wage increases as soon as the economic conditions of the enterprise improve. This movement, far from leading to decreased profitability, contributes to increase workers' motivation and enterprise productivity. This aspect is particularly important in a context in which continuously falling real wages have had a very large negative effect on workers' productivity (Vaughan-Whitehead, 1995), a phenomenon which has unfortunately been completely neglected in the literature on transition economies.

In other words, workers seem to follow a much better and balanced policy in terms both of wage growth and employment reduction, trying to limit the two main costs of transition for employees, that is, unemployment and falling real wages. The timing and the nature of the adjustment, based on more severe wage restrictions but lower employment adjustment in the short term for improving both employment and wage prospects in the long run, would thus tend to be different from the restructuring strategies followed by other enterprises. This balanced approach observed in most chapters of this book would tend to contradict – at least on wage and employment expectations – the assumption that the 'deficiencies of employee-owned firms would be exacerbated by the specific circumstances of transition' (Earle and Estrin, 1996, p. 15).

This policy contrasts strikingly with excessive policies often implemented by other newly privatized enterprises, with massive lay-off programmes implemented immediately, or with systematically restricted wage increases, generally following the national 'shock therapy' policy, imposing both falls in real wages and growing unemployment during the transition, with large detrimental effects on productivity, but also on consumption (Vaughan-Whitehead, 1995).

9 CONCLUSION

Although limited empirical evidence has so far been accumulated on workers' and management ownership in Central and Eastern Europe, this method of privatization has been systematically criticized in the first years of reform. This privatization form was rarely proposed – or even mentioned – in policy documents, and when it was its negative effects were systematically presented while its potential advantages were completely ignored. According to the OECD (1993, p. 80), the transfer of a firm to its workers does not necessarily lead to 'the strengthening of its long-term viability because, as Yugoslavia's experience of the last four decades has proved, workers are generally more interested in current income than in long-term gains'.

More recently, the 1996 World Bank Development Report stressed that the acquisition by insiders of most of the ownership in Russia is 'worrisome' (World Bank, 1996, p. 58), and that 'employee-owned firms may weaken corporate governance; insiders are generally not able to bring new skills and new capital to the company, and they may deter outsiders with skills and capital from investing. Managers or employees may simply prevent outsiders from buying shares. Moreover, insiders may vote to pay higher salaries even if that reduces profits' (World Bank, 1996, pp. 54–55).

Despite this adverse approach, most governments in the region have included employee ownership among the possible privatization methods. The present volume provides empirical evidence which shows that most of the theoretical assumptions and arguments against these schemes were unfounded. This does not mean that the risks theoretically expected from such schemes are not present, but that they have been largely overstressed. In many cases, worker and management ownership has appeared to be a quick privatization method, as in Russia, so contradicting those who believed that the distribution of vouchers to all citizens was the only practical solution for implementing rapid privatization.

Examples in this volume also show that employee-owned enterprises do not systematically prevent unemployment and restructuring and do not systematically pay higher wages instead of investing in the long-term industrial capacity of the enterprise. On the contrary, they were found to have many positive features, thus showing that workers are not necessarily poor at running privatized enterprises and at making use of privatized assets.

First, employee ownership was found in most cases to efficiently ensure one of the main objectives of privatization in Central and Eastern Europe – which motivated the drive for rapid privatization in many countries – namely, decentralization and the breaking away from state control. The management of these enterprises appeared in several cases to be more insulated from political power than other enterprises, so acquiring a new autonomy and eliminating the paternalistic relationship between the state and the firm which was typical of the previous system.

Second, these schemes were found to have the potential to increase workers' motivation and productivity. Case studies, but also statistical evidence from the large enterprise surveys presented in this book, show higher worker motivation and productivity, good profitability rates, and low absenteeism and labour turnover rates in those enterprises.

Third, this privatization method in many cases appeared to help in promoting a new type of enterprise, in which employment, wage, investment and restructuring policies seem to be implemented by workers and management in a more balanced and gradual way. Although these employee-owned enterprises carry out restructuring and lay-offs when necessary, they also try to avoid systematic employment reductions, through production rationalization, training, and temporarily lower wages, in order to progressively increase productivity, profitability and workers' living standards in the long run. This route for higher worker motivation and productivity contrasts with the severe policy of massive unemployment carried out in other enterprises and systematically favoured in the first years of the transition.

On the basis of the evidence provided in this book, we can conclude that the fears expressed by some scholars and policy advisers regarding the negative implications of employee ownership in Central and Eastern Europe are not justified and certainly exaggerated, considering the limited evidence accumulated so far in support of their views. It is also important to consider that this was in many countries the most feasible (and so the fastest) method of privatization. Whatever the actual implications, employee ownership (even if dominant) is in any case a better alternative to the status quo – maintenance of state ownership or undefined property rights (Earle and Estrin, 1996). The widespread belief that the conditions in Central and Eastern Europe for acquisitions by insiders were too generous thus seems unwarranted;[22] had the terms been less generous, today we would have a much smaller number of privatized firms in most transition economies.

Despite these advantages our empirical investigation identified that employee share-ownership also presents clear weaknesses. The most serious of these – and confirmed in a number of the countries covered by this study – is the lack of fresh capital, which has obvious consequences in respect of investment and the introduction of new technologies and production techniques. Although this book provides good examples of active investment strategies followed by worker-owned enterprises – for instance in the Baltic countries or in Ukraine, thus showing that the management of those enterprises is not less keen on maximizing profits in the long run – they have, however, to face a general problem of liquidity and access to finance.

The best route to solving this problem seems to be to develop employee share-ownership in combination with other property forms, and in particular with domestic and foreign private capital. The example of the mixed company in Lviv presented in Chapter 9 on Ukraine emphasizes that a combination of employee share-ownership, which contributes to enhancing workers' motivation and productivity, with foreign investment, which brings new technologies and access to new foreign markets, could be very effective. While employee share-ownership can help motivate workers temporarily to accept lower wages, longer working hours and increased effort and productivity, foreign investors can bring fresh capital, leading to new investments in the newly privatized enterprise, so also securing revenues for the state. Foreign investors also have easier access to modern technologies, an access that domestic private investors in the region have problems obtaining. At the same time, such ownership may provide greater access to foreign managerial skills. Our findings thus emphasize the need to promote mixed enterprises and to privatize enterprises through different but complementary privatization methods. The involvement of banking and financial institutions could also greatly contribute to support the investment plans of employee-owned enterprises. The example of the huge co-operative complex of Mondragon in Spain shows how successful this type of property and organizational form could become when directly supported by an adequate banking and institutional infrastructure system (Thomas and Logan, 1982).

The examples of Russia and the Baltic countries also emphasize the advantages of combining mass privatization with employee share-ownership.

---

[22] This belief has led several Central and East European governments (Estonia, Latvia, Serbia, Croatia, Slovenia) to introduce more restrictive conditions for employee ownership than those stipulated initially.

The convertibility of privatization vouchers into employee shares might help to avoid the problems identified with the promotion of the vouchers option alone, such as the lack of revenues to the state, the dispersion of owners, and the concentration of wealth in mutual funds.

Rather than giving a dominant role to one particular form of privatization – whether employee share-ownership, mass privatization, or foreign investment – a multi-track approach to privatization should be followed including employees' and managers' buy-outs, acquisitions by investment funds selling certificates to the public, public offers of shares, and sales to citizens or foreigners.

Recent experience with privatization in transition economies has clearly shown that there is no 'ideal' approach which ensures the realization of all main objectives of privatization at the same time – corporate governance, speed, revenues, and fairness. Nevertheless, the most important ultimate objective of privatization, whose achievement today is also the most uncertain – improvement of corporate governance – seems easier to realize if a multitrack approach is adopted. According to recent EBRD research based on interviews with assorted brokerages and fund managers (King, 1996), countries which have used a combination of approaches (Poland and Hungary) would now be ahead as regards some indicators of corporate governance of those (primarily Russia, but also the Czech Republic) which took a single-track approach. Countries which took the privatization fast track seem to be paying for it now. The Czech experience has shown why privatization alone does not necessarily lead to effective corporate governance and improved enterprise performance, since active owners and a responsive market that rewards results and punishes the laggards are still lacking (King, 1996).

The combination of different property forms and shared governance with a mutual or horizontal monitoring process would push workers to promote long-term economic interests, but would also ensure that workers will not be losers in the transition process.

In other words, it would contribute to the creation in these countries of an original mixture of property forms, with greater involvement and commitment on the part of employees. At the same time, this form of employee capitalism would make sure that economic objectives continue to be pursued alongside the preservation of basic social protection and decent working conditions and living standards.

REFERENCES

Acs, Z. and F. FitzRoy (1994), 'A constitution for privatizing large Eastern enterprise', *Economics of Transition*, Vol. 2, No. 1, 83–94.

Alchian, A. and Demsetz, H. (1972), 'Production, information costs, an economic organization', *American Economic Review*, Vol. 62, No. 5, 777–95.

Aoki, M. (1995), 'Controlling insider control: Issues of corporate governance in transition economies', in M. Aoki and H. K. Kim (eds), (1995).

Aoki, M. and Kim, H. K. (1995), 'Overview', in M. Aoki and H. K. Kim (eds.), (1995).

Aoki, M. and Kim, H. K. (eds), (1995), *Corporate Governance in Transition economies*, Washington DC, Economic Development Institute of the World Bank.

Ash T. and P. Hare (1994), 'Privatization in the Russian Federation: changing enterprise behaviour in the transition period', *Cambridge Journal of Economics*, Vol. 18, 619–34.

Bartlett, W. and M. Uvalic (1986), 'Labour-managed firms, employee participation and profit-sharing – Theoretical perspectives and European experience', Management Bibliographies and Reviews, Vol. 12, No. 4.

Ben-Ner, A. (1992), *Organizational Reform in Central and Eastern Europe: A Comparative Perspective*, Leuvens Institute Discussion Papers on Economic Transformation: Policy, Institutions and Structure, WP No. 8/1992, Katholieke Universiteit Leuven.

Ben-Ner, A.and J.M. Montias (1994), 'Economic System Reforms and Privatization in Romania', in Estrin (1994).

Blanchard, O., R. Dornbusch, P. Krugman, R. Layard and L. Summers (1991), *Reforms in Eastern Europe*, Cambridge MA, MIT Press.

Blinder, A.S. (ed.) (1990), *Paying for Productivity – A Look at the Evidence*, Washington, DC, The Brookings Institute.

Bogetic, Z. and M. Conte (1992), *Privatizing Eastern European Economies: A Critical Review and Proposal*, World Bank Discussion Paper, Report No. IDP-119, Washington, December.

Bonin, J. P. and Putterman, L. (1987), *Economics of Co-operation and the Labour-Managed Economy*, Harwood Academic Publishers.

Bonin, J. P, Jones, D. C. and Putterman, L. (1993), 'Theoretical and empirical studies of producer co-operatives: Will ever the twain meet?', *Journal of Economic Literature*, Vol. XXXI, September, 1290–1320.

Bradley, K. and Estrin, S. (1987), 'Profit-sharing in the retail trade sector: the relative performance of the John Lewis Partnership', Discussion Paper No. 279, London School of Economics, Centre for Labour Economics.

Bradley, K. and Gelb, A. (1983), *Worker Capitalism: The New Industrial Relations*, Heinemann Educational Books.

Cable, J. R. and FitzRoy, F. R. (1980), 'Productive efficiency, incentives and employee participation. Some preliminary results for West Germany', *Kyklos*, Vol. 33, No. 1.

Chilosi, A. (1995), 'Social and political aspects of privatization', Conference paper, Opatija, October.

Conte, M. and Svejnar, J. (1990), 'The performance effects of employee ownership plans', in A. Blinder (1990).

Council of the European Communities General Secretariat (1992), 'Press Release 8134/92 (Presse 147) of the 1601st meeting of the Council – Economic and Financial Questions', Brussels, 27 July.

Daviddi, R. (ed.) (1995), *Property Rights and Privatization in the Transition to a Market Economy – A Comparative Review,* Maastricht, European Institute of Public Administration.

Defourney, J., Estrin, S. and Jones, D. C. (1985), 'The effects of worker participation upon productivity in French producer co-operatives', *International Journal of Industrial Organization,* Vol. 3, No. 2, 197-217.

Earle, J. and Estrin, S. (1996), 'Employee ownership in transition', in R. Frydman, C. Gray and A. Rapaczynski (eds.), *Corporate Governance in Central Europe and Russia – Insiders and the State, Vol. 2,* Budapest and New York, World Bank–CEU Press.

Earle, J., Estrin, S. and L. Leshchenko (1995), 'Ownership structures, patterns of control and enterprise behaviour in Russia, working paper, Central European University, November.

Ellerman, D. (1993), 'Management and employee buy-outs in Central and Eastern Europe: Introduction', in D. Ellerman (ed.), *Management and Employee Buy-outs as a Technique of Privatization,* Ljubljana, CEEPN Workshop Series No. 3.

Estrin, S. (1994), *Privatization in Central and Eastern Europe,* Harlow, Longman.

Estrin, S. (1996), 'Privatization in Central and Eastern Europe', Centre for Economic and Transformation – CERT Discussion Paper No. 96/5, Heriot-Watt University, Edinburgh.

Estrin, S. and Jones, D.C. (1988), 'Workers' participation, employee ownership and productivity: Results from French producer co-operatives', London School of Economics and Hamilton College, November.

Estrin, S. and Wilson, N. (1986), 'The micro-economic effects of profit-sharing: the British experience', Discussion Paper No. 247, London School of Economics, Centre for Labour Economics.

Estrin, S., Jones, D.C. and Svejnar, J. (1987), 'The productivity effects of worker participation: producer co-operatives in Western economies', *Journal of Comparative Economics,* Vol. 11, 40-61.

Estrin, S., Grout, P. and Wadhwani, S. (1987), 'Profit-sharing and employee share ownership', *Economic Policy, A European Forum,* No. 4, April.

EBRD (1995), *Transition Report 1995,* London.

European Commission (1989), 'Communication from the Commission concerning its Action Programme relating to the implementation of the Community Charter of basic social rights of workers', COM (89) 568 final, Brussels, 29 November.

FitzRoy, F. R. and Kraft, K. (1986), 'Profitability and profit-sharing', *Journal of Industrial Economics,* Vol. 35, No. 2, 113-30.

FitzRoy, F. R. and Kraft, K. (1987), 'Co-operation, productivity and profit-sharing', *Quarterly Journal of Economics,* 102, February.

Grout, P. (1985), 'Employee share-ownership', University of Birmingham.

Hansmann, H. (1990), 'When does worker ownership work? ESOPs, law firms, codetermination, and economic democracy', *The Yale Law Journal,* Vol. 99, No. 8, 1749-1816.

Jensen, M.C. and Meckling, W. H. (1979), 'Rights and production functions: an application to Labour-managed firms and codetermination', *Journal of Business,* Vol. 52, No. 4, 469-506.

Jones, D.C. and Svejnar, J. (1985), 'Participation, profit-sharing, worker ownership and efficiency in Italian producer co-operatives', *Economica,* Vol. 55, 449-65.

Jones, D. and T. Kato (1993), 'The productivity effects of Employee Stock Ownership Plans and Bonuses: Evidence from Japanese panel data', *Industrial and Labour Relations Review.*

King, N. (1996), 'Who's steering?', *Central European Economic Review*, Vol. IV, No. 2, March.

Kornai, J. (1990), *The Road to a Free Economy – Shifting from a Socialist System: The Example of Hungary*, New York: W.W. Norton.

Kruse, D. (1991), 'Profit-sharing and employment variability: Micro-economic evidence on the Weitzman theory', *Industrial and Labour Relations Review*, Vol. 44, April.

Kruse, D. (1993), 'Profit Sharing: Does it Make a Difference?', W.E. Upjohn Institute.

Lee, B. W. (1988), 'Productivity and employee ownership: the case of Sweden', Ph. D. dissertation, Uppsala University, Sweden.

Lipton, D. and J. Sachs (1990), 'Creating a market economy in Eastern Europe: The case of Poland', Brookings Papers on Economic Activity, 1 (1990), 75–147.

Meade, J.E. (1972), The theory of labour-managed firms and of profit sharing', *Economic Journal*, Vol. 82, Supplement, 402-28.

Meade, J.E. (1989), *Agathotopia: The Economics of Partnership*, Aberdeen, Aberdeen University Press.

Mertlik, P. (1995), 'Czech privatization: from public ownership to public ownership in five years?', Paper presented at the Conference of the European Association for Evolutionary Political Economy, Cracow, October.

Milovanovic, M. (1992), 'Preuredjenje vlasnistva putem ESOP-a', *Ekonomska misao*, Vol. 25, No. 4, 491-509.

MRP (Employee Stock Ownership Plan, Hungary) (1994), Foundation and National Alliance of MRPs, Newsletter No. 3.

Munteanu, C. (1995), 'Employees' share-ownership in Central and East European privatization – The case of Romania', Paper prepared for the ILO-CEET project on Insiders' Privatization in Central and Eastern Europe, October.

Mygind, N. (ed.) (1995), *Privatization and Financial Participation in the Baltic Countries*, Copenhagen, Copenhagen Business School.

Nuti, D.M. (1988), 'On traditional co-operatives and James Meade's labour-capital partnership', Florence, European University Institute, Working Paper No. 88/337.

Nuti, D.M. (1995a), 'Mass privatization: costs and benefits of instant capitalism', in R. Daviddi (1995).

Nuti, D.M. (1995b), 'Employeeism: Corporate governance and employee share ownership in transition economies', Conference paper, Reggio Emilia, May 5.

OECD (1993), *Methods of Privatizing Large Enterprises*, OECD–CCET, Paris.

OECD (1995), *Trends and Policies in Privatization*, OECD Centre for Co-operation with the Economies in Transition (CCET), Vol. 2, No. 2, Paris.

Pejovich, S. (1969), 'The firm, monetary policy and property rights in a planned economy', *Western Economic Journal*, Vol. 7, No. 3, 193-200.

Roland, G. (1995), 'Political economy issues of ownership transformation in Eastern Europe', in M. Aoki and H. K. Kim (eds), (1995).

Sertel, M. R. (1982), *Workers and Incentives*, Amsterdam, North Holland.

Spineewyn, F. and J. Svejnar (1990), 'Optimal membership, employment and income distribution in a unionized and labor managed firm', in *Journal of Labor Economics*, 8(3), pp. 317–39, 1990.

Stiglitz, J.E. (1995), *Whither Socialism?*, Cambridge MA, MIT Press.

Sutela, P. (1995), 'Successes and failures of privatization in Russia', paper presented at the Fifth EACES Trento Workshop, March.

Thomas, H. and C. Logan (1982), *Mondragon: An Economic Analysis*, London, Allen and Unwin.

Uvalic, M. (1991), The PEPPER Report: Promotion of Employee Participation in

Profits and Enterprise Results in the Member States of the European Community, (in English, French and German), Social Europe Supplement No. 3/91, Luxembourg, Office for Official Publications of the European Communities.

Uvalic, M. (1992), *Investment and Property Rights in Yugoslavia – The Long Transition to a Market Economy*, Cambridge, Cambridge University Press.

Uvalic, M. (1994), 'Privatization in disintegrating East European States: the case of former Yugoslavia', Florence, European University Institute Working Paper RSC No. 94/11; also in R. Daviddi (ed.), (1995).

Uvalic, M. (1995), 'Employee ownership: international experience and prospects for Yugoslavia', paper prepared for the National Bank of the Federal Republic of Yugoslavia.

Vanek, J. (1970), *The General Theory of Labor-Managed Market Economies*, Ithaca, Cornell University Press.

Vaughan-Whitehead, D. (1992), *Interessement, Participation, Actionnariat – Impacts Economiques dans l'Entreprise*, Paris, Economica.

Vaughan-Whitehead, D. et al. (1995), *Workers' Financial Participation. East–West Experiences*, ILO Labour Management Series No. 80, Geneva.

Vaughan-Whitehead, D. (ed.) (1995), *Reforming Wage Policy in Central and Eastern Europe*, ILO/European Commission.

Ward, B. (1958), 'The firm in Illyria: Market socialism', *American Economic Review*, Vol. 48, No. 4, 566-89.

Weitzman, M. (1984), *The Share Economy*, Cambridge MA, Harvard University Press.

Weitzman, M. (1995), 'Incentive effects of profit-sharing', Conference paper, Reggio Emilia, May 5.

Weitzman, M. and Kruse, D.L. (1990), 'Profit sharing and productivity', in A. S. Blinder (ed.), (1990).

World Bank (1994), Russian Federation Enterprise Support Project, June.

World Bank (1996), *World Development Report 1996 – From Plan to Market*, Washington D.C., June.

Wilson, N. (ed.) (1992), *ESOPs: Their Role in Corporate Finance and Performance*, London, Macmillan Publishers Ltd.

Zec, M., B. Mijatovic, D. Djuricin, N. Savic (eds), (1994), 'Privatizacija – Nuznost ili sloboda izbora', Belgrade, Jugoslovenski pregled and Institute of Economics.

2. Employee Ownership in the Baltic Countries

Niels Mygind

1 INTRODUCTION

One of the surprising results of the transition to a market economy in Eastern Europe is the high incidence of different forms of insider ownership. Some enterprises were taken over by the management, but a considerable number were taken over by a broader group of employees. We shall refer to insider ownership characterized by a broad group of other employees owning more of an enterprise than management as employee ownership. Different forms of insider ownership have been quite important in such countries in transition as Poland, Russia, Slovenia, and Ukraine. Similarly, in the Baltic countries insider ownership in the form of both employee and management ownership has played a considerable role. It was developed, however, to a different extent – with, for example, much larger growth in Lithuania – and took different forms in the three countries.

The aim of the present chapter is to provide an overview of the development and economic performance of different forms of insider ownership in the Baltic countries, with particular emphasis on employee ownership. The material for this chapter was collected in the course of a research project on Privatization and Financial Participation (PFPB) undertaken by the European Commission (ACE–PHARE). This allowed us to collect a rich body of information and data on employee ownership in the Baltic countries.

In Section 2 the background conditions in the three Baltic countries are outlined, with the emphasis on their common features but also their observed differences. Section 3 analyses political developments relating to employee ownership. In Section 4 developments in legislation and the promotion of employee ownership are described. In Section 5 results of an analysis of the performance of enterprises with different property forms are presented, focusing particularly on economic results in employee-owned enterprises. We conclude with an outline of prospects for the further development of employee ownership.

Privatization Surprises in Transition Economies

2 BACKGROUND CONDITIONS OF EMPLOYEE OWNERSHIP

To understand the situation in the Baltic countries we must outline both their similarities and their differences. For this purpose it is useful to employ a classification of four subsystems (further elaborated in Mygind, 1994), and to take into account a range of external factors (*Table 2.1*).

Table 2.1 Background conditions, Estonia, Latvia and Lithuania pre-1988–90

		Estonia			Latvia			Lithuania		
		1988	1989	1990	1988	1989	1990	1988	1989	1990
Institutional System*										
History,	co-ops	256	969	2 087	245	1 190	4 086	503	1 569	4 495
foreign	jobs	4 500	21 500	42 100	5 200	28 700	134 800	5 900	25 500	81 400
dominance	sales**	8	102	385	10	190	1 079	13	118	652
Centres for	% of									
experiment	turnover	–	0.9	3.3	–	1.0	5.6	–	0.5	1.6
during										
perestroika				Leasing			Leasing			Leasing

Social System*	Estonia	Latvia	Lithuania
Ethnic change during Soviet occupation	Emigration and deportations of Estonians and immigration of Russians increased the non-Estonian-speaking minority to 39% in 1989; majority of workers are non-Estonian	Emigration and deportations of Latvians and immigration of Russians increased the non-Latvian-speaking minority to 48% in 1989; majority of workers are non-Latvian	Emigration of Lithuanians, but no large immigration of Russians. Movement of labour from agriculture to new industries Non-Lithuanian-speaking minority: 21% in 1989

Value System	Estonia	Latvia	Lithuania
Language	Finnish/Agrarian	Baltic	Baltic
Religion	Protestant	Protestant	Catholic
Foreign influence	mainly German	mainly German	mainly Polish/traditional

Production System	Estonia	Latvia	Lithuania
Industrialization Surrounding world all three dependent on 'trade' with rest of USSR	quite early strong ties with Finland	quite early	Soviet industrialization

Notes:
* Arkadie et al. (1991).
** Million roubles.
*** Hanson (1990).

Under this four-system classification the *institutional system* is the formal set of rules governing the political process and the co-ordination of the economy. This institutional system was in all three countries dominated by the Soviet command system based on state-owned enterprises mainly controlled by the All Union authorities in Moscow, some enterprises being controlled by local authorities. The economic experiments under Gorbachev had an impact in all three countries, most significantly in Estonia. These experiments involved some steps in the direction of employee ownership. Workers' Councils formally received some right of control at the enterprise level. New co-operatives with the participation of some employees as members were developed, especially in Estonia (*Table 2.1*). Many of the experiments, including the special 'small state enterprises' in Estonia, could be used by insiders particularly at the management level to initiate so-called 'wild privatization' by means of which state-owned assets were more or less legally transferred to their control.

The *social system* comprises the different social groups and their interaction. Here, the main difference was that the Russian-speaking minority constituted a relatively large group in Estonia and Latvia. This was particularly true of industrial workers among whom the native population was a minority. In Lithuania, the Russian minority was less than 10 per cent of the population.

The *value system* – 'culture' – also distinguishes Estonia and Latvia which are Protestant and have a more modern, Germanic culture, and Lithuania which is Catholic and more influenced by Polish examples and traditional values. This difference points in the direction of more individualistic values in the northern countries versus more collectivist values in Lithuania.

The *production system* includes such national assets as natural resources, physical means of production, and know-how. This system also distinguishes Lithuania from the other two because industrialization was more developed in Estonia and Latvia before the Soviet planning system took over: there is more emphasis on large heavy industry with Soviet-type enterprises in Lithuania. All three countries were strongly integrated in the Soviet division of labour, making them very much dependent on partners in the former USSR.

As far as external conditions are concerned, the geographic and linguistic proximity between Estonia and Finland provided a better starting point for Estonia in its turn to the West (Dellenbrant, 1992).

3 POLITICAL DEVELOPMENTS AND EMPLOYEE OWNERSHIP

To understand how background conditions may be transformed into 'change' in the institutional system it is necessary to analyse the political developments

Table 2.2 Political development, privatization and employee ownership, Estonia, Latvia and Lithuania, 1989–95

Baltic	Estonia	Latvia	Lithuania
Fight for independence Economic policy: from experiments to preparation for a 'mixed economy'	IME programme, May 1989: mixed economy with 'peoples enterprises'. Employee ownership seen as instrument for liberalizing enterprises from Soviet rule. Employee ownership gets lower priority as demands for independence and market economy gain ground.	Workers' Council: some role at the enterprise level; weak labour organizations.	Early preparation of reform, emp.shares in Feb. 1990, egalitarian values =>voucher privatization in Feb. 1991. Restitution important in agriculture for citizens living in Lithuania
After independence before elections National forces split, complex choices on citizenship, constitution, economic policy => unclear interests, volatility.	Fight between *national line* for voucher-privatization and restitution, and *technocratic line* favouring direct sale of enterprises. Small privatization: concessions for employees new conflicts, from May 1992. June 1992 introduction of KROON; no citizenship or voting rights for Russians; liberal economic policy; slow privatization.	Using part of old constitution; no citizenship or voting rights for Russians; fast privatization in agriculture (few Russians); government–parliament in deadlock on citizenship and economic policy. Decentralized priv.: municipalities in charge of small priv.; branch ministries in charge of large priv.; some scope for insiders; more empha-sis on restitution.	Minorities full citizenship; unions somewhat involved; protests from employees in early privatization =>30% shares to employees at preferential prices; other preferences for insiders, mainly supported by strong industrial lobby.
After first elections More homogenous and well defined interests. Russian troops out: August 1993 in Lithuania; August 1994 in Estonia and Latvia.	Election, September 1992: new constitution approved, centre-right government programme: ultraliberal focus on the West, hard line nationalism. THA-privatization introduced in summer 1992, no concessions for employees. Sept. 1994 prime minister steps down after scandal.	Election, June 1993; centre-right gov., privatization centralized with key role for privatization agency from summer 1994; slow start for voucher system. July 1994: gov. crisis Sept. 1994: centre-left gov.	Election, Oct./ Nov. 1992; presidential election February 1993, Labour party majority, election Oct./Nov. 1992, presidential election February 1993, Labour party majority, support from workers and agro-workers dissatisfied with privatization policy.

Table 2.2 cont.

	Estonia	Latvia	Lithuania
	Election October 1995: opposition wins, centre-left; privatization policy unchanged.	Dec. 1994: 1st int. tender; 1995: public offerings. Election October 1995: no clear majority; political deadlock; coalition with centre-left; nationalist government.	Preference for employee ownership Employee shares rise to 50%. Privatization slows down in 1993, but accelerates in 1994; voucher programme finished 1995. Managers, old networks, still in strong position, foreign capital remains limited.

Source: Mygind (1996).

which determined the path of transition, including the choice of privatization methods. The political process is the main link between the initial conditions and the transition of the institutional system.

The early start of the economic and political transition in all three countries was closely related to the struggle for independence. The republican leadership was most radical in Lithuania, which may be partly explained by the presence of only a relatively small Russian minority. In the aftermath of the August 1991 coup, the national question played a particularly important role in Estonia and Latvia, leading to a vacuum on the left of the political spectrum. Because the majority of industrial workers were Russian-speaking with very limited political power, workers were split and unions weak. Hence, the political debate in the first years of transition did not focus on economic problems, but rather on national sovereignty. In Estonia, this tendency was combined with quite early and quite radical reforms closely related to a rapid turn to the West which was made easier by the proximity to Finland; in Latvia, a similar pressure for rapid economic reforms did not exist. Here, the national question was to a larger extent a barrier which for a long period brought the political system to a standstill.

This development can be closely connected to the role and relative strength of different social groups. Concerning the question of employee ownership it is relevant to focus mainly on employees. In Estonia and Latvia this group was split between the native speaking and the Russian-speaking groups. In the first stages of transition they could use such leverage as was afforded by the Workers' Councils. Particularly in Estonia, these councils had some influence, but they were split in a pro-Russian and a pro-Estonian organization quite early on (Terk, 1996). During the transition Russian-speaking employees in particular lost influence. This was probably an important factor behind the decreasing importance of employee ownership in the beginning of the 1990s. At the same time, the trade unions were very weak and unable to promote employee ownership.

In the early years of transition, when employees still had some power at the enterprise level, the managers often made alliances with them to implement different forms of insider take-over. During the transition, management gained more power and also built up capital resources so that they were able to effect take-overs without involving the broader group of employees. In Estonia, this was combined with a quite early shift in the direction of direct enterprise sales promoted by the Estonian Privatization Agency. In this way the bureaucrats quite early on implemented a 'technocratic' line favouring take-overs by a core investor, often based on foreign owners or the existing management team. This policy was not affected significantly by the shifts in government. The election in 1992 brought an ultra-liberal, nationalist govern-ment to power. The election in 1995 constituted a reaction to the ultra-liberal policy and resulted in a centrist government. However, the new government continued the previous privatization policy, including a quite ambitious programme for the privatization of public utilities.

In Latvia the process was slower. The decentralized type of privatization led to an alliance between bureaucrats in the ministries and enterprise managements. The initial poor transparency of the privatization process was probably an advantage for insiders, and in some cases broader groups of employees may have been involved. Although there was a change in the legislation on small privatization limiting the advantages of insiders in early 1992, the tendency of local administrations to prefer insiders continued. This changed in 1994 with the reorganization of privatization giving the Latvian Privatization Agency a key role, limiting the role of managers and their networks in the ministries. At the same time, more emphasis on foreign investment with international tenders – starting in autumn 1994 – meant more competition among potential owners. The privatization process went more slowly than expected, and the banking crisis which began in the summer of 1995 created another obstacle. The election in October 1995 was a delayed reaction to the economic crisis, but it did not result in a clearer political situation. The political deadlock continued, first with months of negotiations on the formation of the new government, and later in a broad government based on alliances which did not bode well for stability and decisive action.

In Lithuania, the main directions of privatization were already decided and were being implemented in 1991 in a period in which strongly egalitarian norms still dominated among the leading politicians (Cicinskas, 1994). At this stage, the unions were quite active, making demands about distribution and some sort of employee ownership. The result was a strong emphasis on a voucher system and on preferences for employees. This political tendency was reinforced by the election towards the end of 1992. Unlike the two Northern Baltic countries this election constituted a strong reaction against the ruling politicians and the steep fall in production and living standards. While the previous government had taken some steps in the direction of giving foreign investors a larger role, this policy was only sporadically implemented and had little impact on the privatization process. The victorious Labour Party extended the policy of employee preferences in the privatization process. Managements usually had to make alliances with broader groups of employees if they wanted to take over their enterprise.

4 LEGISLATION AND THE IMPLEMENTATION OF PRIVATIZATION

The legislation and implementation of privatization which were of importance for employee ownership are summarized in *Table 2.3*.

Estonia started very early in 1987 with the first transformation of state ownership in the form of 'semi-private' 'small state-owned enterprises'; the 'new co-operatives' also developed quite early and rapidly in Estonia. It may be assumed that these enterprises were mainly taken over by their managers.

Employee ownership played a considerable role, however, in the political debate and this was to some extent reflected in the legislation and implemented in the early years of transition. The first cases of employee ownership were the leased enterprises under the Soviet legislation of 1989 (Frydman et al., 1993). In July 1991 this law was amended in accordance with Estonian rules and around 200 of such enterprises were started. Legislation on 'People's enterprises' was also adopted in 1991. These enterprises were collectively owned by the employees and in the initial political debate many people expected this type to be the dominant form of ownership in the years to come. However, only seven enterprises were established with full employee ownership (Terk, 1996). When Estonia got its independence in August 1991, the political climate turned against employee ownership. Small privatization started in January 1991 with large concessions for employee ownership. The initial legislation favoured insiders, but from May 1992 most of these preferences were at least formally taken away. Before the change in policy, seven large experimental privatizations had been implemented with a strong element of employee ownership. This development is yet another sign of the change in policy with regard to employee ownership. It is estimated that around 80 per cent of the first wave of 450 small enterprises were taken over by insiders before the change in policy (Kein and Tali, 1994).

In the summer of 1992 the preferential treatment of employees was stopped; the large privatization implemented by the Estonian Privatization Enterprise,

Table 2.3 Overview of privatization and employee ownership, Estonia, Latvia and Lithuania, 1990–95

Period	Estonia	Latvia	Lithuania
Before full independence	'Small state enterprises' and new co-operatives, mostly man.-owned. Soviet leasing systems in 12 large employee-owned enterprises. Estonian leasing adopted in July 1991 and experienced in 200 management-owned enterprises. Legislation on 'people's enterprises' in 1991, leading to 7 fully employee-owned enterprises.	New co-operatives mostly man. -owned. Soviet leasing systems. In large privatization leasing applied in 200–300 enterprises.	New co-operatives mostly management-owned Soviet leasing systems. 60 majority employee-owned enterprises. Temporary law on employee-shares in 1990-91. 3% of the assets in 1991. Small and large privatization starts in 1991.
First stage after independence	Small privatization with insider preferences (Jan.1991–May 1992) 7 large experiments with full employee ownership. 450 employee-owned small enterprises. Change in policy in May 1992: less concessions for employees (May 1992 – June 1993) less employee ownership.	Small privatization in 1992-1993, with preferences for employee ownership. 200 employee-owned enterprises. 6 large experiments in 1991, mainly employee-owned. Decentralized privatization (1992–94) 200 insider-owned.	Privatization programme promotes shares for employees. 30% rsvd. from 1992 50% rsvd. from 1993 Payment mainly by vouchers. From 1992 reserves could be used for employee shares. Increasing employee ownership in large privatization. By July 1994 all industrial joint-stock companies have majority employee ownership.
Second stage	Large priv. by EPA (Nov. 1992–Dec. 1995). 200–300 insider-owned, mainly by management. 200–300 foreign owned, vouchers used for minority shares from end of 1994.	Large priv. by LPA (1994-95) few insider take-overs, increasing role for foreigners, vouchers used for some public offerings.	Sales to foreigners of minor importance. From 1996 the remaining state-owned enterprises to be sold by Privatization Agency for cash.

Source: Mygind, 1996.

later the Estonian Privatization Agency, did not give employees any preferential treatment. This type of privatization was based on a tender process in which the buyers' capital contribution and investment guarantees played an important role. In this way, existing capital owners were given a clear advantage. By this time, most managements had accumulated some capital and it was also possible for them to acquire loans in the rapidly developing system of private banks. Furthermore, domestic capital was allowed to buy in instalments. The managers' alliance with the broad group of employees was no longer necessary. In addition, foreign capital gained increasing access during this late stage of large privatization; it is estimated that foreign investors obtained around 40 per cent of privatized assets (*Baltic Independent,* 19 February 1994).

The high proportion of assets owned by foreigners is also confirmed by the data from the ownership survey of 414 enterprises with different property forms and different sized groups with five or more employees in all branches of the economy. The survey was carried out in January 1995 by the EC project in co-operation with the Statistical Office of Estonia. The main results are summarized below.

When we normalize the sample for the whole economy we find that foreign ownership in privatized industry represents 52 per cent of the capital. For the whole privatized Estonian economy it represents 37 per cent of the assets.

The frequency of employee ownership is quite high, with majority insider ownership covering around 36 per cent of private enterprises. Of these, about half are owned mainly by management and the other half by a broader group of employees; 40 per cent of enterprises covering 29 per cent of employees have no employee ownership. We estimate that in the private sector as a whole one in four employees owns shares in his enterprise.

Agriculture has the highest frequency of employee ownership, with around 50 per cent of enterprises being owned by a broad group of employees. Construction, fishing, and mining have similar percentages. In manufacturing, textiles, leather, petroleum and chemicals, majority ownership by a broad group of employees is also relatively frequent. The degree of employee ownership is relatively low in sectors such as wholesale trade, transport, and financial services.

Between the time of privatization and 1 January 1995, there was no tendency for insiders to sell their shares, but some other tendencies are worth noting. First, the number of cases of both no insider ownership and full insider ownership fell. Second, managers tended to be the buyers and other employees the sellers, as a consequence of which managers increased their shareholdings: the number of majority management owned enterprises increased from 76 to 88 per cent, while the number of majority employee-owned enterprises fell from 102 to 82 per cent. Third, in the enterprises with majority employee ownership, about half the employees are not owners. In agriculture, fishing, and mining the percentage is 25 per cent or lower. Fourth, in 65 per cent of the small enterprises with employee ownership the distribution was found to be relatively equal among owner employees, and in 31 per cent of large enterprises with more than 99 employees. In large enterprises about half the cases indicate a very unequal distribution with differences typically of more than 1:10. Finally, broad employee ownership of capital does not necessarily mean that the employees have a similar degree of control. Non-voting employee shares are prevalent, particularly where there is a high degree of broad employee ownership; 50 per cent of large enterprises with majority employee ownership had this type of governance structure.

The early stages of transition in *Latvia* have many similarities with developments in Estonia. Many new co-operatives were established, and leasing in accordance with Soviet legislation was also important. As in Estonia, the first legislation on small privatization included some employee concessions, but they were also formally removed in 1992. In contrast to Estonia, however, it seems that employee concessions were continued into 1993 by many municipalities (Vojevoda and Rumpis, 1993).

Large privatization formally included some concessions for employees, enabling them to buy 10–20 per cent of the shares in their enterprise (Frydman et al., 1993). However, the most significant advantage was probably the decentralized organization of the privatization process giving a key role to different ministries, which meant that the existing networks could be used to the advantage of insiders. This might explain why one of the most frequently utilized privatization forms was leasing, a method mainly used by insiders. Up until 1994, however, privatization was rather slow: this type of privatization included only around 200–300 enterprises of which most were insider take-overs, probably mainly by management. Still, this included more large enterprises than was the case in Estonia. There was a longer period during which insiders were able to benefit from this type of privatization. In spring/summer 1994 the privatization process was centralized in the hands of the Latvian Privatization Agency, and more emphasis was placed on foreign capital, and also on vouchers distributed mainly to Latvian citizens. The strategy of the Latvian Privatization Agency was, as in Estonia, first to find a core investor by way of tender, and then to sell the minority shares for vouchers in public offerings. Three enterprises were sold by this method in the first months of 1995 and 13 companies were privatized in the second round in mid-1995.

The general data collected by the Latvian Department of Statistics include information on the distribution of ownership between the state, municipalities, domestic outsiders, foreigners, and insiders. The survey covers all enterprises with 20 or more employees and a random sample of smaller enterprises. We have results for 5,585 enterprises for January 1995. The ownership distribution is quite interesting: typically one group of owners owns more than 50 per cent of the enterprise. Only 3 per cent of enterprises had mixed ownership in the sense that no group of owners had a majority; 16 per cent of the 5,589 enterprises were owned mainly by the state and municipalities, 4.4 per cent were owned by foreigners, 26 per cent were owned by domestic outsiders, and in 51 per cent of the enterprises insiders owned more than 50 per cent. A subsample of 685 enterprises shows that more than 80 per cent of the insider-owned enterprises were 100 per cent owned by insiders. The incidence of majority insider ownership was also found to increase as enterprise size decreases measured by number of employees: 67 per cent of enterprises with 1–4 employees were majority insider-owned; for enterprises with more than 500 employees, the figure is only 18 per cent. In this group, state ownership dominates. We do not have figures distinguishing insiders as managers and other employees, but based on earlier information we expect that the bulk, particularly of small insider enterprises, are mainly owned by managers.

In the first years of transition *Lithuania* had the fastest privatization process of the Baltic countries, mainly due to the promotion of employee ownership as the main mode of privatization. Privatization in accordance with Soviet legislation in the form of new co-operatives and leasing was probably not as developed as in Estonia and Latvia, but the Lithuanian legislation for both small and large privatization ('LIPSP Programme') was passed at the start of 1991: implementation started in the second part of 1991. This meant that the early egalitarian orientation had a strong influence on the major part of Lithuanian privatization.

In 1990–91, a temporary *Act on Employee Shares* was introduced. This provided the first opportunity to distribute shares to employees. The progress of employee ownership took off when preferences for employees were built into the privatization programme for large enterprises in 1992. Employees could buy 30 per cent of the shares in their enterprise for vouchers and cash in the first round. The price for employees was set at the 'initial price', which meant that they could get their part of the shares at a relatively low price. Because of the only partial indexation of the price of the assets and of the value of the vouchers, the advantage of employees increased over time (Martinavicius, 1996). In 1993, the share of enterprises in which employees could buy shares at a favourable price was increased to 50 per cent. The 20 per cent of extra shares reserved for employees did not have any voting rights, but later in the process it was made possible for the general meeting of the enterprises to convert these shares into normal voting shares.

Programmes for the sale of state-owned enterprises to foreigners were introduced as early as 1992, but until 1995 were used only in a limited number of cases. Restitution was not a viable option for industrial enterprises either. Therefore, employee ownership was an important element in the privatization, especially of large enterprises in Lithuania. The privatization programme did not include special preferences for employees in small privatization. Because of inside information and the access to purchasing resources in the form of vouchers, however, insiders have probably also had a relatively strong position in this part of privatization. It should be noted that, although small privatization included around half of the 6,000 enterprises to be privatized in the privatization programme, the small enterprises only covered a small percentage of total assets and the total number of employees.

More detailed information about the privatization process and the spread of employee ownership from the database of the Department of Privatization in the Ministry of Economy shows a clear trend. In the first period, up to the end of 1992, employees got a relatively small part of the shares; 67 per cent of enterprises had no employee ownership after the initial privatization. In 1993 and 1994 less than 5 per cent had no employee ownership, and the percentage of enterprises with majority employee ownership increased from 3 per cent in 1991–92 to 65 per cent in 1993, and further to 91–92 per cent in 1994–95. This development indicates the increasing support for employee take-overs.

The ownership survey, undertaken in July 1994 by the Department of Statistics in Lithuania, got responses from 357 industrial enterprises which confirm the wide extension of employee ownership in large enterprises in Lithuania. By July 1994 only 1 per cent of these enterprises still had no employee ownership, 29 per cent of the enterprises had 31–50 per cent employee ownership, and 27 per cent of the enterprises had majority employee ownership.

In only 13 per cent of the cases of some insider ownership does the management own more than the rest of the employees. These results are in considerable contrast to Estonia where management owned more than other employees in most cases. It is also worth noting that on average 87 per cent of management and 73 per cent of employees are owners.

It can be concluded that Lithuania has much more employee ownership than its neighbours: nearly all enterprises have an element of employee ownership, the broad group of employees has a much stronger position in relation to management, and there are fewer non-owners among employees as a whole.

5 ANALYSIS OF ECONOMIC PERFORMANCE

5.1 Presentation of Data Sets in the Three Countries

This section presents a short summary of some of the preliminary results of the study of economic performance of groups of enterprises with different ownership structures. After a short introduction to the data sets used for the analysis of economic performance we describe briefly the special starting conditions for different groups. These starting conditions, in combination with ownership structure, determine economic results. The restructuring of production has immediate effects on sales growth and on the adjustment of employment which will be analysed in the following sections. The degree of efficiency in using resources will be analysed in the following section on productivity. Given the level of productivity, the wage level, analysed in the next section, determines the profitability of the enterprise. Retained profits and external finance are important for deep restructuring in the form of investment. This is discussed in the following sections. The presentation is concluded by an overview showing the interaction between the different elements in the three countries. The data sets used for the analysis of the economic performance of employee-owned enterprises compared to other ownership types are presented in Box 2.1.

Box 2.1 Enterprise surveys and data samples, Estonia, Latvia and Lithuania, 1994–95

Estonia

A stratified random sample of 414 enterprises was surveyed in January 1995 on ownership distribution. This data set was supplemented with 227 state-owned enterprises and 25 foreign-owned enterprises, resulting in a total data set of 666 enterprises. For these enterprises we collected financial data for 1993 and 1994, and for a subset also specific information on wage and investment levels, and sources of finance in 1994.

Latvia

We have total data set of 5,585 enterprises, including summary information on ownership groups broken down into the state, municipalities, insiders, and foreign and domestic outsiders. This data set also includes some data on employment and wage levels. A subset of 685 enterprises with 20 or more employees includes a broad range of financial variables from 1994.

Lithuania

357 large manufacturing enterprises included in the database at the statistical department were surveyed on ownership distribution in July 1994, and again in July 1995. In the second round 127 enterprises from construction and trade were also included. For these enterprises we have financial data for some variables dating back to 1992.

5.2 Starting Conditions of Enterprises Promoting Employee Ownership

The institutional framework described in Section 3 reveals that some of the early starters in both Estonia and Latvia are likely to have enjoyed a rather favourable situation. It can be expected that insiders have taken over some of the best performing enterprises in the first rounds of privatization. This may well have happened also in Lithuania. But unlike the two Northern countries, the legislation in Lithuania gradually improved the position of employees. In fact, outsiders had the best opportunities in the early phase of privatization.

Some of the privatized firms formally appear to be newly established enterprises: this was the case for most of the enterprises taken over on a leasing basis in Estonia and Latvia. In the Estonian sample the bulk of privatizations took place in 1993 and 1994, while most of the 'directly established' enterprises started in 1991–92, the period in which leasing and different forms of spin-off were the typical privatization methods: a new company was established as a legal entity, and then this entity leased the assets of the state-owned company. In other cases a group of insiders – often the management – were able to transfer assets from state-owned enterprises by means of special contracts to newly established private companies in their ownership. Both cases are privatization processes, but in the statistical information these enterprises are counted as *de novo* companies. This represents such a major statistical problem that we will not present results distinguishing between privatized and *de novo* enterprises.

It is difficult to uncover the initial position of the enterprise because often we do not have data about its performance before privatization. Furthermore, the available data derive from a period when the economic changes took place very rapidly; when there were changes in currency and calculation methods, and very high inflation, etc.; all factors which render economic data less reliable. However, a few indicators are worth mentioning.

In Estonia, we have relatively little information on profitability before privatization, and we do not have any significant results indicating that insiders took over the most profitable companies. The relation between choice of ownership and size of company in terms of number of employees is also rather weak. There is no observable tendency for employee ownership to be more frequent in smaller enterprises than in larger ones. As previously noted, only management ownership is significantly negatively related to number of employees. For worker ownership there is some indication of the opposite tendency.

There is a strong tendency for the degree of employee ownership to increase as the amount of capital per employee falls. In half the enterprises with the lowest capital per employee, managers own 24 per cent, other employees 31 per cent, other Estonian citizens 31 per cent, the state 3 per cent, and foreigners 10 per cent; in the 10 per cent of enterprises with the highest capital per employee foreigners own 61 per cent and insiders only 0.2 per cent. The low capital per employee was typical particularly of the early stages of privatization. Combined with legislative support this is the background of the high proportion of employee ownership in enterprises privatized in 1990 and 1991.

Capital intensity was lowest for majority insider ownership and somewhat higher for minority insider ownership, but still lower than for the remaining categories of state and outside ownership. Foreign-owned enterprises had the highest capital intensity. The observations related to capital intensity cover also the years after privatization. But since this variable takes years to change, we assume that the tendency also covers the time before privatization. The main explanation for the tendency is probably that employees had the financial possibilities to take over only less capital intensive enterprises. Another explanation could be that the assets were undervalued, especially in cases in which insiders took over their company. As explained earlier, this was included in the legislation in the early phase of small privatization in Estonia, and it may have been the case also in some of the early large privatizations.

In *Latvia*, we cannot distinguish between management ownership and broad employee ownership. As mentioned earlier, Latvia has a very high incidence of insider ownership, especially in the case of small enterprises. We do not have information on profitability before 1994, but there may have been a trend towards the selection of best enterprises by insiders. As regards capital intensity, the tendency is as clear as in Estonia: enterprises with majority foreign ownership have the highest asset value per employee, although state enterprises also have a high capital intensity. This can be explained by the postponed privatization of large capital-intensive enterprises in Latvia. For state- and foreign-owned enterprises only 12 per cent and 9 per cent had total assets per capita lower than 1,000 Lats, but 34 per cent and 35 per cent had assets higher than 5,000 Lats. For the remaining enterprises owned by insiders and domestic outsiders 29–35 per cent were at the lower end and only 12–17 per cent at the higher end of capital intensity. In a multivariate analysis combining the effects of different branches, state- and foreign-owned companies also have significantly higher capital intensity.

In *Lithuania*, management ownership had a higher incidence in small enterprises, but employee ownership was also quite frequent in large enterprises. There seems not to have been a selection bias according to profitability. Profit figures from 1992 – which for most enterprises was before privatization – show that insider ownership, measured in July 1995, was characterized by below average profit margins. The relation to capital intensity is not as clear as in Estonia and Latvia: the group of enterprises with the highest assets per employee is in state-dominated ownership, with insider ownership lying between 25 and 50 per cent. The insider-dominated groups lie around the average, also taking into account the tendency for lower capital intensity to be combined with smaller size which seems to be a feature of enterprises with employee ownership in Lithuania. In Lithuania high capital intensity has not blocked employee take-overs. The main explanation is the voucher privatization method for large enterprises, combined with the preferential price offered for employees before the public offering of their enterprise.

5.3 Performance after Privatization in terms of Sales Growth

From a theoretical point of view we expect private enterprises to adjust better to the market than state-owned enterprises. For nearly all enterprises an initial drop in sales was unavoidable because production had to adjust to completely new conditions concerning cost structure on the input side and revenue potential on the demand side (Mygind, 1994). After a shorter or longer adjustment period with changes in production methods, products, and marketing, it would again be possible to increase production in many enterprises. This depends both on the branch of industry, human resources, and motivation. The incentives are not expected to be strong enough in state-owned companies. This is the main reason behind the theoretical prediction that they find it more difficult to turn the development in sales in a positive direction. On the other hand, it is expected that foreign-owned companies will be able to improve sales quite rapidly because of large investments and new expertise.

We have quantitative evidence from Lithuania on the increase in sales in 1993–94. The average increase for the 372 enterprises was 52 per cent, which indicates a fall measured in fixed prices since average inflation over the period was 70 per cent. The foreign companies were performing best. Management-dominated enterprises seem to do well and employee-dominated about average. State-owned enterprises were also about average, but with large variations between different groups. In terms of sales growth, domestic outside-owned enterprises tend to perform worse than average.

5.4 Employment Adjustments

The theoretical predictions about employment adjustment are straightforward in the sense that employees also consider their job security and the preservation of their firm specific human capital when they make decisions as owners, especially in a situation characterized by unemployment and lay-offs.

In *Estonia*, a multivariate analysis showed that state-owned enterprises were more reluctant to reduce their workforce. There was also some indication that this was the case for majority employee-owned enterprises, and that employees to a certain extent used wages as a buffer in this respect. For the upward adjustment of employment the results show a tendency to increase employment more in majority employee-owned enterprises. This contradicts the theory, but might be explained by the enterprises taking back some of the employees who had been laid off in an earlier round. The same tendency may be observed in respect of management-dominated ownership, but this is not surprising from a theoretical point of view.

The average change in employment from 1993 to 1994 shows that state-owned, outside-owned, and minority employee-owned enterprises had falling employment, majority employee-owned enterprises had stable employment, enterprises with management ownership had a 9–13 per cent increase, and foreign-owned enterprises had a 40 per cent increase in employment.

In *Latvia*, at given levels of sales and wages the multivariate analysis shows lower employment in insider-owned enterprises than in state-owned enterprises. This means that, up to 1994, insider-owned companies cut down employment more than state-owned enterprises.

In *Lithuania*, the preliminary results of the multivariate analysis show higher levels of employment for given levels of value added and wages. When the employment for an earlier period is included as an independent variable the results show that employee-dominated enterprises experience more sluggish labour force adjustment than state-owned enterprises (Jones and Mygind, 1996a).

This tendency can also be observed for simple averages. The fall in employment each year from 1992 to July 1995 and for the whole period is smaller for employee-dominated ownership and about average for management-dominated ownership. The outsider group generally experienced a steeper fall in employment, however, with a tendency for reduced falls when the degree of insider ownership increases. This tendency is not found for state-owned enterprises which, in most cases, have smaller than average falls.

5.5 Productivity

Productivity growth largely depends on the quality of the management and its ability to combine the resources of the enterprise in an efficient way. Another important factor is employee motivation. Here, the alignment of interests as owners and employees and the incentive effect of owning their enterprise point toward higher productivity for employee-owned enterprises, while the lack of managerial experience, conflicts among employees (Hansmann, 1988), lack of control (Alchian and Demsetz, 1972), and free riding point in the other direction. It is assumed also that downward adjustment of labour will be sluggish, implying lower productivity for employee-owned enterprises.

We have some evidence from all three countries, for which the preliminary results of the production function analysis are reported in Jones and Mygind (1996a).

In *Estonia*, a multivariate analysis showed that state-owned companies have lower productivity, while foreign and minority insider-owned enterprises have higher productivity than enterprises owned by local outsiders. Other calculations confirm that a higher degree of employee and management ownership corresponds to higher productivity.

In *Latvia*, an estimation based on net turnover shows that foreign and insider ownership has a significantly higher level of sales with given inputs of capital and labour compared to state-owned enterprises.

For *Lithuania*, we have also some averages for labour productivity based on the July 1995 ownership distribution. The results for 1993 and 1994 show that the group with dominant employee ownership in particular has high labour productivity, though management ownership also yields above average results. Furthermore, there is a clear tendency towards higher productivity when the degree of insider ownership increases, with regard to both state-dominated and outside-dominated ownership.

5.6 Wage Levels

Just as employees are expected to favour stakeholder interests concerning employment they are also expected to opt for higher wages than would have been the case for other types of ownership (Nuti, 1995). Behind this argument is also the assumption that employees have a relatively short time-horizon concerning savings in their enterprise and a high aversion to risk. In combination with an imperfect capital market this means that they prefer income paid out as wages, and in some cases as dividends, to accumulating large surpluses in the enterprise. On the other hand, there will be a trade-off between wage levels and job security (Earle and Estrin, 1995). It can be expected that employees will be more flexible in their wage demands when they receive the residual surplus and make the relevant decisions. In the depressed economy characteristic of early transition this will typically mean lower wages in employee-owned enterprises. We therefore have two opposite tendencies with regard to the relationship between employee ownership and wage policy, on which we have been trying to collect some data in Estonia and Lithuania.

For *Estonia* we have detailed wage data for 404 enterprises, based on information for different occupational groups in October 1994. The results are shown in *Figure 2.1* for three groups: managers; specialists and skilled workers; and unskilled workers. The figures are weighted so that different gender proportions do not affect the results. Wage levels for all three occupational groups are relatively low in state-owned enterprises and in enterprises with majority insider ownership. For enterprises with minority insider ownership wages for workers and professionals are also quite low, while managers' wages are higher. The highest wage levels for managers

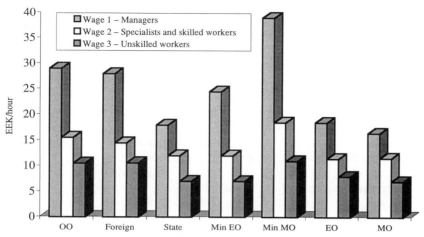

Note: Insider ownership, *IO*, is divided into employee ownership, *EO*, and management ownership, *MO*; OO = outside ownership (MinIO = minority IO, MinMO = minority MO, MinEO = minority EO).

Figure 2.1 Average hourly wages for three occupational groups in Estonia, 1994

were found in enterprises with minority management ownership. Note that this was also the group with the highest factor productivity. There might be special factors influencing this group of enterprises. Enterprises in domestic and foreign outside ownership were found to have relatively high wage levels.

In a multivariate analysis controlling for branches and location the tendency described above is confirmed, with wages for managers and unskilled workers being significantly lower in majority insider-owned enterprises.

In *Lithuania*, the results for average wage levels in different ownership groups for 1992 and 1993 do not show any clear tendencies, except that foreign enterprises clearly have the highest wage levels. This is also the case for 1994, but with insider-dominated companies also having a quite high average wage level that year. There are clear tendencies both in the state-owned and outside-owned enterprises indicating that the greater the share owned by employees the higher the wages. There is no clear variation related to size, but considerable variation between branches; enterprises in construction and in trade pay quite high average wages. In construction – with the highest wage level around 50 per cent above the national average – employee-owned companies are 20 per cent and management-dominated companies 15 per cent above the branch wage average. In trade, the general tendency is somewhat fragmented with insider-dominated enterprises paying between 4 per cent and 20 per cent below the average for the branch.

For Lithuania we have also variables showing dividends per employee, which in the case of employee ownership is clearly another way of remunerating employees. On average they made up only 5.5 per cent of wages in 1993 and 2 per cent in 1994; for employee-dominated enterprises they represented 7 per cent and 3 per cent, with a clear tendency for higher dividends in predominantly employee-owned enterprises or with minority insider ownership. This, however, does not necessarily mean that employees are taking cash out of the enterprise; they may be using dividends to buy some of the remaining state-owned shares. It is worth noting the high level of dividends in foreign-owned enterprises in 1993, indicating an early repatriation of profits and the positive returns that employees could get from combining employee ownership with foreign investment.

5.7 Profitability

If employees pay excessive wages this should directly result in low levels of profitability. We also obtained some results from the three countries.

In *Estonia*, the preliminary results on returns on total assets are based on a multivariate model with controls for branch and location. For the 1993 data this model shows lower returns in state-owned enterprises, but no significant variation for the other ownership types. For 1994 again state-owned enterprises are also found to have lower returns. All enterprises with insider ownership are found to have significantly higher returns than outside ownership, the two categories with management ownership having the highest returns on assets. Simple averages show the same tendency. Worth noting is the fact that foreign ownership has a relatively low return on assets, which might be explained by high capital intensity which has not yet been paid off.

In *Latvia*, the preliminary results in a multivariate model which controlled for branch, number of employees, total assets, and capital intensity indicates that both inside and domestic outside ownership have significantly higher returns than state ownership, while the highest return on assets is found in the category of 50–99.9 per cent inside ownership. Surprisingly, foreign ownership does not have results significantly different from state-owned enterprises. The results of a simple distribution of returns on assets for different owner categories are given in *Table 2.4*.

It can be seen from *Table 2.4* that insider-owned enterprises have a more favourable profit distribution than other types. State-owned enterprises perform the worst. In *Lithuania*, we collected averages both for profit margins and return on total assets. Profit margin seems not to vary much from the national average for insider-dominated enterprises in 1992 and 1993, indicating that there would be no selection bias according to profitability.[1] In

---

[1] Profit margin is defined as operating surplus (not including financial revenues and costs) as a percentage of turnover.

Table 2.4 Return on assets by form of ownership, Latvia 1994 (%)

	State	Foreign	Insider 50–99.9%	Insider 100%	Domestic outside	Total
Number of enterprises	121	55	59	288	159	682
–10%	35	29	25	25	30	29
–10%–0%	28	31	20	15	16	19
0%–10%	22	16	24	23	30	24
10%–25%	12	16	12	18	11	15
+25%–	3	8	19	19	13	13
Total	100	100	100	100	100	100

1994 employee-owned enterprises seemed to do significantly better than other enterprises. This was also the case for outside-dominated enterprises with a high degree of employee ownership. The general fall in profit margin – which was found in all types of enterprise – from 1992 to 1994 can be explained mainly by the depressed economy, although it may also be partly caused by new statistical definitions, return on assets being based on profits inclusive of revenues and costs. On this basis, employee-owned enterprises did quite well in 1994 in relation to other ownership groups. State-owned and outside-owned enterprises with high insider ownership also did better than average, while management-owned enterprises are about average, and all other enterprise forms – that is, without significant employee ownership – were found to be below the average.

5.8 Finance

In order to restructure production it is necessary to adjust fixed capital, which in most cases entails considerable investment. The question of finance is, therefore, crucial for many enterprises. This finance capacity can be generated from internally accumulated profits or from the issue of new shares. Both of these sources will show up as an increase in the net worth of the enterprise. Capital can also be generated by loans from credit institutions. From a theoretical point of view it can be expected that insider ownership will have to rely mainly on internally accumulated capital because of bank fears that insiders – especially employees – will follow stakeholder interests which are different from those of capital holders (Nuti, 1995). This limits also the possibility of share issues to external minority shareholders, while majority shareholders might have difficulties in getting access to employee-owned enterprises since they are often of a closed type.

Privatization Surprises in Transition Economies

Table 2.5 Financial investment sources in Estonia, 1994 (%)

Source	State	Min. emp.-owned	Min. man.-owned	Maj. emp.-owned	Maj. man.-owned	Dom. outside owned	Foreign owned	All property forms
No. of enterprises	104	23	13	29	19	42	26	256
Internal	88	90	62	73	76	84	64	81
Private	1	4	23	8	10	2	6	5
Bank	2	6	15	12	9	11	15	7
Foreign	1	0	0	7	0	3	8	3
State	8	0	0	0	5	0	7	4
Total	100	100	100	100	100	100	100	100

The external loan capital supplied to an enterprise can be measured by the ratio of debt to assets. The growth of this ratio cannot be explained, however, by an inflow of external investment capital alone. The debt might be due to short-term supplier credits created because of obligations that the enterprise has not been able to pay. We therefore have to look both at the debt–asset ratio and the specific type of debt. We thus also include an investigation of bank loans as a percentage of total loans.

The most direct information on investment finance has been collected in *Estonia*. The statistical department carried out a survey of investment in the course of which enterprises were asked to specify the relative capital contributions from six sources: internally generated funds, domestic private capital, finance from banks, foreign capital, state funds, and 'other sources'. *Table 2.5* presents simple unweighted averages for the relative contributions from these sources for 1994 for 256 enterprises which were also included in our ownership sample.

Table 2.5 shows that the vast majority of funds for investment – around 80 per cent – were generated internally.[2] In fact, 71 per cent of all enterprises relied entirely on internal funds; another 10 per cent financed their investments entirely from funds from only one of the other five sources; only around 20 per cent of companies used mixed financial sources. It seems that companies with insider ownership use at least as much private and bank capital as do domestically outside-owned companies. There is no indication that access to external finance for investment was especially difficult for insider-owned companies.

---

[2] Note that the table shows averages; it does not depict individual enterprises.

Looking at the total capital structure of the different groups of enterprises using accounting data, we find that the debt–asset ratio for the majority of insider-owned enterprises (ratio of 66 per cent) was on average higher than for externally owned enterprises (47 per cent), as well as for foreign- and state-owned enterprises. Minority employee-owned enterprises, however, constitute an exemption with only 42 per cent. The average amount of bank loans as a percentage of total loans was also generally higher for both majority and minority insider-owned companies (between 29 per cent and 36 per cent) compared to the overall average of 25 per cent. State-owned companies were found to have significantly lower share of bank loans (15 per cent), while for outside domestic and foreign enterprises bank loans represented 28 per cent of total debt. It seems therefore that the theoretical prediction of problems for insiders in obtaining bank loans was not well founded.

The debt–asset ratio has also been investigated in a multivariate analysis with capital intensity and return on assets in the preceding periods as explanatory variables, and branch and location as control variables. This analysis confirms that insider ownership – with the exception of minority employee ownership – has a significantly higher debt ratio than external ownership. Bank loans as a percentage of total debt are significantly higher for all insider ownership types.

In *Latvia*, a multivariate analysis with specifications similar to those used for Estonia shows that the debt ratio for insider-owned enterprises is also significantly higher than for state-owned enterprises. The proportion of bank loans to total debt does not seem to change significantly on the basis of insider ownership. Only 7 per cent of the state-owned and 8 per cent of the outside-owned enterprises have a debt ratio higher than 100 per cent; for foreign ownership the same figure is 24 per cent, and for insider ownership 14–19 per cent.

Debt in *Lithuania* was divided into long- and short-term debt. Long-term debt was found to be generally very low for all enterprises. Insiders are around average, but there is considerable variation between enterprises. At the start of 1994 short-term debt as a proportion of total assets was 49 per cent on average for all enterprises, but fell to 34 per cent at the end of the year. Here again there was nothing to distinguish insider ownership from the rest. Financial liabilities – mainly bank loans – in proportion to total debt, however, seem to be lower for insider-dominated enterprises, especially in the case of employee ownership. This would tend to confirm that insider-owned enterprises find it more difficult to obtain bank loans than other enterprises.

5.9 Investment

As predicted by the theory and confirmed in the preceding section employee-owned enterprises may have particular problems in obtaining external finance.

Furthermore, they may have a higher preference for short-term increases in income. They may also be more risk averse and, at the same time, concentrate risk in their own enterprise. The result may be lower investment, so lowering their ability to restructure the enterprise (Earle and Estrin, 1995).

In *Estonia*, data from the special investment survey are considered to be the most reliable. As a measure of gross investment we have also used the change in fixed assets plus depreciation. A preliminary multivariate analysis with controls for branch and location shows that foreign-owned enterprises have the highest level of investment. Higher investment levels were also observed for 1993 in majority insider-owned enterprises, though for 1994 the results become more indeterminate. Foreign-owned enterprises continued to have relatively high investment levels, while for state-owned enterprises the investment level was significantly lower. For the different groups of insider-owned enterprises, however, no significant results were found.

In *Latvia*, a similar multivariate analysis shows that insider-owned and foreign-owned enterprises have a statistically significant higher level of investment than comparable state-owned enterprises. For domestic outside-owned enterprises the parameter is also positive compared to state ownership, although not significant.

For *Lithuania*, we have results on investment for 1994 in relation to total assets and per employee. Both measures show that insider-owned enterprises have slightly lower investment levels and that foreign- and outside-owned enterprises with low insider ownership have higher levels. The measure of investment per employee shows that state-owned enterprises with insider ownership also have high levels of investment. We also observed a clear tendency towards higher investment in enterprises with a higher number of employees. Average investment per employee in enterprises with 20–99 employees was 586 Litas in 1994, while it was 1,782 Litas in enterprises with more than 500 employees. This explains some of the low results we found for investment in management-dominated ownership, mainly observed in small enterprises. But the general picture is that insider ownership enterprises in Lithuania seem to be affected by a lack of external finance to a higher degree than other types of ownership.

5.10 Overview of Economic Performance

To obtain a clear overview of the general tendencies it is necessary to understand the relation between the different variables. *Table 2.6* presents comparative results. It is difficult to make comparative generalizations because of differences between countries and specific types of ownership structure. In *Latvia*, for example, we have not been able to distinguish between employee and management ownership. From the earlier described

Table 2.6 Economic performance of employee ownership compared to other types, Estonia, Latvia and Lithuania, 1992–95

	Estonia	Latvia	Lithuania
Preconditions			
capital intensity	EO low, MO low	IO lower	EO, MO comparable to OO
size	EO average, MO low	IO smaller	MO smaller
profitability	no difference	no information	no difference
Sales growth	no information	no information	MO higher EO average lower in OO
Change in employment	less reductions in EO higher increases in EO and MO	more reductions in IO	less reductions in EO average in MO higher reductions in OO
Productivity	higher in MinIO higher in EO and MO	higher in IO compared to state-owned	higher in EO, MO and MinIO
Wages	lower in EO and MO higher to managers in MinMO	no information	higher in EO and MO higher in MinIO
Profitability	higher in EO and MO	higher in IO	EO and Min EO higher, average in MO
Finance			
debt/assets	higher in EO and MO	higher in IO	no difference
bankloans/debt	higher in EO and MO		lower in EO and MO
Investment	average in EO and MO	higher in IO compared to state	lower in EO and MO

Note: Insider ownership, IO, is divided into employee ownership, EO, and management ownership, MO; OO = outside ownership (MinIO = minority IO, MinMO = minority MO, MinEO = minority EO).

institutional background, however, and from the difficulties we had in finding employee-owned enterprises for case studies we can assume that the bulk of the Latvian insider-dominated enterprises are in fact owned, or at least dominated, by the management.

Concerning the starting conditions we found that management-dominated enterprises tended to be relatively small. This was not the case for broader employee ownership. Both types were found to suffer from low capital intensity in Estonia and Latvia. This was not the case in Lithuania, probably because of the favourable conditions which were offered to employees to take over both large and capital-intensive enterprises. Although the institutional background should indicate that, especially in Estonia and Latvia, the initial profit potential should be higher in insider-owned enterprises, our data cannot confirm such a tendency for any of the three countries.

The success of restructuring can be measured by the ability of enterprises to transform an initial fall in sales into new growth. At the current stage of our analysis we have empirical data only from Lithuania on sales growth from 1993 to 1994. The results show that management-owned enterprises tend to do better than other enterprises, while sales growth in employee-dominated enterprises was comparable to the average for all groups.

For *Lithuania,* there is some parallel with the development in employment in the same period, although employee-owned enterprises in particular – in accordance with the theoretical predictions – seem to be more sluggish in their downward adjustment of the labour force. This is confirmed by the results from Estonia, while the relatively high labour force reductions in Latvia confirm the prediction that management-dominated enterprises tend to implement steeper downward adjustments of the labour force. Somewhat surprising is the steeper labour force increase in the majority employee-owned enterprises compared to other enterprises belonging to the part of the Estonian sample with increasing employment.

This tendency towards a slower reduction in the labour force in employee-owned enterprises could result in lower productivity. This is, however, not confirmed by the data. Productivity for employee-owned enterprises was about average in Estonia and Lithuania. Management ownership was also performing about average in Estonia, but was found to be more efficient in Latvia, and surprisingly less efficient in Lithuania. These differences are difficult to explain at the current stage of our research. For Lithuania, however, the results on labour productivity show a high level for both employee- and management-dominated ownership, and also for minority insider ownership. This means that the greater development of insider ownership in Lithuania led to significant and positive performance results. There is no doubt that employee motivation and the alignment of interests (of owners, managers and employees) here play a decisive role in enhancing productivity levels. These effects are stronger than the negative effect that might be expected from the more sluggish reduction of the labour force.

The results on wage levels show different patterns in the three countries. In Estonia, downward flexibility of wages seems to prevail in employee-owned enterprises. In connection with the sluggish downward adjustment of employment, this means that lower wages are traded off against job security in employee-owned enterprises. In Lithuania, wage levels were found to be higher for both employee- and management-owned enterprises, and for other types with a large minority of employee shares.

It seems, however, that labour productivity in the Lithuanian cases has been high enough to allow these relatively high wages, so that wages have not diluted enterprise profitability. In fact, profitability (measured as operating profits on turnover and as net profits on total assets) shows relatively higher levels for employee-owned enterprises. Still, for Lithuania, enterprises with a considerable employee minority share also generated higher profitability rates. For Estonia, both employee- and management-owned enterprises experienced profitability rates above the average, a similar result also being found for insider-owned enterprises in Latvia. It is worth noting that the profitability of insider-owned enterprises in Latvia was higher than for domestic outside-owned enterprises and, more remarkably, also higher than for foreign-owned enterprises.

Analysis of the financial structure of different groups of enterprises showed that the debt–asset ratio was higher for insider-owned enterprises in both Estonia and Latvia, and about average in Lithuania. For this group of enterprises bank loans measured in relation to total debt were also surprisingly high in Estonia, but in Lithuania they were relatively low. These enterprises have a tendency to rely on internally generated capital for investment. In fact, the evidence from Estonia shows that 80 per cent of investments in such enterprises are financed internally.

In Estonia both employee- and management-owned enterprises had an average level of investment. This was also the case for the insider-dominated enterprises in Latvia. For Lithuania, however, our preliminary results indicate lower investment, both for management- and employee-dominated enterprises. The Lithuanian results might be explained by either the lack of external finance or a lower willingness to invest. Further analysis is required in order to go more deeply into these questions.

6 CONCLUSION

What are the conditions which have determined the development of employee ownership in the privatization process in the Baltic countries? What can be learned from the economic performance of employee-owned enterprises in these three countries?

It is difficult to identify a direct link between the specific background conditions of these three countries and the development of employee-ownership. Nevertheless, when the dynamic process of transition from a planned to a market economy, from dictatorship to democracy, from Soviet occupation to independence is analysed some links can be identified, closely connected to political developments in the three countries. The *value system* and the *social system* determine the political climate and the political process which in turn determine the changes in the *institutional system* – the new legislation, the choice of privatization models, and the implementation of the privatization process. The ethnic differences – for instance, as part of the *social system* – have had an important influence on this process. Although initial conditions in the *institutional system* were not so different between the three countries, the number of differences increased during the transition process, clearly leading to different developments in employee ownership in the three countries.

Cultural values are also difficult to identify. It is tempting, however, to assume that collective and egalitarian values are more important in the Catholic Lithuania than in the other two, more individual-oriented countries. This cultural difference is probably one explanation of the higher emphasis on vouchers and employee ownership in Lithuania.

The population is also more homogenous with the same culture, ethnic and religious background in Lithuania, while Estonia and Latvia seem to be suffering from the split between the Russian-oriented and the native populations. This is a good example of the close connection between the *social system* and the *value system*. The cultural split has meant that the broad group of employees was weakened in the process of independence and the further economic and political transition. This is the basic explanation behind the change in policy limiting advantages for employees in Estonia and Latvia, a process which did not happen in Lithuania, where there was no 'national question' to distract the political debate from the economic problems of transition, and where the workers were not weakened by an ethnic split. The Labour Party came to power and the conditions for further support for employee ownership were improved.

The development of the *institutional system* is at the core of the transition and plays a key role in the privatization process and preparation of the legal framework for the initiation and development of employee ownership. The massive development of insider ownership in the Baltic countries was due to the adoption of the following:

- *Discounts on the purchase price.* Employees have been able to buy shares for a price which was normally below the market price paid by other buyers. This system was used in the initial stages of small privatization in Estonia and Latvia, and in large privatization in Lithuania.
- The *leasing systems* dominant in the initial phase in all three countries, and also in the later stage in Latvia, have often included a preferential price for employees.
- *Vouchers* distributed to the general population have also been used for the purchase of enterprises. This system played an important role in Lithuania, and also became important after 1995 in the two other countries, especially in Estonia.

The implementation of the legislation is much dependent on the role and power of different agents. The organization of privatization through decentralized systems gave insider workers and management a quite strong position, enabling them to use their networks of contacts with municipalities and branch ministries. The municipalities had a role in small privatization in all three countries, especially in Latvia before 1994. The centralization of power in the Privatization Agency at the second stage of the privatization process, which first took place in Estonia, diminished the power of insiders.

The legislation and its implementation, combined with the distribution of capital, also determine the strength of other buyers. Here the possibilities for foreign capital are especially important, including the general legislative framework for foreign capital and the economic situation, particularly in respect of the production system. Estonia has put most emphasis on foreign capital. Foreigners have, in turn, favourably evaluated the economic situation in Estonia, where they became strong competitors of domestic investors and insiders.

We have some preliminary results concerning the dynamics of ownership structures. Both in Estonia and in Lithuania there seems to be a quite strong tendency for broad employee ownership to become less frequent and management ownership to become the prevalent property form. In Lithuania, there was at first a tendency towards increased employee ownership closely linked to the possibility for employees to use reserves and profits for increasing their shareholding. This tendency was modified and in 1995 overtaken by a tendency for employees to sell their shares to managers and outsiders. No doubt this property structure will experience further development as the transition continues.

The analysis of economic performance has as yet yielded only preliminary results. In spite of some variation, we can conclude that there is no indication that employee ownership entails worse economic performance than in the case of comparable enterprises in the private sector. There is also no evidence for the often cited conclusion that an insider take-over is only 'half-way privatization', perpetuating many of the defects of the previous system. Employee-owned enterprises may be a little more reluctant to reduce employment, but productivity and profitability seem often to be better than at most other enterprises. We also found that production in these enterprises has been restructured at least as much as in other kinds of enterprise, and that products and production methods have been adjusted to meet the new market conditions, both on the cost and the revenue side. Deep restructuring in the form of investment is about average, but here especially employee-owned enterprises have sometimes had to contend with the unwillingness of banks to provide loans.

REFERENCES

Alchian A. and H. Demsetz (1972), 'Production, Information Cost, and Economic Organization', *American Economic Review*, December, 62 (5), 777–95.

Arkadie B.V. et al. (1991), *Economic Survey of the Baltic Republics*, Stockholm.

Bonin J., D. Jones and L. Putterman (1993), 'Theoretical and Empirical Studies of Producer Co-operatives: Will the Twain Ever Meet?', *Journal of Economic Literature*, 31 (Sept.), 1290–1320.

Cicinskas J. (1994), 'Economic Development in Lithuania After Independence', in J. Å. Dellenbrant and O. Nørgaard (eds), *The Politics of Transition in the Baltic States – Democratization and Economic Reform Policies*, Umeå Universitet, Research Report No. 2, 1994.

Dellenbrant J. Å. (1992), 'Estonia's Economic Development 1940–1990 in Comparison with Finland's', chapter 10 in Åslund (ed.), *Market Socialism or the Restoration of Capitalism,*. Cambridge University Press.

Earle J.S. and S. Estrin (1995), 'Employee Ownership in Transition', Center for International Security and Arms Control, Stanford University.

Earle J.S., S. Estrin and L.L. Leshchenko (1995),'Ownership Structures, Patterns of Control and Enterprise Behavior in Russia', working paper, Central European University, November.

Frydman et al. (1993), *The Privatization Process in Russia, Ukraine and the Baltic States*, CEU Privatization Reports, Vol II, Budapest, NY.

Hansmann, H (1988),'Ownership of the Firm', *Journal of Law, Economics, and Organization*, 4(2), 267–304.

Hanson, P. (1990), *The Baltic States*, The Economist Intelligence Unit – Briefing, London.

Jemeljanovs O. (1996), Privatization in Latvia in Figures, in (Mygind, 1996).

Jones D. and N. Mygind (1996a), 'Employee Ownership and the Effects on Productive Efficiency and Employment: Evidence from the Baltics', working paper PFPB–project, CEES/CBS and Hamilton College.

Jones D. and N. Mygind (1996b), 'Employee Ownership and the Effects on Wage-level and Profitability: Evidence from the Baltics', working paper PFPB-project, CEES/CBS and Hamilton College.

Jones D. and N. Mygind (1996c), 'Employee Ownership and the Effects on Finance and Investment: Evidence from the Baltics', working paper PFPB-project, CEES/CBS and Hamilton College.

Kein A. and V. Tali (1994), 'The Process of Ownership Reform and Privatization', paper for the Institute of Economics, Estonian Academy of Sciences.

Martinavicius J. (1996), 'Privatization in Lithuania: The legislative and political environment and the results achieved', in (Mygind, 1996).

Mygind N. (1994), *Omvæltning i Øst*, Samfundslitteratur, Copenhagen, translated in *Societies in Transition*, Copenhagen Business School .

Mygind, N. (ed.) (1996), *Privatization and Financial Participation in the Baltic Countries*, Copenhagen Business School.

Nuti D.M. (1995), 'Employeeism: Corporate Governance and Employee Share Ownership in Transitional Economies', working paper, University of Rome, London Business School.

Shteinbuka I. (1996), Privatization in Latvia and the role of employee ownership, in (Mygind, 1996).

Terk E. (1996), 'Employee ownership and the political debate in Estonia 1987–94', in (Mygind, 1996).

The Baltic Independent, (weekly paper), Tallinn.
Vojevoda L. and L. Rumpis (1993), 'Small Privatization in Latvia', paper, Institute of Economics, Latvian Academy of Sciences.

3. Employee Ownership and Participation in Bulgaria, 1989 to Mid–1996

Charles Rock and Mark Klinedinst

1 INTRODUCTION[1]

The development of employee ownership in Bulgaria, as in the other post-socialist economies, has depended on how quickly state-owned enterprises and other assets have been privatized. In general it has been quite a slow process, and particularly so in respect of manufacturing enterprises.

One of the main reasons for the slow pace of privatization in Bulgaria has been the rancorous and erratic development of its political situation. Bulgaria experienced a significant polarization immediately after the fall of the dictator Zhivkov in November 1989, with anti-communists forming the Union of Democratic Forces (UDF) on one side, and the reformed communist party becoming the Bulgarian Socialist Party (BSP) on the other. This bipolar division has largely remained in place, with neither pole able to dominate entirely, at least until the December 1994 elections when the BSP won an absolute majority in Parliament, something the UDF has never managed to do.[2]

[1] The authors would like to thank the many Bulgarian managers and workers who, as interviewees, must remain anonymous – as we promised. In addition, invaluable help came from the Central Union of Workers' Production Co-operatives, National Confederation of Independent Trade Unions of Bulgaria (CITUB) and local affiliates, individuals affiliated with the Confederation of Labour 'Podkrepa', the Center for the Study of Democracy, and the Regional Statistical Office in Pernik; also thanks to all the other providers of help on this topic: Galya Kanazireva, Grisha Gradev, Veli Grudkova, Albena Koleva, Aneta Mihailova, Svilen Parvulov, Todor Tanev, and Elena Zhileva. For support on the surveys on Bulgarian enterprises we would like to thank the National Science Foundation (NSF) and Derek Jones, the ILO, the Institute for Social and Trade Union Research in Sofia, and the Bulgarian National Social Research Council. Charles Rock would like to acknowledge an IREX (International Research and Exchanges) grant for a stay in Bulgaria in 1991–92, also grants from the C.A. Johnson and J. Critchfield Foundations for several research trips to Bulgaria.

[2] The UDF government of 1991–92 was in effective coalition with the Movements for Rights and Freedoms associated with the Turkish minority rights movement. The MRF has, since 1991,

Influenced by politics, the privatization process has changed and slowed down as ruling parties have come and gone. Privatization in the post-socialist economies involves the redistribution of the majority of the nation's productive assets, and so determines economic influence in the new economic order. Although the anti-communist UDF, which governed from October 1991 to December 1992, was very liberal economically, it feared that those former communists who had accumulated financial assets in the past would become the most influential new capitalists by out-bidding other Bulgarians if privatization were to proceed on the basis of a simple auctioning-off of assets. No other minority or technocratic government (early 1991, 1993–94) could boast a better record. While proclaiming the need for rapid privatization, they too failed to move forward quickly because of the intense suspicions elicited by privatization. The BSP government has, since December 1994, moved no more rapidly on major privatizations than its predecessors. Those few Bulgarian organizations with privatization as their first priority have not been strong enough to influence the process. All political parties in every government since 1989 – all of which have claimed to be in favour of rapid privatization – have wanted first to place their own appointees in government ministries and agencies (administering the state-owned enterprises) and on the enterprise boards and managements of the state-owned enterprises before proceeding to privatize them, thus further slowing the privatization process.

These power shifts have also retarded the legislative initiatives necessary for privatization to proceed. When passed, these laws have frequently been amended or contradicted by later legislation and government decrees. Finally, existing laws have been interpreted and administered differently as governments or cabinet officials have changed. This uncertain legal, economic, and political environment has also contributed to the relative lack of interest in Bulgaria on the part of foreign investors.[3]

2 LEGAL REFORMS, EMPLOYEE OWNERSHIP AND PARTICIPATION IN ENTERPRISES

2.1 First Legal Foundations

In this section we provide a brief chronology of legal and administrative

been in parliament continuously, with less than 10% of the vote. Other small parties have also managed to obtain some parliamentary representation, notably the Agrarians, a business ideology party, and some social democratic dissenters from the UDF.

[3] Since the beginning of 1990, only about US\$ 500 million has been invested by foreigners in Bulgaria. This is less than one-tenth of the amount invested in Hungary and one-fifth of that invested in the Czech Republic during the same period.

reforms. These are relevant to an understanding of the environment in which privatization and employee financial and decision-making participation has taken place.

By the late 1970s nearly all productive assets in Bulgaria had been nationalized. At the same time, serious economic difficulties were becoming evident which led to some moderate reforms. There was an attempt to get enterprises to respond more actively to markets in the early 1980s, but this seems to have had little success. To improve employee morale and productivity incentives, and following lengthy discussions with the trade union and others, the *Labour Code* was revised in 1986. One element of the new code was a clause which allowed an enterprise's trade unionists to ratify or reject the state-selected enterprise general manager. Other parts of the code invited employees to become involved in reforming the enterprise to improve productivity. In some cases the employees took the new code seriously and tried to reform their enterprise, but sooner or later this was perceived as a threat to the management and/or the Communist Party's hegemony and the reform attempts were thwarted.[4]

Another reform took place in 1987, when new co-operative enterprises with formal autonomy were once again made legal. They were seen as a means of reducing labour bottlenecks in agriculture. This reform seems to have had little impact on the economy before the other political changes began in 1989.[5]

In January 1989 (almost a year before the political revolution) the communist government promulgated *Decree 56* re-establishing the right to engage in private enterprise (but still subordinate to and in concordance with central planning).[6] It also permitted the sale of state-owned enterprise assets.

---

[4] Enterprise interviews, 1991–92; see also Jones and Meurs (1991). The clause allowing workers selection veto of enterprise executives came into direct contradiction with stipulations for shareholder/owner control in the new Commercial Code passed in the summer of 1992, at least until the Labour Code was revised again in January 1993.

[5] Interviews, 1991–92. Few new, autonomous agricultural labour co-operatives were formed after 1987. However, especially after 1989, this regulation seems to have been used for 'student' co-operatives which were engaged in limited retailing, services and later, even for importing, due to the tax privileges all co-operatives enjoyed. Many of these 'student' co-operatives were quite hierarchical organizations with little relationship to the egalitarianism of traditional co-operatives. For a full discussion of the differences between the old co-operative system and the post-1991 rules, as well as other matters concerning co-operatives, see Meurs and Rock (1994).

[6] An amendment to Decree 56 permitted the transformation of state-owned entities into state-owned corporations. Unless prohibited by the responsible government ministry, the new corporate Board of Directors had the ability both to set the valuation of any new stock certificates and to distribute them as desired. This type of activity, easily subject to abuse and insider dealing, occurred during the earliest period of 'wild' or 'secret' privatization of 1989–90. Any arrangements made then (or at any time) in this manner were jeopardized by the 1992 Privatization Law which effectively made any prior privatization steps by state enterprises – if done in unfair manner – subject to reversal.

In effect this decree was an entirely new commercial code. The decree (Article 21) also permitted state-owned enterprise management boards to issue stock to employees with more than a year's job tenure, up to a limited amount. These shares could be transferred only to other employees in the firm. Some enterprise managements (and in a few cases, notably tourism, some employees) were able to use this decree to engage in usually small-scale, spontaneous or 'wild' privatizations in the period up to the summer of 1990. These were brought to a halt by a presidential decree.[7]

From December 1990 until December 1992 economic liberals headed the key ministries of Finance, and Trade and Industry. Using existing laws, ministries and a special privatization agency were able to auction a limited number of retail and service enterprises. No special attention was paid to employee ownership and none developed out of this handful of auctions.

In mid-1991 a new Commercial Code was passed. It basically resurrected the pre-communist code which followed the Central European pattern similar to German commercial laws (with both a supervisory board and a management board for large joint stock companies). This law allows several types of business enterprise with significant flexibility, making Bulgaria legally similar to Western capitalist countries. Among the permitted forms of association are: both publicly listed and closed joint-stock limited liability companies; both unlimited and limited liability partnerships; sole proprietorships; individual traders; state-owned enterprises of all types; and associated hybrids of these. None of these forms precludes employee ownership, at least not minority ownership for employees.

Still in 1991 a new *Act on Co-operatives* was also passed which, along with the laws on the restitution of nationalized property, gave co-operative employees the right to gain control of their enterprises. Co-operative members may retain individual rights or may own property collectively, although retaining the right to withdraw specific property values from the co-operative when leaving. Since nearly all of the old co-operatives had been effectively taken over by the government under communism, the restitution of nationalized property was also important to co-operatives and their members who wished to reclaim co-operative property (Meurs and Rock, 1994).

The restitution of nationalized property was made legally possible in early 1991. Subsequently, the government (national and local) has given back a great deal of real estate to former owners or their heirs. This process was

---

[7] This August 1990 decision was made by Zhelyu Zhelev, the new compromise and non-Communist President, elected by the members the Grand National Assembly (i.e. the constitutional assembly of June 1990–October 1991). Later, in the 1992 Privatization Law, all previous privatizations were jeopardized by a clause allowing review of and abrogation of any prior privatization because of illegitimate dealing or other fraud.

Box 3.1 Summary of government promotion of employee ownership, Bulgaria

Before Laws were passed allowing the issue of stock by state-owned enterprises
1989   to be sold to their employees. Supplemental regulations in *Law-Decree
        No. 56* of January 1989.

1991   *Act on Co-operatives* facilitating employee ownership.

1992   *Act on Privatization* giving price reductions to employees wishing to
        purchase stock in their own enterprise. The law did not allow employees
        voting rights for three years after purchase.

1994   Revision of the 1992 *Act on Privatization* improving the ability of
        employees in smaller state enterprises to purchase their company if they
        could organize themselves. It also gave employees the right to immediate
        voting rights.

---

relatively easy in cases where little change had occurred in the specific real
property; improvements, consolidations, and construction caused compli-
cations. In any case, by the end of 1995 the government and privatization
authorities claimed they had returned the majority of real property to its true
owners. This law also facilitated the restitution of both real property (land and
buildings) as well as other productive assets to the former production co-
operatives and their employees (past and present).

2.2 The 1992 Act on Privatization

The main *Act on Privatization* was enacted in the middle of 1992. This law
established the procedures for privatizing all state enterprises (at least those
not being directly restituted to former owners). The law provided for a State
Privatization Agency to manage 'large' privatizations, and for ministries and
local authorities to manage 'small' privatizations.

The basic privatization strategy involved several overlapping steps. First,
state-owned enterprises would be 'de-monopolized' by breaking up the giant
conglomerates into units which would not have dominance in any sector
(1990–91). Second, the state-owned enterprises would be 'corporatized'; that
is, they would be legally transformed into a state-owned joint stock or sole
proprietorship enterprise falling under the commercial code (1991–92). State-
owned enterprises were to be given more autonomy – this was
'marketization', which included their subjection to the new market
environment and the end of subsidization through 'soft budget constraints'
and other mechanisms. Finally, state-owned enterprises would be privatized
through the procedures outlined in the law after 'expert' auditors had
established the market value of the business.

The 1992 *Act on Privatization* specified two basic types of 'preference' or price reduction on assets purchased by employees, depending on the type of commercial enterprise in which these assets became embodied. In any case, the maximum total price reduction for shares for an employee was limited to the equivalent of one year's salary, no matter what type of enterprise.

For large state-owned enterprises transformed into companies, employees (as a group) could buy no more than 20% of all enterprise shares or one-fifth of the total value of the enterprise. They would pay for these shares, if they chose to buy any at all, at a 50% discount on the experts' valuation price.

For directly state-owned enterprises (non-stock enterprises) and for small units (less than 10 million leva) other rules applied which, in theory, allowed the employees to purchase the enterprise. Employee purchase was subject to a 30% discount. At least 30% of the eligible employees had to take part in the bid to privatize the unit in order to receive the price reduction (calculated on the basis of the winning bid). This procedure was also available for a bankrupt state-owned enterprise.

Other features of the 1992 *Act on Privatization* are worth mentioning. From the employees' standpoint one major drawback was the fact that their cut-price shares would carry no voting rights for three years after purchase. This reduced the effective value of the stock since other share owners would fully control the enterprise, and could disadvantage the employee shareholders. On the other hand, a positive feature of the law was its flexibility regarding the selection of the winner, since other factors besides price could be taken into consideration, such as job retention and creation, future investment, and export potential. Leasing and rental arrangements, and management contracts with options to purchase could be used instead of immediate sale. Any relevant group (the State Privatization Agency or SPA, the government, ministries, local authorities, managers and employees) can initiate a privatization process. Also, the law allowed restitution by the equivalent compensation of former owners.[8]

Despite the high hopes of 1992, the challenges of privatization proved to be much more difficult than anyone had imagined.[9] There was much less interest on the part of foreigners in purchasing state-owned enterprise assets than had been envisaged. Furthermore, governments were reluctant to sell assets to anyone suspected of using 'dirty money'. The 1992 law made it mandatory for Bulgarian purchasers to reveal the sources or methods through which they had acquired their money. The economy progressively collapsed throughout 1992

---

[8] This is in contrast to the post-socialist economies (e.g. East Germany) where disputes are numerous and bitter over the possession of specific pieces of property.

[9] The delays were aggravated by the fact that the 1992 Privatization Law was incomplete. Several other regulations and procedures (e.g. valuation methodology) had to be legislated or decreed in order for the process to operate. For details on these see Rock (1992 and 1994b).

and 1993, so continually eroding the value of almost all economic assets in Bulgaria and rendering it even more difficult to predict future enterprise values. For many Bulgarians, with no experience of fluctuating capital values in a market economy, the valuation process seemed quite arbitrary, and there were frequent press reports implying 'rigged' deals and corrupt officials. Following the 1992 legislation, no credit facilities were created for helping domestic purchasers of state-owned enterprises or their assets. De-monopolization was difficult if not impossible in some sectors, so that after 1992 there was even some re-joining of separated parts and 're-monopolizations.'

By the end of 1993 there had been barely 100 enterprise privatizations of any significant size, about half carried out at the national level and the rest at local government level. Virtually no one considered this an adequate outcome. A small number of these privatizations involved employee ownership purchases.[10]

2.3 The 1994 Amended *Act on Privatization*

Since the privatization of state-owned enterprises was proceeding very slowly, parliament revisited the 1992 law. A major reworking of the 1992 *Act on Privatization* in mid-1994 amended several sections and added others. There were important changes, for the most part facilitating the purchase of their company – that is, the smaller state and municipal enterprises – by employees on condition that they were able to organize themselves. Other changes affected all privatizations.

- One important change was the removal of the 3-year non-voting period for employee shares. This change increased the value of the shares to employees (monetary value plus decision-making power), but had no effect on the price they paid;
- Second, shares must be held for a minimum of three years before they may be sold without restriction;
- Third, the maximum price reduction for each employee buying shares was increased to the equivalent of two years' wages (and not less than the average wage);
- Although the 1992 legislation did not prohibit management and/or employee buy-outs (MEBOs) of public enterprises, in practice it was not a major element in the privatization process. The 1994 changes explicitly recognized this as another method of privatization. Similarly, although the 1992 law theoretically permitted special non-market

---

[10] PA (Bulgarian Privatization Agency) (1995b) and interviews 1993. No hard data seem to be available on the extent or characteristics of employee share ownership at that time.

negotiated arrangements, in practice these were seen as somehow incompatible with the general thrust of the law;

- A fifth change in 1994 explicitly recognized the possibility of restricted negotiations (limited to one or a few parties) with no public offering;
- Sixth, on this same pattern, buy-outs by instalment payments as a method of deferred purchase were now expressly recognized.[11]

The changes concerning instalment purchase were most relevant for smaller public enterprises or parts of enterprises. Smaller enterprises (valued below 10 million leva for manufacturing and service firms, and below 5 million leva for trade and retailing) could be purchased by all employees in a special negotiated non-competitive procedure. The employees could take advantage of the preference (price reduction for some shares) and purchase the enterprise at the authorized experts' valuation price.

Employees must make a 10% (manufacturing and services) or a 30% downpayment and then the state effectively finances the remainder for a period of up to six years. Employees may pay the rest off over several years with due payments increasing at only half the rate of inflation; in this manner the real value of the purchase price is deflated by half the total inflation rate.[12] This change meant that the state would finance and substantially reduce the real purchase price (in effect a state loan with a negative rate of interest).

---

[11] In the 1992 law 'stages' of purchase and sale were mentioned, or the Cabinet could determine the 'mode of payment' and the Minister of Finance was mentioned as having the right to set up instalment purchasing although 'adjusted to the base lending rate.' Hence, the 1992 law was quite confusing as to what was legally possible; the 1994 changes made things much clearer.

[12] For MEBOs in manufacturing or service units valued up to 10 million leva, a down payment of 10% is due on closing the deal. The total price to be paid for the enterprise is reduced by the concession. The sum of all employees' concessions is a maximum of 20% of the price of the whole enterprise; exactly how much depends on the number of employees participating in the buy-out and on the sum of their wages for two years. The remaining payments for completion of the enterprise buy-out begin after a one-year 'grace period' with no inflation adjustment. The first instalment payment is due no later than 24 months after closing the deal. After the no-adjustment year, each year the principal still due is increased by half the inflation rate. Thus the nominal value of instalment payments increases while the real value decreases each year by 50% of that year's annual inflation rate. In summary, the purchase involves the downpayment, plus 5 instalment payments in the second through sixth years. For MEBOs in trade the system is similar with a few differences: (i) the maximum value of the unit is 5 million leva; (ii) the amount of downpayment on closing is 30%; (iii) there is no one-year grace period, so that instalment payments begin no later than 12 months after closing: the purchase is completed within 5 years of beginning the deal. Both types may alternatively choose to make all payments within a two-year period after the downpayment. If they choose this, there is no upward adjustment for inflation in the payments. The only difference here is that in manufacturing and services enterprises, there is one payment due at the end of two years, while for trade enterprises, they must make an instalment payment in both years of the two-year period.

There have been occasional reports of attempts by interested outsiders to influence some of the valuations of some of these smaller enterprises by 'expert' auditors (that is, to increase the value) in order to make it less likely that employees would bid for their firm. Since this legal revision, however, the employee buy-out has become a popular method of privatization for small public enterprises or parts of them throughout the country. The enterprises are mainly those owned by municipal governments. Municipal governments have been relatively successful in speeding up the rate of privatization of municipal property and enterprises since 1993.

No precise data are available on the number of MEBOs which have occurred on the basis of this methodology, in part because individuals leasing public property or having tenants' rights can also use this method to purchase the enterprise.[13] This negotiated privatization (of a particular kind, through Article 35 of the *Act on Privatization*) has become increasingly popular since mid-1994. By the end of 1995 more than half of all new municipal privatizations were employing a negotiated privatization method. Unfortunately there are no comprehensive data on the relative proportion of deals which are MEBOs versus the proportion involving lessees or tenants. In any case, the growing importance of these deals was already evident by the end of 1995 – almost 30% of all (cumulative, 1992–95) privatizations completed by municipalities involved this method (Bulgarian Privatization Agency (PA), 1995a, p. 3).

2.4 'Mass Privatization' Provisions in 1994

One other important change in the 1994 remaking of the *Act on Privatization*, was a provision for 'mass' privatization. During 1992–94, the privatization of the largest firms remained problematic. Only an extremely small percentage of the large state-owned enterprises – enterprises in services, trade, and manufacturing – had been privatized using the 1992 law.[14] Because of these evident difficulties with the large-enterprise privatization process, discussions of mass privatization had begun even in 1991–92. Bulgarians were exposed to all sorts of possible mass privatization schemes through observing other post-socialist economies, from suggestions from international financial organizations, and from the visits of unsolicited adviser-gurus from the West. In the 1994 amendment process the principle of mass privatization was enacted; the details of the specific procedure, however, were left for further government action.

---

[13] They do not, however, benefit from the preferential (price reduction) aspects of the legislation.

[14] This depends on one's definition of 'separate' enterprises, but even the optimists conclude that at best only a little over 10% of the large enterprises had been privatized by the end of 1995.

Prime Minister Lyuben Berov along with his 'non-partisan' government (in power from the beginning of 1993 until late 1994) had strongly promoted the idea of a mass privatization scheme. His government was still trying to create the final accompanying regulations when government support collapsed and he resigned in autumn 1994. He was replaced by Reneta Injova, former head of the Privatization Agency, who took on the interim prime ministership in a caretaker role for the few months before the new parliamentary elections in December 1994. Any hope of a substantial result from the mass privatization debates was put on hold until after the elections.

The elections gave the Bulgarian Socialist Party an absolute majority in the 240-seat parliament. After many months setting up the government and attending to other priorities, the government turned its attention to the mass privatization problem. In part because of external pressures, proposed techniques of mass privatization were passed. The government finally adopted enabling regulations for mass privatization in August 1995. These regulations (through universally available coupons) were intended to do two things: rapidly to privatize enterprises and to help attract new funds to these privatized enterprises. The mass privatization procedures allow both coupons or cash to be used to buy shares in these enterprises. The discussions on the regulations indicate that employees may take their coupons and use them to replace cash contributions in purchasing the reduced price shares set aside for them in their own enterprises. It is also intended that employees at smaller enterprises be able to use coupons to replace cash in any attempt at a collective buy-out, though at present it is not clear how this will take place. If there is a time limit on coupon use an employee takes a risk holding on to the coupons for the purpose of purchasing shares in his own enterprise. If the privatization process for one's own enterprise is delayed beyond the coupon time limit one risks forfeiture of the coupon value.[15]

In January 1996 coupon books went on sale in Bulgaria. Coupon rights were offered for sale for 500 leva to each adult Bulgarian. This would buy coupons with a par (book) value of 25,000 leva.[16] Employees could purchase these coupons and use them to pay the preferential (discounted) price under other provisions of the regular *Act on Privatization*. In this way, the coupons added a second kind of discount through which employees could obtain ownership.

Some 1,000 state-owned enterprises have apparently been part of this mass privatization. Because of the uncertainties of the mass privatization process,

[15] RFE/RL, 1 August 1995. Interviews.

[16] In June 1996 this 500 leva was less than US$5; the par value of the coupons is only about $250. If one used purchasing power parity, the real value in Bulgaria would still be substantial (at least a few months' salary equivalent). At the original time of proposal some two years ago, the exchange value was more than double.

however, the coupons have not sold well. People lack confidence in the mass privatization process – especially the exact timing and methods of transformation of coupons into ownership stakes. It appears that perhaps 50% of eligible adults have purchased the coupon vouchers.[17]

2.5 Current Obstacles to Employee Ownership Development

Credit – in respect of both its availability and affordability – is probably the biggest single economic obstacle to the growth of employee ownership in Bulgaria. The 1992 *Act on Privatization* provided for some privatization revenues to be ploughed back into a mutual fund to support social security and to help 'provide Bulgarian citizens with free purchases'. This clause seems not to have had any subsequent effect.

The financing issue, at least for smaller enterprises, was addressed in the 1994 revisions to the basic *Act on Privatization*. Employee groups in various smaller enterprises have taken advantage of the implicit state financing and succeeded in purchasing their enterprise. Even with this change many employees are still reluctant to become partly liable for future 'repayments' when the necessary resources cannot be guaranteed in advance (enterprise net revenues and/or personal income generated from the enterprise). Most employees have little personal savings and few people in Bulgaria have any experience of borrowing against illiquid assets such as their house. Interest rates for borrowers are unaffordably high. There are no provisions specifically designed to help employees obtain external credit for purchasing shares in their own companies.

There is relatively little experience of evaluating investments or enterprises among the general public. Fear of financial fraud is pervasive after press reports of investment schemes which have gone wrong both in Bulgaria and in other post-socialist countries.[18] The trade union confederations admit their lack of resources adequately to advise workforces facing privatization. The unfamiliarity with employee ownership, the lack of experience in business finance, the lack of knowledge among employees and managers about business operations in a market environment, and the general lack of leadership among employees can together be considered the second major obstacle to the rapid development of employee ownership in Bulgaria.

---

[17] After slow sales in the first few weeks of coupon marketing, the number purchased was only approaching 20% of the possible buyers. The government decided to extend by a month the period for purchasing the coupons. By May 1996 about 40% of eligible adults were reported as having purchased the coupons. The government once again extended the purchase period into June 1996. (OMRI, Part II, April–June, 1996).

[18] The bank and foreign exchange crisis of 1996 exacerbated the level of mistrust.

Within the scope of the legislation on privatization substantial flexibility is afforded the state, the SPA, and other agencies, ministries, and local authorities in charge of administering specific privatizations. The willingness of these administrative units to promote and facilitate employee ownership has varied over time (with changing governments and individual administrators). When an administration favours employee ownership it has the right to consider other variables besides the bid price in deciding to whom it will sell a particular enterprise. There are examples of enterprises which have been sold to employee groups which did not make the highest monetary bid, but instead offered the authorities additional economic benefits from employee enterprise control. During 1995–96 several municipalities have apparently begun to use the MEBO mechanism with growing frequency; other privatization authorities are also paying more attention to the use of employee ownership as a key privatization method, at least for small units.

Employee ownership is very limited at present. Currently – mid-1996 – we estimate that only about 5% of Bulgarian employees formally own a stake in their enterprise.[19] Furthermore, we believe that this proportion is unlikely to grow higher than 25% by the end of the privatization process.

3 TYPES OF ENTERPRISE WITH EMPLOYEE OWNERSHIP

This section is based on case studies and enterprise interviews, media and independent organizations' reports, plus the initial analysis of results from a panel survey of manufacturing enterprises. It briefly describes the types of firm which have emerged so far in Bulgaria with some employee ownership (see summary in Box 3.2).[20] This chapter takes a broad view of 'ownership':

[19] We base this very rough estimate on a combination of the following considerations: the measured labour force in Bulgaria is now less than 3 million, with about 15% measured unemployed. We estimated the number of privatized firms with some employee ownership (in about half – 241 – of the major privatizations of SOEs, in the co-operative businesses, and in MEBOs of small and medium-sized privatizations), average sizes, and the estimated average proportion of employees involved in actually buying shares in their privatized enterprise. In the 1993 round of our enterprise panel survey in the manufacturing sector, co-operative employees are about 4% of the total, but not all co-operative workers may own a share; ownership in other property forms is estimated to be something less than 1–2% of workers in the manufacturing sector (manufacturing now accounts for about one-fourth of the labour force). The CUWPC claims some 50,000 employees in their affiliated co-operative firms.

[20] The 1992 Commercial Code (Trade Act) of Bulgaria allows for the following business organizations: sole proprietorships with unlimited liability; general (unlimited liability) partnerships; limited partnerships (both general and limited liability partners); limited liability companies (shares for owners); joint stock companies (either publicly traded or closely-held forms);

Box 3.2 Summary of employee ownership forms, Bulgaria, 1996

Types of employee ownership

- Co-operative enterprises directly and democratically controlled by employees; co-operative subsidiaries indirectly controlled by co-operative members and central organizations.
- Small egalitarian partnerships.
- Majority employee-owned small businesses (large partnerships with limited liability, limited liability companies, and a few cases of closely held joint stock companies); also minority employee-owned small firms.
- Minority employee-owned large-scale businesses (limited liability and joint stock companies) with mainly foreign, but also Bulgarian outside owners.

Types of informal employee participation in decision-making and in enterprise performance

- Partnerships with informal employee participation.
- Stock companies and other limited liability companies with formal and informal channels of employee participation, usually connected to the role of trade union organizations in the enterprise (both state-owned enterprises and a few privatized former public enterprises).
- Range of pay incentive schemes across all forms of association.

---

beside the formal legal ownership of enterprises we also include the right to participate in control and decision-making, as well as the receipt of compensation beyond a fixed wage (or piece rate) in net enterprise returns, or in rare cases, in capital gains.[21]

3.1 Sole Proprietorship

This type of organization is inherently a single-owner enterprise. Nevertheless, some small enterprises have implicit employee ownership by virtue of the fact that many of these businesses are family affairs. Formally

---

partnerships limited by shares; as well as hybrid associations and holding companies. A separate co-operative law from 1991 creates this additional form of business organization. Moreover, non-profit organizations enjoy a separate legal statute and can also engage in commerce. The differences among the forms concern: (i) whether or not there is limited liability; (ii) the use of shares or other legal forms and rules of property control; (iii) the minimum owners' capital required by law; (iv) tax regulations; (v) the required structure of governance; (vi) the right to raise corporate capital publicly (joint stock companies); and (vii) the requirement to get consensus from all owners to sell participation shares (limited liability corporations).

[21] We look specifically at participation in management in Section 6 below. Here the primary focus is on formal ownership of shares.

they are owned by one person, but in practice other members of the family are effective owners in the sense that spouses, children and sometimes other relatives share in decision-making, in current net returns (through higher individual earnings) and, over time, in any capital appreciation through inheritance. This is the case, for example, with a Sofia restaurant started in early 1993 by one family who moved from the Black Sea coast to the capital. The restaurant employs the entire immediate family along with other relatives.

A second type of sole proprietorship with complicated ownership characteristics involves businesses which are wholly-owned subsidiaries of the national Central Co-operative Union (CCU) or affiliated consumer co-operative unions. After 1989 this union became independent of party and state control. Members of local co-operatives (predominantly in smaller cities and rural areas) elect representatives to local and regional co-operative unions, which in turn may administer their own subsidiaries. Such regional unions have some control over the national union, which also has some subsidiaries. These subsidiary enterprises are mainly in catering, retailing, agro-processing and the like, although a few are in manufacturing. Most of the employees in these enterprises are also members of local co-operatives, so that they have some, albeit indirect, influence on the management of the subsidiary in which they work. In the Western literature on co-operatives, this arrangement also exists, but few people regard it as 'employee ownership' in any significant sense.[22]

3.2 Partnerships

Many new businesses have been started as two- or three-person partnerships. When they remain small, and with all employees as partners, they are effectively co-operative enterprises. In other cases, as the partnership adds additional staff, Bulgarian partnerships have generally evolved into more hierarchically organized enterprises. One successful market research and polling partnership started as an egalitarian operation. It has now expanded to include a workforce of more than a dozen and the two original partners act as joint chief executives, although with a significant amount of employee participation in decision-making. The partners have also promised staff members that they will share in any increase in enterprise net revenues (after basic salaries have been covered).

---

[22] These co-operative union-owned businesses are also connected by commercial relations with the former agricultural collectives and their successor organizations. They are also partially controlled by local government, in part due to lack of clarity on property rights and confusion on enterprise governance.

3.3 Co-operatives

The July 1991 Bulgarian *Act on Co-operatives* requires a one member–one vote system. The law does not, however, require all employees to be members. Nor does it prohibit non-employee members; past members of the co-operative have equal rights to participate in governance if they choose to do so. Not only may past members remain non-working members, but previous and current owners of any property incorporated into the co-operative also have rights to participate in organizing the co-operative.[23]

There are over 400 employees' production co-operatives (mainly in light industry, such as clothing, furniture, fur and leather goods, confectionery) which have become autonomous units under the 1991 co-operative law and the decree on the restitution of nationalized property. More than 300 of these production co-operatives have voluntarily become members of the Central Union of Employees' Production Co-operatives (CUWPC). This union, which was resurrected in 1989, helps member co-operatives with marketing, staff development, state relations and legislation, and other problems.[24]

Few of the employees' co-operatives have non-member employees. In part this is due to the severe economic depression in manufacturing from 1990 onward. The need for labour reductions has been a dominant problem facing enterprises with drastic falls in sales. Any problems with non-member employees are likely to arise at some point in the future. Non-members do exist in a few co-ops. Since wages are relatively low in most of these co-ops, and most have required members to make a capital contribution (frequently equal to less than a month's salary) to retain membership, some of these non-member employees have chosen not to exercise their legal right to become a member in order to avoid this financial contribution. In general, however, the co-operatives have faced the problem of lay-offs rather than hiring. Making an initial capital contribution is often perceived as influencing decisions about whether one keeps one's job.

A major problem which continues for more than a quarter of these co-operatives is the lack of clear property rights over the assets which had been previously nationalized, or over assets attached to enterprises newly created by state investment after nationalization.

---

[23] The 1991 co-operative law was written mainly with agricultural co-operatives or collectives in mind; many of the law's features do not fit the circumstances of workers' production co-operatives. A major difficulty remaining in 1995 is the lack of records for proving who should qualify for membership.

[24] This organization had been abolished in 1971 as all co-operatives were either folded into the single Central Co-operative Union (CCU) federation or transformed into regular state-owned enterprises. It was recreated as the organization for representing and promoting workers' production co-operatives in 1989–90.

A second problem perceived by many co-operatives is the need for new investment in modern technology. Outside loans are seen as expensive and inaccessible. Another source is current member-employees. Current members are usually reluctant to make further contributions, however, since these would simply be unsecured loans to a business in difficulties; because of the fall in real incomes since 1989 blue-collar employees have little in the way of surplus financial assets.[25]

3.4 Employee Ownership of Equity in Limited Liability Companies and of Shares in Joint Stock Commercial Enterprises

The early legal reforms in post-socialist Bulgaria enabled employees to own corporate shares, just like any other citizen. Most employee ownership of joint stock companies or limited liability companies has resulted from privatization procedures which give employees price concessions. These ownership shares are purchased as individually held property. Employee ownership of shares has occurred in both larger enterprise and small and medium-sized enterprise privatization. In general, in the bigger firms only some employees acquire shares, and even then only a minority block of total company equity is available to them. As regards small privatization, especially after the 1994 amendments to the *Act on Privatization*, there has been a growing number of small firm privatizations in which managers and employees have purchased the entire enterprise. Below we first summarize the results of the privatization of larger enterprises, then the smaller ones.

The *Act on Privatization* of 1992 (and the 1994 amended version) provided for employee concessions (such as price reductions) in purchasing a limited portion of the shares during the privatization of larger enterprises. Although this has occurred in about half of the large-scale enterprise privatizations, in no case known to the authors has a majority of the employees purchased a majority of shares. By the end of 1995, of the 500 or so larger privatizations, there were 241 cases (about 45% of the total) in which managers and employees participated in share purchases (PA, 1996, p. 3). For medium-sized (over 10 million leva) and larger firms, cases in which 100% of a company's capital assets were transferred to employee ownership have been very rare. The largest firm in which employees own a majority is one of the biggest Bulgarian export–import trading companies; about a third of the employees participated in the purchase.

---

[25] This is one reason for advocating a 'democratic worker-owned corporation' special statute with special capital accounts (see Ellerman, 1990). Such a statute would change the nature of any additional members' investments in their own firm and perhaps help raise a limited amount of capital financing. See section 7.4 of the paper and point (a) beneath it.

Most frequently, only a portion of the total workforce has exercised the option to purchase reduced price shares. Typically it involves from one-quarter to two-thirds of the workforce; 100% participation is rare. The mandated price reduction limits employees to a total of 20% of any single large enterprise's equity. The employees have purchased the maximum 20% in a number of cases. In many other cases in which the total enterprise valuation is extremely high employees have bought only 1% or 2% (even when taking full advantage of the available concessions).[26]

In a handful of (smaller) medium-sized firms employees have established a special legal entity to buy the enterprise. This appears to be orchestrated primarily by management which ends up controlling a dominant or majority stake in the privatized enterprise. Employees have bought shares in privatization deals involving both foreign investors and exclusively Bulgarian buyers, though to a lesser extent.

An individual employee is entitled to only a limited price reduction according to the law and its amendments; and hence is only permitted to buy a small portion of the available shares, at least at a reduced price. In a few privatizations employees have not purchased any of the shares set aside for them. This has usually been in enterprises in very poor financial and productive health.

The 1992 law also provided for employees in smaller state- and municipal-owned enterprises to purchase equity in their firms in the course of privatization. As already mentioned, the employees of smaller enterprises may combine to make a purchase offer for the business. This arrangement requires financing, which is where the 1994 amendments to the law seem to have been most helpful. This type of employee ownership has been initiated with increasing frequency since the end of 1994, but still in only a small portion of the numerous small privatizations.[27] The employees and/or management must organize themselves and produce an offer and business plan to buy the enterprise, making a substantial downpayment (10% or 30% of the purchase price). This downpayment risks forfeiture if the employees are unable to raise monies for payment of the remainder of the purchase price. One attempt in 1994–95 by a group of employees to buy their enterprise – an automobile service centre – led to just such a forfeiture, which was widely publicized and made employee groups more sceptical of attempts to organize employee buy-outs.[28]

---

[26] This discussion is based on interviews with a number of researchers, unionists, and labour organizations by the authors in 1995 and 1996. The consensus estimates are that, for large and medium-sized privatized enterprises, about 50% of the employees participate in purchasing shares and that they buy only around 5% of their enterprise equity.

[27] There are no official and comprehensive data on the different types of buyers of privatized enterprises, at least in categories relevant to this point.

[28] Knowledge of this problem made it difficult for a similar business to get employees to put forward the cash to pay the downpayment on their own enterprise. Finally, the leader of the workers'

So far, the majority of small enterprise employee buy-outs appear to have been in the service sector, involving enterprises privatized by local authorities. The interest in employee buy-outs has intensified greatly since mid 1995; hence, past trends may not efficiently predict future developments in privatization methodology. No data are available on the distribution of share ownership among employees in MEBOs.

3.5 Quasi-full Employee Ownership in Some Public Services

There have been a small number of experiments in what we might call the 'traditional' public service sectors, the first being a dental clinic controlled by a municipal government. Employees were given the right to rearrange the clinic into a half-public, half-private operation. Employees do not formally 'own' the clinic, but received full control as long as they provided the mandatory public service to which they had traditionally been limited. In addition they established a private service alongside the public one. The operation was controlled by the employees democratically and net revenues were shared on the basis of an incentive system related to contributions to the private and public services rendered by the clinic. Other dentistry and health-care clinics around the country are considering similar ventures.[29]

4 ATTITUDES TO EMPLOYEE OWNERSHIP

4.1 General Situation

Beside the political parties and the churches, the main publicly known organizations in Bulgaria are those representing employees, private business owners, and state enterprise employers and managers.[30] There is a rapidly growing number of informal civic interest groups. There is also an increasing number of non-profit organizations with their own agenda.

There is no significant public opposition to the concept of employee ownership, nor to the current concessions and limitations under current law. In fact, most public opinion polls show a majority of the population in favour of employees obtaining some ownership in their enterprises. The privatization process is generally perceived to have proceeded very slowly so far.

---

group had to demonstrate his faith in the venture by purchasing several times more stock than the other employees. This ultimately resulted in a quite democratically managed service enterprise with a little less than 100 employees, all but one of whom participated in the buy-out.

[29] This example is examined in detail in a case study in Rock (1992).

[30] For an extended institutional analysis of various forms of business and labour organization in Bulgaria in 1989–94, see Rock (1994a).

Employee ownership is seen as one way of speeding it up and perhaps limiting the influence of the increasingly powerful domestic financial conglomerates. Few people have any concrete ideas about the role of employee ownership in increasing employee participation in decision-making or improving enterprise efficiency.

Among the formal organizations there are a few strong supporters of employee ownership and some moderate opponents, while most have remained uncommitted. In the employee ownership debates the formally organized groups most involved (ranked here in order of decreasing influence on legislative and executive decisions) have been: political parties, trade union organizations and business interest groups.

4.2 Political Parties

The Bulgarian Socialist Party has not publicly opposed employee ownership. In 1990, as the BSP evolved from the collapse of the old communist party organization, employee ownership was not an issue. Only as the struggles over the 1992 *Act on Privatization* occurred did some in the party speak out in favour of the general principle of employees owning a substantial interest in their enterprises, though it did not become a key issue. Following its attainment of an outright majority in parliament in the December 1994 elections the BSP has persisted with existing policies and left the employee ownership provisions of the 1992/1994 *Act on Privatization* intact. Beyond this the BSP has accepted provisions allowing the use of mass privatization coupons for purchasing enterprise equity (in the mass coupon privatization regulations made in the summer of 1995).

In practice the BSP government has permitted the more favourable (for employee share ownership) provisions and methods to be used, especially by municipal governments involved in small privatization.

The Union of Democratic Forces (UDF) is an alliance that originated in the more than one dozen party formations of 1989–90 and has continually evolved throughout the post-socialist period. As a result opinions on employee ownership have been diverse and have changed over time for many factions and individuals from the economic crisis of 1989 to the present. Let us summarize the views of the major factions.

The most liberal, laissez-faire wing of the UDF, represented to a significant extent in the UDF Government of 1991–92, was generally hostile to any forms of ownership or procedure which transferred property to communists, including individuals and organizations held over from existing communist structures, as well as any opportunists with 'dirty money' accumulated illegally during the old regime. This entailed a basic hostility towards measures to facilitate employee ownership. Employee ownership meant power for the trade union organizations, predominantly CITUB, the largest, and also the heir to the old communist monopoly trade union confederation.

Furthermore, for the economic advisers of the ultra-liberal UDF faction, employee ownership was not considered a part of mainstream free-market theory which involved traditional 'entrepreneurs.' Since it would be government mandated, employee ownership would very likely do more harm than good; it was seen to create inefficiencies, some of which were similar to the incentive and efficiency problems of the old socialist system. Employee ownership is still seen by this group as a largely irrelevant issue compared to other elements of a well-functioning market economy. Nevertheless, this ideology was not dominant during the drafting of the 1992 *Act on Privatization*. The law allowed employee ownership, but only up to 20% of an enterprise and without voting rights.

Part of the pressure for employee concessions came from the more social democratic elements of the original UDF coalition.[31] This has coalesced with other groups who look more to Germany, France and some other northern European countries as more attractive models of modern capitalism. These groups are friendly to various, usually moderate, levels of employee ownership. They view it as one element among many able to promote a better economic transition. Ideas similar to these were accepted by the Berov government of 1993–94. This government's period of office coincided with growing interest in employee ownership. This has most notably been coupled with the desire of municipal governments to privatize their enterprises and properties more rapidly. MEBOs have been considered as a useful mechanism to achieve this goal.

4.3 Trade Union Organizations

Employee ownership has remained a secondary issue for both of the two main Bulgarian trade union confederations. Their main concerns in the post-socialist era have been: legislation affecting work and trade unions; the collective bargaining process and particularly issues of wages, benefits and

---

[31] Some of these elements have since split from the UDF and, like other groups with different origins, are still trying to create a social democratic 'centre' for Bulgarian political life. In addition to these people, sources close to the government and parliament at the time of the debates on the original 1992 Privatization Law related that an important additional impulse to include employee ownership in the law came from advisers from the major international financial institutions. These institutions, absolutely dominant in the major funding packages for post-socialist transition in Bulgaria and elsewhere, had previously been hostile to mandated employee ownership in privatization. Early reports from 1990 and 1991 indicated that they neither found employee ownership theoretically attractive nor did they believe that outside investors wanted such a burden when they purchased former state enterprises. From interviews we could observe that their attitudes have apparently evolved since then.

working conditions; organizational development of the confederations themselves and protection/assertion of their property rights; and relations with foreign labour unions, international trade union organizations and international agencies.

The heir of the old monopoly union, the Confederation of Independent Trade Unions of Bulgaria (CITUB), has generally viewed employee ownership favourably. Employee ownership was part of the confederation's standpoint on privatization issues even before the 1992 *Act on Privatization*.[32] CITUB is in favour of greater aid to employees involved in privatization and employee ownership. Currently, as the pace of privatization seems likely to increase, CITUB realizes it does not have adequate resources to deal with all the concerns its members will raise about the possibility of buying shares. CITUB would like more staff experts in various business fields in order to give employees sound advice. The lack of capacity is particularly problematic for the largest state-owned enterprises with extremely complicated economic situations, and where CITUB is well represented.

The other major trade union confederation, 'Podkrepa', was relatively uninterested in employee ownership until the 1992 *Act on Privatization* incorporated employee concessions. Before then most Podkrepa advisers argued that the first step in the economic transition was the creation of 'real capitalist owners' to help construct a 'normal economy'. After a stratum of real owners had come into being the trade unions could reduce their political interventions and concentrate on collective bargaining. Since 1992 its official position has evolved to a more open pro-employee ownership viewpoint such that its current position is similar to that of CITUB. Also like CITUB, Podkrepa supports additional aid and financial arrangements to employees trying to buy stakes in their firms and greater employee concessions in privatization. Podkrepa also lacks resources and expertise to give adequate advice to its local affiliates and individual members about privatization.

The general arguments used by the trade union confederations to favour employee ownership include greater fairness for employees in the difficult transition, improved incentives for good working habits, and efficiency improvements for the whole enterprise. They point out that, in any case, there are not enough purchasers of Bulgarian state-owned enterprises.

4.4 Employers' Organizations

Business organizations have come to the issue of employee ownership only

---

[32] This is partly due to the long-time interest in worker participation of Professor Krastyu Petkov, CITUB leader since 1990, and an industrial relations sociologist by training, who had developed a strong interest in worker participation in decision-making by the early 1980s.

recently. Some sectoral organizations connected to state enterprises and their managers have favoured more possibilities for management buy-outs and leasing arrangements. An example of this early in the transition period involved managers in the tourism sector. This sectoral organization publicly advocated management and employee buy-outs as a suitable means of helping the state effectively to divest itself of many properties in the sector. Despite this example, management groups and their organizations have in general tended to favour the possibilities of joint ventures with foreign businesses, providing immediate capital infusion and/or new technologies. If employee ownership were to reduce foreign investors' interest in Bulgarian firms these organizations might be more antagonistic towards employee ownership.

Organizations representing the private business sector have barely addressed employee ownership during the transition period. One – the Union for Private Economic Enterprise – has argued against anything which might delay privatization or drive away potential buyers.

Most foreign businesses have not overtly criticized employee ownership in Bulgaria. In fact, some foreign investors have supported a minority share for their employees. In at least one case the foreign buyers created a credit mechanism in order to allow the employees to buy some of their enterprise's stock.

4.5 Workers' Attitudes

A survey of more than 4,000 manufacturing workers carried out in late Spring 1992 sought to uncover their willingness to invest money in their own enterprise. The responses revealed that only about 25% were willing to invest

Table 3.1 Employees' willingness to invest in their own enterprise, Bulgaria, 1992 (%)

Amount they were willing to invest in their own enterprise (leva)	From Savings	Through Deferred Wages
0	20.1	20.9
1–500	6.0	6.1
501–1000	8.2	2.3
1001–2000	5.1	2.1
2001–3000	1.8	1.8
3001–5000	3.9	4.3
More than 5000	5.3	9.1
No response	49.6	53.3

Source: Employees' survey carried out by the authors, 1992.

in their manufacturing firm at that point. We should remember that mid-1992 was nearly the worst point of the economic transition in terms of the fall in real wages, and also that the manufacturing sector was the most severely affected by the collapse in demand. Note also that at this time, 1,000 leva was slightly more than the gross monthly wages of a typical worker.

5 ECONOMIC EFFECTS OF EMPLOYEE OWNERSHIP AND EMPLOYEE PARTICIPATION IN DECISION-MAKING

A number of empirical studies in the West lead one to conclude that the most positive economic effects (such as value added per employee) have occurred in firms where employee ownership or the structures of the enterprise include both (i) significant levels of employee participation in decision-making, and (ii) important levels of employee financial participation (compensation of employees reflecting enterprise profitability on a regular and frequent basis). The presence of only one of these features tends to achieve less consistent results.[33] Based on the evidence available to us these results are not contradicted by Bulgarian experiences.

5.1 Survey on Employee Attitudes

Bulgarian employee attitudes concerning the effects of owning shares in their enterprise support the potential benefits viewpoint. In the same 1992 survey of manufacturing, employees were asked how share ownership would change their behaviour. Their responses are presented in *Table 3.2*.

Interviews at several enterprises during 1991–95 support the idea that when substantive employee participation in decision-making is combined with compensation based on economic results the efficiency of the enterprise is usually enhanced. In one case, labour productivity increased by a factor of three in eighteen months; in another it doubled over two years. Both of these enterprises are in the service sector. These conclusions are complicated by some technological change, but interviews with elected managers and employees still lead to the conclusion that labour motivation and employee efficiency have seen important improvements.[34] One of these enterprise case studies can help illustrate our points.

---

[33] See the survey articles in Alan Blinder (ed.) (1990). See also Bonin, Jones, and Putterman (1994).

[34] The new technology in these cases has reduced the necessary effort in certain tasks, and perhaps improved the quality of some services, but has not changed the time required to complete work operations.

Table 3.2 Employees' behaviour concerning share ownership, Bulgaria, 1992 (%)

'If I owned shares in my own enterprise, I would...'	Work harder	Not permit laziness	Co-operate with management	Ensure quality output
Strongly disagree	9.4	5.6	5.0	4.9
Disagree	6.0	3.8	3.2	2.6
Disagree somewhat	6.1	4.4	4.8	3.4
Agree somewhat	13.1	10.5	12.7	7.8
Agree	23.6	25.0	27.6	23.7
Strongly agree	29.9	39.1	34.5	46.0
No response	11.9	11.6	12.2	11.6
Total	100.0	100.0	100.0	100.0

Source: Employee survey, 1992.

5.2 A Case Study of an Employee-owned Enterprise: Central Auto Service (CSA)

Central Auto Service is an auto and small truck servicing centre in one of the major cities in Bulgaria. It was the first of its type in the city, opening up in 1961 in a well situated locale near to the major national road (and international trucking route) passing out of the city. At the beginning of 1990, along with all the other service stations in the Motor Technical Division state enterprise, CSA was separated into a independent company. At this time CSA had over one hundred employees. Several auto service and petrol stations were sold in the first auctions of state property in 1991. The state-appointed management of CSA carried out a deliberate policy of debt accumulation, client neglect, shoddy quality control and non-maintenance so that they could subsequently buy it on the cheap. However, estimates made of the assets and liabilities prevented this. Aware of the manager's strategy, employees used their powers under the 1986 Labour Code to dismiss him and in mid-1991 elected as chief executive in his stead a veteran mechanic of some 20 years experience. For the next two and a half years CSA remained a 100% state-owned enterprise and was able to repay most of the debts accumulated by the previous management. Due to a revenue shortage, however, the company was unable to pay all its operating costs (for example, central heating). Client confidence and loyalty was rebuilt over many months through hard work and innovative policies (such as free repairs for pensioners) thereby inducing these customers to provide testimonials as a means of free advertising.

At the end of 1993 the elected manager began conversations with the Ministry of Trade and Transport about the possibility of privatizing CSA. Meanwhile, employees were regularly kept informed of developments. The manager was able to convince the Ministry that the value of CSA was not in the buildings or equipment (little had been done to the buildings in 30 years and the equipment was very old). The real estate, due to its strategic location, did have independent value. The really important value of the company was in the employees – in their skills, experience, and good reputation.

The Ministry decided to privatize CSA by tender (not auction) for interested parties who would make proposals in terms of a business development strategy as well as a bid price. The experts' prior evaluation of the company assets set the initial price at 12 million leva. The manager spent many weeks creating an exhaustive business plan with detailed steps for developing the business and retaining employees. The manager and employees met many times to hammer out the arrangements for their bid and the share of each employee in the bid (and hence ownership). The other employees (all but one of the remaining 75 employees) agreed to support the new manager's plan and authorized him to make the final bid price for them. At the same time, another group of employees at a different auto service station suffered a major loss. They had put down 10% of the price of their company but had been unable to finance the rest of the purchase. They lost their downpayment and their company to another buyer. This news was known at CSA and worried the employees greatly. In order to demonstrate his confidence in the buy-out strategy, the manager agreed to increase his personal investment to almost four times that of the other employees.

The manager bid slightly more than the 12 million leva appraisal value. Their bid was not the highest, but the other bidders had presented only sketchy plans for business development, and ultimately the Ministry agreed to the deal with the workforce. To pay for the enterprise, the employees first looked to the banks for a loan, but they all wanted a mortgage on the property as collateral, which was unacceptable to the employees. The workforce collected savings and other personal funds and the Ministry allowed the permissible 30% discount (in the 1992 *Act on Privatization*) for a buy-out. The remainder came from a signature loan from the State Bank which was signed by all 76 employees (joint liability). The Ministry sold the company to the individual employees (natural persons rather than legal entities), who set up a limited liability company.

The distribution of shares is somewhat unequal. Some employees used only their legal concession (a price reduction equal to no more than a year's wages) for purchasing shares, while others contributed additional funds. The highest investment share was the 5.5% of equity bought by the manager. Voting at the company general assembly is based on the number of shares owned.

According to the company agreement, shares may not be sold to outsiders (non-employees); sale may occur only with the unanimous consent of all shareholders. So far there have been no share sales.

The employees have been willing to make additional investments in better equipment (for example, lease-purchase of a pneumatic pump and distribution lines for power tools). The owners of new cars have tended so far to go to their competitors because of their more modern image. In order to meet this challenge CSA has recently invested in an Italian-made automatic car-wash machine and customers may buy a subscription booklet for it with a special digitalized access card. This brings more affluent car owners to the service station on a regular basis. The manager hopes to open a petrol station alongside the existing repair business. CSA has developed a niche in the market by continuing to specialize in Eastern bloc-made vehicles. In part, CSA has been successful by guaranteeing work done and gathering additional testimonials from well-known public figures satisfied with service and price. The manager has become a recognized figure in the city.

In the past the workforce had 'primitive' work attitudes. Now, working conditions are good and the manager has an open-door policy at all times; mechanics can come to see him with their problems. The manager spends two hours of each workday on the shop floor conferring with employees about the problems of the business. The working habits of the youngest employees are the easiest to change. Theft of company property – a serious problem when CSA was a state-owned enterprise – is no longer a significant problem. When equipment breaks down employees no longer just sit around waiting for someone else to repair it, but will try to repair it themselves or will seek alternative means to carry out their work. The manager and several of the employees interviewed claimed that the workforce has an entirely new attitude to work. The company has adopted individualized supplemental wage incentives based on performance; these premiums can be from 10% to 40% of the basic wage. In addition, CSA has contracts with two vocational schools for training new employees.

The major problems facing CSA appear to be financial. The burden of payment on the debt incurred by purchasing the company is heavy. In order to remain competitive with new market entrants, CSA needs to invest in new equipment; but credit is very expensive. This conflicts also with the company's desire to make significant new investments (car dealership, car rental company, rehabilitation of company shops). On the positive side, CSA has rebuilt its operations and now has about 8–10% of the city's auto repair business.

CSA is open 16 hours a day, six days a week. The company fully employs the workforce. They are even considering remaining open at night.

5.3 More Mixed Results at Manufacturing Companies Fully Owned by the Employees

In the case of employee-owned manufacturing firms a lack of orders appears to be the main constraint on efficiency improvements. Fully employee-owned and controlled enterprises (mainly co-operatives) have been reluctant to lay off employees even in the face of drastically declining demand. This means that measured labour productivity (measured in value or physical terms) in these firms has declined, but due to lack of orders and not necessarily due to employee ownership. Significant falls in labour productivity have occurred throughout the manufacturing sector – in all types of enterprise – over most of the transition period. This decline has occurred also in state-owned manufacturing enterprises, almost all of which have not reduced their labour force in line with reductions in output. Any measurable effects from ownership or participation may well be masked by these huge falls in sales and output.

Co-operative manufacturers have tended also to be located in light industry producing non-necessary items that people purchase with discretionary income. In the early years of the transition, as prices rose rapidly, households had to dedicate a much larger portion of their disposable income to food purchases (almost 50%). Discretionary expenditure fell even more than other spending, making the demand deficiency problem for many co-operatives more severe than for the average manufacturer.

No comprehensive study has yet been made of the effects of employee ownership on enterprise performance in Bulgaria, though there is some anecdotal evidence of improved results reported by individuals and in the press. Generalization on the basis of these results is difficult since the severity of the post-socialist economic downturn has resulted in a much lower level of current output (i.e. the latest available year's performance compared to 1989 or 1990), while various other factors have complicated the research.

In manufacturing, a nationally representative panel survey of enterprises has produced preliminary multiple regression results which indicate that greater levels of employee financial participation (profit-sharing, gain-sharing) contribute to positive economic performance.[35]

---

[35] This is a panel survey of 500 enterprises with data for 1989–92; data for 1993–94 are being processed and data for 1995 are under collection. Working papers dealing with the data are available from the authors and collaborators on the study (e.g. Jones, Klinedinst, and Rock, 1996). These surveys are also used in the subsequent discussion of worker participation; much of the use there is based only on the descriptive analysis of survey data. After pilot tests in 1991 and 1992, the first phase of the surveys was done in a nationally and sectorally representative sample of 500 state and co-operative manufacturing enterprises in mid-1992.

Owning a share of one's enterprise does not in itself improve enterprise results. When sales are low, there is little financial surplus to distribute among owner-employees. There has as yet been no financial pay-off to employee ownership in most cases. Traditional patterns of work and of supervision and subordination often persist even when employees have become partial or full owners of the enterprise. Often employees purchase shares to improve their employment prospects; many people want to continue in their present jobs. They are not much concerned with longer-term returns on this investment; it seems to be regarded by some as a lottery ticket which also provides a work opportunity.

Nevertheless, as appears to be the case in the advanced industrialized countries, employee participation in decision-making and greater employee influence in the enterprise may be necessary components of improved economic performance. Employee ownership correlates positively, but imperfectly, with increased participation.

6 EMPLOYEE PARTICIPATION IN DECISION-MAKING

The level of employee participation in decision-making and informative meetings with management varies enormously. In majority employee-owned companies, there is a high average level of participation. In privatized enterprises with little or no employee share-ownership, and in non-privatized state-owned companies, the level of participation appears to be positively correlated with the level of unionization. It is influenced also by the attitudes of the management group; technology and workforce skill levels also influence the internal patterns of decision-making and consultation. In some enterprises, employees participate in weekly meetings with managers and deal with virtually all issues facing the enterprise. In other enterprises, there is little employee involvement in decision-making, with relatively infrequent meetings, usually only in extraordinary circumstances.[36] As we have already mentioned, the 1986 Labour Code gave workers substantial formal rights in the selection of top managers and participation in the decision-making process in general. This was contradicted by the 1992 Commercial Code. The 1993 revision of the Labour Code finally eliminated the participatory features of the 1986 law.[37]

[36] According to an ongoing nationally representative study of Bulgarian manufacturing enterprises, employee participation in decision-making is significant in a substantial minority of enterprises (almost all remain SOEs). Financial participation (profit-sharing, gains-sharing) is much more widespread. (Jones, Klinedinst, and Rock, 1996).

[37] The 1 January 1993 revision recognized the right of workers to participate in management 'only in instances provided by the law' (Article 7). This revised code does not mention any such

Both the reports of workers and surveys of enterprise top managers indicate that between 1989 and 1993 worker participation in decision-making was quite limited.[38] It seems that neither the level nor the breadth of this influence was greatly altered by the political and economic changes of the period. In general, co-operative enterprises had significant levels of worker influence on decision-making, according to the surveys.[39]

Estimates for 1989–92 seem to show a positive correlation between higher levels of worker influence in decision-making and greater intra-enterprise equality of income distribution. There appears to be no relation between participation and levels of investment, and only a very tentative relation to the relative speed at which workers were laid off during the sales downturn. In general, no great difference has been measured in enterprise performance (for example, value added) according to the level of worker influence on decision-making. Much more important influences on positive enterprise performance include market share and financial participation (incentive compensation schemes).[40]

Since 1992 overall worker participation in decision-making in Bulgaria has not increased much. From case studies conducted over the last three years, however, it seems that the degree of worker involvement in enterprises continues to vary greatly. In most workers' production co-operatives there are regular formal channels for worker involvement in decision-making and the assessment of information relevant to the enterprise. There are also other meetings which are voluntary. Workers do not always choose to participate in the voluntary meetings; they are most likely to do so when these concern wages and benefits. In state-owned enterprises one finds examples of worker

instances; it does recognize trade union organizations and their right to collectively bargain with enterprise management/owners' representatives.

[38] We are concentrating on influence and participation connected to ownership. Workers were frequently able to exert influence on decisions (e.g. removing an unacceptable manager, revising compensation packages, getting payment of unpaid wages for prior work) through trade union actions. Demonstrations were organized to condemn a decision after it was taken. Workers used strikes and strike threats and were quite often successful in bringing a change of mind by managers (or other controlling authorities like the Minister of Industry).

[39] According to a 1992 representative survey of managers in manufacturing, in 1989 about 15% of managers ranked worker influence (compared to management) in their own enterprise at a high level – choosing top scores of 5 or 6 on a six-point scale of influence. Concerning worker decision-making power in 1992, about 20% of the managers chose these same rankings of worker influence. Workers were surveyed at these same enterprises. They perceive their own power over decisions to be less significant; these differing perspectives on the same situation are similar to surveys done in Western countries. Nevertheless, despite these different perceptions of the decision-making power of workers, both managers and workers perceive the same trend of increased influence during 1989–92.

[40] These are preliminary results based on two rounds of survey panel data on a representative sample of manufacturing firms (Jones, Klinedinst, and Rock, 1996). The survey of enterprises continues to collect data and this may lead to firmer conclusions.

involvement which are quite similar to the co-operatives, with regular meetings between workers and managers. Inside these enterprises there is usually a good relationship between the workers' trade union representatives and management. In many instances, workers have contributed to making the enterprise more effective in response to the new market and new product demands. In contrast, in other state-owned enterprises there is little regular contact between higher management and the workforce; this appears to be more frequently true of the largest enterprises. In private, 'traditional' capitalist enterprises, substantial worker participation appears to be non-existent, although in many small enterprises there are informal relations with some characteristics of worker participation and influence.

Where workers have gained majority control of the enterprise – this includes some co-operatives and a few companies – the nature of worker participation has changed dramatically. Most owner-employees take some advantage of their right to participate in the running of their enterprise. Nevertheless, the severity of the economic situation leads many workers in the most severely hit employee-owned firms to despair of making much difference in their enterprise's struggle to survive. Even in workers' co-operatives the workers are often looking for other employment since they perceive little income or job security from their current jobs.

7 RECOMMENDATIONS

The economic situation in Bulgaria is difficult, but employee ownership still holds out some hope, we believe, for improving economic effectiveness through its influence on employee motivation and enterprise productivity.

The logic of our analysis is based on the following chain of causality. Employee ownership generally leads to greater involvement of employees in the net results of their enterprise, for example, through profit-sharing schemes.[41] Ownership also implies participation at the highest level of decision-making in the enterprise (that is, on the Board).[42] When employees share some of the net financial results of the enterprise and are involved in

[41] There are many ways to link workers' compensation to the net results of their enterprise. Ownership of shares is one. Perhaps its main drawback is that normally dividends are paid only annually and may not give frequent enough feedback to workers on how the firm is doing. Also, dividends may be zero some years, and not always due to the lack of net earnings. However, employee ownership may lead to more participation of workers in enterprise decisions about how to connect compensation to economic performance in order to produce the most positive effects on labour motivation and efficiency. Thus workers and/or their representatives can jointly design an optimal incentive system.

[42] This high-level participation through share ownership is not usually sufficient to have a significant effect. Participation may need to occur at different levels in the enterprise (e.g. on the

decision-making there is a greater likelihood of positive economic effects. Improvements in labour motivation, individual and collective work efficiency, quality output, and other effects may all ensue, enhancing the performance of the enterprise as a whole.[43] We may hope for higher productivity, a greater ability to compete in difficult markets, and general improvements in employee and even social welfare.

If the political powers in Bulgaria agree with this argument there are a series of proposals which might help realize the potential benefits of employee ownership. The Government should support expanded reforms to increase employee ownership and make it more likely to spread, for example, by making it cheaper and easier. (See Section 7.1.)

Since the potential benefits depend on the quality of decision-making in the firm, there should also be some support to help increase the general awareness and specific expertise in Bulgaria about employee ownership and participation in enterprises. Information access, special training, skills development in business and enterprise decision-making, and organization building are all important for workers, managers, trade unions and others. We address these possibilities in Section 7.2.

There are also arguments to be made for flexibility in commercial law to promote more organizational experimentation in developing effective enterprises with highly motivated and effective employees. Other reforms may make it more attractive for enterprises to create employee ownership opportunities. Moreover, if the political actors are convinced of the positive effects of broader participation in economic life, they may consider a range of further reforms. These matters are dealt with in section 7.3.

Before we turn to our specific proposals, it is important to stress the need for a clear legal and economic environment. Stable, transparent and effectively applied laws and practices must prevail in the economy. Legal stability is just as crucial for a well-functioning market economy as relative price stability. The reduction of uncertainty makes people better able to plan and act economically. At present, the following legislative action is needed:

i)   rapid and binding decisions on property rights so that enterprises can quickly find out what belongs to them and what does not (property privatization often involves decisions on the restitution of portions previously nationalized);

Board, on management decisions of strategy, as well as everyday work processes) in order to get the full benefits of participation for economic performance.

[43] This is based on the brief review of the empirical literature (and supported by some theoretical arguments) we summarized at the start of Section 5. Better results come from a combination of financial and decision-making participation.

ii)   clear, non-contradictory and stable legislation on commerce, property, ownership rights and the duties of different economic actors.

These features can improve the predictability of the environment for all enterprises and economic actors. The benefits are not exclusive to employee owners or their enterprises. We believe that the following recommendations should be given priority.

7.1 Reducing Costs and Improving Credit for Employee Ownership

If employee-owned shares become cheaper, more employees will probably take advantage of opportunities to purchase them. In this regard improved access to credit is another change which would almost certainly expand employee ownership.

7.1.1 Reducing the cost to employees of employee ownership

This might include:

i)   greater reductions in the price of enterprise shares for employees;
ii)   clear rights for employees to use the mass privatization coupons for the purchase of shares in their own enterprise (still at a reduced price) with no time limit on the use of the coupons.

7.1.2 Improving credit access for employees

This could involve:

i)   more flexibility in the terms of payment for enterprise shares by extending the repayment terms of existing or new financing;[44]
ii)   employee stock ownership laws as in the USA and other countries (to facilitate employee purchase of shares through internal funding, tax advantages for enterprises and financial institutions making loans for this purpose);[45]
iii)   resurrection and active use of the previously planned state-established fund to help Bulgarian citizens to acquire property (at present,

[44] The amendments to the 1994 revision of the Privatization Law were an important step in the right direction. Nevertheless, further flexibility in the schedule of instalment payments should be allowed. Some small and medium-sized enterprises, purchased through MEBOs, may be able to survive only if the repayment schedule is longer than 6 years.

[45] There are some interesting facts to be learned from both the intensive study of one's own country and by looking at others. The US situation has seen Employee Ownership amended by

privatization revenues appear to have been swamped by the large government budget deficit);[46]

iv)   government credit guarantees (on repayment of loans to employees to purchase shares) would attract more lenders into the market;[47]

v)   establishment of special investment fund(s) to purchase shares as a 'friendly outsider' helping to hold shares while employees save or get funds from elsewhere to purchase shares in their own company (this could be connected to the already legislated pension fund allocation from the sale of enterprises to the public).

7.2 Information, Training and Skills Development

Employees, trade union officials, and managers all desire more training and information about employee ownership and how it may enhance the performance of enterprises and benefit all of them. Most managers (and employees) in Bulgaria need more help in business skills development. Enterprises with employee ownership must also become familiar with these things. Developing leadership within the firm also needs practical skills in the trade or product.

Better and more comprehensive information can help employees to evaluate rationally the decision to buy shares. They may learn of other advantages besides those they tend to emphasize in surveys. Information can also reveal potential problems and disadvantages ahead of time. More effective participatory structures can be created within enterprises by well-informed employees and managers. They have some economic interests in common and may be able to improve effectiveness by building on these common interests. Trade unions will need to refashion their activities and expertise – to move beyond traditional concerns with collective bargaining, wages and benefits – if they are to remain relevant for employee owners or co-operative members.

---

the national government at least once a year since the landmark ERISA legislation of 1974 which connected tax deferral treatment for worker benefits to special arrangements for financing employee stock purchases. This is why the USA has had such a phenomenal growth in employee ownership over the last two decades. See Joseph Blasi (1988), on US employee ownership. The main organization in the USA monitoring employee ownership developments is the National Center for Employee Ownership (NCEO), Oakland, California which publishes an informative newsletter and journal on the subject.

[46] The Sofia Municipal Privatization Authority has also created an infrastructure investment fund out of its privatization receipts. This could be expanded to help finance employee ownership (PA, 1995a).

[47] The employee shares could serve as collateral for the loans.

7.2.1 Information, training and skills development concerning employee ownership issues

This could include:

i)   training/workshops on legal aspects of employee ownership – employees need to understand in a general way the rights and consequences of ownership;

ii) training/workshops for trade unionists on the expanded/different role of trade unions in enterprises with employee ownership – trade unions must still collectively bargain and protect employees, but now they must also give advice and debate with employees about employee ownership;

iii) collecting and disseminating empirical information on specific economic and financial problems faced by enterprises with employee ownership or other non-traditional structures;[48]

iv) establishment of a national non-profit organization to focus on employee ownership (and perhaps employee participation in general);

v)   funds are required in order that Bulgarian organizations and individuals may join international groups and organizations working on employee ownership and participation;

vi) training and workshops on organizational development to help participants take advantage of positive effects of employee ownership and employee participation in management; and to avoid negative group dynamics in employee-controlled firms.

7.2.2 Information, training and skills development for employees, trade unionists, and even managers concerning business practices and concerns

This could include:

i)   ensuring that employees and/or their representatives have equal access to the existing training centres/study visits for general business skills and information/contact desks to help them engage in business;

ii) specific training for employees and employee groups in business skills aimed at improving the financial analysis of enterprises (important in evaluating possible stock purchases and annual reports);

---

[48] There are many arguments for having a non-profit or co-operative organization specializing in worker ownership and worker participation. This allows the organization to focus on somewhat different matters than traditional trade unions. It is possible for a trade union organization to run these things internally. In Bulgaria, at present, the trade unions do not have the financial resources to do so alone.

iii)   help with the development of general business skills (marketing, accounting, product development, management, etc.) so that employees can be effective participants in the enterprise and evaluate management as other investors do;

iv)   help with staff training for effective planning and practical implementation of complex decisions – organizational development for more effective work and decision-making.

7.3 Support for More Employee Involvement – Ownership as an Initial Step towards Expanded Financial and Decision-making Participation and Enhanced Economic Democracy

A more active strategy for expanding employee ownership would also encourage the greater democratization of enterprises and other economic institutions. Some of these proposals already exist in some Western economies. Many analysts believe that such reforms can make further improvements in employee motivation, improve management and enterprise performance, and develop a market-based system perceived as fair and accessible to many more people than the current economic arrangements.

7.3.1 Legislation to increase the variety and flexibility of forms of business organization with employee ownership

The following would be needed:

i)   employee stock-ownership laws with incentives to develop participatory management arrangements;

ii)   legislation to increase the possibilities of combining ownership with financial participation, employee participation in decision-making, and possibly democratic governance – for example, a mechanism to allow a collective of employees to purchase a block of stock and to organize it into a trust such as the Democratic Employee-owned Trust Enterprise statutes – co-operative legislation to permit internal individual capital accounts like those in the Mondragon co-operatives (Spain) and in several states of the USA (with corporate income tax deductibility for enterprise set-asides to accounts, and individual income tax deferrals until the individual actually withdraws his allocated funds from the enterprise accounts);[49]

---

[49] The internal capital accounts are most easily accessible in David Ellerman (1990). Easy to understand materials on the arrangements and how they affect accounting are available from ICA /Somerville consultants.

iii)   a co-operative statute with maximum flexibility for dynamic development (although current law is quite flexible in some ways, collective ownership provisions – for example – make co-operatives less able to survive business recessions, since they are required to pay out capital to departing members).

7.3.2 Legislation with increased tax and other advantages for employee ownership and participation:

i)   employee stock ownership laws as in the USA and other countries (with tax advantages for setting up employee ownership plans to facilitate employee purchases of shares using internal funding, special tax relief to financial institutions making loans for this purpose);[50]

ii)   maintenance of co-operative statute which allows avoidance of corporate income tax.

7.3.3 Development of support organizations for employee ownership and participation

The aim would be to provide information, education, and consulting to enterprises/employees to help with development of employee ownership/ control of enterprises, as follows:

i)   organization of non-profit umbrella groups (such as the Central Union of Employees' Production Co-operatives for current workers' co-operatives) to help groups, such as employee ownership firms, co-operatives, firms with participation programmes;

ii)   organizing regular conferences to exhibit cases of effective programmes or enterprises with employee ownership and participation;

7.3.4 Creation of investment funds with a special interest in employee-owned firms:

i)   establishment of special 'friendly outsider' investment fund(s) to purchase shares and, ultimately, to help pass along majority control to

---

[50] The US situation has seen employee ownership laws amended by the national government at least once a year since the landmark ERISA legislation of 1974 which connected tax deferral treatment for worker benefits to special arrangements for financing employee stock purchases. Many of the revisions have been to prevent unforeseen abuses by entrepreneurs and others. The special law of 1974 is the main reason the USA has had such a phenomenal growth in employee ownership (over 10% of all private sector workers) over the last two decades. See Blasi (1988) on US employee ownership; for current news the NCEO newsletter has regular updates.

employees who may own only a minority of shares (this mechanism could be brought into being now with part of the already legislated pension fund allocation from privatization revenues);

ii)   establishment of a quasi-public investment fund, with publicly elected Board, which would hold shares (minority holder, with dividends going to pension system or other public benefit) and which could assess management and economic performance in employee-owned companies and monitor abuses

7.3.5 Further legal measures to promote democracy in the workplace

The aim would be to promote a systematic combination of financial and decision-making participation in more companies with fewer conflicts of interest through:

i)   creation of mechanisms to allow a collective of employees to purchase a block of stock and to organize it into a democratically controlled trust;[51]

ii)   legislation to permit the existence of internal individual capital accounts like those in the Mondragon co-operatives (Spain) and in several states of the USA (with corporate income tax deductibility for enterprise set-asides to individual accounts, and individual income tax deferrals until the individual actually withdraws his allocated funds from the enterprise accounts).[52]

8 CONCLUSION

Although employee ownership may be able to improve economic performance and its coverage of workers little may result from employee share ownership alone if they look on ownership as a low-cost financial asset and not much else. We have seen cases in which ownership has led to substantial positive changes in an enterprise, and other enterprises in which

---

[51] Such Democratic Worker Owned Trust Enterprise arrangements have been set up in the USA. Their features and the reasoning behind them is found in Ellerman (1990); he also considers their use in Eastern Europe in one chapter.

[52] The individual internal capital accounts are described in many works about the famous Mondragon co-operative system of northern Spain/Basque region. There is a Harvard Business School case study on them by David Ellerman which includes a brief discussion of their financial arrangements. The most easily understood materials on the internal individual capital account arrangements and how they affect accounting and governance are available from ICA Somerville consulting group.

share ownership, and even majority control by employees, has yet to have perceptible effects. Some of the proposals we have offered could help to make ownership into something more.

We are well aware of the obstacles which at present stand in the way of many of our ideas. Some may not be feasible for political reasons, others may fail due to economic or cultural factors. Obviously local people – those in power, those with roots in these organizations, and others – will ultimately determine the fate of any practical reform measure. That is right and proper, for they are the ones who will suffer the costs or enjoy the benefits. Finally, only if Bulgarians are well-informed can they make these decisions for themselves in a thoughtful, intelligent manner.

REFERENCES

Blasi, Joseph (1988), *Employee Ownership: Revolution or Rip-off?* Cambridge, Mass.: Ballinger.

Blinder, A. (ed.) (1990), *Paying for Productivity: A Look at the Evidence*, Washington, DC: The Brookings Institution.

Bonin, John, Derek Jones and Louis Putterman (1994), 'Theoretical and Empirical Studies of Producers' Co-operatives: When Will the Twain Meet?' *Journal of Economic Literature.*

Economic and Industrial Democracy (1993), Special Issue on 'Financial Participation', **14** (2), May.

Ellerman, D. (1990), *The Democratic Employee-Owned Firm: A New Model for East and West*, Boston: Unwin Hyman.

ICA (Industrial Co-operative Association – consulting group) Somerville, Mass., Miscellaneous documents, technical guides, 1980–95.

Jones, Derek C. (1994), 'Restructuring Enterprises in Bulgaria: The role of corporate governance,' working paper, mimeo, 3 May 1994.

————— (1987), 'Alternative Sharing Arrangements: a Review of the Evidence of their Effects and some Policy Implications for the US,' Economic and Industrial Democracy, 8:4 (November 1987), 489–516.

Jones, Derek and Kosali Ilayperuma (1994), 'The Determinants of Employee Participation During Fading Communism and Early Transition,' Hamilton College Department of Economics Working Paper # 94/4.

Jones, Derek, Mark Klinedinst and Charles Rock, (1996), 'Determinants of Firm Performance in Bulgaria,' Working Paper. Presented at ACES meeting.

Jones, Derek and Mieke Meurs, (1991), 'Employee Participation and Employee Self-Management in Bulgaria,' *Comparative Economic Studies*, (December).

Jones, Derek and Charles Rock, (1994) 'Privatization in Bulgaria,' in Saul Estrin (ed.), *Privatization in Central and Eastern Europe*, London: Longmans.

Keremidchiev, Spartak (ca.1990), 'Employees' Ownership in Bulgaria – Wishes and Possibilities', mimeo, 10pp., Sofia, Bulgaria.

Klinedinst, Mark and Charles Rock, (1994) 'Wage Determination in Bulgaria, 1990–92', paper presented at the International Association for the Economics of Self-management, Portoroz, Slovenia, June, 1994.

Meidner, R., with A. Hedborg and G. Ford (1978), *Employee Investment Funds: An Approach to Collective Capital Formation*, London: George Allen and Unwin.

Meurs, Mieke and Charles Rock (1994), 'Bulgarian Co-operatives and Economic Transformation,' *Co-opératives et Developpement*, (Montreal), Vol. 26, numéro 1/94-95, 103–119.

Mygind, Niels (1992),'The Choice of Ownership,' *Economic and Industrial Democracy*, **13** (3).

Mygind, Niels and Charles Rock (1993), 'Financial Participation and the Democratization of Work,' *Economic and Industrial Democracy*, **14** (2), 163–83.

NCEO (National Center for Employee Ownership), Oakland, California, Employee Ownership newsletters, reports.

NSI (National Statistical Institute of Bulgaria), (1995a), 'Statisticheski Godishnik [Statistical Yearbook] 1995,' Sofia: NSI, 1995.

————— (1995b), 'Privatizatsia v Bulgaria: 2' Sofia: NSI, Feb.1995.

————— (1994), 'Current Economic Business, May 1994,' Sofia: NSI.

OMRI, (Open Media Research Institute; formerly RFE/RL), (miscellaneous dates), Daily Digest, Part II, 'Survey of News in East-Central and South-eastern Europe,' daily Internet version.

PA (Bulgarian Privatization Agency) (1995a), *Information Bulletin*, No. 11, Nov. 1995.

————— (1995b), 'Privatization in Bulgaria,' Report of Vessilin Blagoev, Executive Director, Mimeo, Sofia: PA, Nov. 1995.

————— (1996), 'Privatization in Bulgaria,' Report of Vessilin Blagoev, Executive Director, mimeo, Sofia: PA, 1996. Parvulov, Svilen (1991), 'Employee Participation in Privatization: Likely Developments in Bulgaria', paper presented at the International Association for the Economics of Self-management conference, Cornell University, Ithaca, NY, August 1991.

Petkov, Krastyu and Grigor Gradev (1995), 'Bulgaria', in J. Thirkell, R. Scase, and S. Vickerstaff et al. (eds), *Labour Relations and Political Change in Eastern Europe*, 31-60, Ithaca, NY: ILR Press, Cornell University.

Republic of Bulgaria, (1993), 'The Labour Code.'

————— (1992 and 1994 [amended]), 'Transformation and Privatization of State-Owned and Municipal-Owned Enterprises Act,' (*Act on Privatization*), 23 April, 1992 (SG No.38/1992)

————— (1992) 'The Trade Act' (the commercial code).

————— (1991) 'Law on Co-operatives.'

————— (1991) 'The Constitution of the Republic of Bulgaria.'

(People's) Republic of Bulgaria, (1989), 'Decree 56' January 1989.

RFE/RL (see OMRI).

Rock, Charles P. (1994a), 'Interest Representation and the Evolution of Industrial and Labour Relations in Bulgaria, 1989–93,' in special issue on 'The Building of Interest Representation in Eastern Europe,' of *EMERGO: Journal of Transforming Economies and Societies*, (Krakow), **1** (2) (Autumn 1994), 83–102.

————— (1994b), 'Employment and Privatization in Bulgaria's Reforms,' (1994), Interdepartmental Project on Structural Adjustment Working Paper Series, International Labour Organization; Geneva.

————— (1993) 'Employees' Ownership: Prospects in Bulgaria,' (May 1993). Study for the International Labour Organization, Employment and Active Labour Market Policies Division, for special conference on Labour Markets in Bulgaria, Sofia, May, 1993.

————— (1993b) 'The Primacy of Politics Over the Economics of Workplace Democracy,' in S. Mahalingam, S.C. Smith, J.-E. Askildsen, and D. Vaughan-Whitehead (eds), *Labour Managed Market Economy*, New Delhi: Mittal Publications, 184–89.

————— (1992), 'Employment, Labour and Privatization in Bulgaria's Reforms: 1989 to mid–92,' Unpublished manuscript, July, 1992.

Uvalic, Milica (1993), 'Employees' Financial Participation in the European Community,' *Economic and Industrial Democracy*, **14** (2).

Vaughan-Whitehead, Daniel (1993) 'Employees' Financial Participation: An East-West Comparative Perspective,' *Economic and Industrial Democracy*, **14** (2).

4. The Demise of Employee Ownership in the Czech Privatization Programme?

Josef Kotrba

1 INTRODUCTION

In the Czech Republic (and, of course, in the former Czechoslovakia as a whole), employee ownership and financial participation have rich traditions. Employee control of enterprises was part of the reform package of 1968 and, prior to the communist take-over in 1948, the country had a dense network of co-operatives in industry, trade and financial services. Last but not least, many Czech thinkers were interested in the question of employee ownership, largely inspired by the Czech ex-patriot Jaroslav Vanek.

Despite this, employees have played a far smaller role in Czech privatization, the management of state-owned enterprises and the restructuring process than in many other countries in the region. The most important reason for this is probably the tight control exercised by the government over state-owned enterprises prior to transition. We will devote considerable attention to the historical development of power-sharing in state-owned enterprises prior to 1989 (Section 2). Section 3 describes the development of employee participation both prior to privatization and in joint-stock companies. Section 4 details the discussions which took place around the design of privatization policy, while Section 5 describes the policies actually adopted and the privatization process itself. Section 6 concentrates on employee ownership and financial participation within the privatization process. Section 7 describes spontaneously established employee-owned enterprises and the use of partial employee ownership in existing companies. We will then attempt to draw some conclusions.

2 THE PARTIAL REFORMS OF 1988

The former Czechoslovakia, in contrast with other Central European countries, had the following specific features:

- an extremely high degree of state involvement in the economy (virtually no private sector and a co-operative sector with limited autonomy, if any);
- a strong central presence in state-owned enterprises;
- internal and external macroeconomic stability.

It seems that it was the – relatively – good macroeconomic situation which enabled the communist government to postpone major reforms until its fall in 1989. For our purposes, however, the most important point is the strong control exercised by the state over state-owned enterprises. Unlike Poland, where even under martial law employees retained considerable influence over enterprise management (at least in terms of a veto on changes affecting their welfare), Czechoslovakia had no independent trade unions and extremely obedient official ones: workers had little, if any power within the enterprise. Management control over state-owned enterprises was just as limited; investment decisions in particular were entirely in the hands of the state, and the mandatory state plans were very detailed as regards both output and input.[1]

The high degree of centralization necessarily led to a great deal of rigidity and inefficiency, a situation of which the communist leaders were fully aware. The attempt at political and economic reform in 1968, which led to Soviet invasion and mass purges within the communist party and society as a whole, inculcated in the new leadership an unusually strong resistance to reform, partly because their legitimacy derived directly from the anti-reform purges and partly because would-be reformers were loath to emulate their predecessors of 1968. In the late 1980s, the influence of Gorbachev's 'perestroika' was strong enough to propel the communist government into partial reform, the declared aim of which was the decentralization of decision-making – in particular, the strengthening of the role of state-owned enterprises and the elimination of the intermediate level of higher 'productive economic units', groups of state-owned enterprises from the same industry; excessive horizontal integration was to be replaced by more vertical integration.

The new role of state-owned enterprises was defined in the *Act on State-owned Enterprises* of 6 June 1988. The Act – indeed, the whole reform concept of 1987–88, preserved largely intact the pre-reform state of affairs: the state planning authorities were still entitled to impose obligatory requirements on state-owned enterprises (although indirect methods were to

---

[1] Mlcoch (1990) argues that the information gap endowed the managements of state-owned enterprises (SOE) with considerable power in what he calls the 'planning game', or bargaining between management and central planners. Even if we accept this, management power was indirect and far from that of an ultimate decision-maker.

be preferred), the branch ministries were still the ultimate decision-makers in terms of the merger, liquidation, founding, and so on, of state-owned enterprises, and the state retained the power of discretionary decision-making in respect of the redistribution of financial resources. On the other hand, the law introduced limited employee participation in enterprise management: state-owned enterprise employees were given the right to elect the General Manager and a Workers' Council. The Workers' Council (a third of the members of which were elected on the proposal of the General Manager) was supposed to approve strategic measures.

The employee participation introduced under the partial reforms of 1988 was extremely weak. The right to elect the General Manager was merely formal; employees were not allowed to propose a candidate (he was nominated by the relevant branch ministry), while the Workers' Council was not entitled to propose his dismissal. Actual developments in the period 1988–89 were even less reform-oriented than had been anticipated. Instead of decentralization, 'productive economic units' were transformed into state-owned enterprises, leading in fact to a higher degree of *centralization*. Central planning and the subsidization of poorly performing enterprises remained intact. Not surprisingly, employee participation played only an insignificant role in state-owned enterprises, if any.[2]

3 EMPLOYEE PARTICIPATION AFTER 1989

Shortly after the collapse of the communist regime in November 1989, there was a short period during which employees exercised a strong influence on the management of state-owned enterprises: despite the fact that the *Act on State-owned Enterprises* did not allow employees to dismiss managers, at many enterprises employees did vote in favour of 'proposals' to dismiss managers, proposals which the founding branch ministries usually obeyed. This wave of employee-driven dismissals – which peaked around mid-1990 – was almost entirely politically motivated. Indeed, most of the changes were made not under the aegis of so-called 'workers' collectives' (a term used in the 1988 law on state-owned enterprises), but by enterprise-based groups related to the Civic Forum, a broad coalition of non-communist forces.

In the second quarter of 1990, the government decided to stabilize the situation within state-owned enterprises, not only because the management instability of the latter threatened economic performance, but also because the government was planning a mass privatization programme – an early draft of which was approved in April 1990 – which was incompatible with the transfer

---

2 See Zieleniec (1988) for a critical analysis of state-owned enterprise reform measures.

of a high degree of power to employees. The new *Act on State-owned Enterprises* (approved on 19 April 1990 and effective as of 1 May of that year) reduced the extent of employee management participation to a 50 per cent representation on the state-owned enterprise's Supervisory Board, the remaining board members being nominated by the founding branch ministry. Supervisory Board responsibilities included discussion of enterprise development, management and accounting supervision, the profit allocation, and liquidation, merger and division. The Boards were also allowed to propose to the branch ministry the dismissal of the state-owned enterprise's General Manager.

A different situation prevailed in the case of state-owned enterprises established or transformed in the form of a (state-owned) joint-stock Company. Employee participation in the Supervisory Boards of such enterprises was mandatory only if the workforce was greater than 200; furthermore, employees were entitled to provide only one-third of Board members.[3] This form of employee participation remains in force today; since the adoption of the general Commercial Code,[4] employee representatives on Supervisory Boards are obligatory for companies with more than 50 employees, their number varying between one-third and one-half of the Board's membership.

Since most state-owned companies were either privatized in the form of joint-stock companies or transformed into joint-stock companies without privatization, the one-third representation on Supervisory Boards has become more and more important in the course of the 1990s. The importance of employee representatives, as well as of Supervisory Boards as such, varies dramatically from company to company. In some important companies, the Supervisory Board elects and may dismiss the Chief Executive Officer and the management, fixes their wages and bonuses and approves all crucial management decisions (this follows the so-called German model). In such companies, especially those privatized on the basis of voucher privatization, with several partial owners represented in the Board, employee representatives play an important role. However, in many companies the Supervisory Board has little if any power.

Since the approval of *Act on Joint-stock Companies* (18 April 1990), the Czech legal system has also introduced employee shares. The law of 1990 allowed joint-stock companies (at that time mostly state owned) to issue free or discounted employee shares with the same rights as regular shares, with the sole difference that retiring or departing employees had to sell their shares to the company. The Commercial Code, which superseded the Act on Joint-stock

---

[3] According to the Law on Joint-stock Companies approved on 18 April 1990 (effective as of 1 May 1990).

[4] Adopted on 5 November 1991 and effective as of 1 January 1992.

Companies (from 1 January 1992) limited the volume of discounted (from their face value) employee shares to 5 per cent of the enterprise's equity capital. The rights pertaining to employee shares may be different to those of regular issues, an option which has indeed been taken up by most enterprises.

4 THE DEBATE ON THE PRIVATIZATION PROGRAMME AND WORKERS' OWNERSHIP

In early 1990 the discussion began about the scope and form of large-scale privatization. The most important of the competing sets of proposals under discussion were the following:[5]

a)   Privatization should be restricted to smaller units. Large enterprises should be separated from the state (for example, by forming public holding companies subject to parliamentary control) and all efforts made to improve management. Privatization should be based on the enterprise's business plan and focus on attracting new capital or foreign strategic partners.

b)   With the exception of small businesses, enterprise ownership rights should be transferred to employees. This could be done in 'big bang' fashion by declaring the firms to be worker-owned, or by the gradual introduction of some form of employee stock ownership plans – ESOPs.

c)   Assets should be distributed free of charge or for a nominal sum to all citizens.[6] The primary goal should be the speed of privatization and its social acceptability (perceived fairness). Management and restructuring problems will be tackled in due course by the new owners. So-called spontaneous privatization (the surreptitious – and illegal – acquisition of enterprises and enterprise assets by management) should be stopped.

Proposals characterized by worker participation and ownership – category b) above – have enjoyed historical predominance in Czechoslovakia. The 1968 economic reforms, interrupted by the Soviet tanks, contained a spontaneous element of employee control. The co-operative movement also has long historical traditions. After the 1989 'velvet revolution', proposals of this kind were backed by a number of political parties and other groups.

---

5   See Kotrba and Svejnar (1994) for more detail on the pre-privatization discussion.

6   Borensztein and Kumar (1991) in their classification of privatization proposals mention only one that does not fall into this category. This reflects to a great extent the orientation of the papers and proposals published in the West.

Management by workers figured prominently in the Social Democratic Party's election programme in both the 1990 and 1992 elections; ESOPs were an important element in the 1992 programme of the Liberal Social Union and to some extent in that of the Communist Party. Employee ownership was also extensively discussed by the (religiously oriented) Czechoslovak People's Party in 1990; it was also advocated by Ota Sik, a prominent economist active in the 1968 reform process (Sik, 1990) and, in 1990, an economic advisor to president Vaclav Havel. There were also some special interest groups, such as the Movement for a Self-managed Society, whose proposals were based on ideas drawn from the large Czech literature on self-management and directly inspired by Jaroslav Vanek, a leading researcher and propagator of such ideas (Vanek, 1990). Last but not least, until the summer of 1990, ESOP plans were discussed within the government, employee ownership being listed as a possible privatization method in some of the early 1990 government documents on the subject.

After the election victory of the Civic Forum in June 1990, a movement broadly oriented towards the introduction of a market economy, the proposals concerning ESOPs and employee management of enterprises lost part of their support as private property-based reforms attained greater popular appeal. Moreover, the Civic Forum was committed to the idea of voucher privatization, which also reduced the appeal of employee ownership to the general public: in this way everybody would become an owner, not just the employees of a particular enterprise.

5 THE ADOPTED PROGRAMME

The adopted large-scale privatization programme was based on the straightforward transfer of privatized firms to new owners – no particular rights for employees or incumbent managers were specified, nor was privatization linked with restructuring. On the other hand, it was quite flexible in terms of the privatization methods it permitted. The programme allowed direct sale, auction, transformation into a joint-stock company, the sale or voucher distribution of shares, and a combination of these. Within the voucher scheme citizens could either allocate their vouchers to mutual funds or use them to bid for shares in specific enterprises.

The privatization of each state-owned enterprise was based on an approved privatization plan, which had to contain a detailed description of the assets to be privatized which may or may be identical with the enterprise as it was then constituted: the plan may relate to only part of a state-owned enterprise or to several such enterprises or to a combination of parts of different enterprises. It should also specify the number and composition of the resulting privatization units (recombined from privatized assets), and the status of these units (limited liability companies, joint-stock companies, plain physical assets and so on).[7] The plan also had to propose a method of privatization in accordance with the five permissible options:

1) transformation of a state-owned enterprise into a joint-stock company and subsequent transfer of shares;
2) direct sale to a predetermined buyer;
3) public auction or public tender;
4) free transfer to municipal ownership; and
5) free transfer to social security, health insurance and other publicly beneficial institutions.

The transformation of a state-owned enterprise into a joint-stock company (which was the most important method and used in the case of large state-owned enterprises) was subject to a number of options. Shares could be:

a) distributed through voucher privatization to Czech citizens;
b) sold directly to a domestic or foreign owner;
c) sold through an intermediary (stock exchange or financial institution);
d) transferred free to municipalities and health insurance companies;
e) sold to employees in the form of employee shares;
f) issued to former owners against their restitution claims;
g) kept temporarily or permanently by the National Property Fund. While temporary National Property Fund ownership usually indicates that negotiations with a foreign or domestic partner are under way and that the shares will be sold after agreement is reached, the purpose of permanent ownership is to retain central control over key enterprises.

Any domestic or foreign natural person or legal entity was allowed to submit a privatization plan in respect of any company listed for privatization.[8] The only exception was state-owned enterprise managements which were obliged to prepare a so-called basic plan to be submitted by a given deadline (for the first wave, basic plans were to be submitted by 30 November 1991 and competing plans by 20 January 1992). As may be seen from *Table 4.1* the

[7] Kotrba (1995) gives a detailed description of the privatization of a sample of 200 enterprises with the focus on organizational changes and the impact of the kind of entity which submitted the winning privatization plan. Lizal, Singer and Švejnar (1995) provide theoretical and empirical analysis of reasons for the frequent break-up of privatized state-owned enterprises.

[8] In June 1991, the government approved the list of enterprises to be privatized in the first and second privatization waves, those which were to be liquidated and those which were to be privatized at a later date.

Table 4.1 Privatization plans by applicant,[1] Czech Republic, 1994

Applicant[2]	Total	Approved	Rejected	To be decided
SOE management	5 315	2 815	1 954	546
Lower management	699	204	453	42
Potential buyer	13 809	2 386	7 534	3 889
Restitution claimant	638	173	427	38
Ministry	503	378	72	53
Consulting firm	512	103	349	60
Trade unions	33	6	26	1
Employees	1 199	236	498	465
Regional bodies	1 896	228	1 464	204
Other applicants	2 010	208	1 630	172
Total	26 614	6 737	14 407	5 470

Source: Ministry of Privatization of the Czech Republic.
1) As of 31 December 1994.
2) Selected groups of those submitting plans; other groups include District Privatization Committees, District and Municipal Authorities and others.

most successful group of bidders was state-owned enterprise managements, which had both more plans approved than any other group and the best ratio of approved plans to those submitted. However, this should not be taken to indicate that state-owned enterprise managements were the real winners in the privatization process. First, many companies the managements of which had originally proposed privatization ended up in external hands: for example, most of the plans for voucher privatization were submitted by managements. Second, the extremely high approval rate derives largely from the fact that, in many cases, the management was the only bidder. On the other hand, potential buyers concentrated on the most attractive firms, so that most of the real competition for particular enterprises was among non-management bidders.

Employees played a limited role, largely restricted to small firms or to parts of firms. Trade unions usually privatized small vacation facilities which typically had been owned by state-owned enterprises under communism.

The submitted privatization plans were scrutinized by the Ministry of Privatization with the exception of direct sales to a predetermined buyer; in such cases, the decision was taken by the government. The decision-making process was, in some cases, rather lengthy: some plans from the first wave of privatization (with a submission deadline of late 1991) still had not been decided by mid-1995 – the fate of most enterprises, particularly those taking part in the first wave of voucher privatization, had been decided early in 1992.

As already mentioned, the privatization scheme allowed complex plans to decompose and recombine existing state-owned enterprises. In reality, the greater part of state-owned enterprises were privatized as a single unit (most break-ups took place prior to privatization, in late 1990 and early 1991). On the other hand, many enterprises were decomposed into many individual units which were then privatized separately, some on the basis of different submitted privatization plans. For example, between 1991 and the end of 1994, the privatization authorities approved the privatization of 1,235 industrial enterprises. The number of plans approved was 1,824 and the number of privatization units 3,568 – on average, slightly less than 3 units per original state-owned enterprise.

Most large state-owned enterprises were privatized as joint-stock companies; the average size of units privatized in the form of a joint-stock company was far greater than that of those privatized by other methods. From the point of view of employee participation, this is quite important because of the resulting level of employee representation on the supervisory boards; as we will see in following section, partial employee ownership did play a role in these companies.

As to the other methods, public auctions were used mostly for the privatization of small parts of enterprises, frequently only selected assets. However, some small firms were auctioned as a whole – in this case no special rights were afforded employees or management. Public tenders were initially used to sell small and medium-sized enterprises; later they became progressively important in the sale of blocks of shares in partly privatized large firms (in *Table 4.2* such cases are included not under 'Public tender' but under '(transformation into) joint-stock company'). Managers were frequently important bidders, and, in the absence of strong (particularly foreign) competition, they usually turned out the winners. The same holds for direct sales – in this case, the buyer was predetermined in the approved privatization plan. Free transfers of property were used above all for the privatization of such non-productive assets as housing facilities, kindergartens, idle land or municipal utilities. In most cases the property was transferred from privatized state-owned enterprises to municipalities.

The best known privatization method yielding shares in joint-stock companies in the Czech Republic is voucher privatization.[9] Voucher privatization was organized as follows:

1)   the privatization authorities issued a list of enterprises to be privatized for vouchers, giving a rough estimate of the book value of the assets to be privatized;

---

[9] For more details, see e.g. Kotrba and Svejnar (1994) or Singer and Svejnar (1994).

Table 4.2 Large-scale privatization, Czech Republic, 1992–95[1]

Privatization Method	Plans			
	Approved		Implemented	
	Units	Assets	Units	Assets
Public auction	2 128	9 314	777	6 767
Public tender	1 394	33 001	570	18 432
Direct sale	11 343	91 653	4 611	55 171
Joint-stock company[2]	1 883	768 101	1 737	754 652
Free transfer	4 857	55 749	3 281	29 787
Total[3]	21 605	957 818	10 976	864 809

Source: Ministry for Privatization of the Czech Republic .
1) As of 31 December 1995. Property is given in CSK million (1$ = CSK 27) – valuations are based on book value which may of course differ from market value.
2) Plans for joint-stock companies are taken as implemented after their registration; shares may not be sold at the time of 'implementation'.
3) Not including restitutions implemented through the National Property Fund.

2) Czech citizens could then register their vouchers for an administrative fee of CSK 1,000;
3) any legal entity could, under the conditions laid down in the law, register an Investment Privatization Fund (with status of an independent joint-stock company), or an open or closed mutual fund;
4) the privatization authorities published a list of registered Funds;
5) in 'Round Zero' vouchers could be assigned to Investment Funds. Those who did not assign their vouchers to Funds had to place their vouchers individually;
6) the privatization authorities published a list of privatized enterprises giving information on their most important economic indicators, such as the number of shares offered, and share prices in terms of investment 'points' (each voucher represented 1,000 investment points). In the first round, the prices were uniform; in subsequent rounds, the prices were adjusted upwards (if there was great demand for the share) or downwards (if there was little or no demand).
7) in every round, private individuals and Funds bid for selected shares on the basis of a given price. If the demand for a given share was smaller than or equal to its supply, shares were assigned to the bidders. Otherwise, shares remained unplaced and investment points remained with their owners;

8) when the process had run its course (that is, when only a small fraction of privatization points remained unplaced), the bidding procedure was terminated and the remaining vouchers declared void. The privatization authorities had some discretion as regards when the bidding should be terminated; in both waves of voucher privatization, the number of rounds was small (5 in the first wave, 6 in the second), as was the number of unused points (around 1 per cent);

9) after the bidding rounds had ended, the shares were transferred to individuals or Investment Privatization Funds;

10) the Investment Privatization Funds then issued their own shares and distributed them among their investors.

Although undoubtedly faster than standard privatization methods, voucher privatization was by no means instant: the whole process took at least two years: 6 to 8 months were needed to collect and approve privatization plans, the distribution and registration of vouchers, 'Round Zero' and bidding for shares took more than 12 months, and another couple of months were required before the shares were transferred to their owners.

6 EMPLOYEE OWNERSHIP AND PRIVATIZATION

As already mentioned in Section 3, special legal provisions apply to employee shares. Employee shares could have been issued as a part of the privatization of state-owned enterprises. The rules and procedures were as follows:

1) the privatization plan could propose that part of the shares in a privatized state-owned enterprise be issued as employee shares;

2) the Ministry of Privatization – if it approved the plan as a whole – approved the issue of employee shares up to 10 per cent of equity capital; the Fund of National Property transformed the state-owned enterprise into a joint-stock company and held all its shares, including employee shares;

3) the privatized enterprise bought employee shares at their nominal value (usually CSK 1,000);

4) the privatized enterprise distributed employee shares in accordance with its status (approved by two-thirds of the shareholders present at the Annual General Meeting).

The issue of employee shares was proposed by a (non-negligible) minority of state-owned enterprises privatized in the form of joint-stock companies: out of 1,688 companies transformed in this manner, 480 proposed (and got approval

Table 4.3 Privatization of shares in joint-stock companies,[1] Czech Republic, 1994

Method of privatization	Book value[2]	% of total
Shares already privatized	478 182.65	67.73
– vouchers, first and second wave	342 859.32	48.23
– sold	49 194.83	6.92
– transferred to RIF	19 505.71	2.74
– transferred free of charge	49 111.23	6.91
Shares still held by FNP	232 079.90	32.64
– to be held permanently	68 101.88	9.63
– to be held temporarily	111 670.26	14.09
Shares in joint-stock company to be established	322.00	0.05
New shares in a joint-stock company which has increased its equity	787.01	0.11
Total equity of privatized joint-stock companies	711 049.56	100.00

Source: National Property Fund of the Czech Republic.
1) As of 31 December 1994 (shares from the second wave of voucher privatization were transferred in February 1995; that is why so many shares are still listed as owned by the FNP).
2) CSK million; most shares have a nominal value of CSK 1,000.

for) the privatization of part of their shares as employee shares. As *Table 4.3* indicates, in the event only a minority exercised this option. The main reason for this was incorrect evaluation of assets and so of the enterprise's equity capital: in some firms, stated equity capital exceeded the real value of the firm by ten times or more; although, in other cases, real value exceeded stated equity value. This is also reflected in the stock market: some shares with a face value of CSK 1,000 were in early 1996 being traded at around CSK 50, others for several thousand. As a result, officially overvalued firms (those with shares traded at CSK 50) had nothing to gain by purchasing their employee shares from the National Property Fund for CSK 1,000. Other enterprises, such as Cokoladovny, partly sold to the Swiss giant Nestlé, whose shares are traded at CSK 2–4,000 per share (with a face value of CSK 1,000) did exercise their right to buy the employee shares included in their privatization plan.

Voucher privatization provided another opportunity for employee owner-ship. Although the Czech privatization process did not give employees the right to buy shares in their own company under favourable conditions (as in Russia), it did not prevent them from utilizing their vouchers to the same end. Some companies encouraged their employees to invest in their shares; a good

Table 4.4 Employee shares in the first and second waves of privatization, Czech Republic, 1995

Employee shares		No. of shares	No. of companies
First Wave:	Approved	2 757 100	220
	Purchased	1 112 406	82
Second Wave:	Approved	2 416 870	260
	Purchased	920 856	89
Total approved		5 173 970	280
Total purchased[1]		2 033 262	171
All joint-stock companies privatized[2]		748 218 044	1 688

1) As of 7 February 1995.
2) As of 31 December 1995. The figure refers to all joint-stock company shares approved for privatization, including shares not yet sold and strategically held by the state.

example is ZPS Zlin, a machinery producer exporting to the advanced industrial countries. The ZPS Shareholders' Association, which was formed by its employees, retirees and local residents, plays an important role as one of the largest shareholders in co-operation with the enterprise management. ZPS Zlin is one of the most successful companies in the Czech Republic.[10]

Other large industrial companies have founded their own investment privatization funds with the intention of attracting employees. These funds later invested in their founding company and in other enterprises in the same industry. The most important industrial companies which founded such funds are from Slovakia, the largest being VSZ (East Slovak Steelworks), the major employer in the East Slovakia region.

7 WORKERS' OWNERSHIP IN PRIVATE COMPANIES

Many companies – state-owned or privatized, fully private or joint ventures – have chosen to introduce some form of employee ownership. Some have issued employee shares representing 5 per cent or less of their equity capital (as laid down in the Commercial Code), others have given employees the right to buy new issues of regular shares under favourable conditions. There are also companies which are (or were) controlled fully or predominantly by employees.

10 ZPS also planned to issue employee shares, although a legal dispute with the Fund of National Property nipped this in the bud.

The most important fully or predominantly employee-owned companies are newspaper publishers. Several newspapers, originally (pre-1989) published by communist party-related organizations, were 'privatized' by their employees in the following way: the employees (led by the management) established a separate publishing company. At some point, the workforce left their former employer *en masse* and announced to their readers that the new enterprise will print in effect the same newspaper but under a slightly different title. In one case, the incumbent publisher tried to continue publishing the original title (*Zemedelske noviny* or 'Agricultural News', published by the Ministry of Agriculture); all other publishers agreed to sell or lease their rights to the new publisher, including the daily with the highest circulation, *Mlada Fronta*. *Rude pravo*, the daily of the Central Committee of the Communist Party, was privatized in the same way, but without any employee ownership: the new publisher was fully owned by its editor-in-chief and director.

The former dissident monthly *Lidove noviny*, which became a daily in 1990 and was re-established as a company controlled by the Association for *Lidove noviny*, was transformed into an employee-owned joint-stock company. Every employee (as well as the contributors to *Lidove noviny*'s illegal predecessor) was given the right to purchase up to 1.5 per cent of the shares at a discount. At the end of 1992, over two-thirds of the shares were owned by employees and their relatives, the rest being held by the Association.

Partly because of economic difficulties (the newspaper market became very competitive in the early 1990s), and partly because no one wanted to continue to run them on an employee-owned basis over the long term, all the important employee-owned newspapers were sold to foreign publishing groups: starting with *Mlada Fronta* – sold to French publisher Hersant – and ending with *Lidove noviny* which was sold to Swiss publisher Ringier, when the employees decided to sell first part of the shares, and then the majority of them to another owner. By 1990, none of the national dailies remained in the hands of their employees.

Many important banks have used employee co-ownership to stabilize and improve staff motivation. The second largest bank in the country, Komercni banka, has given its employees the opportunity to subscribe a limited portion of a new share issue below the price at which it was offered to existing shareholders – when the issue was announced, the discount on the market price was 50 per cent.[11] Although more than 60 per cent of employees exercised this option, their share of the company remained rather small – less than 1 per cent. Many employees also purchased shares in the bank in the course of voucher privatization. The participation of employee-owners is as low as that of other small share-holders. Komercni banka's general

---

[11] This measure, intended to be employee friendly, has some irony in it; during the subscription period the Czech stock market collapsed and the price fell below even the discounted price.

shareholders' meetings were attended in 1994, 1995 and 1996 by 200 to 300 shareholders, approximately three-quarters of them being small, non-institutional shareholders, some of them employees. No shareholders' association or other body was formed to represent the interests of employee-shareholders until 1996. Despite the disappointment caused by the price development of the shares sold to employees in 1994 the bank maintains that partial ownership represents an important means of motivation, especially for managers, and is considering introducing a share option plan in 1996.

A similar proportion of shares was sold to employees at Ceskoslovenska Obchodni Banka (CSOB), another of the six largest banks, and at some smaller banks (Pragobanka and others).

8 CONCLUSION

Employee ownership and management participation has enjoyed less official support in the Czech Republic than in some other countries in the region. On the other hand, the government has not discriminated against it. Employee participation in large privatized, formerly state-owned enterprises is similar to that in Germany and Austria.

Czech privatization has focused heavily on voucher privatization, the free distribution of shares among citizens. The system was based on nationwide centralized auctions in which everybody was free to bid for any firm during a determined period of time. Unlike the Russian voucher privatization it did not encourage employees to bid for shares in their firm, with the result that mass employee ownership did not develop. The vast majority of the participants in voucher privatization have chosen to use their vouchers through special financial intermediaries, investment privatization funds. These funds, many founded by banks, have become the most important owners of privatized companies. Since these funds may not own more than 20 per cent of the shares in a single company voucher privatization has resulted in dispersed ownership. Moreover, investments funds have turned out to be passive owners. As a result, a process of ownership changes (namely concentration of ownership) started soon after the end of the voucher privatization process. This is not far from the intention of the scheme's architects, who assumed that the initial distribution of shares was not important, since the market would create the optimal ownership structure after privatization. In fact, the ownership transformation process has proven to be quite lengthy. In 1996 it was speeded up when several investment funds were transformed into holding companies.

Employee ownership was originally intended to become a complementary privatization method to voucher privatization. Each company could have assigned up to 10 per cent of its shares for sale to employees at book value.

The major obstacle to employee ownership turned out to be an unintended one: the valuation of enterprises on the basis of a book value that was highly inaccurate, in fact well above the market, so that neither privatized enterprises nor employees opted to use this possibility. The condition that enterprises be evaluated on the basis of their book value was not applied in a discriminatory manner: at the beginning, it was also used in the case of direct sales and as the minimum price in tenders. Also, employee shares were not the only casualties of exaggerated book values – it is still wreaking havoc with the accounts of many investment privatization funds.

Nevertheless, employee ownership has played a role in Czech privatization. Moreover, many companies are actively using employee shares to stabilize and motivate their labour force. There is no reason to expect a mass conversion of companies to employee ownership, but it will probably continue to play a small if significant role in the Czech economy.

REFERENCES

Borensztein, E. and Kuman, M. (1991), *Proposals for Privatization in Eastern Europe, IMF Staff Papers*, Vol. 38, No. 2.

Kotrba, J. (1995), 'The Privatization Process in the Czech Republic: Players and Winners', in Svejnar, J. (ed.), *The Czech Republic and Economic Transition in Eastern Europe,* Academic Press.

Kotrba, J. and Svejnar, J. (1994), *Rapid and Multifaceted Privatization: Experience of the Czech and Slovak Republics,* MOCT-MOST 4.

Lizal, L., Singer, M. and Svejnar, J. (1995), 'Manager Interests, Breakups and Performance of State Enterprises in Transition', in Svejnar (1995).

Mlcoch, L. (1990), *Behaviour of Czechoslovak Enterprise Sector* (in Czech), Working paper, Institute of Economics, Czechoslovak Academy of Sciences.

Sik, O. (ed.) (1990), *Socialism Today*, London: Macmillan.

Singer, M. and Svejnar, J. (1994), 'Using Vouchers to Privatize an Economy: The Czech and Slovak Case', *Economics of Transition* 2 (1)

Svejnar, J. (1989), A Framework for the Economic Transformation of Czechoslovakia, *PlanEcon Report*, Vol. V, No. 52.

Svejnar, J. (ed.) (1995), *The Czech Republic and Economic Transition in Eastern Europe,* Academic Press.

Vanek, J. (1990), Beware of the Yeast of the Pharisees, *Economic Analysis and Worker's Management*, Vol. 24, No. 1.

Zieleniec, J. (ed.) (1988), *Socialist Enterprise and Planned Management* (in Czech), Working paper, Institute of Economics, Czechoslovak Academy of Sciences.

5. Successful Waves of Employee Ownership in Hungary

György Lajtai

1 INTRODUCTION

Contrary to other countries of Central and Eastern Europe the share of the private sector in Hungarian GDP was relatively high (up to 10 per cent) before the main body of privatization measures was launched. Radical change came in the period from 1990 to 1993, when privatization became the central pillar in the economic policy of the first democratically elected government for forty years. The key year was 1993: by that time, the value of production and services in the private sector had exceeded that of the state, as shown in *Figure 5.1*.

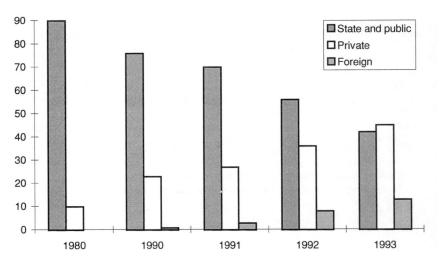

Figure 5.1 Contributions to GDP by form of ownership, Hungary, 1980–93 (%)

Arrival at this point was not easy. Hungarian politics and public debate were loud with discussion of the extent, speed and control of the privatization process, along with the precise nature of 'desirable investors', the concessions that should be given to different groups of buyers and the proportion of privatization income that should be allocated to the state budget.

2 MAIN FEATURES AND DATES OF PRIVATIZATION IN HUNGARY

The history of privatization in Hungary can be divided into the following periods:

- 1989–90: spontaneous privatization;
- 1991–92: large, centrally organized privatization;
- 1993–94: concessionary privatization schemes for domestic investors;
- 1995–96: 'privatization for cash'.

It is worth taking a brief look at the main outlines of these periods and the privatization policies followed in them.

2.1 The Beginning of Privatization: Spontaneity and Local Initiatives

The first privatization law, the first regulatory framework for privatization, was in fact drafted by the last single-party parliament. The law was both cautious and progressive. It was cautious in that privatization was allowed only in the case of the subsidiaries (plants, regional units) of large state conglomerates. On the other hand, the law was very progressive because the management of the parent company had a free hand to organize joint ventures or domestic mixed (state and privately owned) companies on the basis of contributions in kind (in the form of state property) made to the new enterprises.

This 'free hand' was made even freer by the manner in which most state companies were run at this time. In the early 1980s, ideologically motivated company councils were elected by the employees in the majority of state companies. These company councils had wide decision-making powers (such as the selection of the general manager and decisions concerning investments, wage increases and borrowing).

In tandem with the introduction of this law, the control of the central state bureaucracies (the branch ministries) was radically reduced. There were substantial job cuts in the ministries in order physically to prevent them from excessive interference in enterprise activity. Under these circumstances, the top managers in the company council-led enterprises had considerable room to manoeuvre as regards the future organization of the companies they managed, not to mention their own personal futures.

Although there were many examples of fruitful, mutually advantageous privatization at this time, many transactions raised suspicions among the general public. The contribution of company assets to semi-private companies at a rate well below their market value, and the separation and 'privatization' of the most profitable enterprise units, markets and trading networks, while letting the rest of the business slide into bankruptcy brought about a considerable devaluation of state property.

Because of the increasing public dissatisfaction (employee protests, press reports) and the criticism directed by the newly-elected conservative government of József Antall at the technocratic and economic elite of the old regime, legislation concerning both privatization and the management of the process became a central issue of the government programme and the new institutional structure of state administration.

2.2 The Centrally-managed Privatization Programme of 1992

After almost a year of fierce debate among the coalition parties, the first general privatization legislation was accepted in mid-1992. Prior to this, a new state agency, the State Property Agency, had been established to bring transactions involving state property under tighter control. At the same time, the last remnants of the authority of branch ministry officials over the management of state companies were eliminated and the powers of the State Property Agency were consolidated. Company councils were gradually dissolved and a substantial part of the managements of state enterprises was replaced on the grounds of incompetence and mismanagement.

In the meantime, the emphasis in the privatization process was shifted from the peripheral units of state companies to the large strongholds of the Hungarian economy, that is, to the company centres.

The only exceptions were the public utilities (telecommunications, energy), where the social consequences of privatization required more careful consideration and the restructuring of state regulation prior to privatization.

This hasty concentration of privatization on the most valuable parts of the Hungarian economy can be explained by several important factors:

1)   On the demand side, Hungary had an advantage vis-à-vis its post-communist neighbours, both in respect of its economic reform process and its legal environment which was more suited to the transition to a market economy. Both strategic and financial investors were keen to obtain a stake in the Hungarian economy.

2)   On the supply side, the Hungarian economy was deeply shocked by the collapse of the former COMECON markets: most state enterprises suffered a profound financial crisis caused by increasing indebtedness owing to the time lag between this rapid market collapse and the gradual adjustment to it (employment, fixed costs, trading contacts, and so on).

3)   The high level of indebtedness characteristic of the Hungarian economy as a whole, the origins of which date back to the spectacular borrowing practices of the last single-party governments.

Because of the rapid market reorientation and the financial crisis in both the micro- and the macroeconomy it was vital that fresh capital be obtained from Western investors in every possible form: greenfield investments, joint ventures and the purchase of state assets resulting in the 100 per cent foreign ownership of some state enterprises.

The results of the so-called 'first privatization round' – aimed at the most substantial foreign investors – were inconclusive. The companies were selected by the State Property Agency from industries believed most likely to attract foreign investors, such as the largest chain of department stores, Centrum, and the largest road transport company, Volan. Some of the companies selected were not sold in the envisaged period of time, partly because they had lost their market position as a result of the transition in Eastern Europe (for example, some chemical and footwear companies), partly because the price was too high (as happened with the large hotel and department store chains).

Participation of foreign investors in the privatization process increased in 1992–93 (*Figure 5.2*), especially in food processing and consumer goods (brewing, tobacco, vegetable oil, sugar) which had a secure domestic market position (*Figure 5.4*). This gave rise to sharp criticisms from domestic agricultural producers, who accused the government of selling strategic consumer industries and trade networks to foreigners.

They were not placated by the retail trade and services privatization programme aimed at Hungarian investors and supplemented by preferential privatization credit instruments.

Increasing dissatisfaction with the low participation of domestic investors in the privatization process, and the decreasing trend of privatization sales (*Figure 5.3*) caused by a diminution of interest on the part of foreign investors led to a general revaluation of privatization policy at the end of 1992. One of the most important outcomes of this revaluation was the new system of financial concessions for those participating in the privatization process.

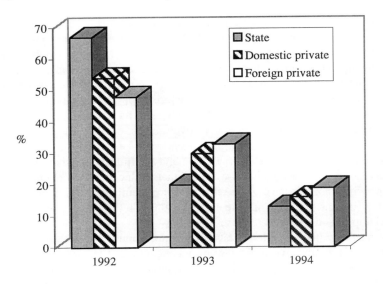

Figure 5.2 Share of ownership sectors in total equity, Hungary, 1992–94

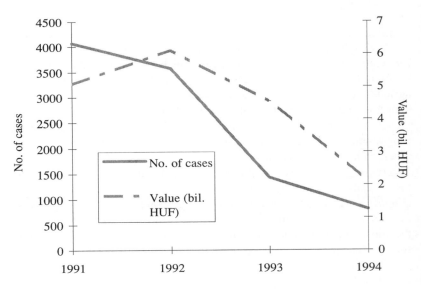

Figure 5.3 Small businesses sold by the State Property Agency, 1991–94

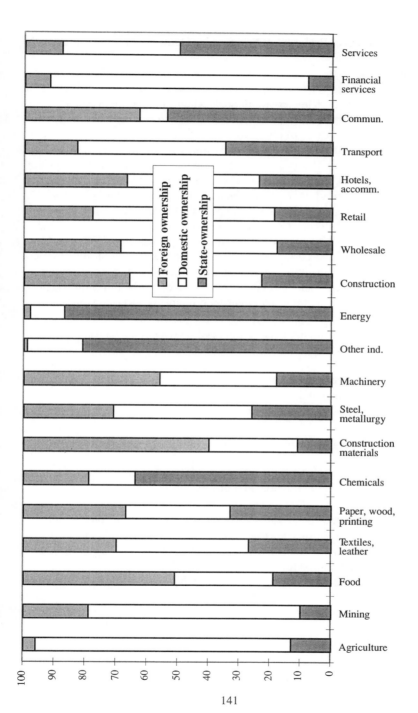

Figure 5.4 Structure of ownership by industry, Hungary, 1994 (%)

2.3 The Launch of Preferential Schemes for Domestic Investors in 1993–94

The upgrading of the role of domestic investors in the privatization process renewed the evergreen debate about large-scale or mass privatization schemes. The main characteristic of such schemes is the involvement of the population in privatization by the distribution of shares over a relatively short period of time either free of charge or at concessionary rates.

What motivated the Hungarian government to choose the form of privatization that it did was its ideological opposition to any kind of voucher-type solution to mass privatization. The key element in Hungarian privatization practice hitherto had been the issue of tenders, inviting potential investors to engage in rounds of competitive bidding; the most important factor from the government's point of view was the sheer size of the offer.

However, in the third year of privatization, after clear imbalances began to emerge regarding the participation of different players (domestic, foreign, strategic, financial, institutional and small investors) in the redistribution of ownership in Hungary and, last but not least, in view of the impending general election, the government revised its earlier principles concerning the access of the wider population to state assets under privatization.

The privatization methods and financial concessions which were now introduced targeted the following social groups:

- the employees of privatized companies;
- domestic small and medium entrepreneurs;
- small investors looking for opportunities on the Budapest Stock Exchange;
- those politically and/or economically persecuted under communism.

Members of these groups were offered a wide range of means to facilitate their participation in the privatization process.

- The employees of privatized companies were able to buy minority – maximum stake of 10–15 per cent – shares in them. The price of such shares was set at half their market value, and in the case of employee shares with limited trading rights at only 10 per cent.
- A new law on *Employee Share Ownership Programmes* (ESOPs) was enacted, providing long-term, low interest credit and an additional corporate tax benefit resource to finance privatization by employees; that is, to buy either minority or majority stakes in their companies. Majority shares were obtainable for ESOP schemes, however, only in the case of participation in the regular competitive bidding process.
- Hungarian citizens (new or existing entrepreneurs) were given the

opportunity to borrow money from commercial banks at preferential interest rates and to buy state assets or shares over a long period (up to a maximum of 15 years). This credit resource is refinanced by the National Bank of Hungary.

• Persons persecuted by the communist regime either politically or economically (through the confiscation or 'nationalization' of private property) were compensated with so-called *compensation notes* which could be used to buy state property at a favourable rate. Later, these notes were listed on the Budapest Stock Exchange and could be exchanged for cash.

• A special *mass privatization scheme* was developed with the professional and financial assistance of the British Know How Fund, to invent a market-type solution for the wide involvement of the Hungarian public into the privatization process. The Small Investors Share Ownership Programme was concentrating on selling company shares listed in the Budapest Stock Exchange, allowing a five-year interest-free instalment payment benefit to buy shares for the less wealthy part of the public.

The changing priorities as regards privatization are well reflected in *Figure 5.2* which shows the evolution of the share of each ownership form in total equity, which indicates the increasing role of domestic private buyers. *Figure 5.5* also shows that the overall effects of the changes made in respect of the available privatization tools was spectacular: while between 1989 and 1992 two-thirds of privatization sales revenue was in foreign currency, in 1993 two-thirds of investors paid in Hungarian forints: in the course of only one year, the share of domestic investors in the privatization process had increased by nearly 50%, while the participation of outside investors had decreased by nearly one-sixth (*Figure 5.5*). This was made possible by the preferential financial instruments made available only to Hungarian citizens: the privatization loan, the Employee Stock Ownership Programme and compensation notes.

These artificial financial schemes, however, soon revealed a long-standing distortion of the capital structure of most state companies, namely their constant liquidity problems and lack of investment resources. The new private owners, who typically had to use all their cash resources even partly to 'buy out the state' and incurred onerous credit burdens to make up the difference, soon began to experience grave financial crises. Moreover, this financial burden later increased: for the first three years after privatization investors enjoy a grace period during which they pay only the interest on a loan. *Figure 5.6* shows that while, by 1993, the new private sector had overtaken the state sector in sales terms, it kept pace with it as regards loss-making and inefficiency.

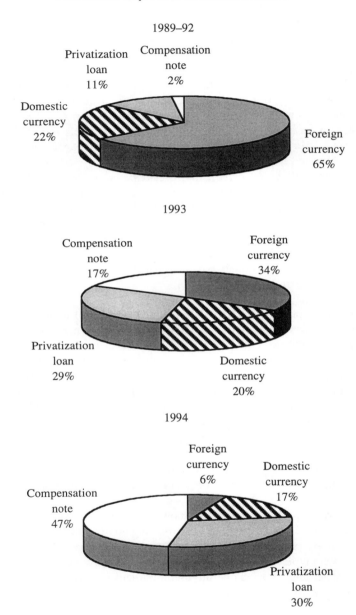

Figure 5.5 Sources of payment for state property, Hungary, 1989–94

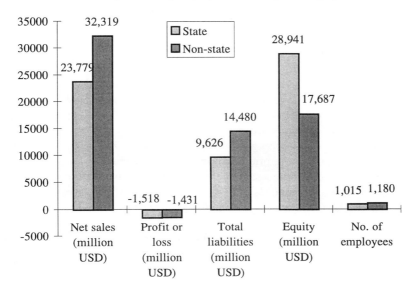

Figure 5.6 Comparison of characteristics of private and public sectors, Hungary, 1993

2.4 The New Privatization Law in 1995

The growing number of post-privatization bankruptcies affecting those who had bought assets by means of leveraged buy-outs and the growing balance of payments deficit demanded a new approach to privatization, elaborated by the new socialist–liberal coalition government.

The new privatization law passed in May 1995 laid down the following priorities for the future management of privatization:

- the capital increases necessary for enterprises under privatization should be ensured;
- enterprise restructuring should be encouraged – privatization revenues should be used to make financial injections into newly privatized enterprises;
- the domestic capital market should be developed;
- the interest of foreign investors in privatization should be both maintained and further encouraged;
- the acquisition of property by domestic entrepreneurs should be promoted;
- workplaces must be preserved and new jobs created;
- employee ownership and management buy-outs should be promoted;

• appropriate property should be made available in exchange for compensation notes.

The most important difference between the privatization priorities of the new government and those of its predecessor is the preference now given to institutional financial investors to the detriment of strategic ones. Another – ideologically unexpected – step was the suspension of the mass privatization programme on the grounds that the state budget urgently needed cash. A third development was the support given to *management buy-outs* in contrast to the previous, almost exclusive prioritization of ESOP schemes.

These moves were compensated, however, by benefits given to employees affected by a privatization deal. The new privatization regulations strongly emphasize the involvement of employee representatives (trade unions, company councils) in the privatization process.

Trade unions representing workers affected by a particular privatization deal should be informed about the social conditions of the deal by the seller 30 days before the issue of the tender, and again 30 days before the final decision is made about the winner. If the company assets sold include real estate servicing the social needs of employees, the seller must come to an agreement with the relevant trade union concerning the future utilization of these assets by the new owner.

In some cases – which will be approved by the board of the privatization agency – the willingness of a bidder to assume responsibilities pertaining to reorganization, capital increase, technical development, restructuring and employment will take priority over the size of his cash offer. Such non-cash related priorities should, of course, be made clear when the privatization tender is issued.

It is important to understand, however, that the new privatization law has not altered the basic philosophy of the Hungarian privatization process: first, that it should be based on market-type solutions with commercial sales, while such instruments of mass privatization as the free, or almost free, distribution of state property to the population should not be employed; second, Hungary has avoided the in-kind indemnification of earlier private owners and so the lengthy legal proceedings that this usually entails.

The main argument in favour of this approach is that privatization based on individual sales offers an earlier opportunity to find responsible private owners, although it is slower than privatization by distributing shares. Commercial sales also prefer financially stronger investors, especially foreign investors, who may play a positive role in the restructuring of state enterprises which typically lack financial resources, technology and the requisite management skills. It must be added, however, that foreign investors have tended to be most active in the takeover of the most attractive part of state enterprises, those with a strong position in the domestic market (for example, consumer goods, food, civil engineering, retail, tourism).

The crises which hit such industries as machine making, steel, textiles, meat and canning were generally neglected. These state-owned companies lost their market value rapidly, at the rate of about 20 per cent per year.

3 THE PROMOTION OF WORKER OWNERSHIP IN PRIVATIZATION

3.1 Government, Trade Unions and Employers

The conservative government's original attitude to employee ownership as a means of privatization was rather lukewarm. While the need for some concessionary instruments could not be gainsaid, the main emphasis was on minimizing the employees' stake in an enterprise and so their influence on decision-making. The government aimed at an average ownership share of less than 10 per cent, which under Hungarian company law is the point at which specific voting rights are mandatory. The most important rights pertaining to a 10 per cent stake are the right to call an extraordinary shareholders' meeting and the right to have items placed on the agenda. Majority employee ownership was regarded as extremely undesirable and by no means to be supported by government incentives.

A change in the official standpoint took place in the middle of the government's term of office with the promulgation of a separate law on employee ownership and on the financial benefits required to facilitate ESOPs.

The main cause of this 'about-turn' in privatization policy was the increasing public dissatisfaction with the conservative government overall and especially with its handling of the privatization process.

Domestic entrepreneurs were critical because of the difficulties they had competing with the financially much stronger foreign investors in purchasing companies with good prospects. They demanded preferential privatization credits in order to make up for their lack of capital. The one-sided revenue orientation of privatization, the failure actively to manage state enterprises not yet privatized and the abrupt liberalization of the domestic market resulted in a rapid rise in unemployment and in a deterioration of the companies under privatization. The new private owners, especially the domestic ones, took an often intransigent attitude, not only trying to eliminate trade union activity, but also collective bargaining and the system of collective agreements. They cancelled the old collective agreements and delayed the conclusion of new ones. This occurred at one of our case studies – described later in Section 4 – a paper mill, bought by a Greek investor, in which the employees had a 20 per cent stake.

Although the government recognized the need for a prompt response to public concern it could not easily overcome its strong negative feelings about the larger trade union centres in Hungary – it regarded them as the successors of the old communist trade unions – and so looked for innovative ways in which employees' interests could be represented.

Employee ownership seemed to be an appropriate tool for this purpose because it created a new institution for this purpose, the ESOP organization.

They also hoped to weaken the position of the traditional trade unions by promoting the long-term interest of owners in increasing the value of their shares as against the short-term wage and social benefit-oriented approach. The ESOP law was put together in a relatively short time drawing on the rich practical and professional experience of the American ESOP schemes and incentives.

The main difference between the US and the Hungarian solutions was that the Hungarian rules gave financial benefits (favourable government credit sources) only to ESOPs linked to cases of privatization (excluding the change of ownership between a private owner and an ESOP organization), and excluding the possibility of keeping the acquired shares in the common ownership of the ESOP organization: every share must be distributed to individual employees by the end of the repayment of the ESOP loan.

The *trade unions*, the other main influences as regards employee participation – despite the clear intentions of the government – were definitely in favour of employee ownership and financial benefits to promote the extension of employee share ownership. The main reason for this was their conviction that it would not undermine their position. Trade unions in most enterprises had been strong enough before privatization to obtain a role in the preparation of ESOP programmes and on the boards of ESOP organizations. They had also discovered that industrial relations at ESOP companies tended to be far more developed than elsewhere. To cite one of the preliminary conclusions of the case studies described in the last section of the present chapter, there is no ESOP company in which employee ownership has weakened the position of the trade unions. Although the introduction of an ESOP did not strengthen trade union activity if it was already weak, strong trade union organizations were maintained.

The *management* proved to be the key factor in most ESOP initiatives. The original government motivation – to strike a blow against the dubious management structures inherited from the previous regime – here worked against them. Managers deprived of the financial means and official support necessary to enable them to buy out their companies became the most dedicated educators, agitators and organizers of ESOP schemes.

Such enforced co-operation between differently motivated partners in some cases later caused tension between the new co-owners. This occurred in those cases in which the ESOP was in reality a hidden management buy-out, or when the management tried to reroute the ESOP scheme towards MBO privatization.

3.2 Legal Foundations and Financial Concessions

The rules and concessions pertaining to employee ownership can be separated into two major groups:

1.   General facilities, such as the partial circumvention of the competitive principle binding for outside investors, but at the cost of exclusively minority shareholdings for employees.
2.   The ESOP scheme, which is a way of financing employee buy-outs as part of the overall competitive bidding process, allowing employees both majority and minority ownership, although the former was possible only if they had offered the highest price.

3.2.1 General concessions for minority ownership

The concession in question is a price discount of up to 50 per cent of the market price of the share (the market price is the one paid by the majority owner) only for company employees. The total discount should not exceed 150 per cent of the national minimum wage, multiplied by the number of employees applying for shares. Besides the 50 per cent price discount, the state makes possible the delayed payment (over a maximum of three years) of the rest of the reduced price in the form of instalments at a preferential interest rate.

The shares acquired by employees on this basis should not exceed 15 per cent of the total equity of the company. These shares are normal shares: they are freely tradable after repayment of the loan to the seller.

There is a special type of employee share called the 'workers' share', which is tradable only among the employees of the given company; because of this, the price discount can amount to 90 per cent. The proportion of these workers' shares in the total equity of the company cannot exceed 10 per cent.

3.2.2 The ESOP scheme

ESOP buy-outs can be used to privatize any company, on condition that:

•   at least 40% of the enterprise's full-time employees join the organization set up to manage the deal; and
•   the ESOP organization wins the competitive tender.

The central element of the ESOP buy-out is, of course, the financial concession system provided for it by the state with:

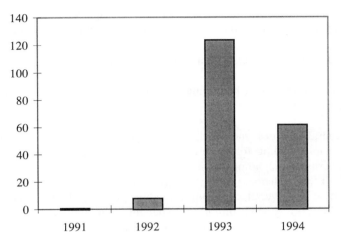

Figure 5.7 Number of ESOPs in privatization, Hungary, 1991–94

- a long-term (maximum 15 years) credit for 98 per cent of the sales price;
- a preferential interest rate (at present, 20 per cent of the market rate);
- a tax concession, in the form of tax exemption up to a maximum 20 per cent of the enterprise's annual pre-tax profit, if it is transferred to the ESOP organization with the purpose of repaying the loan.

The shares bought on credit can be transferred to individual employees only step by step, at the same rate at which the privatization loan is repaid. Shares which have not yet been paid for represent collateral for the bank, and the relevant voting rights are exercised by representatives of the ESOP organization. ESOP organizations draw their membership from all employees participating in the privatization programme (as already mentioned, at least 40 per cent of all full-time employees). The ESOP organization elects a 3–7 member presidium which exercises its voting rights at the general meeting of shareholders and appoints representatives to the board of directors of the company.

The new privatization law seriously restricted the financial benefits available for ESOPs: an ESOP loan can finance a maximum of 50 million HUF (around US$ 400,000) or – if the price is lower – a maximum of 50% of the selling price. These provisions are clearly intended to limit the scope of ESOP buy-outs to small and medium-sized enterprises: most experts predict a sharp decline in the proportion of privatization deals made on this basis.

The data presented on the extent of ESOPs in *Figure 5.7* – representing the situation when the old ESOP rules were still in force – clearly demonstrate that ESOPs have been hitherto the most popular and successful privatization

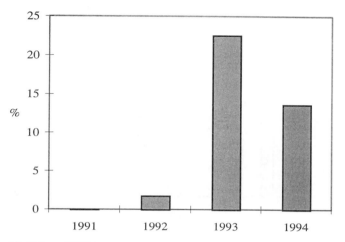

Figure 5.8 Value of ESOPs in total privatization income, Hungary, 1991–94

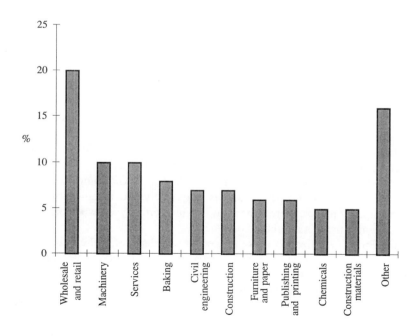

Figure 5.9 Value of ESOP sales in total privatization, by sector, Hungary, 1991–94

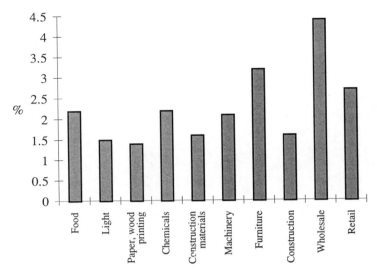

Figure 5.10 Industries with ESOPs with more than 1% of total equity, Hungary, 1994
Source: Tax Office Data Base, 1994.

instruments. By spring 1995, around 180 companies had been privatized either partially or totally using an ESOP scheme. The value of ESOPs represented more than 20 per cent of total privatization income in 1993 and nearly 16 per cent in 1994 *(Figure 5.8)*.

If we look at the breakdown of *ESOP privatization cases by industry (Table 5.1)*, we can see that ESOP schemes were particularly frequent in the commercial sector, machine manufacture, services (car repairs, cleaning) and the food industry (bakeries). The highest percentage of ESOPs in equity is observed in wholesale, retail, and furniture *(Figure 5.10)*.

By studying the *ownership structure* of the 180 ESOP companies we can also observe that ESOP ownership is only rarely accompanied by foreign ownership. Moreover, there is no case in which employee ownership reaches 10 per cent if there is a foreign co-owner.

If the ESOP organization is not the owner of the shares in their entirety, the usual co-owners are the enterprise management or the state. State co-ownership is typical when employees could not get enough credit or when too much credit had to be obtained in order to buy out the enterprise as a whole. In such cases, the usual share of the ESOP is 51 per cent, the minority stake being left with the state.

The *distribution of ESOP schemes among enterprises with different levels of equity* shows a higher concentration around enterprises at the upper end of the

Table 5.1 Proportion of ESOPs by sector, Hungary, 1994 (% of total no. of ESOPs)

Sector	%
Wholesale and retail trade	20
Machine making	10
Services	10
Baking	8
Civil engineering	7
Construction	7
Furniture and paper	6
Publishing and printing	6
Chemicals	5
Construction materials	5
Other	16
Total	100

Source: SPA.

Table 5.2 Distribution of ESOP enterprises by size of equity, Hungary, 1994

Equity (million HUF)	%
0–50	17.5
51–100	10.7
101–200	16.8
201–500	28.2
Greater than 500	26.8
Total	100.0

Source: SPA.

Table 5.3 The proportion of loans in financing ESOP shares, Hungary, 1994

Equity (million HUF)	%
0–50	65
51–100	45
101–200	58
201–500	62
Greater than 500	56

Source: SPA.

scale (*Table 5.2*). The data on the *utilization of financial concessions* demonstrate that preferential credit instruments were employed very evenly in the privatization of enterprises with different levels of equity (*Table 5.3*).

This uneven distribution by equity size is due to the fact that small companies were much easier to buy for outside (including domestic) investors. On the other hand, many larger companies which did not attract the interest of foreign investors were purchased on the strength of privatization loans made available to ESOP–MBO consortia, often on the basis of old customer relationships.

Tables 5.2 and *5.3* clearly show that the restrictions of the new privatization law on the borrowing capacity of ESOP organizations prevented employees from achieving majority ownership in medium-sized and large companies. But do the experiences of ESOP-owned companies justify the limitations of the new privatization law? What are the basic characteristics of the social and business activities of employee-owned firms? The next section seeks to answer these questions on the basis of company examples.

4 LESSONS FROM SIX ENTERPRISES WITH EMPLOYEE OWNERSHIP

The main topics investigated during the enterprise visits were the following:

- the motivations of employees and managers when deciding about an employee buy-out;
- the financial conditions of the purchase and the basic rules of the distribution of employee shares;
- the performance of the ESOP company after privatization;
- the formation of labour relations in the company, paying particular attention to co-operation between the management, the ESOP organization and the trade unions; and
- the ownership rights of employees.

The case studies covered six companies whose main data are presented in *Table 5.4*. The companies are medium-sized by Hungarian standards (as measured by equity value) and belong to industries (trade, construction, paper, furniture, chemicals) where ESOPs have above-average representation (see *Box 5.1*).

Table 5.4 Characteristics of the six enterprises with employee ownership, Hungary, 1994

Company	Year of priv.	Share of ESOPs in ownership (%)	Value of equity (M HUF)	Turnover (M HUF)	No. of employees 1994
1	1993	100.0	641	3 976	227
2	1992	86.0	406	902	135
3	1993	64.0	1 683	2 623	899
4	1993	50.5	1 103	2 972	396
5	1993	29.0	1 621	7 213	1 150
6	1992	20.0	–	–	–

Note: M = million.

Box 5.1 Introduction to the six companies examined

Company 1

Wholesale company of agricultural products situated 100 km east of the capital, in a rich, highly developed agricultural region. Before privatization it belonged to a national concern with affiliate companies all over the country. The company was making a good profit at the time of privatization; furthermore, they paid twice the average salary in the region. Their high profitability also allowed them to borrow money from the bank to purchase the firm. Management supported employee ownership to avoid becoming a subordinate distribution plant of a foreign (probably Austrian) wholesale company.

Company 2

Woven carpet making company situated in the same town as Company 1. Just before privatization the company was hit by a serious crisis in both its local and export markets. They were in debt and loss-making which pushed down the price of the company. Despite the low price, however, because of the depressed market situation there was no competitive bid. Employees also hesitated about whether to participate in the purchase, so that the management acquired a 51 per cent stake. Since that time the market situation has changed considerably for the better, and now many employees regret that they did not buy more shares earlier. The management is unwilling to surrender majority ownership.

Company 3

Chemical company situated in Budapest selling products at a lower price than its large multinational competitors, mostly for the domestic household market.

Privatization was marked chiefly by the State Property Agency's choice of a *closed tender* to keep away multinational strategic investors, who by this time had established strong positions in the Hungarian household cleaning market. In the end there was only *one bid* for the company, from the ESOP–MBO consortium. The wide production profile and the environmental risks scared off potential outside investors. The company has a highly labour-intensive production structure compared to its competitors.

The participation rate of employees in the ESOP scheme was 90 per cent. The most important factor convincing employees to participate in the privatization was the example of the top management who paid 15 per cent in cash for the shares, a much higher portion than the 2 per cent paid by the average employee.

Company 4

A highly prestigious construction company situated in the capital. As a state firm they specialized in the building of large public buildings (ministries, theatres, hotels). There is a very strong trade union organization at the company which also has a strong position on the ownership body. At the beginning management was against employee ownership. Their attitude was changed by the arrogant behaviour towards them of foreign investors. At the time of privatization the firm had a favourable liquidity position, though this has since worsened, and the management intends to tighten the conditions of the collective agreement.

Company 5

Plastic-manufacturing company situated in the Budapest area. ESOP-type privatization was initiated by the trade unions which surveyed employees in order to assess their intentions. The company is the main employer in the region; the majority of employees have worked there for a long time. There were serious doubts about the intentions of potential Western investors, the main fears being a narrowing of profile and downsizing. More than 80 per cent of the employees participated in the ESOP programme without the need for an intensive campaign of persuasion. The example of the chief executive was also important: he began his career 40 years ago as a blue-collar worker at the company. The strategy of the management is to form joint-venture affiliate companies with various competitors in different production sectors, with 50 per cent co-ownership.

Company 6

A paper mill situated 30 km from the capital. It was formerly a plant of a big, multi-plant state concern. The plant had struggled hard for a number of years to split from the parent company. One of the reasons for its eventual privatization was its profitability in contrast to the loss-making parent. Another important factor was the role of the plant in the region, where they are by far the biggest employers. The trade unions were anxious to achieve employee-led privatization to lessen the danger of mass lay-offs. Because of the company's capital-intensive profile the State Property Agency insisted on the inclusion of a financially strong strategic investor in the mill's privatization.

A compromise was agreed: a majority stake was sold to a foreign strategic investor and a 20 per cent stake to employees. The foreign owner froze wages for 12 months (during a period of 28 per cent inflation) and offered to buy employee shares at a rate 9 times higher than their nominal value. Most employees accepted the offer and sold the shares. Since then the economic and social situation has worsened considerably.

At present, the owners and the employees are in grave conflict, the latter having neither shares nor a collective agreement.

4.1 The Main Motives behind Employee Ownership

The most common reason given by employees for assuming the (limited) risk of ownership was the wish to avoid the uncertainty entailed by the presence of an outside owner. On this point the interests of management and employees were the same, although for different reasons. *Employees* stressed the importance of stable employment conditions, especially when the enterprise they worked for was the sole or principal employer in the region. The role of employment security among the factors motivating employee ownership was particularly important at one of the rare companies with ESOP and foreign co-ownership (Company 6). Until privatization, the employees had struggled to obtain at least a 25 per cent share in the company. They put strong pressure on the State Property Agency to secure this share on the basis of the normal competitive bidding process. Finally they managed to obtain a 20 per cent share at a preferential price (around 10 per cent of the market price).

Six months later, when they were sure that the foreign partner had no lay-offs in mind – at least in the short-term – the employees sold their shares to the foreign co-owner at an average profit equal to six months' salary.

What is more interesting is that in the majority of cases with worker ownership employees expressed a commitment to the present management. There were cases in which employees were, at the beginning, reluctant to participate in the ESOP programme: what convinced them was the relatively high financial risk assumed by the management (for instance, in Companies 2 and 3). Another common feature of ESOP firms is that both employees and managers had been working at their enterprise for longer than the industrial seniority average.

The *management* put the emphasis on a commitment to the present profile of the companies they had developed over a number of years. In a couple of cases they stressed the danger of becoming a mere internal supplier of the foreign mother company of the new owner (Companies 1, 3 and 5 to different extents). Managers also pointed to the hostile, sometimes disdainful manner in which the representatives of the potential investors often treated the Hungarian partners (see Company 4). There were other cases in which the management was at an advanced stage of negotiations about the sale of the firm when the hidden intentions of the outside investor came to light, at which the Hungarians changed their mind and developed a competitive bid to privatize the company through the ESOP scheme.

The desire of enterprise managements to retain autonomy derives from the history of company supervision in the state sector. As mentioned earlier, only a few years before privatization started state company managers had obtained a relatively high degree of independence from the authorities. Many were not willing to relinquish this newly won autonomy for another type of dependency.

In at least 50 per cent of the visited enterprises the ESOP take-over was the only way in which privatization could take place, since no outside investor had expressed an interest. The reason for this lack of interest was usually low profitability, loss making, recession in the sector, or environmental problems.

4.2 The Distribution of Shares and Financial Concessions

The ESOP scheme makes it possible to obtain almost complete ownership (up to a maximum of 98 per cent) on the basis of preferential credits and tax exemptions. The distribution of shares paid for in this way is therefore crucial to the fairness and efficiency of the system.

The ESOP law did not prescribe any central, obligatory or even recommended way in which ESOP shares should be divided – the only legal precondition was that 40 per cent of employees must participate. The most common principle developed by ESOP organizations on the basis of which shares would be divided among members was a combination of the number of years' service and the wages accumulated over that time. In most cases, there was an upper limit on the number of shares each person could obtain under the scheme (for example, not more than 2 per cent of the total value of the shares). But the level of the limit was flexible enough sometimes to grant concessions to managers thus leading to the implementation of what were essentially management buy-outs instead of ESOPs. This happened, for example, when the top 20 managers at a particular enterprise acquired 47 per cent of the shares due to the accepted distribution scheme.

There is, however, an inherent tendency for ESOP ownership to become concentrated in ever fewer hands, because only shares sold by the state are available on a concessionary basis (low-interest credit and tax exemptions). New employees can obtain on a preferential basis only the shares of employees who leave the company, while the financial assistance available for this purpose continues to diminish. Needless to say, ownership tends to concentrate in the hands of the fortunate employees and managers who were working for the privatized company when the state shares were sold.

4.3 Performance Trends after Privatization

The fact that the privatization process is still relatively young made it difficult to draw far-reaching conclusions on the performance of the companies under study (*Table 5.5*).

The most general statement we can make is that, on average, enterprise performance has not worsened since privatization. Pre-tax profit and wage efficiency (as calculated in the productivity ratio) increased in four out of six cases, stagnated in one and decreased in one, although even this enterprise has a positive bottom-line figure and a profit/equity ratio higher than the industrial average.

The main problems that seem to emerge are linked to indebtedness and investment activity. The debt ratio (total debt/equity) is increasing, though it is still only about 50 per cent of the industrial average.

As regards new investments, none of the six companies had increased investment activity (investment expenditure/total assets) since privatization.

Can this increasing indebtedness and low investment activity be explained by the relatively generous employment and wage policies of these firms?

It cannot be denied that labour costs in these enterprises were not kept under control in the year of privatization. This was the only year in which the wage efficiency indicator (pre-tax profit/wage costs) worsened. The obvious explanation for this is the desire of management to make it easier for employees to make the necessary cash investment in ESOP shares. After privatization, although wage growth at every ESOP enterprise was above the industrial average, in most cases it did not climb above the consumer price index; and at only one enterprise did wage growth exceed profit growth. This shows that most of the enterprises in the study pursued a careful wage policy, in order not to undermine their financial stability.

The employment policy of the ESOP firms has been even more encouraging. There were substantial lay-offs – on average 20 per cent of the workforce – in the year of privatization; after privatization on average a further 5 per cent of the workforce was laid off annually. This shows that ESOP firms are willing to implement the necessary labour rationalization.

The final conclusion is that, although the ESOP firms in the study did experience higher labour costs than the industrial average, these were the result of productivity increases. In any case, the poor capital resources of these firms, inherited from the previous regime, could have not been ameliorated by savings in labour costs.

Table 5.5 Performance of the six ESOP companies since privatization, Hungary, 1993–95

Company	Year of privatization (1993 or late 1992)	1994	1995 (projected)	1994/ 1993	1995/ 1993
Net sales*					
1.	2 393	2 972	3 286	1.24	1.37
2.	3 154	3 976	3 620	1.26	1.14
3.	4 389	7 213	5 700	1.64	1.29
4.	278	902	950	3.24	3.41
5.	2 310	2 623	3 000	1.13	1.29
6.	4 200	4 800	–	1.14	–
Pre-tax profit*					
1.	145	167	210	1.15	1.44
2.	271	161	100	0.59	0.36
3.	86	118	76	1.37	0.88
4.	3	50	55	16.60	18.30
5.	33	80	110	2.42	3.33
6.	270	704	–	2.60	–
No. of employees					
1.	449	396	400	0.80	0.89
2.	218	227	225	1.04	1.03
3.	1 327	1 150	–	0.86	–
4.	199	135	168	0.67	0.84
5.	1 121	899	852	0.80	0.76
6.	1 100	1 000	–	0.90	–
Labour costs*					
1.	180	200	240	1.11	1.33
2.	140	163	154	1.16	1.10
3.	527	680	750	1.29	1.40
4.	43	119	147	2.76	3.41
5.	418	424	450	1.01	1.07
6.	–	–	–	–	–

* Million HUF

Source: Interviews.

The shortage of resources for working capital and technological development is still one of the great challenges that employee-owned enterprises must face. To tackle it, ESOP firms have adopted a number of strategies, for example, narrowing their business profile (dropping less profitable activities) or mobilizing unused assets, including those serving social purposes (such as the sale of company-owned holiday apartments, kindergartens, sports facilities, and so on).

Another alternative is to involve outside investors. Efforts in this direction, however, have not yet been successful. Although financial investors tend to be comfortable with ESOP owners (especially Western European investors), in the case of overseas capital funds the profitability or growth potential of the enterprise was not attractive enough.

An interesting interim solution may be the establishment of joint ventures with strategic investors on a fifty-fifty ownership basis. This model would avoid the abandonment of majority employee ownership in the Hungarian mother company and guarantee the influence requested by the outside partner in the joint venture.

4.4 Labour Relations and Management Policy

The main characteristics of ESOP companies as regards labour relations are a 'soft' labour policy and highly developed collective bargaining.

A soft labour policy does not necessarily entail tolerance of over-employment or excessive labour costs. It is rather a question of emphasis. For ESOP enterprises lay-offs were found to be the last resort, after all other avenues have been pursued, such as a search for new markets and the flexible reallocation of employees (for example, many white-collar employees had to be allocated blue-collar jobs in order to remain in employment). To facilitate their flexible labour policy these enterprises actively utilize internal training and retraining facilities. In 50 per cent of the companies visited significant training programmes had been implemented.

The other notable difference between ESOP companies and other privatized companies is the role of collective bargaining in the prevention and resolution of labour disputes. One of our preliminary assumptions was that in ESOP firms the ESOP organization would be actively involved in the resolution of labour disputes, mostly on behalf of the employees. In reality, the traditional channels of collective negotiation are functioning smoothly in these firms, and labour relations are managed extremely well on the old trade union–management basis. The management in almost all cases is careful not to admit day-to-day labour issues to owners' meetings, a goal which they achieve by correct and fair treatment of the trade unions and a constructive intention to conclude collective agreements.

In only one case was a different approach taken, namely an attempt on the part of the management to undermine trade union influence by overturning the old bargaining rules. The unions simply shifted the dispute to the ESOP meeting, at which the management had to step back.

On the other hand, if the trade unions at an enterprise are so weak that they are left out of the preparation of the ESOP programme, employee ownership can lead to their demise. This process is enhanced when the management 'takes over trade union functions', using ESOP meetings to replace the traditional institutions of employee interest representation.

The effect of employee ownership on managerial behaviour is most clearly seen in the attitude of managers to the rest of the workforce. The most important factor here is communication skills, primarily oral. Employees need explanations – usually in the form of question-and-answer type discussions – and they are keen to think of the general manager as a partner. In recognition of the importance of management–employee communications, management training to develop negotiation skills was found in most of the ESOP companies visited.

The other outstanding effect of employee ownership on management style is its curbing of management remuneration and other benefits. In a situation of financial instability and limited real wage growth it is crucial that the management avoid extravagance (for example, as regards office furniture, company cars, salaries and bonuses). Since management remuneration is a perquisite of the board of directors, on which the ESOP organization is represented, nothing can be kept hidden in this regard. This differs sharply from the practice of other privatized companies, at which the details of management compensation packages are confidential and almost always much more favourable than those of employees. The obvious danger here is that ESOP companies might lose their top managers or have difficulties in recruiting new ones. The modest incentives at the top will also limit those available to lower level management. Many general managers at ESOP companies complained about how difficult it was to recruit young, foreign-language-speaking professionals.

In some companies efforts have been made to promote detailed wage differentiation. A prerequisite of this was the restructuring of working practices, with the introduction of group work and group performance calculation methods. The management at these enterprises emphasized the importance of breaking down ownership participation into the contributions to profitability of different employee groups. In most ESOP companies, however, traditional working practices remain in place, and the hierarchical management system and wage formation are untouched.

4.5 The Exercise of Ownership Rights

Most employees at ESOP companies still do not exercise the rights which their partial ownership has given them. Needless to say, to expect anything else after only a couple of years would be unrealistic. ESOP shares come into individual employee ownership very slowly, at the rate at which the privatization credit is repaid. In most cases, only 5–7 per cent of the shares have been paid for, the rest serving as collateral for the bank. For the same reason, most employee-owners have not yet earned much in the form of dividends. The small dividends are also often spent on repaying the loan. Because the repayment period is usually 10–15 years, it will be a long time before most employees receive a tangible return on their investment.

In this situation, the two main ways in which employees can exercise their ownership rights are the influence they have on the 'hiring and firing' of top management and their ability to obtain valuable information on the situation of the company through the ESOP organization. These possibilities should not be underestimated under current Hungarian circumstances. At companies where employees have sold their 20 per cent share, trade union officials tend to experience great difficulty in obtaining information on economic indicators and future management strategy, and in getting involved in decision-making concerning employment matters.

By contrast, in all the ESOP firms studied the management was fully aware of the importance of frequent communication with the employees. What may be criticized is the quality of communication, being predominantly oral. Written information is very rare: no background statistics or calculations are provided, and if some general statistics are available, no explanation is attached to help employees to understand the information given orally. For example, employees are unable to assess the historical performance of the company and have difficulties continuing discussions among themselves about the strategic options of their firm.

Nowhere was there an educational programme to help at least the ESOP representatives to become acquainted with the basics of company economics, business strategy, balance sheet analysis or capital market terms. The usual reasons for this were that it is too expensive, that there is no time for it or that no one was interested. Probably the real reason is that the majority of managers do not really want employees, or employee representatives, to be involved in strategic decision-making. Managers are convinced that the knowledge, culture and interests of employees would not allow them to participate effectively in this area and they do not hold out much hope that this will change. The present situation, in which employees exercise direct ownership rights only once or twice a year at the general shareholders' meetings, is quite satisfactory. As a consequence, management–employee relations tend to be confined to personal relations between the president of the ESOP organization and the general manager. This situation is somewhat enlivened by the fact that at most companies employees – with the assistance of local trade unions – elect independent-minded, outspoken personalities to the top positions of their ESOP organization. This is important in a situation characterized by conflicts of interest: the same person who is president of the ESOP organization and an influential member of the board of directors is also an employee. Some ESOP firms are trying to resolve this difficult situation by inviting outside professionals on to the board of directors as representatives of the ESOP organization. This offers a very promising way of combining the representation of employee ownership rights with professionalism.

Let us conclude with a story that says a great deal about the supposed incompetence of employees as regards economic issues. In 1995 a very dangerous crisis developed at one of the companies visited, threatening the company with insolvency. The probable outcome of this liquidity crisis, however, would not be the loss of jobs, but 'only' the loss of the shares serving as collateral on the privatization loan. The management was unwilling at first to inform the employees of this situation, fearing that panic would set in. Finally, they decided that 'honesty is the best policy'. As a result, at the end of that year, the firm realized record profits and was able to pay off a substantial portion of its debts. Although there was no obvious explanation for this abrupt growth in profits, the management is convinced that the prospect of losing their shares shocked the workforce into achieving a much higher level of performance.

5 CONCLUSION

The 'golden age' of ESOP schemes in the Hungarian privatization process was 1993–94, when medium-sized companies in trade, services, the food industry, construction and construction materials were on offer. The motivation for the introduction of ESOP schemes was the maintenance of employment and the protection of the autonomy of firms on the domestic market.

In the companies examined we found little evidence of the efficiency disadvantage attributed by many authors to the 'soft' labour policy allegedly followed by firms in employee ownership. The real problem is in fact undercapitalization, which is complicated by the indebtedness due to privatization borrowing. Industrial relations are well institutionalized in these companies; the division of interest representation between ownership and labour issues has been well drawn. In cases of conflict between workers and management the ESOP organizations have played a constructive mediating role.

6. Employee Ownership in Polish Privatizations

Domenico Mario Nuti

1 INTRODUCTION

Large-scale privatization of state assets is the distinctive feature of the recent transformation of Central East European economies, with respect to all earlier attempts at reforming the Soviet type system. Poland was among the first in announcing it (September 1989) and launching it (with the Act on the Privatization of State Enterprises, 13 July 1990); Hungary's earlier initiative (1988) was designed to regulate spontaneous private appropriation by insiders rather than to radically transform the system, while Yugoslavia's 1989 privatization law applied to a different ownership regime. On the eve of transformation Poland already had a significant private sector, not only in agriculture but also in non-agricultural sectors. In 1989 private agriculture amounted to 75 per cent of the land, about 10 per cent of GDP and 21 per cent of employment (Rapacki and Linz, 1992); in the 1980s non-agricultural private activities trebled to about 10 per cent of GDP and employment, including manufacturing as well as traditionally private activities such as trade, catering and services.

In 1990-95 the Polish private sector expanded fast, reaching over 60 per cent of employment, but primarily through what has been variously called 'organic growth' or 'grass-roots privatization', that is, the growth of existing private activities and the rise and growth of *de novo* firms, rather than through the fast transfer of state assets to private new owners, domestic or foreign. In many ways such transfer has followed a different course from that originally anticipated.

First, the privatization process has been *slower* than planned. The early 1990 target of privatizing 50 per cent of state enterprises by the end of 1992, later moved to the end of 1995 (Rapacki, 1995, p. 57; Monkiewicz, 1995), has not been achieved. By end-1995 there were still over half of the initial state-owned enterprises (4,563 out of 8,453), not to count wholly Treasury-owned joint-stock and other limited liability companies (*jednoosobowa spolka Skarbu Panstwa*, or jsSP) and incomplete privatizations; completed privatizations amounted to only about one fifth (*Table 6.1*). The market value of the residual state sector is controversial, but its book value is of the order of 75 billion zlotys;[1] in 1995 among the 100 largest Polish enterprises, 19 were state owned, 35 were wholly Treasury-owned joint-stock companies, and 17 were mixed ownership companies with dominant state ownership (OECD, 1996).

Second, privatization has followed a *multi-track course* through the accretion of new methods adopted to overcome unexpected difficulties as they arose. Initially the dominant method was to be a Western-style 'indirect' or 'capital' privatization, involving open sales of shares and the search for a strategic outside investor. This proved to be slower, costlier and harder than anticipated: in the words of Janusz Lewandowski, twice Minister for Privatization, 'In the transition, privatization is a process whereby assets whose real owners are not known and whose real value is uncertain are sold to people who do not have the money to buy them'. To resolve the problems of lack of liquid savings – vapourized by high inflation at the inception of the Polish transformation – and of asset valuation, a mass privatization scheme was devised, which technically is another form of 'capital' privatization. This track was held up by political and technical delays (Nuti, 1995), launched by the *Act on National Investment Funds* (NIFs) and their privatization (30 April 1993), and implemented in 1996. It involves the distribution to adult Poles, on request and for a token payment, of certificates in 15 NIFs, to which 60 per cent of the shares of 512 'commercialized' state enterprises have been allocated (OECD, 1996, Annex IV).

Meanwhile, many insolvent state enterprises were being closed down and sold off to private buyers, as a whole or in bits and pieces, according to Article 19 of the old *Act on State Enterprises* of 25 September 1981.[2] Other, economically viable state enterprises were being sold or leased, also as a whole or in parts, to private buyers and consortia of buyers, with priority granted to new companies formed with employee participation; this was allowed by the 1990 Privatization Law, Article 37 (enterprise assets could also be contributed to a new company, without preference for employees). The two processes reflected radically different, indeed opposite, underlying economic

[1] All zloty values given here are in post-denomination units, i.e. pre-1995 zlotys have been divided by 10,000.

[2] Insolvent state enterprises can also be made bankrupt (Article 24 of the Act on state enterprises) on the basis of bankruptcy procedures (Decree of 24-10-1934 of the President of the Polish Republic). Article 19 liquidation differs from bankruptcy procedures primarily because it can only be applied if there are 'grounds for stating' that liquidation net revenues are sufficient to satisfy all creditors' claims.

Table 6.1 Progress of ownership transfer, Poland 1990–95 (cumulative number of enterprises at the end of each year)

	1990	1991	1992	1993	1994	1995
Total number of state-owned enterprises	8 453	8 228	7 245	5 924	4 955	4 563
Liquidation						
Started	49	989	1 576	1 999	2 287	2 507
Completed	0	201	561	893	1 248	1 450
Article 19 of the SOE Law						
Started	18	540	857	1 082	1 845	1 358
Completed	0	19	86	186	303	396
Article 37 of the Privatization Law						
Started	31	449	719	917	1 042	1 149
Completed	0	182	475	707	945	1 054
Converted into joint-stock companies	38	260	480	527	723	958
Capital privatization	6	27	51	99	134	160
Public offerings	5	11	12	15	19	22
Trade Sales	1	16	39	81	110	132
Mixed methods	0	0	0	3	5	6
Total						
Started	93	1 276	2 107	2 625	3 144	3 625
Completed	6	228	612	992	1 382	1 610
Income from privatization (flows)*	–	170.9	484.4	780.4	1 594.8	2 641.7
Leasing and sale of liquidated assets*	–	46.4	171.8	287.0	322.9	406.2
Capital privatization*	–	124.5	308.7	439.4	846.7	1 714.2
Bank privatization*	–	0.0	3.9	54.0	425.2	521.3

* Million zlotys.
Source: Ministry of Ownership Transformation. From OECD, 1996.

Privatization Surprises in Transition Economies

Table 6.2 Enterprises involved in ownership transformations by sector, Poland, end-1995, and their growth rates in 1995

Sectors	Total		Article 19 Liquidation		Article 37 Liquidation		jsSP	
	No.	growth (%)	No.	growth (%)	No.	growth (%)	No.	growth (%)
National economy	3 465	15.1	1 358	9.1	1149	10.3	958	32.5
Industry	1 594	19.5	411	3.8	388	10.9	795	35.2
Construction	861	10.2	367	15.0	383	5.8	111	11.0
Agriculture	340	12.6	270	9.8	67	24.1	3	50.0
Forestry	18	5.9	9	0	6	0	3	50.0
Transport	175	9.4	126	2.4	30	30.4	19	35.7
Communic.	1	0	0	–	1	0	0	–
Trade	311	12.7	99	8.8	189	10.5	23	64.3
Other	165	18.7	76	24.6	85	13.3	4	33.3

See text for the definition of headings.
Source: MPW, 1996.

Table 6.3 Ownership transformations according to privatization method and employment size at end-1995, Poland

Number of employees	Total	jsSP				Liquidation		
	Total	Total	Art. 5	Art. 6	Art. 7	Total	Art. 37	Art. 19
Total	3 465	958	387	230	341	2 507	1 149	1 358
Up to 50	299	1	0	0	1	298	52	246
51-200	1 495	42	16	0	26	1 453	597	856
201-500	663	184	77	19	88	479	309	170
over 500	1 008	731	294	211	226	277	191	86

Source: MPW, 1996.
Note: Wholly Treasury-owned joint-stock companies (jsSP) have resulted from Articles 5 and 6 of the July 1990 Act on the Privatization of State Enterprises, and from Article 7 of the Act on National Investment Funds. 'Liquidation' took place under Article 37 of the July 1990 Law (restructuring privatization) and Article 19 of the old Act on State Enterprises of September 1981.

situations; however, they had in common the so-called 'liquidation' of state enterprises, in the literal technical sense of their cancellation by the Tribunal from the registry of state enterprises. This is why these two forms of 'direct' privatization are often lumped together in Polish classifications.[3] A significant difference between the two kinds of 'liquidation' is the much higher rate of completion for Article 37 privatization (92 per cent versus 29 per cent of Article 19 procedures, *Table 6.1*).

Further channels of privatization were opened by the Law on Financial Re-structuring of State Enterprises and Banks of 3 February 1993,[4] which leads to privatization through debt–equity swaps, often as a pre-condition of access to central funds; technically this is yet another form of 'capital' privatization. An Act on the Commercialization of State Enterprises, involving their generalized transformation into joint-stock companies, regardless of their privatization prospects, has had a difficult course and by mid-1996 is not yet operational: approved by Parliament, hit by a Presidential veto overturned by Parliament, successfully denounced to the Constitutional Tribunal, this law is to be reconsidered in a new draft.

In Polish practice, state enterprises 'involved in ownership transformation' are defined to include those registered as jsSPs, those whose Article 37 liquidation has been initiated (regardless of approval by the Ministry for Ownership Transformation or MPW), and those whose Article 19 liquidation has been initiated by their Founding Organ. At the end of 1995 the relative weights of the three categories was 26.8 per cent, 33.2 per cent and 40 per cent (see also *Table 6.2*, from MPW, 1996, whose data have been slightly revised by the Ministry with respect to those in *Table 6.1*).

Third, *all Polish privatization tracks involved some form, often very significant, of employee ownership.* This unexpected and important feature of privatization in Poland, replicated almost everywhere else in transition economies except for the Czech and Slovak republics, is the object of this chapter, reviewing the modes and reasons for employee ownership (Section 2), the implications predicted by theory (Section 3), actual performance (Section 4) and problems and prospects (Section 5).

---

[3] By the end of 1995, out of all enterprises privatized under Article 37, 18.8% were sold (mostly quick sales of bad enterprises otherwise subject to Article 19 liquidation); 5.6 % were contributed to new companies; 68.6% were leased and the remaining 7% used a mixture of these methods.

[4] At the initiative of either creditors or the debtor enterprise, in case of actual or prospective inability to service outstanding debt.

2 EMPLOYEE OWNERSHIP: MODES AND MOTIVES

Employees of enterprises privatized following the 'indirect' or 'capital' track were offered 20 per cent of capital equity at half price, subject to a maximum of one year's wage; this was later transformed into a 10 per cent free share, subsequently raised to 15 per cent. Moreover, four such enterprises were the object of managers' and employees' buy-outs (MEBOs). In general 15 per cent of the capital of state enterprises privatized through mass privatization, as well as other commercialized enterprises, is reserved to employees (and in some cases also to farmers and fishermen who had a contractual relation with the enterprise).

'Direct' privatization, sometimes called 'restructuring' privatization, also led to employee ownership. By the end of 1994 nine enterprises were sold/leased to employees and managers under Article 19 liquidation, but the most common channel for employee ownership was Article 37 liquidation, which turned out to be the single fastest privatization track (Gomulka and Jasinski, 1994). Typically these MEBOs were management-led, rather than pure employee or management buy-outs (Filatotchev et al., 1996, p. 68). Out of a total of 140 enterprises sold under Article 37, employees became sole owners of nine enterprises and dominant shareholders in another 20 (Filatotchev et al. 1996, p. 72). Mostly, however, MEBOs took the form of a lease-purchase agreement, or rather a lease with an option to purchase, by a company established by at least 50 per cent of employees; ownership would be transferred after cumulative rentals matched the stipulated capital value and interest. 'Being the least conflictual, this [employee leasing] was the most frequent form of direct privatization. To the end of 1995 788 enterprises followed this track, corresponding to 68.6 per cent of directly privatized enterprises' (MPW, 1996, p. 24).

The most significant aspect of these MEBOs is credit, both by 'Founding Organs' agreeing on delayed payments, and by others for the provision of employees' initial downpayment of 20 per cent of the book value of the enterprise. Apart from employee savings, this downpayment was financed from a variety of sources: banks and non-bank financial intermediaries (such as venture capital firms), credit from enterprise own funds, special enterprise funds set up to support employee ownership.[5]

In general, the sectors more significantly affected by MEBOs and other forms of employee ownership have not been those which required restructuring most badly, such as mining, metallurgy and power generation, but instead those more traditionally favourable to employee ownership and participation, such as construction, trade and services (Jarosz, 1994a and b;

---

[5] Apparently 30 per cent of initial finance came from such special funds (Filatotchev et al., 1996, from a study of 142 companies reported in *Zycie Gospodarcze*, No. 14, 1994).

Table 6.2 also provides some indication of sectoral trends, incomplete due to excessive aggregation of the industrial sector).

Polish experiences with employee ownership match those of most transition economies. The last thing that the new post-communist leaders everywhere – from Balcerowicz to Gaidar – wished to promote was precisely the emergence of significant forms of employee ownership. This was reminiscent of Yugoslav self-management, Western socialist programmes and the search for a 'Third Way' – intermediate between straight capitalism and the old Soviet-type system – which they firmly rejected. Thus in 1990 the Polish Privatization Minister Krzysztof Lis actually wrote to the British Embassy complaining that the support given by the British Know How Fund to employees' companies was against Polish government policy (Kowalik, 1994). In June 1991 Leonid Grigoryev and Evgeny Yasin regarded the birth of an employee-controlled economy as one of the dangers of voucher privatization (quoted in Sutela, 1994). The Russian Privatization Minister Anatoly Chubais (1993) stressed that the Russian government was strongly opposed to any privatization procedures that would imply a give-away of enterprise shares to insiders. At the Davos Forum of March 1994 Grigory Yavlinsky could refer to Russian mass privatization, dominated by employee and managerial ownership, as 'a form of socialization'.

After all, wage employment – as opposed to workers' ownership/ entrepreneurship, whether full or partial – was one of the few features of a market economy that was already in place under the old system. All that was needed to turn the existing near-market for labour[6] into a genuine market was to remove de-facto 'job rights protection' (entitlements to existing jobs, which were never a legal right and therefore could be removed without any change in legislation) and create large-scale unemployment in order to discipline wage demands and introduce flexibility in labour redeployment. In spite of free trade unions, collective bargaining, income policies and social pacts, sooner or later this was done, or is being done, practically everywhere.

Yet significant, large-scale, unexpected forms of employee ownership emerged in the transition, with few exceptions such as the former

---

[6] Even at the height of Stalinism state enterprises had to offer a wage level and structure matching their labour demands; they were subject to wage-bill ceilings but had a fair amount of flexibility in their wage policy, through the grading of jobs and of employees and through fringe benefits as well as in wage-fixing. The difference with respect to capitalism was primarily in the state of the labour market, i.e. the full and often over-full employment which prevailed in the centrally planned economy. While undoubtedly consistent with government policies, this was obtained as a by-product of 'tight' or 'taut' planning, i.e. endemic excess demand for goods and services at administered prices fixed below market-clearing levels, rather than as a result of specific measures of employment creation and protection. Apart from full/over-full employment, the wage contract in the traditional Soviet-type economy was basically the same as in the market economy.

Czechoslovak Federal Republic – in spite of its pre-War tradition and the impressive intellectual input of Jan and Jaroslav Vanek.[7] Partly this unexpected development was the result of public policy measures forced on the new governments by the need to implement a quick and smooth transition, partly it happened by default (for employee ownership in the transition, see Smith, 1993; Schaffer, 1996).

Employee ownership had to be introduced for a variety of reasons:

i)   To reverse the effects of earlier attempts at reforming the old system that had introduced employee self-management, notably in Poland and to a smaller extent in Hungary (of course in addition to Yugoslavia; in Romania self-management had been formally introduced but had gone nowhere).
      Paradoxically these earlier attempts at reform became an obstacle to subsequent transition, which could only be overcome by converting self-management into co-ownership. Privatization of state enterprises with self-management provisions required employees to surrender their 100 per cent entitlement to, say, 20 per cent of property rights (that part of property rights that involved the right to appoint and dismiss managers, to use and control capital, and the right to appropriate some of the results). For them to do so willingly employees had to be given instead, say, 20 per cent of full property rights (including the entitlement to any increase in capital value and the free disposal of capital, which they did not have before).
ii)   As a natural consequence of transition, employee ownership was also introduced with the transformation of former pseudo-co-operatives (public sector co-operatives) into genuine co-operatives run by elected officials and independent from central organs; this was an early development in the Polish transition (which are not considered here).
iii) To win over employee support for the transition in spite of concern for its short-run adverse effects on real wages and on mass unemployment.

In addition, unintended employee ownership also happened, by default, given:

a)   the low and often negative value (at the ruling fixed wage rates but not for more flexible participatory earnings) of some state enterprises for which there could not have been other takers. In Polish parlance this is

---

[7] See Kotrba, Chapter 4 in this volume. On general trends in other transition economies see the other contributions to this volume; see also Estrin (1994), and particular chapters by Gomulka and Jasinski on Poland, Carlin on Germany, Ben-Ner and Montias on Romania, Canning and Hare on Hungary, Bim et al. on Russia; see also Lissovolik (1995).

the case of enterprises 'liquidated' under Article 37 of the Privatization Law, which, otherwise, would have been liquidated for insolvency under Article 19 of the old Act on State Enterprises.

b)   the shortage of domestic capital, which placed employees (especially in view of their inside information) in a good position with respect to domestic outsiders, while alternative external buyers frequently evoked xenophobic reactions; and

c)   employees' and managers' natural inclination, in the absence of information about other enterprises and other localities, simply to automatically select the one which they knew best and was most important for their livelihood, or, at most, enterprises in the same locality – what Peter Murrell (1994) calls the 'balkanization of ownership'. In Poland this was a much less important factor than in those transition economies – like Russia – where mass privatization vouchers could be used to buy an interest in one's enterprise on privileged terms.

3 THEORETICAL PREDICTIONS

From theoretical literature on various forms of employee ownership a number of ready-made predictions can be drawn which will be listed here before reviewing their verification in the Polish case (Section 4).

In general the acquisition of a non-controlling interest by managers and employees in their own enterprises can be regarded as a positive development which encourages productivity, better labour relations, economic democracy; the diffusion of employee ownership is encouraged in the European Community (Uvalic, 1991). The acquisition of a *controlling* interest, however, is capable of having devastating effects on earnings, employment, efficiency and restructuring.

First, employees may use their controlling power to maintain employment levels higher than those compatible with profit maximization at the going wage rate. When this happens workers will be dismissed only if their wages are higher than the value of their average product, not necessarily if wages are higher than the value of their marginal product. On the positive side, there will be a lower unemployment level than otherwise, as a result of what is effectively a form of work-sharing within employee-controlled enterprises. On the negative side, such work-sharing at the microeconomic level will be less efficient than economy-wide work-sharing, because there will be no tendency for the value of labour's marginal product to be equalized throughout the economy; indeed employees might be kept on even when their marginal product is negative.

Second, employees may use their controlling power to raise earnings (including fringe benefits in kind, both individual and collective) above the going wage rate to the point of bringing profits down to zero or even incurring losses, eating up equity capital right down to the point of bare solvency, that is, of zero capital value of the enterprise – even if budget constraints are hard (if they are not, losses may be inflicted also on suppliers). Other shareholders can be effectively disenfranchised and expropriated. No additional equity capital will be available from outside on that basis; the enterprise will have to rely on internal finance for its growth, and naturally its viability will be limited to the sectors or techniques with less than average risk, size or capital per man.

Capacity restructuring, if any, will be much slower than otherwise, in the short run because of obstacles to labour shedding, in the medium to long run because of lower self-financed investment, lower access to loans and no access to external equity capital. If the resulting trade-offs between employment, efficiency and capacity restructuring – which ultimately involve a trade-off between lower short-term social costs and higher cost and longer duration of necessary restructuring – were actually acceptable to governments, all would be well in the best of all possible worlds. The trouble is that such trade-offs are uncontrollable and unpredictable, and therefore unlikely to coincide with government preferences; they are the result of an *absence* of government policy, without the justification of a laissez-faire approach, because such phenomena are policy-induced and interfere with market processes rather than being their natural result.

The probability of such adverse implications of employee ownership is not an increasing function of the degree of their ownership and/or control. Nuti (1995) has shown that such adverse implications are the 'catastrophic' consequence of *a controlling interest being exercised – whether individually or collectively – by those employee-shareholders who individually hold a share of equity capital smaller than their share in wage labour.* Only those employee-shareholders, in fact, gain more as employees from higher wages and continued employment than they lose as shareholders; other employee-shareholders have no incentive to behave any differently from other shareholders.

Predicting what might happen in a given enterprise with employee ownership thus meets considerable difficulties. First, whether or not a given share of the votes is a controlling interest is not always known a priori: over 50 per cent of the votes may not be enough if the vote is dispersed among disinterested holders, while considerably less than 50 per cent may be sufficient to exercise control when the rest of the votes are dispersed or disinterested; in other words, a potential controlling interest may remain unused. Second, available information about share distribution is never related to earnings distribution, in the only way that would indicate whether employee ownership can make a difference, even potentially. As far as one can see, no empirical investigation to date – East or West – has collected information about the relative size of individual employee shares in equity and in earnings. *For both reasons, we should expect empirical studies of enterprises with significant employee ownership to be fairly inconclusive.*

In these conditions the best we can do is to venture some plausible conjectures. First, since as a rule managers are bound to hold higher individual shares than other employees, and enjoy incentives unrelated (or indeed negatively related) to the level of earnings of other employees, managerial holdings are best excluded from aggregate employee shareholdings for the purposes of assessing whether they can amount to a controlling interest diverting the company away from profit maximization.

Second, more generally, the higher the concentration of employee share ownership, the less likely it is that an enterprise with substantial employee ownership will behave differently from otherwise equivalent enterprises.

Third, in the course of time the employee-controlled enterprise is bound to easily revert to an ordinary company, when a sufficient number of employee-shareholders raise their equity stake over their share in total earnings, or cease to be employees, or shareholders.[8]

It should be stressed that the problems that might arise with an employee-owned enterprise are the same that would arise with shareholders who have another stake in the company other than equity, for example as suppliers, buyers, creditors, debtors, competitors, etc. (see Nuti, 1995). At the same time, such problems should not be confused with those of the standard co-operative or self-managed firm, where members are not full co-owners but only share the right to use enterprise capital and to appropriate net value added. The only features co-operatives and employee-owned enterprises have in common are a greater suitability to activities characterized by a lower than average capital intensity, riskiness and enterprise size, and a restricted access to risk capital. Otherwise employee-owned enterprises, unlike co-operatives or self-managed enterprises, do not have an incentive to restrict employment, to over-exploit a monopoly position, to respond sluggishly and possibly 'perversely' to price changes, to distribute rather than reinvest profits or to exhibit a bias for labour-saving projects (see Nuti, 1992).

4 ACTUAL PERFORMANCE

Evidence on the impact of employee ownership on actual enterprise performance in Poland is practically limited to MEBOs, since other forms of

---

[8] Unless employee-shareholders happen to sell their stock to employees who still fail to reach an equity stake at least as high as their share in earnings – a fairly contrived supposition.

privatizations have led to weaker forms of employee ownership, fairly uniformly distributed among privatized state enterprises at the time of privatization and not yet sufficiently diversified. Neither standard Polish classification (exemplified in *Tables 6.1* and *6.2*), nor major studies of Polish privatization such as Belka et al., 1994, single out enterprises characterized by significant employee ownership. Nevertheless a number of empirical studies are available on Polish MEBOs: Jarosz, 1994a and b; Szomburg, 1994; Estrin et al., 1994 (a comparative study of an enterprise sample from Poland, Hungary and Czechoslovakia); Rapacki, 1995; see also Estrin, 1996; Filatotchev et al., 1996; Woodward 1996.

Profitability of Polish MEBO enterprises appears to have been relatively better (though not very significantly) than that of other enterprises, whether otherwise privatized, or still in Treasury ownership, or in the traditional state sector. Thus in 1994 MEBOs recorded a profit rate on current costs of 7.4 per cent as opposed to 7.2 per cent for capital privatization, 6.2 per cent for Treasury-owned enterprises and 5.1 per cent for the public sector as a whole. Net profit margins bear identical relationships, correspondingly 3.7 per cent, 2.9 per cent, 2.8 per cent, 2.5 per cent (Rapacki, 1995).

It would be premature to conclude, from these data, that Polish employee-owned firms are more efficient than residual state enterprises or traditional private firms. First there is generalized consensus that the higher margin is due not to MEBOs' better performance but to the fact that MEBOs were self-selected by employees precisely on the basis of their prospective cash flow being sufficiently attractive (Rapacki, 1995; Estrin, 1996; Filatotchev et al., 1996). Indeed, gross mark-ups differ significantly, being much higher for MEBOs, presumably in order to enable them to bear the burden of lease/purchase costs. Second, on average the performance of MEBO companies deteriorated over time; the number of loss-making enterprises rose from 4.4 per cent in 1991 to 13.2 per cent in 1992 (see Filatotchev et al., 1996). Third, there was considerable variability in such firms' performance, from the four very successful firms now listed in the Warsaw Stock Exchange to seven leased firms which went bankrupt before the end of 1994. By and large the more successful have been medium-sized (over 300 employees) industrial enterprises less exposed to competition, whereas small firms (under 100 employees) operating in a very competitive environment such as trade have experienced severe difficulties (Filatotchev et al., 1996; Jarosz, 1994a and b; Szomburg, 1994; on the employment size distribution of privatized enterprises, see *Table 6.3*).

In the MEBO samples available, wages appear to have initially risen faster than in similar firms, only to be more contained than average in subsequent periods. Contrary to expectations, employment has been considerably more flexible than in other state firms, whether privatized or not, and in the economy as a whole, also falling faster than prior to privatization (although often employment fell significantly immediately before privatization). The highest wage increases have been obtained in the enterprises that experienced the largest employment decline (Jarosz, 1994a and b; Filatotchev et al., 1996). This combination of employment, wage levels and trends, suggests that budget constraints have hardened just as in other privatized firms (which is not a surprise because they have hardened also in state enterprises, see Belka et al., 1994); that causality may have gone from labour shedding to higher wages, rather than the other way round; that employee control – if present – has not dominated wage and employment policy, apart from a possible initial over-generosity which may have been due to an accommodating managerial attitude rather than to opportunism by employee-shareholders.

Investment in the MEBO enterprises was generally lower than in similar enterprises, due to the burden of lease payments, high interest and the inability to offer enterprise assets as collateral before the ownership transfer (see Jarosz, 1994a and b). Financial institutions appear to have been aware of the greater risk of lending to enterprises controlled by insiders (see the previous section): apparently the nine main Polish commercial banks usually rated exclusive insider ownership as a greater risk than partial ownership with foreign or other outsider participation (Solarz, 1994).

5 PROBLEMS AND PROSPECTS

Unresolved problems of employee ownership in Poland, especially for its stronger version of MEBOs, include governance conflicts, financial constraints to growth, institutional instability. Prospects for a further growth of employee shareholding in Poland are poor.

Governance problems here concern not so much, or not only, owners' control over managers, but the resolution of possible conflicts between those shareholders who are also employees or managers and other shareholders who are not. The government, even when retaining an interest as lessor, seems unsuitable to resolve these conflicts, since the lease or sale has occurred precisely because of its earlier inability to exercise effective control. The best solution is perhaps the reduction of the total share held by small insiders; a recent proposal to make at least 20 per cent of the capital to outside investors (Filatotchev et al., 1996, p. 82) is a move to add an external voice and reduce the weight of all insiders, but does not discriminate between small and large inside shareholders and, consequently, does not go far enough.

Access to finance, both for funding a MEBO and financing subsequent investment, is particularly difficult and costly. From the point of view of externally financing a MEBO, 'the appropriate candidate for such a transaction is an enterprise in a mature industrial sector, with stable and significant cash flow and with low investment needs' (Filatotchev et al., 1996, p. 79); other enterprises are much less attractive candidates. Internal investment finance is greatly squeezed by the financial burden of leasing, exceptionally heavy in spite of privileged interest rates, owing to the exceptionally high, nominal and real, basic interest rates in the transition in general and in Poland in particular (see Nuti, 1996). External finance – as noted above – is discouraged by the inability to offer enterprise assets as collateral before the ownership transfer which only occurs at the end of the purchase-lease agreement. Here it should not be difficult to transfer ownership after cumulative payments have covered, say, half of the enterprise capital value, after which point the value of employees' equity stake should be sufficient to raise and secure a matching amount of external finance (a MPW proposal reducing to one third the minimum repayment sufficient to transfer ownership should be enacted in the near future).

There is not only an a priori presumption (noted above in Section 3) but also empirical evidence, that a controlling employee ownership is a tendentially unstable institution. *Table 6.4* for Poland and, even more so, *Table 6.5* for Russia, clearly demonstrate how the pattern of ownership both shifts from insiders to outsiders, and becomes more concentrated among insiders. As small employee-shareholders cease to be small (relatively to their share in labour earnings), or employees (through retirement or turnover), or shareholders (through sales to outsiders), the employee-controlled enterprise will tend to behave as an ordinary capitalist enterprise with only the small though non-negligible net advantages from employee participation. Partly these trends are affected by limitations to share tradability, with pre-emption rights by insiders and the need for transfers to outsiders to be approved by managements and other enterprise organs; but share liquidity naturally increases with the termination of employment. Ultimately, '. . . buy-outs, which have been a highly pragmatic means of effecting initial privatization, increasingly need to be viewed as a *transitory form of organization*' (Filatotchev et al., 1996, emphasis added).

Table 6.4 Change in ownership structure in Polish enterprises leased by employees.

Type of owner	Average holding end-1991 (%)	Average holding mid-1993 (%)
Employees	75.4	66.9
Managers	9.8	12.0
Outside investors	14.8	21.1

Source: Jarosz, 1994b; from Filatotchev et al., 1996.

Table 6.5 Shareholders by ownership type in Russian joint-stock companies (per cent of equity, 1994–95).

	April 1994	Dec. 1994	March 1995	June 1995	June 1996 forecast
Insiders (total) of which:	62	60	60	56	51
employees	53	49	47	43	35
directors	9	11	13	13	16
Outsiders (total) of which:	21	27	28	33	45
large	11	16	17	22	32
small	10	11	11	11	13
Government	17	13	12	11	4
Total	100	100	100	100	100

Source: RF State Committee for Property Management, 1995; from: Mizobata, 1996.

From several view points – suitability for external financing of MEBOs, sectoral and size suitability – employee ownership does not appear to be a universal solution, in Poland as anywhere else. The downside of its high initial incidence and rate of completion in Poland is the current low rate of new starts; potential candidates and takers have been virtually exhausted. The direct privatization track in general and MEBOs in particular are now regarded in Poland as a 'dead end' (Monkiewicz, 1996). More promising developments in current privatization policies in Poland are represented by generalized commercialization, debt–equity swaps, linking privatization with pension fund reform, raising revenue for the state budget (which in the past has meant capital privatizations with increasing participation of foreign buyers)[9] – rather than the further development of MEBOs and other forms of employee ownership.

REFERENCES

Aslund, A. and R. Layard (eds) (1993), *Change of Economic System in Russia*, London.
Belka, M., S. Estrin, M. Shaffer, I.J. Singh (1994), 'Enterprise adjustment in Poland: evidence from a survey of 200 firms', *LSE–CEP Working Paper* No. 658, London.

---

[9] On the increasing importance of privatization revenue see *Table 6.1*. In 1995 two-thirds of such revenue came from foreign buyers (see OECD, 1996).

Ben-Ner, A. and J.M. Montias (1994), 'Economic system reforms and privatization in Romania', in Estrin (1994).

Bim, A.S., D.C. Jones and T. Weisskopf (1994), 'Privatization in the former Soviet Union and the new Russia', in Estrin (1994).

Blommestein, H. and M. Marrese (eds) (1991), *Transformation of Planned Economies: Property Rights reform and macroeconomic stability*, OECD, Paris.

Canning, A. and P. Hare (1994), 'The privatization process-economic and political aspects of the Hungarian approach', in Estrin (1994).

Carlin, W. (1994), 'Privatization and de-industrialization in East Germany', in S. Estrin (ed.), 1994.

Chubais, A. (1993), 'Main issues of privatization in Russia', in Aslund and Layard (eds) 1993.

Daviddi, R. (ed.) (1995), *Property rights and privatization in the transition to a market economy. A comparative review*, Maastricht, EIPA.

Earle, J. S. and S. Estrin (1995), 'Employee ownership in Transition', in Gray et al. (1995).

Estrin, S. (ed.) (1994), *Privatization in Central and Eastern Europe*, Longman Group UK, Harlow.

Estrin, S. (1996), 'Privatization in Central and Eastern Europe', LBS and CEP–LSE, London.

Estrin, S., A. Gelb and I. Singh (1994), 'Shocks and adjustments by firms in transition: a comparative study', LSE/LBS/World Bank, March.

Filatotchev, I., I. Grosfeld, J. Karsai, M. Wright, T. Buck (1996), 'Buy-outs in Hungary, Poland and Russia: governance and finance issues', *Economics of Transition*, Vol. 4(1), 67–88.

Frydman, R., E. S. Phelps, A. Rapaczynski and A. Schleifer (1993), 'Needed mechanisms of corporate governance and finance in Eastern Europe', *Economics of Transition*, Vol. 2, June 1993, 171–208.

Gomulka, S. and P. Jasinski (1994), 'Privatization in Poland 1989–1993: policies, methods and results', in Estrin (ed.), 1994.

Gray, C., R. Frydman and A. Rapaczynski, (1995), *Corporate governance in transitional economies*, World Bank, Washington.

Jarosz, M. (ed.) (1994a), Employee-owned companies in Poland, PAN–ISP, Warsaw.

Jarosz, M. (ed.) (1994b), Pracownicze Spolki Leasingujace, MPW, Warsaw.

Jones, D. and J. Svejnar (eds.) (1992), *Advances in the Economic Analysis of Participatory and Labour-Managed Firms*, Vol. 4, 1992, JAI Press, Greenwich and London.

Kowalik, T. (1994), 'The social costs of liberalization and privatization in Poland' (mimeo), Warsaw.

Lissovolik, B. (1995), 'Special features of Russian privatization: causes and consequences', in R. Daviddi (ed.), 1995.

Mizobata, S. (1996), 'Characteristics of capitalism in Russia', CREES, Birmingham University.

Monkiewicz, J. (1996), 'W poszukiwaniu strategii przeksztalcen wlasnosciowych', mimeo, Warsaw.

MPW – Ministry of Property Transformations (1996), *Dynamika Przeksztalcen Wlasnosciowych*, No. 27, Warsaw.

Murrel, P. (1994), 'Peremptory privatization', American Economic Association, Annual Conference, Boston, 3–5 January.

Nuti, D.M. (1991), 'Privatization of socialist economies: general issues and the Polish case', in H. Blommestein and M. Marrese (eds.), 1991, 51–68.

Nuti, D.M. (1992), 'Traditional cooperatives and James Meade's Labour–Capital Discriminating Partnerships', in D. Jones–J. Svejnar (eds..), 1992, 1–26

Nuti, D.M. (1994), 'Mass privatization: costs and benefits of instant capitalism', *CISME–LBS Working Papers* No. 9, London, also in R. Daviddi (ed.), 1995.

Nuti, D.M. (1995), 'Corporate governance et actionnariat des salaries', *Economie Internationale* No. 62.

Nuti, D.M. (1996), 'Inflation, interest and exchange rates in the transition', *Economics of Transition*, vol. 4(1), 137–158.

OECD (1996), *Poland Survey 1996*, Paris.

Pagano, U. and R.E. Rowthorn (eds.) (1996), *Democracy and Efficiency in the Economic Enterprise, Routledge Studies in Business Organization and Networks*, London and New York.

Rapacki, R. (1995), 'Privatization in Poland: performance, problems and prospects – a survey article', *Comparative Economic Studies*, Vol. 37 No. 1 Spring, 57–75.

Rapacki, R. and S. J. Linz (1992), 'Privatization in transition economies: Case study of Poland', *Econometric and Economic Theory Papers*, No. 9011, Department of Economics, Michigan State University.

Schaffer, M. (1996), 'Worker participation in socialist and transitional economics', in U. Pagano and R.E. Rowthorn, 1996.

Schliwa, R. (ed.) (1994), *Bottom-up privatization, finance and the role of employers' and workers' organisations in the Czech Republic, Hungary, Poland and Slovakia*, ILO, Geneva.

Smith, S. C. (1993), 'Employee ownership in privatization in developing and reforming countries', George Washington University, April.

Solarz J. (1994), 'The financial sector and bottom-up privatization', in Schliwa (ed.) (1994).

Sutela, P. (1994), 'Insider privatization in Russia: speculations on systemic change', *Review of Economies in Transition–Idantalouksien Katsauksia*, No. 1, Bank of Finland, 5–26.

Szomburg, J. (1994), 'Prywatyzacja w trybie leasingu', IBGR, Gdansk.

Uvalic, M. (1991), *The PEPPER Report: Promotion of Employee Participation in Profits and Enterprise Results in the Member States of the European Community*, revised edition, *Social Europe*, Supplement No. 3.

Woodward, R. (1996), 'Management–Employee Buyouts in Poland', *Studies and Analyses* No. 69, CASE–Centre for Social and Economic Research, Warsaw.

7. Employee Share-ownership in Romania: The Main Path to Privatization

Costea Munteanu

1 INTRODUCTION

Perhaps in no other country in Central and Eastern Europe has privatization based on employee share-ownership become as popular as it has in Romania. On the other hand, in no other country has the method adopted generated more debate.

The statistical importance of privatization by means of employee share-ownership – which in Romania in almost every case has taken the form of the MEBO or Management–Employee Buy-out – is indisputable: by December 1995, out of more than 1,400 companies which had been privatized, 98 per cent had utilized the MEBO method.[1] These enterprises employ approximately 500,000 employees and represent 14% of the whole equity capital of all the state-owned companies which are to be privatized in Romania.

Although it is the most widespread method, the MEBO is also the most disputed. No other legal privatization method – public auction, public offering, direct negotiation or mass privatization – has given rise to more polemic (see next section). Support for the MEBO came especially from members of parliament and the directors of state-owned companies, while some high government officials were against it. Expert opinion is divided, with a preponderance in favour of those emphasizing its disadvantages over its advantages.

---

[1] Another less frequent form of privatization on the basis of employee share-ownership (involving approximately 150 companies) is the sale of shares on the basis of a public offering. In this case, the employees of the company concerned are granted preferential terms in the first round of the public offering: 10% of the shares are offered to employees at a 10% discount.

2 THE PRIVATIZATION PROCESS IN ROMANIA

2.1 Overview

The Romanian authorities have chosen an approach to privatization which acknowledges both the right of citizens to own private property and the state's need to derive revenue from the privatization process. The Romanian legislation stipulates the following:

- The distribution to each Romanian citizen of a share in 30% of Romania's 6,300 companies. This process began in 1992 with the distribution of the so-called Certificates of Ownership (COs), and ended in 1995 with the distribution of the Nominative Privatization Coupons (NPCs) in five Private Ownership Funds (POFs) which had previously received 30% of the equity capital of the share companies.
- The eventual sale of the State Ownership Fund's (SOF) 70% interest in these companies. This goal is to be accomplished by the sale of assets and/or shares; both employees and investors (Romanian and foreign) will be entitled to participate in these sales.

2.2 Legal and Institutional Framework

The process of privatizing Romania's state-owned companies has taken place in three major phases:

1) the conversion of state-owned enterprises into share companies;
2) the allotment of a 30% interest in the capital of these share companies to eligible Romanian citizens;
3) the sale of the unallocated 70% to Romanian and/or foreign investors.

The first step, the conversion of state enterprises into share companies with share capital and autonomous public enterprises ('Régies autonomes' or RAs), was undertaken according to the law on the restructuring of state-owned enterprises (*Act No. 15 of 1990*). The share companies are estimated to represent 53% of all enterprises and 47% of the RAs; about 6,300 share companies and 390 RAs were established. The RAs comprise strategic sectors of the national economy, including the defence industry, rail and urban transport, energy, natural gas and mining. Although these sectors are currently designated to remain in the hands of the state, the particular enterprises included in this category are subject to review.

The second step, the transfer of a 30% ownership to eligible Romanian citizens, is addressed in both the law on company privatization (*Act No. 58 of*

1991) and the law for the acceleration of the privatization process (*Act No. 58 of 1995*). This legislation provides free of charge for all Romanian citizens bearer Certificates of Ownership (COs) and non-bearer Nominative Privatization Coupons (NPCs) representing the unallocated 30% holding of the share capital of the share companies. *Act No. 15 of 1990* also created the National Agency for Privatization, the entity which is responsible for preparing, organizing and co-ordinating the privatization process and the CO and NPC programme.

The third step, regarding the sale of the 70% interest in share companies which were not distributed to individual Romanian citizens is the responsibility of the State Ownership Fund (SOF). This step is also comprised in both *Act No. 58 of 1991* and *Act No. 55 of 1995*.

The chronology of the combined privatization programme by vouchers (COs and NPCs) and by sale has been as follows:

1)   five Private Ownership Funds were created in order to hold and manage the share company shares distributed to individual Romanian citizens;
2)   a sixth fund was created, the State Ownership Fund, in order to hold the state share in these companies and to co-ordinate the restructuring of larger enterprises;
3)   the allocation of share company shares to the five POFs and to the SOF;
4)   the distribution to individual eligible Romanians, free of charge, of COs (in 1992) and NPCs (in 1995) comprising the 30% holding in the share companies by the POFs;
5)   the introduction of general guidelines and procedures for the privatization of the SOF holding by the sale of shares (auctions, public offerings, direct negotiations, MEBO) or of assets;
6)   the free transfer of the shares against COs and NPCs; the process started on 1 October 1995 and is to be followed by the sale of shares for cash at auction once the free transfer has been carried out.

2.3 Employees' Share-ownership

The history of the MEBO in Romania began in March 1992 with a brief visit to Bucharest by a group of experts from the British Know How Fund. Their task was to analyse the ways and means of providing technical assistance with a view to the implementation of this privatization method in Romania. Two months later, a Romanian delegation including five company directors and six union leaders went to Great Britain in order to study a number of cases in which the MEBO method had been successfully applied. This exchange of visits had extremely positive consequences. On the one hand, highly influential Romanian newspapers and journals campaigned to popularize this method. On the other, the authorities realized that this method could be successfully implemented in Romania. The first results of this followed shortly afterwards: by means of the Privatization Law (*Act No. 58 of 1991*) – which includes direct negotiation among permissible privatization methods (the MEBO is a typical form of direct negotiation) – two of the Romanian companies whose directors had visited Great Britain within the framework of the Know-How Fund programme were already privatized by the end of the same year. The process was accelerated by means of the *Pilot Programme for Privatization* developed by the Romanian *National Agency for Privatization*; of the 22 companies which were included in the Pilot Programme (with equity capital of 13 billion lei, or approximately US$ 6 million and 18,500 employees), 15 companies were privatized through the sale of all the shares to the management and employees (MEBO).

Public recognition of the 'MEBO phenomenon' in Romania came later on with the establishment of the methodological norms concerning the standard procedure for the privatization of small companies by means of the sale of shares (usually known as the 'MEBO Procedure'). The MEBO method reached maturity when it was extended to the privatization of the medium-sized and large companies in *Act No. 77 of August 1994* (concerning the association of the employees and management of companies undergoing privatization and known as the 'MEBO Law').

Paradoxically, the completion of the legal framework for the implementation of the MEBO method coincided with a dramatic fall in the number of privatization cases utilizing this method. This was a direct consequence of the draft law concerning the acceleration of the mass privatization programme which the Government submitted for debate in September 1994. Without going into details, it is a special feature of privatization in Romania that mass privatization and privatization by the MEBO method are not complementary (in contrast, for example, to Russia). This explains why most privatizations using the MEBO method were registered before the middle of 1994; after this date, the method declined in importance. The available data show that over 400 companies have concluded privatization contracts with the Private Ownership Funds to which they belong using the MEBO method; surprisingly, they are also included on the list of companies to be included in the mass privatization programme. Normally, all these companies should have continued their privatization by the method already under implementation, namely the MEBO. Experts believe that their inclusion in the mass privatization programme constitutes a new turn in government policy for the purpose of hindering utilization of the MEBO method.

Despite the abovementioned 'incompatibility' between mass privatization and employee share-ownership by the MEBO method, the mass privatization programme may constitute a spontaneous and *sui generis* form of employee share-ownership. At present, a few months after *Act No. 55 of 1995* on the acceleration of the mass privatization process came into force, one of the most critical problems is the relationship between the employees and the company. The current data on the development of the process show that the solution preferred by the more than 3,900 companies which are included in the mass privatization programme is the so-called 'in-the-family' option (employee share-ownership). In many companies the managers have already issued questionnaires in order to find out if the workforce would be interested in buying the company with cash, certificates of ownership (COs) or nominative privatization coupons (NPCs). It is too early to draw conclusions in this connection, but the insistent manner in which managers try to convince employees to invest their financial resources in their companies is noticeable: certificates and coupons for up to 60% of the shares distributed free and cash for the rest of the shares which become private in this way. The acquisition of a stake with cash is regarded as the 'key' to employee and manager share-ownership because this is the only way in which insiders (management and employees) can obtain ownership of the company. An interesting indication of government encouragement of this kind of share-ownership is a recent ordinance granting financial facilities for the cash sale of shares. Although these facilities can be used by insiders and outsiders alike, they are intended to help employees who would otherwise not be in a position to purchase shares sold for cash (because the price is not established on the basis of demand and supply, but with reference to the book value of the company's assets). The downward trend experienced in recent months by the MEBO method could be counterbalanced by employee share-ownership through mass privatization.

It is important to understand that the predominance of the MEBO is due less to its consistency or to the advantages it offers than to the lack of interest in the other available methods (sale of assets, public offering, auction), and the hesitant and inconsistent manner in which the government has so far developed the mass privatization programme. In a context in which the privatization process overall is advancing extremely slowly,[2] the position of the MEBO method seems rather artificial.

A further explanation is the extreme volatility of Romanian politics. The MEBO method harmoniously combines a number of different (ideological) options from a wide range of political opinion. The Social Democrats and the Socialists – who are currently the strongest political forces – support this method because it allows employees to become involved in the management of their company. The Liberals also favour the MEBO because it constitutes

---

[2] It is important to point out that, after more than four years of privatization, private companies represent only 21.9% of all the companies which are to be privatized.

a rapid and simple way of diminishing the role of the state in the Romanian economy. On the other hand, employees prefer this method of privatization for the job security it seems to offer – at least in comparison with other privatization methods – and, again, because of the decision-making opportunities it makes available. In a larger perspective, the MEBO method appeals to employees because it is a means of counterbalancing the tendency of Romanian society to become divided into a small group of persons monopolizing capital ownership and wealth and a large and impoverished mass of employees (and unemployed). Management tends to be interested in the MEBO since it allows them the greatest degree of control after privatization. Finally, some leading economists take the view that an enterprise may be developed more effectively by insiders than by outside investors whose principal interest may well be to 'take-the-money-and-run'.

3 IMPLEMENTATION OF THE MEBO METHOD IN ROMANIA

3.1 Basic Premises

Two basic conditions must be met before a company may become the property of its management and employees. The first is profitability: a company should at least be able to survive in the marketplace. It should have an adequate management team and be able to produce goods or services for which demand exists reasonably efficiently. To this end, the company must present a realistic business plan (according to the 'methodological norms') or feasibility study (according to *Act 77 of 1994*).

Second, the company must exhibit the necessary 'will'. Management and employees must show a determination to take this large step and that they understand its implications. The law requires the establishment of an initiative group constituting the association of the employees' and the management. This association can function (that is, it can organize the constitutive general assembly) only if at least 30% of the company workforce has applied for membership.

3.2 Main Objectives

After meeting the first two conditions, the next step in the process of gaining possession of the company concentrates on the main objectives of privatization:

i)   A realistic business plan or feasibility study must be prepared which must include any necessary restructuring measures.

ii)   A proper valuation of the company must be made in order that the price
        may be agreed with the sellers (the State Ownership Fund and the
        Private Ownership Fund). This is politically delicate and technically
        complex. In fact, success or failure in setting a reasonable price can
        determine the course of the whole acquisition process and indeed the
        continued interest of the employees in buying the company. The
        evaluation process can be long and complex and so the law is very
        detailed on this point.

iii)   How the shares will be distributed and the 'democratic legitimacy' of
        the new company must be determined. In Romania, this is the main
        problem with MEBO privatization: the acquisition of the company by
        its employees will be successful only if all those involved are confident
        that their partners are good-willed. The law states that agreements
        between prospective shareholders on a range of matters – of which the
        distribution of the right to buy shares is perhaps the most important in
        the short term – must be correct and perceived as such.

iv)   A proper post-privatization relationship must be established between
        management and employees. The objective laid down in the MEBO law
        is that employee share-ownership should not obstruct the ability of the
        management to run the company efficiently. This is a familiar problem
        with companies at which employees are also shareholders with
        decision-making rights. Although this difficulty is clearly understood,
        the legal framework remains incomplete: the law does not stipulate that
        specific management–employee agreements must be signed before
        privatization of the company.

3.3 Advantages and Disadvantages

As we have already mentioned, privatization by way of management and
employee share-ownership has been employed in Romania largely in the case
of the small companies, using the standard method stipulated by the
'methodological norms'. These are the main positive effects expected from
promotion of the standard MEBO method:

- the enterprise's productive potential will be reactivated by improving
  management and encouraging effective workforce participation;
- the depletion of assets by theft, disuse, etc. will be halted;
- the illegal competition represented by the network of private companies
  created around state-owned companies and fraudulent use of their
  resources ('wild privatization') will be contained;
- domestic and foreign strategic investors who are more interested in doing
  business with a private company than with a state one will be attracted;

- employee shareholders will develop a mentality more appropriate to a market economy; it is also hoped that enterprises will establish training courses to educate the workforce in this regard;
- tension inside enterprises will be reduced by creating a framework for negotiation on the basis of the full representation of all interests and which could progressively improve social parameters according to the financial results of the company.

The potential disadvantages of the MEBO method stem from the way it has been designed and implemented. The most important shortcomings seem to be the following:

- it dissipates share-ownership, which very much complicates the task of post-privatization corporate governance;
- at least at the beginning, enterprises privatized in this way find it very difficult to finance the investments needed for restructuring;
- it is difficult either to buy or to sell shares in such enterprises, also with a view to obtaining the majority stake.

When the MEBO method was extended to cover medium-sized and large companies (by *Act 77 of 1994*, the so-called 'MEBO Law'), the advantages and disadvantages changed. The advantages of the MEBO method for medium-sized and large companies are as follows:

- the privatization process is more decentralized, it is simpler and more rapid, and administrative costs tend to be relatively low;
- the MEBO has been extremely popular in the case of small companies and the privatization of medium-sized and large companies should therefore be as transparent as possible;
- employee ownership could improve the company's incentive structure because of greater employee involvement in the decision-making process;
- the state may derive large revenues from privatization.

As far as disadvantages are concerned, the following points are worth mentioning:

- employees cannot buy the majority of shares in a medium-sized or large company;
- employee ownership itself is much more problematic in the case of larger enterprises. One of the main difficulties is the tendency of employee-owners to put their interests as employees above their interests as shareholders, particularly in respect of wage levels and lay-offs.

Besides, in Romania, in common with the rest of Central and Eastern Europe, employee-owners have at best limited access to capital, new markets, new technology and modern management, financial administration and marketing techniques, all of which are indispensable in medium-sized and large companies;

- very often the employee–management association is not in a position to pay back the loan taken out to buy out the company;
- secondary transactions could be hindered, delayed or reduced. The management could oblige employees to retain their shares by threatening them with redundancy.

3.4 Risk-taking

Needless to say, adoption of the MEBO privatization method entails a certain amount of risk. Under current Romanian circumstances, the survival and future prospects of a company depend on several important factors:

- the existence of a market for its products or services;
- the presence of a market-oriented management able to identify market needs and trends and willing to take the necessary restructuring, modernization and 'retechnologization' measures;
- the existence of financial means sufficient to implement at least the short-term restructuring and modernization programmes required by the market.

The post-privatization state of a company largely depends on the manner in which these three problems are dealt with. This is why the business plan already mentioned is so important. The plan should comprise an accurate estimation of the financial evolution of the company based on an analysis of the qualitative and quantitative requirements of the market and of the relevant costs. Under these circumstances, the major risk to which company insiders are exposed – especially in such an unstable and unpredictable economic environment – is the high probability that the initial estimations do not correspond to reality.[3]

---

[3] The dominant features of the present economic environment in Romania are the highly volatile character of the legal and institutional framework, the instability and unpredictability of the inflation rate in an emerging product and service market for which there is not enough data on the basis of which to plot its trends, and a labour market offering uncertain information about its real qualification level and about the evolution of the average level of wages in various branches and sectors.

4 THE LEGAL FRAMEWORK OF MEBO PRIVATIZATION

The relevant Romanian legislation defines the Management–Employee Buy-out as a method of buying all or at least the majority of the shares in a company by direct negotiation. The buyer is the employee and management association of the company in question, which is established for this purpose.

The current legal provisions pertaining to the MEBO have evolved over the last three years, and two distinct stages can be identified.

4.1 The Introduction of Privatization by the Sale of Shares (to Insiders as well as Outside Investors)

4.1.1 The ratification of *Act No. 58 of 1991* on company privatization represents the first part of this stage. According to this law – fundamental to Romanian privatization – there are two ways in which insiders can buy shares in the company which employs them:

- by setting up an employee and management association which enjoys preferential rights under the law: (i) when the shares are sold by public offering they can buy, for a limited period, up to 10% of the shares on sale at a discount of 10%; (ii) when the shares are sold by auction, they have the right to buy shares at a price at most 10% lower than the highest bid;
- by direct negotiation.

4.1.2 Government Decree No. 264 of 1992 ratifying the methodological norms concerning the sale of the shares in companies undergoing privatization before the establishment of the Private Ownership Fund (POF) and the State Ownership Fund (SOF). These norms allow an employee and management association to purchase a majority stake of shares in the following ways:

- by using their preferential rights under *Act No. 58*;
- by buying all or the majority of the company's shares by direct negotiation.

4.1.3 Act No. 114 of 1992 on the status of Private Ownership Funds. This law regulates the privatization of companies according to size (small, medium, large). As regards small companies, the law stipulates that a procedure for rapid and large-scale privatization by a standard method must be elaborated. At the same time, the law enables persons possessing certificates of ownership to exchange them for shares in privatized companies. In the case of small companies all the shares of which have been bought by the employees and the management and all the certificates of ownership owned by the latter may be used as means of payment up to a limit of 30% of the equity capital.

4.2 The Promulgation of Legislation Specific to the MEBO Method

By this means, Romania became one of the few countries to have elaborated specific legislation in this area (USA, Great Britain, France, Germany and, since 1992, Hungary).

4.2.1 The Methodological Norms No.1 of 1993 regarding the standard procedure for the privatization of small companies by sale of shares (the 'MEBO Procedure').

According to these norms, and in the absence of other legal provisions to the contrary, the employee and management association established with the aim of ensuring financial backing for the purchase of shares and for organizing the process, is a 'share-ownership pact' which is valid from the perspective of civil and commercial law.[4] In this context, for the first companies which became private using the MEBO method (within the Pilot Privatization Programme), as well as those companies which became private later on in accordance with the methodological norms of 1993, the advantages of the legal concept of the 'share-ownership pact' proved to be important:

- the establishment procedure is much simpler and excludes publicity. It is therefore cheaper and quicker;
- it gives the association a legal personality, a status which is particularly important in relation to the Private Ownership Funds, banks and other financial institutions.

4.2.2 Act No. 77 of 1994 concerning the employee and management associations of privatized companies (the 'MEBO Law').

Although the MEBO Procedure has offered certain advantages for consolidation of the MEBO method, it is still unclear in some places regarding (i) the establishment and functioning of the employee and management association, (ii) the extent to which each employee should contribute to the purchase of the shares and the relevant payment conditions, and (iii) the granting of fiscal advantages and payment facilities in order to encourage privatization using the MEBO method and to protect companies after privatization. Apart from the problems generated by these oversights, the strong parliamentary lobby in favour of extending the MEBO method to

---

[4] The share-ownership pacts are the result of the respective parties' free will and the law does not stipulate their legal form.

medium-sized and large companies forced through the adoption of the MEBO Law in August 1994.

The MEBO Law stipulates that the employees and managers who wish to buy the shares of their own company can organize associations. These associations have the status of a legal entity and involve managers and other employees interested in buying the shares of the state-owned company, as well as former employees. The principal organ of the association is the general assembly of its members and its main executive organ is the board of directors; the activities of the association are carried out in accordance with its bylaws. The association has the legal right to buy the shares of its members' company and enjoys some important privileges. The association is entitled to negotiate with the Private Ownership Fund (POF) to which the company is ascribed and with the State Ownership Fund (SOF),[5] and it concludes the following: the sales contract – after the price has been established by agreement and in accordance with a feasibility study – the initial payment, the distribution of instalments and the interest rate on the loan. The purchase of shares by the association can be performed either (a) on behalf of members who have subscribed to the shares and who pay the association for them (in cash or in exchange for certificates of ownership) or (b) on behalf of all its members, by buying shares which initially are not distributed to each member (payment by instalments facilitated by the SOF or by other credits contracted by the association). The shares which have been subscribed and paid for by individual members are transferred to them immediately; consequently, the members of the association have the right to vote at the annual general meeting in accordance with the number of shares they own. Furthermore, the shares bought by the association on behalf of all its members can serve as collateral for the loans that the association has taken out with the SOF, banks or other financial institutions. These shares are registered in the name of the association and are gradually distributed to their members in accordance with the amount repaid as instalments or for the reimbursement of the loans. The association has the right to vote at the general assembly of the company in accordance with its shares, as stipulated by the company contract. The dividends distributed by the company on shares bought by the association on behalf of all its members and still burdened by loans or unpaid instalments must be used to cover them. The company which was privatized by transferring shares to the employee and management association benefits throughout the period of repayment from a 50% profit tax reduction on its shares. The dividends corresponding to the shares acquired under the MEBO Law are tax-exempt for the period in question. Apart from the already

---

[5] As shareholders in the state company and sellers of the shares to the association, the POF in respect of 30% of the shares and the SOF in respect of 70%.

mentioned fiscal facilities, the employee and management association benefits directly from a range of credit facilities granted by the SOF. These offer the possibility to pay for the shares by instalments under the following circumstances:

•   an initial minimum advance of 20% of the price negotiated with the SOF;
•   the instalments should be paid within a minimum period of 5 years;
•   a negotiable annual interest rate of maximum 10%.[6]

Furthermore, the POF to which the privatized company is allotted under the terms of the MEBO Law must receive certificates of ownership from association members representing at least two-thirds of the 30% quota mentioned above, up to the value that had been agreed upon with it.

Although the conception and general principles of the MEBO Law are identical to those of the MEBO Procedure, the former includes a series of extensions, changes and new elements and sanctions in this way the completion of the difficult process of establishing specific MEBO legislation. While the MEBO Law is intended to act as substitute for the MEBO Procedure, it is worth comparing the two:

1)   Concerning the members of the employee and management association, the MEBO Law stipulates the extension of eligibility to former employees of the company and to pensioners whose last working place it was;
2)   As far as the size of the company is concerned, the MEBO Procedure stipulates that only small companies are appropriate for the employee share-ownership method, while the MEBO Law has no provision of the kind;
3)   While the MEBO Procedure stipulates the net book assets method as the most general way of valuing and negotiating the sale of shares, the MEBO Law introduces the notion of 'feasibility study';
4)   A new element in the MEBO Law relates to the criteria employed to distribute shares within the association. These criteria – length of service, position, wage, other considerations approved by the general meeting – bring into relief the concern for a hierarchy which takes into consideration the contribution in time to the development of the company.

Despite its extensions and improvements the MEBO Law also has several potential defects:

---

[6] The average interest rate has been between 50% and 60% in Romania over the last two years.

1) By extending the category of eligible participants, the law provides some degree of reparation to those who contributed for years to the development of the company. On the other hand, it also increases the number of passive shareholders (pensioners, former employees), who will probably be more interested in dividends than in reinvestment and so recapitalization.[7]

2) The MEBO Law makes so many important fiscal and financial facilities available to the company that individual financial involvement tends to become merely symbolic. Perhaps it would have been better if certain facilities had been conditioned by certain margins of profit reinvestment in the privatized company.

3) Finally, there is a certain overlap between the company management and the leadership of the employee and management association. Consequently, there is a risk that the management – which generally initiates and supports MEBO privatization – will be left out after the share sale has been concluded. At the same time, the existence of an important group of passive shareholders (pensioners and former employees) may tempt various other interest groups both inside and outside the company to seek to manipulate them, so generating prolonged (post-privatization) instability in the decision-making process.

On the other hand, as we have already mentioned, the establishment of a specific legal regime for the promotion of the MEBO Law in Romania (with the support of a large number of MPs) was followed, paradoxically, by a significant fall in the number of companies choosing this privatization method. The main reason for this was the constraints indirectly generated by the parallel launch of the government initiative to accelerate the mass privatization programme. In this way, far fewer companies have been privatized in accordance with the provisions of the MEBO Law than under the MEBO Procedure (Methodological Norms No.1 of 1993). In Section 5 we analyse the post-privatization evolution of companies privatized on the basis of the latter.

5 THE EFFICIENCY OF MEBOS

In the context of a hesitant, inconsistent and often incoherent government policy, the privatization process in Romania is still in a state of relative

---

[7] At present, large-scale decapitalization is the main problem faced by the majority of state companies in Romania.

Table 7.1 The post-privatization situation of 447 MEBO companies, Romania, December 1993–October 1994

Sector	Equity capital (billion lei)	Number of employees	Profit rate (%)	Degree of indebtedness (debt/total income)
Agriculture and food industry (94 firms)				
31.12.1993	51.7	29 601	6.28	0.14
01.10.1994	86.9	22 408	6.44	0.22
Industry (96 firms)				
31.12.1993	43.2	50 910	6.61	0.37
01.10.1994	72.9	47 484	9.05	0.56
Trade and tourism (33 firms)				
31.12.1993	11.7	6 325	4.62	0.73
01.10.1994	13.4	5 921	5.59	0.20
Civil engineering (58 firms)				
31.12.1993	11.1	27 109	8.43	0.25
01.10.1994	34.3	26 613	7.23	0.31
Transport (22 firms)				
31.12.1993	8.2	6 447	10.49	0.18
01.10.1994	28.1	5 991	9.36	0.26
Culture (5 firms)				
31.12.1993	0.4	363	3.04	0.20
01.10.1994	0.4	314	5.12	0.29
144 Firms of local importance				
31.12.1993	21.4	23 023	4.55	0.16
01.10.1994	37.7	21 598	5.27	0.24

Source: Data from the State Ownership Fund.

stagnation. Not even the recently initiated government programme to accelerate mass privatization – which has been widely commented upon by the media, but forcefully rejected by a large part of the political spectrum, business groups and expert opinion – seems to have the necessary force to relaunch privatization. Under these difficult circumstances, privatization based on employee share-ownership has made its own way and has until now been the most dynamic aspect of Romanian privatization.

Nevertheless, the relatively short period which has elapsed since a significant number of companies were privatized using the MEBO method does not allow a profound evaluation of the consequences nor, in a wider perspective, of the post-privatization evolution of the companies concerned. Moreover, few serious studies have been conducted on the post-privatization situation of these companies. This is why the comments and conclusions presented in this section should be regarded as preliminary and, inevitably, subjective.

5.1 Improved Performance according to the Statistics

The main conclusion the data offer us is the following: the changes that have taken place in the structure of share-ownership have led in a relatively short period to a noticeable improvement in the economic performance of the companies privatized by the MEBO method. These companies seem to be among the most profitable in Romania, some of them undergoing a quite remarkable transformation; export activity has increased as never before, production discipline has very much improved.

A survey of 447 MEBO companies concerning the main economic and financial indices for the first three quarters of 1994 (*Table 7.1*) leads to the following preliminary conclusions (Zaman, 1995):

- the profit rate has increased remarkably in industry, trade, tourism, culture and firms of local importance and has fallen slightly in civil engineering and transport;
- in all sectors the number of employees has fallen, which indicates that the MEBO method, instead of creating new jobs, initially leads to lay-offs (especially in the case of companies burdened with overemployment and bureaucracy);
- the degree of indebtedness increased in all cases with the exception of trade and tourism.

Another survey of 240 companies in civil engineering, ready-to-wear clothing, food, trade and furniture, one year after their privatization using the MEBO method, shows that for 232 companies turnover and profit have increased by 15–120%, for six companies the increase was 1–15%, and only in the case of two companies did these indicators fall, mainly because of conflicts between employees and management (Salagean, 1995).

Most of the companies which were privatized using the MEBO method managed to improve their economic performance in an extremely short time; this is not just surprising, it is quite remarkable. Needless to say, one of the principal aims of the Central and East European privatization process as a whole is to improve the economic performance of the privatized companies – the Romanian experience of privatization by means of employee share-ownership seems to be quite encouraging in this respect, at least up to now.

Nevertheless, the post-privatization period seems to be extremely complicated and stressful for MEBO-privatized companies and any final conclusions regarding its success or failure would be premature.

Any improvement in economic performance will be short-lived unless it is the product of a wholesale transformation of the company, and particularly of the mentality of the new employee- and manager-shareholders. From this point of view, the post-privatization development of MEBO-privatized companies has been mixed: some of the companies we studied have been very successful;[8] for many others, the post-privatization period – even if economic and financial performance has improved – has brought with it a series of internal and external challenges.

5.2 A Success Story in Romanian MEBO Privatization

The Romanian companies for which MEBO-type privatization has been a success, without doubt constitute a strong argument in favour of those who claimed from the outset that the Western experience of the MEBO method (especially in Great Britain and the USA) would also work for economies in transition. Analysis of the Romanian success stories confirms all the main claims of MEBO supporters:

- the main aim of MEBO privatization is to improve performance by giving the workforce a stake in the company;
- shareholders who are also employees are more inclined to support restructuring measures with a view to improving long-term productivity because they will benefit more from company longevity than from the making of a 'fast buck' – the individual stakes of shop-floor workers are likely to be insufficient to provide them with much cash income for many years to come;
- the bringing together of the shareholder and the union member in one person brings with it a new attitude to union negotiations: such negotiations will now take place in a wider perspective. The preservation of jobs for its own sake will yield considerable ground to a desire to utilize labour more efficiently with a view to improvements in productivity and quality.

---

[8] The analysis is based mainly on the data and information provided by a series of case studies made by various Romanian researchers or Romanian institutions and on information from the economic press. Some of these data were obtained from the incomplete results of a project in which we have participated, which consisted of a systematic analysis based on a survey of 66 Romanian companies privatized via the MEBO method. Unfortunately, logistic and financial difficulties have hindered completion of this project.

We carried out a case study of the company which was the 'pioneer' in the field of MEBO privatization in Romania. IPCT Bucharest was the first Romanian company to be privatized using the MEBO method. After the overthrow of the Ceaucescu regime in 1989, privatization was the only option for this design and research institute. In the middle of 1991, the company was included in the list of the first 30 enterprises to be privatized before the founding of the Private Ownership Funds and the State Ownership Fund; National Agency for Privatization experts suggested that the MEBO method be used. An algorithm was worked out to determine how shares in the institute should be allocated to its employees, the criteria being position in the institute, wages and length of service. A number of points was allotted to each of these criteria and a minimum allotment. The ratio between the maximum and the minimum number of points obtained by a single employee was 6.

Of the 300 institute employees, 241 bought shares. At present, 51% of these shares are owned by 46 employees, or 19% of the shareholders. Although it was at first agreed that shareholders who left the institute would sell their shares to it, later on they were allowed to retain them for an unlimited period. If an employee wishes to sell his shares, however, he must sell them to the company.

Since privatization, the institute has very much extended its activities and it even offers consulting services concerning the MEBO method.

> We are independent and our survival in this competitive world depends on us. I am very much in favour of this method. If the employees of a company under privatization wish to buy shares in it they should be given the opportunity. If I was asked, I would suggest that this method be applied particularly in the case of less successful enterprises. The state would benefit by getting rid of a company it would otherwise be obliged to support; the employees would benefit by being given an opportunity to procure their own survival. (General Manager, IPCT Bucharest)

At the insistence of the trade union at the institute, the sales contract which was negotiated with the National Agency for Privatization also stipulated measures ensuring some social protection for the employees: the institute could not introduce lay-offs for a period of two years. Since privatization, the strength of the union has decreased and many employees have given up union membership. The number of union members has been reduced to 40% of the workforce. The union has adjusted to the new circumstances and confines itself to industrial relations. As a consequence, union–management conflict has diminished: the two parties decided to work together to promote the interests of the researchers and designers.

'If the politicians wish to end the eternal conflict with the unions, they should facilitate the privatization of as many companies as possible using the MEBO method', suggested the union leader at IPCT Bucharest.

The example of this MEBO shows clearly that the typical features of privatization using employee and management share-ownership are also present in the Romanian experience:

- The acquisition of decision-making powers and the reduction of bureaucracy made possible the elaboration of business strategies which have already been implemented, leading to retechnologization, the working out of a marketing policy, and the introduction of fresh capital, and so on. As a consequence, the post-privatization restructuring of these companies was accelerated and the first signs emerged of a new attitude to work on the part of the workforce.
- Increased security and motivation and an enhanced ability to increase one's income by one's own efforts generated an atmosphere of competition among employees which benefits everyone. This has led to the differentiation of income according to individual contribution and to the elimination of equal profit distribution to all employees. Differentiation according to individual skills has forced employees to assume more personal responsibility.
- The management stake in the company has led to noticeable performance improvements and even the first signs of a genuine management policy.

5.3 Challenges for MEBO-privatized Companies

The mixed post-privatization fortunes of MEBO privatized companies are put into bold relief by the fact that the virtues which form the substance of the success stories become vices for the companies for which privatization – without necessarily failing – has led to some serious problems.

A 'quantitative' evaluation of the MEBO method – comparing the successful cases with the problematic ones – is not helpful; what matters most at this stage of post-privatization development (more than one year after the completion of privatization) is the *nature* of the problems encountered.

I have tried to group the difficulties of the post-privatization period into a few large categories.

5.3.1 The hostile reaction of the public sector represents the main external constraint; it has taken various forms:

- The company's account is blocked by the bank after privatization; the usual excuse is that private companies are subject to different regulations and conditions and that the situation must be resolved before normal service is resumed.

- Public sector suppliers are reluctant to continue working as before – the usual excuse in this case is that the orders of line departments and ministries allow the delivery of some products only according to allocation papers and that scarce products must first be supplied to state companies.
- Public central and local administrations become hostile.
- In some cases inspections are carried out either too frequently or for no reason at all by such institutions as the Finance Ministry, the Government Control Department and the Ministry of Internal Affairs (often not even in accordance with the relevant regulations).
- The Court of Registration delays registration of changes arising in respect of the share-ownership structure of private companies, their regulations and board of directors.

5.3.2 The post-privatization behaviour of the company also raises a range of problems, although not at every company. These include:

- Difficulties in fulfilling the sales contract: under the difficult economic circumstances of 1993–94 and due to the restrictive monetary policy of the National Bank of Romania, the employee and management associations at a number of companies found themselves unable to pay their loan instalments (for instance, the companies that were privatized under the Pilot Programme). Investment was also a major problem.
- Failure to progress in a highly unstable economic environment characterized by scarce and disorganized information. Some recently privatized companies adopted the same commercial strategies and procedures as their competitors, so wasting resources. In the absence of any analysis of market developments and of any attempt to identify gaps production capacity grew out of all proportion in relation to real market developments.
- Competition was misunderstood to signify a 'bellum omnium contra omnes', ruling out such notions as partnership, agreement and association. This behavioural modification, which is the result of privatization, may be difficult to reverse.

5.3.3 The most delicate and the most urgent problems, however, seem to be those of *post-privatization corporate governance.*

These problems at first tend to take the form of organizational conflicts between the members of the employee and management association, related to definition of their rights, duties and responsibilities. The general causes of this are the shortcomings of the company contract and regulations and, above all, lack of knowledge of the prerogatives of shareholders, administrators and employees, the way in which decisions are taken at joint stock companies and, in a wider perspective the functioning of a market economy. The main virtues of the MEBO method in advanced Western economies (harmony among the interests of employees, management, shareholders, unions and company clientele; employee support for restructuring; proper understanding of the double status of employee and shareholder; commitment on all sides to long-term objectives and the obtaining of immediate incomes, etc.) are rare or completely absent when the method is applied in an economy under transition.

Conflict may also arise between employee-shareholders and manager-shareholders over control of the company. The Romanian experience seems to be untypical in this regard. In the majority of Central and East European countries the management runs the company, even if the employees own most of the shares (Blasi, 1994); in the case of Romania, the employees generally own most of the shares and control the company.

This state of affairs takes two main forms:

- *The management team is marginalized* by the constant and inevitably incompetent interference of the employee–shareholders (Popescu-Bogdanesti, 1995). Analysis of the available case studies demonstrates that often even the purchase of the most insignificant things can generate unending debate and suspicion. This tends to distort the decision-making process, so thwarting the very aim of privatization: to improve decision-making flexibility and initiative. Management security – in respect of rewards, decision-making authority, and the evaluation of management performance in an economy under transition – is one of the main problems attendant on privatization in Romania.
- *The employee-shareholders often pursue their interests as employees at the expense of their interests as shareholders.* As a consequence, such necessary adjustments and restructuring measures as a decrease in production volumes, the sale of secondary assets, organizational changes and lay-offs are not taken (Earle, Frydman, and Rapaczynski, 1993).

6 CONCLUSION

The economic performances of the companies concerned one year after their privatization show that the MEBO method has been a success in Romania. From the point of view of corporate governance, however, the situation is rather different. Consequently, the present structure of share-ownership should be regarded as transitional. There is a significant imbalance between employee share-ownership (about 63%) and that of the management (only about 6%), the remaining shares being owned by administrative and technical personnel. Furthermore, managements are faced with diminishing decision-making control and increasing and inept interference, while the unions are becoming irrelevant. This situation tends to be hostile to reform and threatens the long-term development of the company. The present structure of share-ownership will change as the managers and, above all, outside investors, buy out the employee-shareholders. In anticipation of this, much needs to be done in order to normalize the position of employee-shareholders; otherwise, the predictable consolidation of management power and that of external investors will take place to their detriment.

REFERENCES

Blasi, J. (1994), 'The Impact of Privatization on the Enterprise and the Impact of the Enterprise on Reform', paper presented at the Conference on Conversion of the Defence Industry in Russia and Eastern Europe, Bonn, 10–13 August.

Dochia, A. (1995), 'Contributia privatizarii prin MEBO la dezvoltarea sectorului privat. Tei ani de perspectiva' (MEBO-type privatization contribution to private sector development. A three-year perspective), report prepared for the Centre for Political Analysis and Comparative Studies, Bucharest, December.

Earle, J., Frydman, R. and Rapaczynski, A. (1993), 'Transition Policies and the Establishment of a Private Property Regime in Eastern Europe', paper presented at the 18th Panel Meeting of the Economic Policy Forum in Brussels, 22–23 October.

Popescu-Bogdanesti, C. (1995), 'Post-privatizarea - Protectia echipelor de conducere' (Post-Privatization - Protection of Management Teams', in *Tribuna economica* (*Economic Tribune*), No. 7, 16 February.

Salagean, V. (1995), 'MEBO - Bilant si perspectiva' (MEBO - Results and Prospects), in *Adevarul economic* (*The Economic Truth*), No. 36, 2–8 September, 1–3.

Zaman, G. (1995), 'Ritmul privatizarii – Restrictii legislative si financiare' ('Privatization Pace – Legislative and Financial Restrictions'), in *Tribuna economica* (*Economic Tribune*), No. 24, 15 July, 23.

8. Rapid Spread of Employee Ownership in the Privatized Russia

Bogdan Lissovolik

1 INTRODUCTION

Much of Russia's history may serve as a telling example of how extreme forms of coercion and bureaucratization may overpower a whole society. The unbridled interventionism of the Russian state – whether tsarist or communist – was largely the result of a limitless desire for centralized power which generally made impossible the strict observance of 'voluntary exchange' and so the attainment of a true market economy.[1] In fact, the catastrophic passage from tsarism to communism seems to have been in part made possible by the slow progress made towards the decentralization of power and the elimination of restrictions in the course of capitalist development late in the nineteenth century. The institutions necessary for a full-fledged market economy were not allowed to develop naturally, provoking widespread dissatisfaction among social groups which considered themselves politically disenfranchised.

The communists capitalized on Russia's arrested civil development to stage the so-called 'socialist revolution' in October 1917, but were subsequently unable to deliver the across-the-board improvement in living standards which they promised. One of the most appealing benefits pledged by communist ideologues – and later by the countries of 'actually existing' socialism – was the absence of the exploitation of labour by capital. In practice, however, the enormous and all-pervasive administration, particularly in the form of cross-subsidies, made this claim untenable, since no economic agent, from enterprise directors to workers, could have the slightest idea what fraction of the product of their labour they were supposed to receive. The ironic result of this is that so-called 'exploitation' – and so its elimination – is meaningless without the supposedly 'capitalist' principle of voluntary exchange.

[1] See Gerschenkron (1962) and Hewett (1988) for authoritative accounts of the dawn of Russian capitalism and of the Soviet socialist system respectively.

These administrative abuses in part determined the long 'co-operativist' tradition and mentality in Russia. Under both tsarist and socialist absolutism the authorities chose formally to endorse limited co-operative institutions in an attempt to dilute dissatisfaction with their monopolization of economic life (at least until the nineteenth century) and politics, while preserving *de facto* autocracy. Under the tsars this meant collective land holding in the form of the *mir* or commune. Under socialism co-operative organization was, to a limited extent, retained in agriculture (in the form of the collective farm or *kolkhoz*) and in household residential construction. Given the dominant state ownership of the economy and the pervasive constraints imposed by comprehensive central planning, however, the presence of 'co-operativist' decision-making was more formal than real. Nevertheless, co-operative principles were declared 'progressive' and 'useful' during the so-called 'transition to socialism'.

The open disillusionment with central planning which had emerged by the 1980s and the resulting drive towards market-oriented economic transformation put the problem of 'co-operative property' and employee ownership in a new light. At the theoretical level this discussion degenerated into a lively but unrealistic debate about the feasibility and characteristics of a so-called 'third way' between socialism and capitalism. In practice, however, there was a contradiction to be resolved. On the one hand, managers and workers legitimately believed that they had earned the right to become de facto owners of their enterprises. On the other hand, the final goal of the economic transformation was declared to be a 'privatized' economy, or one that would place no restrictions on the pattern and form of ownership.

The course chosen to overcome this problem was the implementation of a well-designed mass privatization programme which would strike a balance between giving the workers their 'fair share' and providing outside investors with the opportunity to participate actively both in the ownership of Russian enterprises and in corporate governance. In the event, the Russian privatization programme has proved quite controversial on both counts, although it would be unfair to declare it a complete failure. While the consensus in Russia is that privatization was anything but fair, it is difficult to conceive how such accusations could be avoided altogether by any form of privatization. Moreover, the chosen privatization strategy ended up by offering many concessions to insiders, thereby giving rise to an ownership structure quite different to that of a typical capitalist economy.[2] The present chapter elaborates on the significance of these developments for the market-oriented transformation of the Russian economy.

[2] In a 'mainstream' capitalist economy, employee ownership usually evolves towards a fairly limited role in terms of its share in output and employment (see Earle and Estrin, 1994).

The rest of the chapter is structured as follows. Section 2 takes up the issue of Russia's uniqueness in the context of its transition to a market economy, with particular reference to privatization. Section 3 outlines the relative prospects of individualist and collectivist principles in respect of Russian market development. Section 4 discusses the possible advantages and disadvantages of employee ownership for enterprises in Russia. Section 5 surveys the main developments in the privatization process and the associated legislation. Section 6 takes a brief look at the basic structure of ownership which is emerging in Russian industry and relates the observed ownership patterns to enterprise behaviour. Section 7 offers some preliminary evidence on enterprise performance in Russia with reference to corporate governance. Finally, Section 8 offers a brief summary of the whole.

2 PRIVATIZATION AND RUSSIAN UNIQUENESS

Since the beginning of the transition in Central and Eastern Europe it has been widely accepted that successful economic transformation requires the privatization of productive assets. Privatization strategy in the region has largely evolved on the basis of schemes aimed at the most *rapid* possible transfer of rights to new owners by way of financially-intermediated give-away schemes.[3] Against this background the Russian voucher privatization programme emerged as one of the most ambitious undertakings of its kind. The ultimate success of privatization efforts would not be measured by their speed, however, but rather by the long-term viability of the privatized businesses, an outcome dependent on many factors, including initial conditions and the success of other reforms, such as stabilization and liberalization.

Russia's particular history of collectivist values notwithstanding, it would be useful to outline its unique development in terms of general economic factors, and against the backdrop of the mainstream model of privatization.[4] This is followed by an analysis of the scope for alternative forms of non-state ownership. We will also describe the differences that distinguish Russia from its neighbours in Central and Eastern Europe because the other transitional economies have received considerable attention in the literature.

Historically, the Russian population – in contrast to the other countries of the region – has no living memory of how a normal market-based economy works. This implies that simpler privatization solutions and techniques would

---

[3] See Lissovolik (1995) for a more detailed description of the mainstream view of privatization.

[4] As shown below, in a broad sense privatization does not necessarily imply a particular pattern of ownership and control, but rather a transfer of assets away from the state sector.

be more effective. The positive development of the private sector, especially at the level of individual businesses, is likely to be slower than in other Central and East European countries because of specific human capital constraints. One probable consequence is a profound differentiation between the younger and the older generation in respect of their grasp of the intricacies of the market economy. This gap is somewhat smaller in the rest of the region, where the older generation remembers the workings of a market economy.

Russia also has a particular *structural* legacy, since it was the only country to undergo industrialization under communist rule.[5] This implies the existence of larger and more ingrained imbalances in its industrial structure, probably implying that a somewhat greater share of its capital stock has to be weeded out in the transitional process. Thus, although the initial fall in output was somewhat less severe in Russia than in the other transition countries, by 1993 its cumulative output loss was already comparable to theirs, a process which continued almost unchecked in 1994.[6] Other important structural issues include the conversion of the defence industries to civilian use and the downsizing of heavy industry.[7]

The sheer *size* of the country makes crucial the attainment of a sustainable balance between central and local authorities. Geographical barriers to the transmission of information are likely to disrupt the privatization process; for example, there is more leeway for local authorities to secretly renege on some commitments without fear of sanction. Such undermining of central authority can be prevented only by way of mutually beneficial and sustainable compromises between various levels of authority.[8] In Russia, complex ethnic tensions and interdependencies further exacerbate the problem. Furthermore, to the extent that regional endowments differ (or are perceived to differ) 'rational self-interest' will intensify local pressures. In Russia this is particularly strong in respect of potential oil wealth, leading the oil-rich republics to become especially active in pushing for greater autonomy, also in connection with privatization.

---

[5] For a brief overview of the structural legacy of Russia see (Lipton and Sachs, 1993).

[6] According to Goskomstat, after the first quarter of 1994 industrial production declined to about 62 per cent of the level of December 1991. By that time (if the former countries of the Soviet Union are excluded), only Albania did worse. Moreover, in contrast to the other economies of Eastern Europe, output growth in Russia has not yet resumed to date (mid-1996). However, the legacy argument should be swallowed with caution in this context, because alongside the structural factors, there were macroeconomic and other reasons for the difference in the growth record. Also, there have been a number of statistical problems with GDP data (see Gavrilenkov and Koen, 1994).

[7] The rest of Eastern Europe is not uniform in these particular respects (for example, one could cite the difference between the Czech and the Slovak Republics). Nevertheless, the Russian economy is invariably an extreme case.

[8] The multilateral bargaining model has been a useful framework for the analysis of privatization in this context (see Rausser and Simon, 1992).

As far as *'culture'* is concerned, the grass-roots entrepreneurial drive of Russians has never been based on private property and its institutions as they evolved in the West. On the contrary, the ideological aversion to the notion of privately owned productive assets already characteristic of the Russian peasantry[9] was carefully nurtured by the communists. Probing deeper into history, the Russian communal system of land holding was far from being fertile soil for the development of private initiative. In the Caucasus, parts of Central Asia and Ukraine the free-market instincts of the population are somewhat more promising, but it remains to be seen, on the one hand whether there are enough enterprising individuals to form a critical mass, and on the other whether the aversion to legality – to a great extent induced by external circumstances – historically characteristic of Russian entrepreneurs will prove too much of a liability. Furthermore, ethnic differentiation as regards the capacity to assimilate market values could have undesirable political repercussions.

The historical background of the cultural determinants of legality is not very encouraging either. In his classic study, Gerschenkron (1962) described the rise of capitalism in Russia in the nineteenth century as follows:

> the standards of honesty in business were. . . disastrously low, the general distrust of the public. . . great. . . in an economy where fraudulent bankruptcy had been almost elevated to the rank of a general business practice. . . Incompetence and corruption of bureaucracy were great. The amount of waste that accompanied the process was formidable. (Gerschenkron, 1962, pp. 19–20)

While Gerschenkron goes on to say that in the course of capitalist development some progress was made in respect of the rule of law it was still small by the time of the establishment of the socialist regime. As far as the post-revolution period is concerned, Litwack (1989) gives an intriguing account of how aversion to legality flourished.

As the above historical experiences are more or less remote, one can only speculate as to their appropriateness to the current situation in Russia. In recent years these experiences have received wide coverage: there has been a surge of information on the period which might influence the mentality of the new Russian entrepreneur. Initial impressions of the progress of 'new capitalism' in Russia do little to refute the possibility, offering many examples of fraudulent activity on a grand scale.[10]

The development of the Russian *political* system was entirely different from the rest of Europe; the already mentioned generational and ethnic differentiation

---

[9] The peasantry constituted around 80 per cent of the Russian population and held nine-tenths of the country's agricultural land in 1917 (*Editor's note*).

[10] Particularly salient examples are a number of scandals with joint-stock companies ('MMM' was the most notorious) which were revealed to have been engaged in Ponzi schemes.

could hinder the progress of market-oriented reforms. The country has almost no experience of democracy, and civil society has never been encouraged. There have been many reports of violations of constitutional powers by virtually all branches of power.[11] Moreover, the political system is at present in a state of legal flux because de facto power has been devolving to the regions, requiring continuous renegotiation of the division of powers. This has given rise to an unstable and contradictory legal framework for the settlement of political conflicts. Privatization could well suffer from this lack of experience and competence, both because the debate has been politicized and because transition economies generally are characterized by 'excessive political control' over assets (Shleifer, 1994). The political situation in Russia is more precarious than elsewhere in the region, being subject to populist pressures which are notoriously oblivious of economic realities.

Although successful change will undoubtedly be difficult there are a number of mitigating factors, particularly in respect of Russia (in contrast to the rest of the former Soviet Union). The enormous resource potential of the country, especially the oil wealth, has brought about positive changes in Russia's terms of trade, initially in relation to the former COMECON countries and subsequently to former members of the CIS (Kazakhstan and Azerbaijan are possible exceptions). This should ease the macroeconomic pressures on reform. In fact, resource-rich regions have turned out to be particularly interested in privatization and efficiency-enhancing measures able to give credibility to their drive. With positive feedback from foreign investors 'virtuous circles' may be generated across the economy. These mitigating factors are by no means sufficient, however, and warrant careful attention on the part of policymakers.[12] Finally, the already mentioned historical remoteness of market experiences means that the controversies which have surrounded the issue of restitution in the rest of Central and Eastern Europe will have no place on the privatization agenda in Russia.

3 PROSPECTS FOR COLLECTIVE DECISION-MAKING IN RUSSIA

Do Russian conditions strengthen or weaken the case for a rapid property-rights-oriented privatization strategy? It seems inevitable – in view of the facts presented in the previous section – that privatization in Russia along the lines of the consensus view is likely to entail greater social costs than elsewhere.

---

[11] *Izvestia*, 15 June 1994.

[12] See Tornell and Velasco (1992) which shows that if the 'tragedy of the commons' problem is not ameliorated, higher productivity of the capital stock may be a curse rather than a blessing.

First, such privatization would involve an abrupt shift towards an 'individualism' that has only the shallowest roots in Russian history which has been predominantly collectivist in orientation, particularly under the communists, who also waged an intensive propaganda campaign to consolidate this tendency throughout the duration of their rule. Apart from the enormous wrench that this shift would represent in Russia, the experiences of other countries suggest that such a departure from collectivist values is not a necessary step towards a market-based economy. This is attested by the Yugoslav variety of socialism, by the relative success of co-operatives in various countries and, more recently, by the Chinese experience of incremental reform. Weitzman (1993) points to the success of township–village enterprises (TVE) in China as an example of a very informal organization (based on co-operativist principles) more concerned with building markets than with sorting out property claims. In this way the new non-state sector might peacefully outgrow the state sector without major setbacks.[13]

Furthermore, if shares are distributed to all individuals as part of a mainstream privatization programme there must necessarily be a long learning period before the majority start to exercise their rights properly (even in terms of individual self-interest), especially if the programme includes some form of financial intermediation. There are obvious institutional limitations which will mean that efficiency gains from privatization in Russia will be slower to materialize, a scenario likely to damage the credibility of any privatization programme.

The challenge is therefore to find a scheme which differs from mainstream privatization in the necessary respects but which is incentive-compatible at the micro level. In Russia there is no indication of a grass-roots collectivist movement like the Chinese TVEs,[14] which could be viewed as *alternative* to the routines and structures which evolved under central planning. It is now evident that reliance on state-owned 'dinosaurs' as vehicles of economic transformation is a recipe for disaster, as it is unlikely to lead to major structural changes. Sporadic microeconomic counter-examples of grass-roots restructuring of existing enterprises might be found,[15] but on the whole the Russian *co-operativist* restructuring movement has made little overall progress.

---

[13] There are some doubts about the validity of the 'irrelevance of property rights' explanation for the success of Chinese TVEs. There is some evidence that local bureaucrats there act as residual income maximizers (see Shleifer, 1994), on which basis the property rights structure turns out to be fairly well defined. If so, 'efficient bureaucracy' is a better explanation of the Chinese miracle.

[14] For a fuller understanding of the following discussion the reader is referred to Weitzman (1993), in which the author underscores the problem of co-operative versus unco-operative behaviour and stresses the relevance of game theory in this context.

[15] One of them is the successful reform of some military enterprises in St Petersburg.

One apparent reason for this failure has been the not-quite-collectivist culture which prevailed in Russia at the time, and which reflected disillusionment with socialist bureaucracy. In addition, Russia is very differentiated in terms of entrepreneurial instincts; while it is more 'co-operativist' than the other countries of Central and Eastern Europe, the opposite tendency is also represented. Section 2 emphasized the generational and ethnic differentiation of the Russian population, on the basis of which we may roughly characterize younger people and people of Asian origin as forming an uncompromising group of 'individualists', while the rest range from 'passive individualists' to 'cautious collectivists'. The strong roots of entrepreneurship in Russia can be seen, however, in the example of Soviet 'co-operative enterprises' (permitted since 1988) which were a manifestation of the 'privatistic drive' long suppressed in parts of the population under socialism, and which were nothing but loopholes for transferring state assets to new private owners.

In fact, the drive towards private enrichment in Russia has been so strong that it cannot be explained by cultural factors alone. One credible explanation emphasizes the interplay between cultural factors and the strength of the state. If no coercion is applied by the state to enforce 'co-operative' principles – recall the disintegration of authority in Russia in contrast with China – the gain to those behaving in a 'non-co-operative' fashion increases monotonically in proportion to the number of those who behave co-operatively. Barring exceptional circumstances, any 'co-operative' equilibrium will eventually be destroyed by the defection of rational agents. Direct mass privatization, by reducing the scope for non-co-operative behaviour – that is, for defection – may involve less, not more, dislocation in the Russian context.

An example (attributed by Stiglitz (1992) to Lawrence Summers) may help illustrate this point. Suppose our economy consists of individuals who are engaged in useful (on balance) productive activity. Suppose further that banknotes start to fall out of the sky (for our purposes, these banknotes are analogous to the opportunity of participating in *spontaneous* privatization). One cannot pick the bills up without hampering the productive process. As it turns out, the best (Pareto-superior) solution – that everyone finishes his work before picking up his banknotes – is not a Nash equilibrium (a set of strategies that are best replies to each other). In this way peoples' energies are diverted to an unproductive quest for windfall gains, resulting in a Pareto-inferior outcome of everyone scrambling after the banknotes.[16]

In practice, the above example would critically depend on the governing institutional arrangements. In the Chinese case, the government oversees the

[16] In our setting, the banknotes are a metaphor for the opportunities offered by economic liberalization, while a mass privatization scheme can be thought of as a careful public assignment of (and an attempt to enforce) individual rights within the area in which the banknotes fall.

process and credibly threatens to punish deviators from the grass-roots collectivist values, so that the outcome of everyone finishing his work first follows. In Central Europe the 'Nash equilibrium' solution would tend to occur. In this region the government should ideally be concerned with an orderly assignment of banknotes (that is, clarification of property rights through rapid privatization), on the assumption that people would stop 'working' and apply themselves to the pursuit of individual gain whatever happened. The cost of punishing deviators would be prohibitive for the government, to say nothing of the European democratic tradition.

One is tempted to say that Russia is an intermediate case in this connection, combining the worst of both worlds. The authorities' lack of credible control makes the Chinese solution unsustainable. Furthermore, while it is true that Russia is more individualistic than China, more importantly, the larger the initial proportion of 'naive collectivists' the greater the amount of 'banknotes' will be collected by individualists, given the low probability/cost of 'punishment'. New individualists will be 'recruited' from the herd of collectivists, and the population ends up being converted to individualism with severe distributional consequences (if the co-operative solution is nevertheless attempted).[17] Moreover, because of the inherited generational and ethnic differentiation and administrative limitations, these distributional consequences would be even worse if the government adopts a non-co-operative solution (namely, privatization) if corruption is not kept in check. Nevertheless, given the political will, such a solution at least offers some chance of limiting the adverse consequences.

To conclude, Russia has to go one way or the other, and it would seem that the 'Chinese' model is neither applicable nor desirable. First, the Russian state is much weaker in its ability to enforce its provisions, so that it cannot effectively 'punish deviators' in many circumstances. Second, such coercion has lost much of its appeal for most Russians. Third, Russian culture tends to be more individualistic.

4 COSTS AND BENEFITS OF EMPLOYEE OWNERSHIP IN RUSSIA: A CONCEPTUAL FRAMEWORK

In the previous section we argued that collective forms of decision-making may not be in themselves a panacea for building the micro-foundations of a market-based economy in Russia. A significant degree of employee ownership, however, cannot be avoided during the transition process, at least

---

[17] Curiously, the outcome (for Russia) is not Pareto-inferior in a strict sense, but any applied economist would clearly prefer to avoid severe distributional implications at all costs.

initially.[18] Furthermore, in some enterprise-specific situations such a pattern of ownership may be useful. A more detailed microeconomic analysis is called for in order to determine the costs and benefits of employee ownership in various settings.

The potential costs of employee ownership for enterprise efficiency are well-known from the academic literature. First, employee-owned firms are presented as unlikely to attract high-quality managers, as the managerial tasks in such a firm would be more demanding and less rewarding. Furthermore, the managerial time-horizon is likely to be short in such firms, as the managers are in constant danger of being removed by the workers. Second, if employee ownership is dispersed among highly heterogeneous agents the opportunity cost of reaching consensus may be very high (Hansmann, 1990). At best, even if no mistakes are made, important decisions may not be taken as promptly as in outsider-controlled firms. Third, employee-owned firms are expected to pay excessive wages, to resist lay-offs, and to exhibit low supply elasticities (Ward, 1958). Fourth, they may have a comparative disadvantage as regards attracting outside investment (Meade, 1972).

The benefits of employee ownership, on the other hand, are likely to accrue in exceptional circumstances, outside the normal working of a market economy; for example, when there are production-specific difficulties in monitoring the performance of a firm externally, a degree of employee ownership may encourage self- and peer group monitoring. Second, in some situations employee ownership may reduce conflict and strategic bargaining between workers and managers, as there is no scope for managerial opportunism versus workers with enterprise-specific skills. Finally, employee ownership has certain advantages for the temporary alleviation of the social fallout, or even re-orientation, of loss-making enterprises, as the scope for wage concessions and comprehensive co-operation between managers and workers is enhanced under this form of ownership.

The above costs and benefits must be related to the conditions prevailing in Russia. At first glance, it seems that for most enterprises employee ownership would exacerbate the problems of transformation. Restructuring – the most crucial aspect of enterprise management in a transition economy – normally requires important outside sources of finance. As already mentioned, these sources are difficult for employee-owned firms to access. Furthermore, such firms are generally not very flexible with respect to output and employment, and this would also be a liability in the volatile environment of emerging markets. Finally, employee turnover (management and workers) is likely to be particularly high during transition, and the difficulties employee-owned firms are

---

[18] Note that employee ownership does not necessarily imply collective decision-making, although frequently these concepts are synonymous.

likely to encounter in their quest for top workers/managers may put them at a disadvantage.

In practice, however, many of these costs may not play a very important role in the Russian economy. For example, sources of finance depend on many external circumstances, such as macroeconomic, political and legal risks. If these are high (as so far in Russia), the *marginal* costs of employee ownership may not be excessive. In addition, the enormous natural and infrastructural barriers to the flow of commodities/information in Russia necessarily limit the development of markets for factors of production, so that human capital outflows occur much more slowly than would otherwise have been the case. Moreover, current conditions in Russia tend to magnify the relative benefits of employee ownership: the fairly large number of loss-making enterprises in Russia (see Section 7) that are, in addition, situated in remote areas are a classic case in which wage flexibility and extremely close co-operation between workers and managers are necessary conditions for enterprise survival.

Employee ownership in the Russian economy may be a mixed blessing, depending on the enterprise. Ultimately, assessment of the role and impact of employee ownership is an empirical matter. In the following sections we attempt to throw some light on the matter by looking at concrete cases.

5 THE RUSSIAN PRIVATIZATION PROGRAMME

5.1 Historical Perspective

So-called pre- or spontaneous privatization began in the Soviet Union under Gorbachev's *perestroika* in 1987–88. The control of firms gradually devolved to enterprise managers, some of whom were able to transfer the ownership of resources to themselves or to their business partners under the guise of joint ventures or co-operatives. Subsequently, the Gorbachev government tried to control this process, but their attempts were half-hearted and riddled with ideological prejudice. In the meantime, the loss of effective government control over resources continued, and no effective steps were taken to keep spontaneous privatization in check. On the other hand, the first privatization measures of the then shadow Russian government were clearly marked by signs of a struggle for power and were basically aimed at shifting responsibility for the process to the local authorities. In 1990–91 small-scale privatization was given the go-ahead, but its progress was slow before 1992.

Privatization began in earnest on the territory of the Russian Federation in July–August 1992, when large and medium-sized firms were selected for public sale. The chosen enterprises were to be transformed into equity-issuing companies to be purchased first by workers and managers using vouchers,

Table 8.1 Market share of privatized enterprises, Russia, 1993–94 (%)

Sector	Apr. 93	Aug. 93	Apr. 94	Jun. 94
Retail trade	52	61	69	75
Catering	47	57	61	66
Personal services	53	63	73	77

Source: Russian Economic Trends, Vol. 3, No. 2, Chapter 9, p. 5, 1994.

second by the public for vouchers, and subsequently by the public for cash. The distribution of vouchers started on 1 October 1992, and involving more than 96 per cent of the population (146 million citizens). The bulk of the vouchers were distributed by the end of the year, and by that time 700 large and nearly 900 medium-sized enterprises had been turned into joint stock companies. From early December 1992 shares began to be sold to the public for vouchers.

According to the GKI (government agency in charge of the voucher process), more than 13,000 large and medium-sized firms were sold in voucher auctions in the 19 months of 'give-away' privatization. Over 40 million Russians became owners of shares in enterprises or investment funds as a result of this scheme. The newly-privatized enterprises employed more than 75 per cent of the industrial workforce. The Russian privatization programme has been the most comprehensive and rapid undertaking of its kind (*Table 8.1*).

A clear sectoral differentiation was observed in terms of the book-value of shares per voucher. Hotels and restaurants were most in demand (0.4 of a thousand rouble share per voucher). Wood-pulp, furniture and food-processing industries also commanded high investor interest (0.9–1.2 thousand roubles per voucher). Least favoured were the water supply, water transport and textile industries (3.6–4.8 thousand roubles per voucher). These implicit valuations roughly corresponded to the relative profitability of these sectors. Precise parallels should be treated with caution, however, since there is a built-in bias in the highly controversial book-value calculations. At the aggregate level this bias would probably lead to an underestimation of the degree of differentiation in the quality of capital stocks.

Voucher privatization was completed on 1 July 1994 and gave way to the second, *post-voucher,* stage. At that point, the government still had important stakes in a number of enterprises. First, more than 7,000 corporatized enterprises were not ready in time for the voucher auctions. Second, the government retained minority stakes (usually 20 per cent or less, with the exception of a few 'strategic' enterprises) in most privatized large and medium-sized firms. Third, a substantial number of strategic enterprises were not privatized altogether under the voucher scheme.

The *Presidential Decree of 23 July 1994* stipulated procedures for privatizing the remaining state enterprises (that is, the residual stakes in state ownership) by investment tenders or cash privatization. The privatized companies were to receive 51 per cent of the proceeds from the sale and the remaining share was to be divided between federal and regional authorities. Enterprise buildings and land were also included in the sale. The progress of post-voucher privatization was far from satisfactory, however. Investment tenders proved to be a non-transparent, unenforceable – and hence very corrupt – way of allocating shares. The use of this method resulted in significant shortfalls of privatization receipts from cash sales against planned targets in 1994 and for much of 1995.

In the second half of 1995 the government made a serious effort to reinvigorate the privatization process. Sales of residual government stakes in a number of attractive companies were accelerated. In some sectors there was a significant opening of sales and investment tenders to foreign investors. Some government-owned stakes in 'strategic' enterprises were handled within the so-called *shares-for-loans* scheme. It was agreed that a number of commercial banks would lend the government, on concessionary terms, around 9 trillion roubles (about US$ 1.8 billion) in exchange for the right to manage the government blocks of shares for a certain period (approximately one year). These shares were also intended to serve as collateral for the loans: if the government failed to repay, the commercial banks would keep the shares.[19]

On paper, the scheme seemed a bargain for the government. It made it possible to finance the budget deficit on extremely favourable terms, seemingly without major risks. In practice, however, given the poor record of fiscal management in Russia, no one really expected the government to pay back the loan. Furthermore, some of the very commercial banks which were supposed to compete for the right to manage the shares were given the responsibility of organizing the auctions. Naturally, these banks took advantage of the opportunity and moved in advance to have their rivals disqualified on technicalities or simply declared themselves the winner of their own auctions even though their bids were significantly lower than those of their rivals. Some of the nation's largest commercial banks – Uneximbank,

---

[19] This is the essence of the scheme – the details are somewhat more complicated. For example, a number of rules were specified for the division of the surplus between the government and the commercial banks if the market value of the shares increased considerably as a result of the interim management by the commercial banks.

Menatep, Imperial – were at the centre of these controversies, which in the end dealt a devastating blow to the credibility of further privatization efforts, both with domestic and foreign investors. As a result, privatization has not made significant progress since the end of 1995, while the results of the shares-for-loans auctions have been seriously questioned by the public.

5.2 The Design of the Voucher Programme

It is clear that the voucher stage of privatization has been the principal determinant of the ownership structure in Russia. But what of the mechanics of the programme? Its implementation was the responsibility of the GKI, a government agency. A Co-ordinating Commission headed by the GKI chairman was set up to oversee the implementation of the programme. The commission also included representatives of the Federal Property Fund, the seller of state-owned enterprises, as well as other government agencies and local governments. A large number of local territorial commissions were subordinate to the national commission and oversaw the day-to-day implementation of the programme. Local branches of the GKI and the Federal Property Fund also figured prominently in this decentralized system.

All large and medium-sized companies had to prepare privatization plans before 1 October 1992. The plans were initially drafted by privatization committees within the companies, then they had to win the approval of the workforce and of the local branches of the GKI. The plan had to stipulate which of the three options offered by the State Privatization Committee had been chosen by the workers. Under the first option employees were given, free of charge, non-voting shares worth 25 per cent of total equity. They had also the option of buying an additional 10 per cent at a 30 per cent discount on book value. Top managers could purchase up to 5 per cent of equity at book value. All these payments could be made in vouchers. Under the second option, a group of employees was allowed to purchase 51 per cent of equity at a price determined by the GKI. Up to half of this amount could be paid in vouchers. The third option (applicable to medium-sized companies only) basically constituted a one-year lease contract with an option to buy 20 per cent of equity at a 30 per cent discount. More than 70 per cent of all the companies privatized for vouchers chose the second option which allowed them to retain control over the enterprise.[20]

After the sale of equity to the employees and managers (so-called 'closed subscription') voucher auctions had to be organized. Initially, very vague

---

[20] The effective control of insiders in post-voucher privatization was to be much smaller than under voucher privatization: 10% of the voting shares and 25% of the non-voting shares were to be given to employees free of charge.

regulations allowed both local property funds and workers and managers to minimize sales at public voucher auctions.[21] A number of presidential edicts attempted to increase the percentage of shares sold at this stage, however, either by directly fixing the percentage that could be sold for vouchers (for example, 80 per cent of all the voting and non-voting shares), or by facilitating the purchase of buildings, land and small municipal enterprises by the economic agents if they complied well with the targets. Regional property committees were responsible for dividing into groups all firms subject to privatization, so that they could be auctioned at a particular date. At the subsequent stage all the documents were transferred to the local property fund, which acted as the legal seller of state-owned enterprises.

Participation in a voucher auction required the submission of one of two types of bid. In a Type 1 bid, only the number of vouchers was stipulated. In a Type 2 bid, the investor indicated the minimum number of shares per voucher he was prepared to accept. This arrangement gave investors flexibility and the chance to withdraw in the face of possible manipulation and mismanagement during the voucher collection period (which could not be shorter than two weeks). After all the bids had been collected, the equilibrium price was determined at an auction in terms of shares per voucher. Although the book value of shares on which the nominal price of the auction was based did not, as a rule, reflect true scarcity, this problem was not so acute, since the auction itself corrected such imbalances. If necessary, shares were split in order to distribute whole shares. This arrangement was intended to protect small investors.

In such a complex and decentralized privatization programme investment intermediaries were relied on to play a key role. Following the rather unsettling experience of unregulated fund activity in the Czech and Slovak privatization process, however, specialized voucher funds in Russia were subject to licensing by the GKI or one of its branches. This was stipulated in the *Presidential Decree on Securities Markets of 8 October 1992*. The regulation was tightened further six months later, when these funds were prohibited from using vouchers for any other purpose than that of selling them at voucher auctions for the shares of privatized enterprises. Furthermore, a 10 per cent ceiling was imposed on the proportion of equity which could be acquired at an auction by a single fund. All in all, around 600 licensed funds were operating in Russia by mid-1993.

It is clear that Russian privatization has much in common with the mass privatization programmes implemented elsewhere in Central and Eastern Europe: the enormous quantity of assets involved, the large number of citizens

---

[21] Local property funds were counting on the revenue the unsold part of shares would bring at subsequent cash auctions.

participating, and the almost free distribution of property claims (subject to a nominal administrative fee). Like the Czechoslovak programme (but unlike the Polish or Romanian), it was 'laissez-faire' or eclectic in that citizens could choose whether to bid directly for privatized shares or to do so through various intermediaries. In fact, the Russian programme was quite extreme in this respect, since vouchers could be retraded freely at any time, and changes of ownership did not have to be recorded. Another distinguishing feature of the Russian programme was its highly decentralized organization. Regional branches of the GKI and regional property funds, as well as local authorities, had substantial leeway in influencing the pace and outcome of privatization. Larger enterprises could lobby successfully for favourable treatment.[22] At times this took the form of an outright challenge to the central authority, as happened in Tatarstan with the issue of local vouchers worth 30,000 roubles each, in addition to the all-Russian vouchers. Decentralized procedures meant that no uniform schedule could be instituted, creating considerable uncertainty about when and what enterprises would be put on sale. Nevertheless, centrally-instigated privatization maintained its momentum across the overwhelming majority of regions.

6 EMERGING OWNERSHIP PATTERNS AND CONTROL STRUCTURES

The privatization process laid the foundations for the peculiar ownership structure of Russian industry. The most important aspect of this has been the prevalence of *insider* ownership, that of workers and managers. As already mentioned, the decentralization of the main procedures has allowed most collectives to claim 51 per cent of the shares, and to purchase additional shares at subsequent open auctions. In many instances, these auctions were heavily manipulated by insiders.[23]

About two-thirds of the 118,000 firms privatized came into worker-majority ownership (see Halligan and Richter, 1995). This was particularly the case in respect of large and medium-sized enterprises. Just after voucher privatization Blasi (1994) concluded that 90 per cent of the privatized firms surveyed had majority employee ownership. Insiders owned 65 per cent of the enterprises

[22] For example, large enterprises in St Petersburg were able to re-schedule the timetable for their privatization in mid-1993 in order to facilitate their acquisition by insiders.

[23] One interesting empirical regularity of the voucher auctions has been the fairly high 'control premium,' as the shares of small enterprises (control over which was easier to obtain) were progressively more in demand than those of larger ones (see *Kommersant-Daily*, September, 1993).

surveyed; outsiders owned 21.5 per cent; while the state retained around 13 per cent. Of the shares held by insiders, 8.6 per cent were in the hands of top managers.

Another distinctive feature is the *dispersion* of ownership. In Russia, block holdings of shares have not played as crucial a role as in most Western countries. Except for the fairly concentrated management stakes, the remaining shares appear to be scattered among employees, voucher investment funds and small outside investors.

The combination of insider bias and dispersed ownership has a number of important implications for the governance of such firms. First, insider domination has clearly introduced an undesirable asymmetry into the balance of forces between insiders and outsiders. Anecdotal evidence points to numerous attempts by outside investors to obtain large stakes in enterprises at voucher or cash auctions which in the end resulted in failure. Even in the infrequent exceptional cases, large outside investors were generally unsuccessful in making their formal stakes count in terms of operating decisions. Apparently, this had negative consequences in terms of the financing available to such enterprises and the quality of administration.

Second, the dispersion of ownership has led to a strengthening of the position of managers in their day-to-day operations, although under central planning enterprise managers already had extensive powers, including a virtual monopoly on comprehensive information regarding the external circumstances influencing input/output conditions. By contrast, workers had no access to such knowledge under socialism, and were apparently slow to realize the importance of depriving the managers of such a monopoly in the emerging market conditions. Even if they had realized this, they would have had to incur Stigler-type costs in ascertaining what they really needed to know and how. On the other hand, since ownership was not sufficiently concentrated among employees the incentives for active participation in decision-making were blunted for individual owners. By default, the power vacuum was apparently filled by the managers.

This has been widely confirmed by survey evidence. Lipsits et al. (1995) reported that 74.1 per cent of Russian workers believed that the top managers were the real owners of their enterprise. The same opinion was shared by 58.4 per cent of the managerial staff. According to the survey, the influence of the managers was exercised through: (1) control over salaries and bonuses; (2) operational control; (3) organization of export production; and (4) control over financial and credit policies. Interestingly, many of the surveyed workers believed that the extent of managerial power was justified. Only 36 per cent of the workers persisted in their aspiration to become collective owners of the enterprise.

The strong managerial position within formal employee majority ownership has been emphasized by most observers of Central and Eastern Europe. Earle and Estrin (1994) dubbed such firms MCEOs or 'managerially controlled employee-owned firms'. In Russia, however, this phenomenon has become much more ingrained than elsewhere in the region. For one thing, the size of the country made possible much greater decentralization in Russia, so giving the managers greater powers vis-à-vis the central authorities. Furthermore, the capital stock in Russia is much more differentiated than in other countries, so that there is more uncertainty with respect to the turnover/profitability characteristics of a given enterprise, providing greater scope for managers to exploit informational asymmetries.

The position of MCEOs is difficult to evaluate. On the one hand, managers become residual income maximizers and are therefore interested in the efficient use of assets. The well known agency problems of employee-managed firms are also somewhat reduced as decision-making becomes more hierarchical. On the other hand, MCEOs may represent a continuation of the property rights vacuum characteristic of the pre-reform period. If this is the case, the horizons of managers are short, and so they are interested in reducing the transparency of their operations in order to reap temporary benefits from their current monopoly position.

In the imperfect information setting of the transition period, the scope for managerial discretion and the concomitant asset stripping can occur regardless of its profitability, for a variety of reasons. In potentially profitable firms, there are pressures for continued 'spontaneous' privatization of core assets. This may occur through additional share issues to top management, and the diversion of earnings into special 'funds' or their channelling through 'pocket banks' in a non-transparent manner. For non-viable firms, the preferred method is to strip 'non-core' assets, for instance through the process of 'supply diversion' of valuable inputs to the side market. Of course, such forms of asset stripping necessarily imply continued bargaining for government subsidies to mend the holes in the enterprise balance sheets. In the longer run, spontaneous privatization of non-viable firms could give rise to a vicious circle of subsidies and the plundering of funds, as the enterprise barely manages to remain afloat. By contrast, spontaneous privatization of potentially viable firms may not be as damaging, since it finally helps to clarify the property rights situation of useful assets. One must still assume, however, that this type of clarification will in the end be accepted as legitimate by society in general and not lead to further legal battles. Obviously, this is a large assumption. Unfortunately, managerial control and entrenchment in Russia is much costlier than it is in other countries, especially the West, because many managers in Russia have skills very different from those needed to restructure privatized firms.

The initial extent of managerial control over enterprises, and the share of insiders in general, seems somewhat excessive in Russia. It was thought, however, that the redistribution of employee-owned shares would proceed fairly quickly in secondary trading, and that the main beneficiaries would be outside investors. The evidence for this has been mixed so far (see Pistor et al., 1994; EBRD, 1995), as the insiders were apparently not selling shares in great numbers. Anecdotal evidence suggests that the reason given most often is again managerial entrenchment. For example, managers have substantial power over the timing and procedure of shareholder meetings. There have also been instances of direct coercion against workers through threats of lay-offs or manipulation of shareholder registers. Of course, this is not the whole picture, as the workers on their part can and do exploit some of the power which accrues to them through formal ownership.[24] On the other hand, managerial ownership of shares may well be understated, both because the process of trading shares *between* insiders appears to be fairly active, and because the official registers and statistics may not reflect adequately insider ownership.[25] The current bias in terms of corporate governance is fairly clear; in Section 7 we examine how it has been affecting performance.

7 PRELIMINARY EVIDENCE ON ENTERPRISE PERFORMANCE

Detailed and meaningful evidence on how different types of privatized enterprise have been adjusting to the conditions of an emerging market economy has been very scarce to date. This is even more so with respect to the impact of employee ownership. As frequently mentioned elsewhere, the official statistics do not adequately capture the new private sector, or the economy derived from spontaneously privatized assets.[26] In addition, the official disaggregation into state and non-state enterprises commonly used by Goskomstat is not sufficient for ascertaining the impact of employee ownership. An alternative is to rely on survey data (see Blasi, 1994). Surveys are also very imperfect, however, because of the sampling bias and because of the possible *ad hoc* distortions induced by the particular question-and-answer structure. Thus, any statistical information has to be complemented – or substituted – by casual empiricism, as well as by inferences from general economic indicators.

---

[24] According to the Russian Privatization Centre, some 13% of managers have been dismissed at the first shareholders' meetings, although Pistor et al. (1994) report a rate of manager dismissals of no more than 3 to 4%.

[25] For example, the EBRD Transition Report of 1995 puts the share of formal management ownership at 17%, which is significantly higher than in Blasi (1994).

[26] By some estimates, the unrecorded economy in Russia amounted to about 40% of the economy as a whole in 1995.

Since most enterprises in Russia are known to be employee-owned and managerially controlled, evidence on general performance would still contain valuable information as to the role of this particular form of ownership and corporate governance in enterprise performance. So far, the overall record of enterprise adjustment in Russia has ranged from mixed to disappointing. At the aggregate level, economic growth has not yet resumed in the economy after six years of decline. This may to a large extent have been due to the fairly slow pace of adjustment at the enterprise level.

If we choose efficient use of assets as a benchmark, the initial information has not yet provided clear-cut evidence that mass privatization has made decision-making at enterprises more 'responsible'. In one of the first serious surveys of newly-private enterprises in Russia it was, among other things, inferred that:

> Half of the firms moved into the private sector in bits and pieces under leaseholds, and half came through the mass privatization programme. In both cases, there was little evidence that managers had sorted through assets, chosen the best, and discarded unwanted parts. (Webster et al., 1995, p. 172)

About 50 per cent of enterprises were seen as just 'muddling through,' struggling to find solvent customers and to cover their operating costs. About a quarter of enterprises were considered clearly promising. The remainder were expected to fail, as they could not even stay afloat.[27] A somewhat more optimistic assessment of enterprise adjustment was given by the Russian Privatization Centre (see OECD, 1995) which argued that more than half of privatized Russian firms had modified their product mix.[28]

According to another survey, the share of loss-making output continued to be very high and even increased in Russia between 1992 and 1995. Some 60 per cent of Russian enterprises reported in 1995 that at least some share of their output was loss-making.[29] The share of enterprises which were in the red on balance was 23 per cent. The loss-making output was more or less evenly distributed across broad sectors (consumer, investment, intermediate goods). The survey indicated the main reasons for continued loss-making production: (1) unexpected relative price shocks (60 per cent of loss-making enterprises); (2) a desire to maintain market share (38 per cent); and (3) a desire to employ idle workers (36 per cent). According to the bulk of the literature, the third reason is a typical response of a labour-managed firm. While the role of this latter explanation is significant, it is not overwhelming, thereby indirectly confirming the strong managerial position vis-à-vis workers.

---

[27] Apparently, this did not depend on any particular pattern of corporate governance, but was rather seen as exogenously determined by the 'inherited' stocks of production factors.

[28] However, this kind of statement is difficult to judge given the vagueness of definition.

[29] *Russian Economic Barometer*, Vol. 4, 1995.

A similar conclusion follows from the survey evidence on so-called 'labour hoarding', which suggests that at the beginning of 1996 about 60 per cent of industrial enterprises suffered from overemployment (as defined by managers of those enterprises).[30] According to the survey, the most important reason given for excess employment was 'social responsibility of the enterprise director' (71 per cent of such enterprises). This does not necessarily indicate effective worker influence on enterprise managers; instead it may indicate the management appetite for government subsidies. By contrast, only 28 per cent of enterprise managers claimed they maintained excess employment in order to 'avoid potential conflict with worker collectives'. Interestingly, state firm managers reported excess employment more frequently (64 per cent) than privatized firms (59 per cent), although the difference was small.

As far as the sources of external finance are concerned, 43 per cent of managers surveyed by Webster et al. (1995) said that they would use business profits; 25 per cent said that they would take long-term loans from banks when available; and 21 per cent said that they would rely on equity from foreign investors. Many managers spoke of equity as the preferred source of financing, however. All this indicates the presence of doubts about access to external finance. To some extent, the actual and expected paucity of such financing has been a result of insider dominance in corporate control. On the other hand, the managers were generally optimistic about the prospects for their own enterprise under conditions of low inflation and stable relative prices.

In a recent survey of relatively successful enterprises in the St Petersburg region,[31] it was revealed that employee ownership was not a significant factor in the performance of those firms. Much of the observed success hinged on the ability of managers to improve discipline and instil a climate of common goals between workers and management. At the same time, many successful directors acted fairly quickly to dismiss the surplus workers, as they realized that resignations-through-attrition would drain their enterprise of its best employees. The behaviour of these fairly successful firms was therefore not connected with employee ownership. The survey also drew the general conclusion that basic, common-sense improvements in the organization of production had enormous potential for turning around Russian firms.

Finally, since 1993 unquestionable progress has been made with hardening of the budget constraints of Russian enterprises. This has been instrumental in the creation of a more stable macroeconomic environment and has also been steadily pushing enterprises toward introducing improvements in their output mix. Unfortunately, the progress towards stabilization was achieved mainly

[30] See Auktsinenok and Kapeliushnikov (1996).
[31] *Expert* (in Russian), 3 June 1996.

through ad hoc cuts in government expenditure, while the streamlining of the tax system has been delayed. As a result, effective tax collection has been dwindling, while ad hoc expenditure reductions have encouraged a culture of non-payment. Inter-enterprise and tax arrears have been growing rapidly, thereby increasing pressure on the government to offer concessions and subsidies. While the pressure for cash injections has so far been largely resisted, concessions in the form of tax arrears and tax exemptions were not. The excessive managerial powers and opportunism already mentioned appear to have increased these adverse pressures, as enterprise directors appear to be primarily interested in reducing the transparency of transactions for continued asset stripping. Hence extensive recourse to arrears, tax offsets and barter transactions.[32] If the government does not take steps to ensure effective tax administration, it will have to abandon macroeconomic stability or prohibitively tax the most promising enterprises. In either case, further structural reform will be delayed.

8 CONCLUSION

For a number of historical and cultural reasons, the idea of comprehensive employee ownership has definitely had some appeal in parts of Russia. By and large, however, it may be unsustainable in the context of economic transition. Specifically, the pervasive rents inherited from the era of central planning have provided enormous opportunities for private gain with the liberalization of economic activity. Even culturally, private enrichment has found receptive ground with at least part of the population, so inhibiting the formation of 'co-operative equilibria'.[33] To a considerable extent, enterprise managers were the primary beneficiaries of this process. Because of informational asymmetry and organizational routines, ordinary workers were generally unable to partake in the rents. On the government side, the weakness, corruptibility and inefficiency of central and regional bureaucracies have not provided effective checks against spontaneous rent appropriation.

One of the aims of the mass privatization programme in Russia has been to ensure some redistributive justice through the free distribution of vouchers to the population. The procedures for auctioning enterprises under the

[32] Survey data indicate that the role of barter transactions has been steadily rising, from about 6–7 per cent in 1992, to 20–25 per cent in 1995, and 30 per cent in 1996 (*Russian Economic Barometer*, No. 2, 1996).

[33] The idea of employee ownership in Russia has also been part of the political process. Its main proponent, Svyatoslav Fedorov, has steadily lost popularity in the course of the transition period: he was left with less than 1 per cent of the vote in the June 1996 presidential election.

programme were highly decentralized, however, and subject to every form of manipulation. As a result, most of the shares were obtained by insiders, with the workers and managers apparently receiving the bulk of privatized shares. In the long term, however, employee ownership will be partly transformed as these shares will be retraded either to the management, or to outside investors. Even in the short term, most of the firms can be viewed as only formally employee-owned; in practice, the managers enjoy a degree of decision-making power much higher than their counterparts in advanced market economies, and perhaps even in the other countries of Central and Eastern Europe. Specifically, survey data indicate that most workers regard their firms as de facto manager-controlled, even if in those firms the workers formally own most of the shares.

The most important question is what this would mean in terms of the pace and quality of industrial restructuring. In principle, managerial control should alleviate some of the problems of employee ownership outlined in the literature, such as overmanning and excessive wages. Unfortunately, the transition process unfolding in Russia has introduced additional problems. Most importantly, considerable variation and continued uncertainty over potential profitability shorten managerial horizons. For example, the managers of troubled enterprises face the imminent threat of bankruptcy, prompting them to secure their personal well-being by disposing of the most valuable assets in a non-transparent manner. At the other end of the spectrum, the managers of potentially profitable enterprises are afraid of prospective future takeover bids from worker-owners or from large outside investors. Moreover, with further development of market institutions the scope for managerial discretion is almost certain to be reduced. All this prompts some managers to extract immediate benefits from their current decision-making monopoly, often at the expense of the enterprise's much-needed adjustment to the conditions of the market.

Early evidence on the performance of enterprises indicates that extensive managerial powers and entrenchment do constitute a problem. By and large, the pace of restructuring has been slow and firms have been unable to tap external sources of financing. Anecdotal evidence suggests that there have been numerous instances of abuse of managerial powers, either in the form of covert acts of privatization or through enhanced salaries or perks secured by the top management. Perhaps the most dangerous implication of this form of corporate governance has been the perpetuation of a lack of transparency in inter-enterprise transactions. Among other things, this has had adverse implications in terms of tax receipts and overall tax culture. At the same time, such enterprises have exerted strong pressure on the government to increase subsidies in order to take up the managerial slack in restructuring. Faced with the prospect of large fiscal imbalances, the Russian government has had to increase the notional tax burden of enterprises, thereby hurting *bona fide* tax-payers and further undermining the tax culture.

Whatever the adequacy of the current arrangement for the interim management of assets, overall progress with the development of market institutions should eventually steer things in the right direction in Russia.[34] Further progress with economic liberalization will be conducive to the dissipation of rents and the concomitant reduction of incentive distortions. Macroeconomic stabilization is likely to clarify the financial health of enterprises and will contribute to a better investment climate. A strengthening of the legal and institutional framework for securities markets will attract outside investment in corporate debt instruments that will in turn act as an additional control device for management. The deepening of the markets for factors of production should improve the turnover of managerial talent, thereby increasing the management quality.

In the meantime, to the extent these markets/institutions are still in an embryonic state, in certain instances the effective strengthening of the position of employees may be warranted. It appears that in situations where co-operation between managers and employees has been more open, firm restructuring has proceeded more successfully. A healthy dose of employee power, and the associated wage flexibility, have also been useful for mitigating employment shocks in regions dominated by so-called 'city-forming' enterprises, and so may have curbed the rise in unemployment nationwide. While, as argued in Section 3, comprehensive employeeism may not be the way of the future for Russia, it does offer temporary relief in important aspects of transition. More permanently, it contributes to a more balanced pattern of corporate governance and control within which workers' rights are likely to be respected under any corporate governance structure.

REFERENCES

Auktsinenok, S. and R. Kapeliushnikov (1996), 'Labour Hoarding in Russian Industry,' *Russian Economic Barometer*, No. 2, 3–11.

Blasi, J., (1994), 'Corporate Governance in Russia,' The World Bank – Central European University conference paper, Washington, December.

Earle, J. and S. Estrin (1994), 'Worker Ownership in Transition,' The World Bank – Central European University conference paper, Washington, December.

---

[34] An exception could occur if the political will to reverse dwindling tax revenues should prove deficient, resulting in either a slippage into high inflation, or in disastrous structural policies under which the best and most promising enterprises would be continuously drained by higher taxes in order to support tax-delinquent firms.

European Bank for Reconstruction and Development (1995), *Transition Report 1995*, London.

Gavrilenkov, Y and V. Koen (1994), 'How Large Was the Output Collapse in Russia? Alternative Estimates and Welfare Implications,' *IMF Working Paper* 94/154, Dec.

Gerschenkron, A. (1962), *Economic Backwardness in a Historical Perspective*, Cambridge Mass., Harvard University Press.

Halligan, L. and A. Richter (1995), 'Restructuring and the Russian Labour Market: 1992–95', mimeo, September.

Hansmann, H. (1990), 'The Viability of Worker Ownership: an Economic Perspective on the Political Structure of the Firm,' in M. Aoki, B. Gustaffson, and O. Williamson (eds), *The Firm as a Nexus for Treaties*, London, Sage Pub., 162–84.

Hewett, E. (1988), *Reforming the Soviet Economy: Equality versus Efficiency*, Brookings Institution, Washington DC.

Lipton, D. and J. Sachs (1993), 'Prospects for Russian Economic Reforms,' *Brookings Papers on Economic Activity*, 1, 165–213.

Lissovolik, B. (1995), 'Special Features of Russian Privatization: Causes and Consequences,' in R. Daviddi (ed.), *Property Rights and Privatization in the Transition to a Market Economy*, European Institute for Public Administration, Maastricht.

Lipsits, I., I. Gourkov and A. Neschadin (1995), 'Russian Enterprises in Search of Survival Elixir,' Working Paper, Expert Institute of the Russian Union of Industrialists and Entrepreneurs, Moscow.

Litwack, J. (1989), 'Discretionary Behaviour and Soviet Economic Reform,' mimeo, Stanford University, December.

Meade, J. (1972), 'The Theory of Labor-Managed Firms and of Profit-sharing,' *Economic Journal*, 82 (325, Supplement), March, 402–28.

Organisation for Economic Co-operation and Development (1995), *OECD Economic Surveys, The Russian Federation*, Paris.

Pistor, K., Frydman, R. and A. Rapaczynski (1994), 'Investing in Insider-Dominated Firms: A Study of Russian Voucher Privatization Funds,' The World Bank – Central European University conference paper, Washington, December.

Rausser, G. and L. Simon (1992), 'The Political Economy of Transition in Eastern Europe: Packaging Enterprises for Privatization,' in C. Clague and G. Rausser (eds), *The Emergence of Market Economies in Eastern Europe*, Cambridge Mass., Basil Blackwell, 245–71.

Shleifer, A., (1994), 'Establishing Property Rights,' The World Bank Annual Conference, April.

Shleifer, A. and D. Vasiliev (1994), 'Management Ownership and Russian Privatization,' The World Bank – Central European University conference paper, Washington, December.

Stiglitz, J. (1992), 'The Design of Financial Systems for the Newly-Emerging Democracies of Eastern Europe,' in C. Clague and G. Rausser (eds), *The Emergence of Market Economies in Eastern Europe*, Cambridge Mass., Basil Blackwell, 161–87.

Tornell, A. and J. Velasco (1992), 'The Tragedy of the Commons and Economic Growth: Why Does Capital Flow from Poor to Rich Countries,' *Journal of Political Economy*, Vol. 100, No. 6, 1208–31.

Ward, B. (1958), 'The Firm in Illyria: Market Syndicalism,' *American Economic Review*, Vol. 48, 566–89.

Webster, L. (with J. Franz, I. Artemiev and H. Wackman) (1995), 'Newly Privatized Enterprises: A Survey,' in I. Lieberman and J. Nellis (eds), *Russia: Creating Private Enterprises and Efficient Markets*, The World Bank, Washington DC.

Weitzman, M. (1993), 'Economic Transition: Can Theory Help?,' *European Economic Review*, 37, 549–55.

9. Employee Ownership alongside Hyper-stagflation in Ukraine: Enterprise Survey Results for 1993–95

Daniel Vaughan-Whitehead*

1 INTRODUCTION

Although privatization is proceeding rapidly in some countries of Central and Eastern Europe, and most governments have been trying to promote various forms of employee share-ownership as part of the process, the impact of this property form on restructuring, economic performance and industrial relations has not been much investigated. The aim of the present chapter is to present some results from an enterprise survey whose first round was carried out in 1994, and the second in 1995. We tried to analyse the effect of employee ownership on enterprises, paying particular attention to its impact on restructuring and employment in the particular crisis context of Ukraine. The horrendous situation in which the Ukrainian economy finds itself might be characterized as hyper-stagflation, in which output has shrunk by up to 50 per cent and inflation in 1993 alone was over 10,000 per cent. Over the same period, wages fell by more than 60 per cent in real terms. We complement our survey results with an example of a successful employee-owned enterprise in Lviv, Western Ukraine.

* I would like to thank Guy Standing and László Zsoldos for their friendly co-operation during the first round of this enterprise survey carried out in 1994, and for allowing me to use, for this first preliminary study, data from the second round carried out in 1995. More detailed results will be presented in a joint comparative paper on the basis of additional statistics and an econometric analysis. I would also like to thank the Ukrainian Ministry of Statistics. Thanks are due finally to Anatoly Fedorenko for the useful information he provided on privatization in Ukraine.

2 EMPLOYEE OWNERSHIP AND PRIVATIZATION

The privatization process was launched in Ukraine in a very difficult economic and social context (*Table 9.1*). Since 1990 the Ukrainian economy has been
characterized by a fall in production – GDP fell by more than 50 per cent in
the five years up to 1995 – hyperinflation and, consequently, a sharp fall in real
wages and living standards. The economy is still also characterized by monopoly enterprises which largely contributed to inflation by raising prices despite
the continuous decline in production. In November 1992 these developments
forced the Ukrainian Parliament to grant the government emergency powers in
order to stabilize the economy and to carry out the initial steps towards market
reforms. The new policy mainly consisted of a restrictive tax-based incomes
policy, however, that rapidly contributed to a further reduction in living standards
without helping to control inflation. The inflation rate rose to over 10,000 per
cent in 1993, while real wages that year fell by nearly 60 per cent to less than
40 per cent of the subsistence minimum. At the same time, the minimum wage
also fell below 5 per cent of the poverty line (Khulikov, 1995).

Privatization was intended to turn most large inefficient state enterprises
towards profitability. It was preceded by the corporatization of enterprises,
which means the transformation of enterprises into 100 per cent state-owned
public joint-stock companies. One of the aims of corporatization was to
induce the transformation of large monopoly state enterprises into several new
small and medium-sized joint-stock enterprises.

The privatization process was officially launched in early 1992 when the
Parliament adopted the *State Privatization Programme* with a set of laws
stipulating the different conditions for small, medium-sized and large state
enterprises (*Table 9.2*), and setting forth the responsibilities of the State
Property Fund (SPF). Citizens' participation is based on the right to receive
one free certificate of privatization issued by the National Bank of Ukraine
and distributed by the State Savings Bank. From August 1993 people were
invited to open 'privatization deposit accounts' and within a year more than
five million people – 10 per cent of the population – had done so. In fact, this
free transfer of property was intended to implement mass privatization in a
relatively short time. The nominal amount of these certificates was fixed at
Krbs 30,000, and was originally intended to involve 40 per cent of state
property; the amount was increased to 70 per cent after a special
parliamentary act in September 1992. The nominal amount of privatization
certificates was also increased from Krbs 30,000 to 65,000 in late 1993 to
compensate for inflation. Some small enterprises have been privatized
exclusively on the basis of privatization certificates.

Employees in enterprises designated for privatization were also given certain
privileges in acquiring the property rights of their enterprises, in combination

Table 9.1 Key economic indicators, Ukraine, 1991–95 (%)

	1991	1992	1993	1994	1995
GDP growth rate	−13.5	−16.8	−14.2	−23.0	−11.8
Industrial production	−4.8	−6.4	−8.0	−27.3	−11.5
Capital investment	−7.1	−36.8	−10.5	−22.8	−35.0
Inflation (CPI)	39.0	210.0	10 255.0	501.0	282.0
Official unemployment	–	–	0.3	0.4	0.5
Labour productivity	−7.3	−8.1	−12.0	−20.0	−4.8
Real average wage					
(Index 1990=100)	87.2	73.6	32.3	27.6	32.0

Source: Ministry of Statistics

Table 9.2 Legislation on privatization, Ukraine, 1991–95

Legislation	Date
Act on the Privatization of the Property of State Enterprises	March 1992
Act on Privatization of Small State Enterprises	March 1992
Act on Privatization Certificates	March 1992
Act on Leasing of Property of State Enterprises	April 1992
Decree on Leasing Arrangements and Privatization	May 1993
Decree on Corporatization of Large Enterprises	June 1993
Presidential Decree on Financial Funds and Companies	February 1994

with their privatization certificates and independently of them. The privatization programme stipulates priority rights in respect of their enterprise, on condition that shares go to workers as individuals and not to the workers' collective. A special privilege was first given to workers for the free transfer of the enterprise's social assets, that is 'facilities created at the cost of assets of social development', such as recreation centres, vacation homes, day-care facilities, and cafeterias. In addition, shares could be bought by workers using the privatization certificates directly placed on their bank accounts. A certain number of additional shares could also be bought in cash by employees through personal savings for a nominal value not exceeding Krbs 15,000, which corresponded to 50 per cent of the original nominal value of the vouchers.[1]

---

[1] Original maximum nominal value of shares was therefore Krbs 45,000 (30,000 in the form of certificates and 15,000 in cash).

Shares that remain after distribution to employees are offered for competitive sale. When an enterprise is to be sold at open auction, the workers may form a buyers' association, which must include at least half of the workforce, and submit an application to become the preferred buyer. They will then have the right to pay by instalments over a period of up to three years, the initial payment being 30 per cent of the purchase cost. The management was also authorized to purchase 5 per cent of shares at nominal price. Labour–management buy-outs have also developed, mainly in small enterprises.

The *Act on the Leasing of State Enterprises of April 1992* also gave workers the right to lease the enterprise and endowed them with a preferential right to buy out their enterprise at a later date. We will see from our enterprise survey results that this last option has been much used by employees and that most leasehold enterprises have in practice been progressively transformed into employee-owned enterprises. In the first phase of privatization approximately 3,500 enterprises were leased to the managers and other employees with buy-out provisions, either free of charge or at a very low price (OECD, 1995, p. 57). After having been severely criticized, however, the provisions of the leasing law were considerably attenuated in 1993: for example, the preferential buy-out option for lessees was eliminated. It has been argued that leasing would slow the process of mass privatization in Ukraine and hinder other potential buyers. Furthermore, the privileges offered to the workers' collective would also lead to the undervaluation of the property to be privatized. We will see if the empirical evidence confirms the inefficiency of this privatization form.

According to the State Property Fund, 1,750 industrial enterprises were privatized in 1993 compared to 36 in 1992. A new stage of privatization started in March 1994. A presidential decree provided for the circulation of paper privatization certificates.[2] Shares in more than 100 joint-stock enterprises were sold to the owners of privatization certificates. About 30 million shares were offered to Ukrainian citizens for purchase. Another decree in November created streamlined methods for the mass privatization of 8,000 enterprises through certificate auctions to be held in 1995. The objective of the State Property Fund was to set up more than 8,000 joint-stock enterprises. In December 1994 a further decree was signed to accelerate small privatization.

By the end of 1995 28 million citizens had received certificates and five million had become owners of shares, entitlements or portions of private property (UNDP, 1996). Privatization certificates were given out until July 1996 and had to be used by the end of the year. By the beginning of 1996

---

[2] 'New Stage of Privatization Kicks Off March 1', in *INTELNEWS*, Kiev, 26 February 1994, p. 2.

approximately 26,000 enterprises had been privatized, most of them in 1995. The targets for the year were not reached, however, with only 25 per cent of the targeted industrial enterprises being privatized. Since he came into power in July 1994 President Leonid Kuchma has demonstrated a firm commitment to the rapid accomplishment of the privatization process. He reiterated in 1996 the need for accelerating privatization, stressing 'the extraordinary socio-economic and political importance of completing primary privatization in 1996' and also insisting on the 'social prospects' of privatization (see his proposed programme in Box 9.1).

Box 9.1 'Speeding up privatization is a necessity of the times.' Speech of the President of Ukraine at the conference on accelerating privatization Kiev, 24 January 1996

The centrepiece of privatization is a radical reform of property relations and, as a result, fundamental change in production relations. Our task is not confined to creating a private owner, not even on a massive scale. We have to create a society of private owners.

This is why the main goal of privatization is not to generate cash for the budget, even though it is an important source of revenue for financing social programmes. The chief purpose of privatization is to match property and an efficient owner, thereby ensuring a dynamic growth of society's productive forces.

Privatization is also a precondition of restructuring the Ukrainian economy with an eye to people's needs. It will also make it possible to turn the input-heavy economy into a resource- and energy-saving one.

Lastly, privatization is designed to mould a modern human being – an active, enterprising personality able to provide a worthy life for him/herself. In fact this is perhaps the single most important task. It is hopeless to try and inculcate market awareness and owner's mentality in the absence of private property and respect for the results of one's own and other people's work and even property as such. Our own history proves that well.

We have to proceed from the fact that privatization makes it possible to increase the individual's responsibility for his own life to a great extent and thus reduce the paternalistic role of the State, which has acquired unprecedented proportions in this country. Also, this is the only real chance to create an economy in which citizens who are unable to provide for themselves would get adequate social security rather than alms.

We must restore people's faith in the necessity, irreversibility and, most importantly, the sound social prospects of privatization. This is why I would name the ideological substantiation of privatization among its priority tasks.

Based on the consequences of today's conference, I would set forth the following strategic objectives:

- greater and wider participation of citizens in privatization;
- supporting the private owner;

- encouragement of small entrepreneurship;
- creation of an organizationally and economically more favourable environment for foreign investments in the Ukrainian economy, giving investors due role on privatization.

In doing this we have to solve, together with the Cabinet of Ministers of Ukraine, a number of concrete and important issues:

1. To strengthen the motivation of Ukrainian tax-payers, work collectives and managers of enterprises to take part in privatization; to raise the responsibility of government officials for timely and satisfactory performance of the tasks of the privatization programme.

2. To take measures aimed at backing up privatization certificates with real property and preventing them from devaluation.

3. To streamline assessments procedures, especially for objects slated for privatization through competitive bidding or auction.

4. To take a more substantiated approach towards establishing additional conditions of privatization, such as their expediency (possibility of implementation, deadlines, etc.).

5. To shorten time needed for privatization.

6. To determine the main aspects and fundamental distinctions of privatization in the agroindustrial complex and lend it a market character.

7. To solve, from the regulatory and organizational point of view, the problem of managing state-owned enterprises and shares of assets of enterprises in mixed ownership.

8. To take measures aimed at elevating the status and broadening the powers of the State Property Fund of Ukraine in comparison with other national economic institutions.

9. To ensure periodic review of the lists of enterprises exempt from privatization and their updating by Parliament, at the same time, on the basis of analysis of the performance of a number of state-owned and communal enterprises, to look into the expediency of transferring them to private ownership. One of the decisive reasons can be bankruptcy of a large state-owned enterprise not included in the exemption list.

10. To streamline existing and develop additional measures for raising the interests of foreign investors in privatization.

11. To pay attention to proposals from international organizations and use their concrete assistance in privatization. The main objective of our co-operation with them is to obtain real returns from jointly launched programmes and projects.

12. To increase government's attention to the status and performance of enterprises during the post-privatization period.

Source: UNDP *Ukraine Human Development Report 1996*, p. 14.

3 EXPECTED EFFECTS OF EMPLOYEE OWNERSHIP ON ENTERPRISES

In our questionnaire we distinguished five different enterprises according to their property form: state-owned, leaseholding, closed joint-stock, open joint-stock, and private. *Closed joint-stock* enterprises normally include state enterprises whose capital has been distributed to a restricted number of shareholders. Most closed joint-stock enterprises in Ukraine are fully owned and managed by their employees. The *open joint-stock* category includes a variety of domestic individual or group investors; these enterprises were also found to have a large percentage of worker share-ownership. *Leasehold* enterprises remain the property of the state while its assets are leased back to its management and workers before being converted into a non-state enterprise, generally a joint-stock company. This property form is thus a temporary measure. *Private* enterprises include newly created and generally small enterprises, as well as some small privatized enterprises. This group of enterprises also includes some partnership with foreign investors. The relatively limited number of private enterprises and, within this category, the limited number of joint-ventures or other forms of partnership with a foreign investor, however, did not allow us to draw conclusions concerning this last property form, but only to provide some tentative evidence from a few enterprise examples.

In order to test the effects of employee ownership, we regrouped all open and closed joint-stock enterprises in which more than 50 per cent of the shares were owned by the employees. In 1994, we obtained a sample of 52 employee-owned enterprises out of 311 enterprises that we then compared to other enterprises – state owned, leaseholding, private and other joint-stock. In 1995 we compared 184 employee-owned enterprises in a total sample of 541 enterprises. This last group mainly included open joint-stock enterprises in which the majority of capital was not owned by the workers, although a few of these firms had distributed some minority capital to them.

Table 9.3 presents some of the effects which might be expected from the five property forms according to the literature (Bartlett and Uvalic, 1986). First, private enterprises and non-employee-owned joint-stock enterprises are expected to implement significant lay-off programmes in their restructuring process after privatization has been completed. Accordingly, the social climate is expected to deteriorate rapidly. Managers can be expected to develop collective agreements and trade union activities to improve the situation, although they might prefer to promote direct participatory practices and to favour direct partnership with the workers. The wages of the remaining labour force are also expected to be higher, particularly in joint ventures with foreign enterprises. By contrast, state-owned enterprises have often been

Table 9.3 *Effects theoretically expected from different property forms, Ukraine*

	State-owned	Lease-hold	Private	Employee-owned joint-stock	Other joint-stock
Wage levels	−	±	+	±	+
Wage differentials	−	−	+	−	+
Flexible wage	−	−	+	+	+
Profit-sharing	−	−	+	+	+
Employment cuts	−	−	+	−	+
Training	−	±	+	±	+
New technologies	−	−	+	−	+
Change in work organization	−	±	+	+	+
Participatory practices	−	±	±	+	±
Trade unions	+	±	±	±	±
Collective agreements	+	+	±	±	±
Exports	−	−	+	−	+
Efficiency	−	±	+	±	+

described as developing 'labour hoarding', maintaining high levels of employment despite falls in output. Wages are particularly low, and no profit-sharing schemes or other payment systems linked to performance have been promoted. As a result of these economic problems and low wages, the social climate is expected to deteriorate even if employment stability contributes to avoiding major social conflicts.

Compared to state-owned enterprises, leaseholding enterprises can help to enhance workers' motivation and productivity, so allowing higher wage increases. At the same time, employees might use their bargaining power to secure employment stability, and accept wage reductions as a sensible alternative to lay-offs. Wage behaviour at this type of enterprise is thus difficult to predict. Workers' influence might also lead to direct participatory practices such as profit-sharing and participation in decision-making. These different elements – higher wages or, alternatively, higher employment stability combined with new participatory practices – might help to improve the social climate. In these firms, no new investment and introduction of new technologies is to be expected, however, due to the lack of profits and new capital, a trend which might be reinforced by the fact that employees have no ownership interest in the fixed assets of their enterprise. The absence of individual property rights might also limit the increase in workers' motivation expected from these schemes. In contrast, private firms, especially foreign companies, are expected to provide new capital and to introduce new technologies, as well as training programmes to adapt the labour force to new technology requirements. They should also help local enterprises to find new markets abroad and so contribute to boosting exports, while implementing large programmes of lay-offs. In contrast, employee-owned enterprises are expected to maintain employment after privatization.

In employee-owned enterprises the effect on wages is difficult to predict. On the one hand, the theoretical literature predicts that employees will pay higher wages, to the detriment of investment and enterprise profitability. On the other hand, they might be ready to accept relatively lower wages to compensate for employment stability. They are also expected to promote different forms of economic democracy, including profit-sharing schemes and other participatory practices, which could contribute to improving the social climate within the enterprise, and to enhancing worker motivation and productivity. Nevertheless, this effect on economic performance might be limited because of the low propensity of employee-owned enterprises to invest in capital intensive products and new technologies, the workers being constrained by a lack of financial resources. Compared with leaseholding enterprises, however, employees have an interest in rapidly increasing their enterprise's value, and in ensuring better maintenance of equipment and introduction of new technologies. We also directly checked by means of our survey whether this relative employment stability was accompanied by training programmes aimed at adapting the labour force to restructuring requirements.

We will now examine whether some of these theoretical effects are confirmed by our two enterprise surveys carried out in Ukraine in 1994 and in 1995. Of course, the aim of this chapter is not to draw definite conclusions but to compare, through empirical evidence, employee-owned enterprises to other property forms in the current restructuring process.

4 SURVEY RESULTS

The first survey was conducted in 1994 in six regions of the country – Kiev city, Kiev region, Donetsk, Kharkov, Lviv and Nikolaev – and provided comparative data on 311 establishments for the period 1993–94. The fieldwork was carried out in collaboration with the Ministry of Statistics of Ukraine. The methodology involved interviews with senior managements and

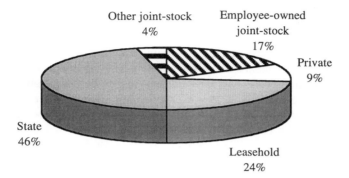

Figure 9.1a Distribution of property forms, Ukrainian Survey, 1994
Source: ILO Ukrainian Labour Flexibility Survey 1 (ULFS1).

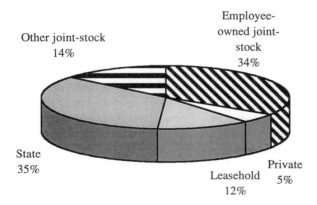

Figure 9.1b Distribution of property forms, Ukraine, All Regions, 1995
Source: ILO Ukrainian Labour Flexibility Survey 2 (ULFS2).

two questionnaires, one statistical part to be completed by various sections of the establishment and another administered orally in discussion with managers, often accompanied by senior staff and union representatives. The second survey carried out in 1995 followed the same pattern, applied to the same enterprises and more than 200 additional enterprises drawn from six other regions. In all, 541 enterprises were covered over the period 1994–95. We put particular emphasis on privatization and various aspects of labour market dynamics.[3] The two samples are not directly comparable, since the second round covered over 200 enterprises more than the first. We obtained results on how establishments with different property forms – state-owned, leasehold, private, employee-owned joint-stock, other joint-stock – behave in terms of employment, wage policy, training, worker participation, and collective agreements. In 1994, 46.6 per cent of establishments were still state-owned, 23.8 per cent were leaseholdings (*ariendas*), 16.7 per cent employee-owned joint-stock, 4 per cent other joint-stock, and 9 per cent private establishments. In terms of property form distribution, there had been considerable restructuring. According to survey results, leaseholding firms were progressively being converted into open joint-stock enterprises. The number of leasehold enterprises diminished over 1994–95, from 24 per cent to 12 per cent, confirming the progressive replacement of this property form. In 1995, 80 per cent of remaining leaseholdings reported that they planned to change property form, while the number of state enterprises had decreased from 45 per cent to 34 per cent of the sample. As can be seen from *Figures 9.1a* and *9.1b*, the categories that grew most were employee-owned enterprises, from 17 per cent in 1994 to 34 per cent in 1995, and other joint-stock enterprises, which increased from 4 per cent to 14 per cent. Surprisingly, the proportion of private enterprises was lower in 1995, although this result is not systematically representative of the economy as a whole.

4.1 The Continuous Economic Slump

Despite privatization, all types of establishment reported a decline in output and sales. The probability of decline was highest in state-owned enterprises, and lowest in private firms and joint-stock enterprises. In 1995 81 per cent of all establishments reported that their sales had declined compared with two years ago. It was not surprising that in 1995 enterprises were operating at well below capacity. In 1994 enterprises reported that they were operating at 66 per cent of capacity, this average falling even further in 1995, to 48.5 per cent. The lowest percentage was in chemicals and the highest in energy. This

---

[3] For complementary results on the Ukrainian enterprise survey for 1993–94, see Standing (1994b); for more details on the survey for 1994–95 see Standing and Zsoldos (1995).

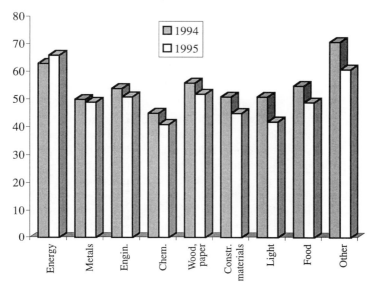

Figure 9.2 Capacity utilization, Ukraine, 1994–95

Source: ULFS1, ULFS2.

extremely low percentage gives an idea of the deep crisis with which Ukrainian industry is confronted. This situation not only reflects the large-scale collapse of external markets, but also the fall in demand on the internal market. Consumption has fallen dramatically since 1991, reflecting an inability to afford anything other than the most basic goods in a situation of falling real wages and stagflation (Khulikov, 1995).

4.2 Employment Changes

It is in this context that we tried to measure the impact of this falling output on employment. The average number of employees was the highest in state-owned enterprises and non-employee-owned joint-stock enterprises, and the lowest in private enterprises. In 1995 the average number of employees was nearly 1,000 in employee-owned joint-stock enterprises (*Figure 9.3*).

The first impressive figure was for employment cuts which on average reached nearly 40 per cent at all enterprises in the first survey over the course of a year. We first tried to identify what was distinct about how these enterprises carried out this process.[4] According to *Figures 9.4a* and *9.4b*, in

---

[4] See Standing and Zsoldos (1995) for more detailed results and on details on employment changes (by industry, by region, by size, etc.).

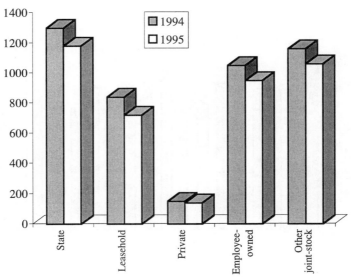

Figure 9.3 Average number of employees, by property form, Ukraine, 1994–95

Source: ULFS1, ULFS2.

1993–94 the fall in employment seems to have been more significant in non-employee-owned joint-stock enterprises and leasehold enterprises, and less in private and employee-owned enterprises. In 1994–95, however, employee-owned enterprises were found to reduce employment significantly, leaseholding enterprises continuing to reduce employment the most. For those believing that there would be employment cuts and restructuring only after privatization, it is worth observing that employment cuts were relatively high in state enterprises. Total employment was cut in state enterprises by nearly 8 per cent in 1993–94 and by nearly 9 per cent in 1994–95. Although employment in employee-owned enterprises fell by only 4 per cent in 1993–94 it fell significantly – by more than 10 per cent – in 1994–95. This might mean that employee-owned enterprises are slower to carry out lay-offs, probably because they try to find other restructuring alternatives before this last resort. In the first years of reform, for instance, a cut in normal working hours was found to be an alternative to releasing workers. Nevertheless, these enterprises would also implement lay-offs if they became indispensable to the future profitability of the enterprise. Private enterprises have maintained employment with small and dynamic new enterprises even creating new jobs. From the sample, joint ventures were found to have decreased their total number of employees by nearly 12 per cent in 1993–94 and by 8 per cent in

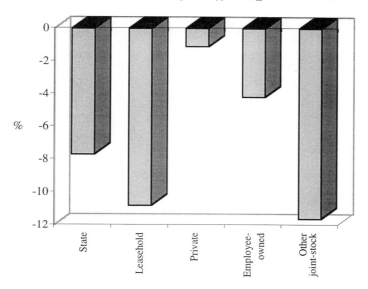

Figure 9.4a Percentage change in employment, by property form, Ukraine, 1993–94 (all workers)

Source: ULFS1.

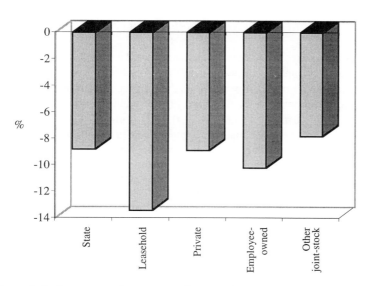

Figure 9.4b Percentage change in employment, by property form, Ukraine, 1994–95 (all workers)

Source: ULFS2.

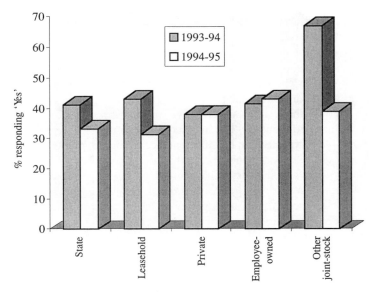

Figure 9.5 Produce same level of output with fewer workers, by property form, Ukraine, 1993–95

Source: ULFS2.

1994–95, thus confirming that some lay-off programmes are to be expected in such enterprises.

Managers were asked whether they could produce the same output with fewer workers and to estimate what percentage they could let go without reducing output (*Figure 9.5*). For all property forms the proportion of enterprises in that situation decreased between the two surveys, but remained at a relatively high level (more than 40 per cent on average). This form of 'labour-hoarding' tended to be lowest in private enterprises and highest in employee-owned joint-stock enterprises and other joint-stock enterprises, a result which probably also reflects differences in employment size – the average number of employees is particularly small in private enterprises and large in labour- and non-employee-owned joint-stock enterprises. We can thus anticipate that these enterprises will shed many more jobs in 1996–97. State and leaseholding enterprises also estimated that they could cut jobs without affecting output.

4.3 Wage Policy

In order to cope with persistent stagflation, in 1994–96 the government continued its central wage regulations, mainly through a rigid tariff system, a tax-based incomes policy involving a punitive tax on high wage rises, and very irregular adjustments of the statutory minimum wage. As a result, the real average wage fell by more than 70 per cent between 1991 and 1995, and the minimum wage of Krbs 60,000 (less than $1 per month) also fell to an indecent 1 per cent of the official poverty line (Khulikov, 1995). This centralized system encouraged firms to shift to non-monetary remuneration and prevented them from linking wages to productivity growth, which might have converted them into an effective mechanism for boosting work motivation and efficiency.[5] The impact of central wage regulations on enterprises was expected to be different according to property form. In particular, it has been commonly argued that privatization would influence the evolution of wages in industry. The main claim is that privatization would lead to higher wages, for several reasons. First, the government's attempts to limit wage increases as part of its policy to limit expenditure could lead to state enterprises holding down wages more than other enterprises. Second, private enterprise would lead to better performance, thus allowing them to share part of the profits with the workers through higher wages. Surprisingly, quite different results were obtained between 1993–94 and 1994–95 (*Figures 9.6a* and *9.6b*). As expected, wages were highest in non-employee-owned joint-stock and private enterprises and relatively lower in state enterprises. In 1994–95 private enterprises were still found to pay the highest wages but wages appeared to be lower in other joint-stock enterprises. In both periods relatively low wages in employee-owned enterprises would tend to support the view that economic democracy does not lead to higher wages, although those enterprises were found to pay substantial other benefits and profit-sharing bonuses (see next section). Leaseholding enterprises were found to pay slightly higher wages than state enterprises, which were found to pay among the lowest wages.

Since various studies on Ukraine have reported that many enterprises do not always pay the wages to which they are committed, or pay them only after a significant delay, it was important to complement our data on wage levels with information on the difficulties enterprises have in this connection. Nearly 50 per cent of enterprises reported problems in paying wages in 1994 and more than 60 per cent in 1995. This proportion was particularly striking in employee-owned enterprises, more than 70 per cent of them admitting that in 1994 they had difficulties in paying wages. While employee-owned enterprises seem to have succeeded in maintaining employment, they were found to pay lower wages and to have great difficulties in paying them at all. In 1994, 69 per cent of state enterprises also had problems in this connection. Enterprises generally solve this problem by getting loans or delaying wage payments. In June 1996 more than Krbs 250 trillion in wages remained

---

[5] 'Reforming wage policy in a hyper-inflationary context', Chapter 4 of *ILO-CEET*, 1995 .

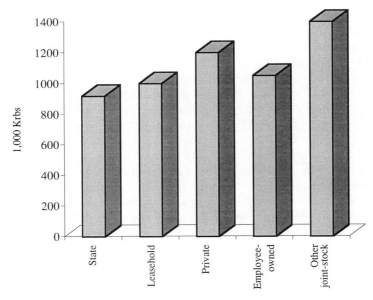

Figure 9.6a Average wages, by property form, Ukraine, 1993–94
Source: ULFS1, ULFS2.

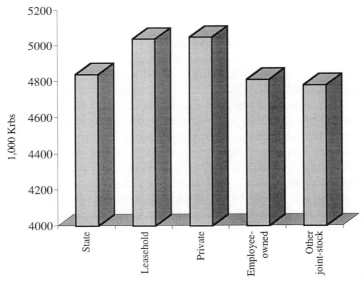

Figure 9.6b Average wages, by property form, Ukraine, 1994–95
Source: ULFS1, ULFS2.

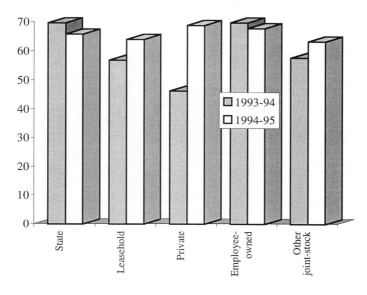

Figure 9.7 Difficulty in paying wages, Ukraine, 1993–95 (% responding 'Yes')
Source: ULFS1, ULFS2.

unpaid. Interviews with local authorities in two regions of Ukraine, Zhitomir (Kiev Region) and Lviv (Western Ukraine) also revealed that most workers were paid well below the official minimum and that wage payments were regularly postponed by several months. From factory visits we were able to observe that the worst situations were in state-owned enterprises, but that such practices were also observable in other types of enterprise: from *Figure 9.7*, for example, we can see that this problem was also widespread among private enterprises. Transformation of enterprises into private businesses does not seem so far to have improved the ability of enterprises to pay wages.[6] This is a worrying phenomenon, since a delay in paying wages in a stagflationary context amounts to substantial additional wage cuts.

We also collected data on wage differentials (*Table 9.4*), which were found to have increased between 1993 and 1995, with the emergence of a distinct category of very low-paid workers, paid less than one-third of the enterprise average wage. In terms of property forms, wage differentials were found to be slightly smaller in employee-owned and leasehold enterprises. Elements of economic democracy and the 'wage solidarity' principle which tend to prevail in employee-owned enterprises may perhaps contribute to limiting the growth

---

[6] Average wages reported by official statistics should be deflated to take account of these processes.

Table 9.4 Occupational wage ratios by property form, Ukraine, 1995 (occupational wages compared with unskilled workers' wages)

	State	Lease	Private	Employee-owned joint-stock	Other joint-stock
Managers	3.75	3.33	4.87	3.39	3.69
Specialists	2.26	2.19	3.61	2.08	2.31
General service	1.29	1.33	2.24	1.39	1.62
Supervisors	2.73	2.44	2.64	2.57	3.14
Technicians	2.02	1.60	1.96	1.73	1.94
Skilled workers	2.18	1.91	3.00	2.00	2.31

Source: ULFS2.

of wage differentials between categories of worker. By contrast, widening wage differentials were observed in private enterprises.

In a context of centralized wage determination based on a wage tariff system, it was also of interest to ascertain whether employee-owned enterprises had succeeded in introducing more flexibility in their payment systems. Most enterprises reported that they had introduced a profit-sharing scheme (*Figure 9.8*), linking part of wages to profits or other economic performance indicators, although this phenomenon seemed to be slightly less widespread in 1995 for all property forms. Nearly 80 per cent of employee-owned enterprises in 1994 reported that they operated some form of profit-sharing, so confirming that employee-owned enterprises tend to introduce various forms of economic democracy. The probability of introducing a profit-sharing scheme was also much higher among employee-owned enterprises in 1995, although to a lesser extent than in 1994. Surprisingly, 56.5 per cent of state enterprises also redistributed some profits to their employees, which probably reflects a tradition of workers sharing part of enterprise profits in Central and Eastern Europe (Vaughan-Whitehead et al., 1995a). This might also be due to the fact that most enterprises, constrained by centralized wage fund control and strict application of the wage tariff system, have tried to develop alternative payment systems – such as profit-sharing – but also fringe benefits in order to pay higher wages. In contrast, less than 30 per cent of private enterprises followed a profit-sharing scheme in 1994–95 (against less than 40 per cent in 1993–94).

Most enterprises also paid production bonuses, with the majority of employee-owned enterprises applying such schemes, showing again their

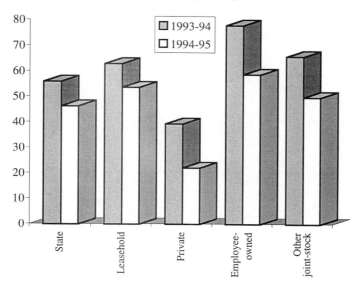

Figure 9.8 Percentage of enterprises operating a profit-sharing scheme, Ukraine, 1993–95 (% responding 'Yes')

Source: ULFS1, ULFS2.

tendency to introduce more flexible payment systems. Enterprises also provided numerous types of social benefit, which in the previous system had traditionally been provided by the enterprise and constituted a large share of total remuneration. Private enterprises in our sample distributed fewer benefits, confirming the expectation that privatization would progressively shift social protection from enterprises to the state. At the same time, benefits were still important in employee-owned enterprises owing to the active role of workers' collectives. These enterprises were thus trying to partly compensate below-average wages by providing various benefits, such as subsidizing food or other consumer goods (*Table 9.5*). This represented an important source of protection for the employees in a period in which several social services previously covered by the state, such as education and health care, have now to be paid by the user, despite the vertiginous fall in living standards.

Table 9.5 *Types of benefits provided, by property form, Ukraine, all regions, 1994–95 (%)*

Benefit type	State		Leasehold		Private		Employee-owned		Other joint-stock	
	1994	1995	1994	1995	1994	1995	1994	1995	1994	1995
Paid vacation	99.0	98.9	100.0	100.0	96.0	100.0	100.0	99.5	100.0	100.0
Additional vacation	88.3	79.6	87.8	86.4	64.3	69.0	92.3	78.1	91.7	76.3
Rest houses	81.6	59.3	81.1	59.1	53.3	34.5	78.8	59.1	83.3	64.9
Sickness benefit	92.0	96.2	100.0	97.0	89.3	96.6	94.2	92.5	81.8	97.4
Paid health services	43.5	27.5	39.1	27.3	35.7	31.0	55.8	31.4	75.0	28.6
Subsidized rent	21.4	16.4	25.6	18.2	10.7	10.3	44.2	19.6	33.3	22.1
Subsidies for kindergartens	31.3	29.5	27.0	22.7	14.2	10.3	42.3	25.5	33.3	16.9
Bonuses	90.1	85.8	94.6	80.3	78.6	65.5	88.5	80.0	100.0	84.4
Profit sharing	–	39.9	–	48.5	–	48.3	–	68.5	–	63.2
Loans	96.9	88.5	97.3	87.9	85.7	86.2	100.0	91.9	100.0	92.2
Retiring assistance	82.2	85.8	86.5	83.3	42.8	58.6	88.5	84.4	75.0	87.0
Supplementary pension	9.0	4.9	10.8	4.5	3.5	3.4	23.1	9.8	25.0	6.5
Possibility for training	73.6	67.8	85.1	69.7	53.6	44.8	84.6	71.2	75.0	66.2
Subsidized food	40.4	35.5	45.9	47.0	17.8	20.7	48.1	32.8	41.7	32.5
Subsidy for canteen or benefit for meal	52.7	44.5	61.6	40.9	25.0	13.8	57.7	41.1	75.0	36.4
Subsidized consumer goods	23.3	14.8	27.0	21.2	17.8	17.2	65.4	20.9	25.0	15.6
Transport subsidies	28.8	24.0	25.7	27.3	28.6	17.2	24.0	18.9	33.3	31.2

Source: ULFS1, ULFS2.

250

4.4 Unionization and Collective Agreements

Figure 9.9 suggests that unionization was highest in joint-stock enterprises, whether employee-owned (97 per cent in 1994) or not (99.5 per cent), and lowest in private enterprises (70 per cent). Trade unionization remains important in state and leasehold enterprises. High unionization in employee-owned enterprises shows that this property form is not incompatible with strong trade unions. Visits to factories in Ukraine clearly showed that trade unions were actively involved in the privatization of their enterprises. As shown in the case study we develop in Section 5, they often helped the workers to become owners of their enterprise, so contradicting theoretical claims that trade unions would be opposed to economic democracy and other forms of direct participation because of fears that their bargaining position would be weakened by a strong and direct employee-management partnership.

Most enterprises reported the conclusion of a collective agreement (*Figure 9.10*) at enterprise level (85 per cent in 1994), while a few also had sectoral or national agreements. Most of these enterprise agreements covered a wide range of issues, such as wage rates, bonuses, benefits, and working time, but also dismissal and release procedures, norms for output performance and internal job mobility and promotion, thus reflecting an intensive collective

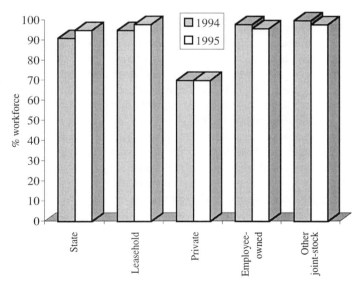

Figure 9.9 Percentage of workers unionized, by property form, Ukraine, 1994–95
Source: ULFS1, ULFS2.

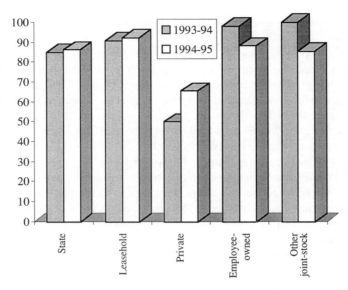

Figure 9.10 Collective agreements reached at enterprise level, by property form, Ukraine, 1993–95 (% responding 'Yes')

Source: ULFS1, ULFS2.

bargaining process. One particularly important result is the much smaller number of collective agreements in private enterprises, and this for all collective bargaining issues included in our survey. This is clearly the sign of less intensive collective bargaining in these enterprises. Less than 50 per cent of them have signed a collective agreement at the enterprise level. We might also add that we identified foreign enterprises that refused to sign enterprise collective agreements with trade unions.

Dismissal agreements were more important in state and leasehold enterprises than in joint-stock or private enterprises. From case studies, it appeared that employee-owned enterprises have a lower propensity to implement lay-offs as the first option, with workers trying to avoid this extreme solution, as was also shown from *Figures 9.4a* and *9.4b* on employment changes.

From *Table 9.6* we can see that the propensity to cover the issue of dismissals through collective agreements in employee-owned enterprises compared to other enterprises was lower in 1993–94, but much higher in 1994–95, thus confirming that employee-owned enterprises also implement lay-offs but tend to delay such decisions and to implement them as the last restructuring option.

Table 9.6 Issues covered by collective agreement, by property form, Ukraine, all regions, 1993 and 1995 (%)

Issue	State		Leasehold		Private		Employee-owned		Other joint-stock	
	1993–94	1994–95	1993–94	1994–95	1993–94	1994–95	1993–94	1994–95	1993–94	1994–95
Wage rates	93.1	94.9	94.6	90.8	64.3	77.8	90.4	95.5	91.6	93.4
Bonuses	87.6	89.2	89.2	93.8	50.0	61.1	75.0	85.0	91.6	88.2
Benefits	86.2	97.7	98.6	98.5	50.0	72.2	75.0	97.8	91.6	100.0
Working time	97.2	98.9	98.6	95.4	57.1	72.2	98.1	96.7	91.6	97.4
Dismissals	74.5	86.2	77.0	73.8	46.4	66.7	57.7	83.1	58.3	76.3
Job mobility	42.7	50.9	44.6	50.8	25.0	44.4	34.6	48.6	50.0	52.0
Promotion	24.1	30.5	20.3	28.6	14.3	29.4	17.3	28.0	25.0	24.0
Output norm	57.9	66.5	64.8	71.4	25.0	55.6	46.0	58.9	58.3	58.7
Release	63.4	63.2	71.6	63.5	25.0	44.4	48.1	70.5	50.0	66.7

Source: ULFS1, ULFS2.

4.5 New Technologies, Work Organization and Training

In 1995 over 40 per cent of enterprises claimed to have introduced new production technologies: this was relatively common in employee-owned and other joint-stock enterprises. This result contradicts theoretical expectations that employee-owned enterprises would be less oriented towards high technology. As expected, private enterprises also have a tendency to introduce new technologies, while less than 30 per cent of state enterprises had done so (*Figure 9.11*). The main change in most enterprises was new production machinery but also computerization and line automation. Computerization was mainly introduced in employee-owned and leasehold enterprises, while state enterprises tended to favour line automation.

Employee-owned enterprises were also found to have a higher propensity to make some change in work organization, confirming their advanced human resources policies. Again, this tendency was lower in state-owned but also in private enterprises (*Figure 9.12*). This may be due to the fact that most private enterprises were newly created, generally small, and had less work organizational problems. In all types of enterprise, the main changes consisted of tightening up the hierarchical structure, rearranging equipment, facilities and materials, and increasing the range of tasks.

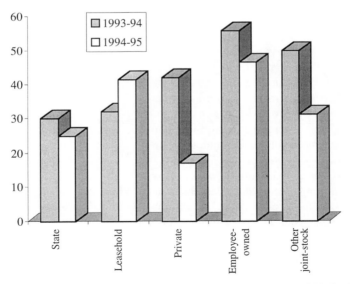

Figure 9.11 Introduced new technology, by property form, Ukraine, 1993–95(% responding 'Yes')

Source: ULFS1, ULFS2.

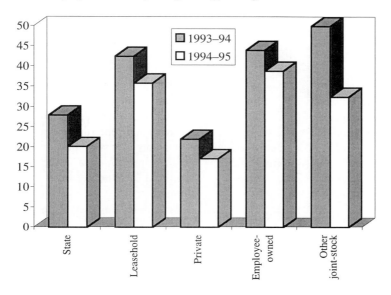

Figure 9.12 Change in work organization, by property form, Ukraine, 1993–95(% responding 'Yes')

Source: ULFS1, ULFS2.

Introduction of new technologies and changes in work organization require important training programmes, which were actively implemented in all companies except private and state enterprises (*Figure 9.13*). Training is also crucial for labour market and employment restructuring and the necessary labour mobility. We divided training into three levels – entry-level training, retraining for improving performance in an existing job or for moving workers between jobs, and training for upgrading; that is, to raise the grade and status of a worker. We found that the training policies of private enterprises were particularly weak with regard to the latter two forms of training; employee-owned, leasehold and other joint-stock enterprises, however, were developing the three forms of training simultaneously, a sign of accelerated internal restructuring. This reflects different ways of carrying out restructuring, employee-owned enterprises encouraging job mobility and retraining before envisaging employment cuts. In fact, those enterprises that had cut employment the most (by more than 20 per cent), were the least likely to be providing training.

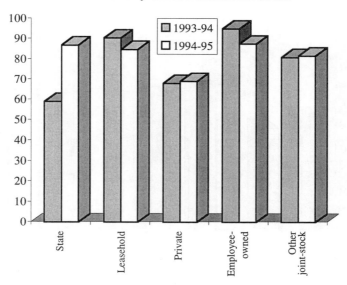

Figure 9.13 Training, by property form, Ukraine, 1993–95 (% responding 'Yes')
Source: ULFS1, ULFS2.

4.6 Economic Performance and Efficiency

From data on sales at constant prices, we tried to provide some estimate of productivity by dividing sales by number of employees. Although it is only an approximate measure of productivity – the variable of value added per employee being much more accurate – it provided interesting comparative results (*Figure 9.14*). Productivity increases appeared to be much more likely in employee-owned enterprises, thus confirming the encouraging effects of employee ownership on economic performance, despite efforts to maintain employment in the restructuring process, and their difficulties in providing new capital and technologies. Although they reported that they could produce the same output with fewer workers, employee-owned enterprises seem to have good productivity rates, probably partly due to the motivational effects of this property form.

Productivity was also above average in leasehold and private enterprises, thus confirming the previously noted dynamism of small private enterprises. Surprisingly, productivity in other joint-stock enterprises was rather low, even lower than in state-owned enterprises, a result which might be due to the large size and sectoral distribution of these enterprises. This result confirms *Figure 9.5*, that these enterprises could produce the same output with much fewer workers, so increasing productivity rates.

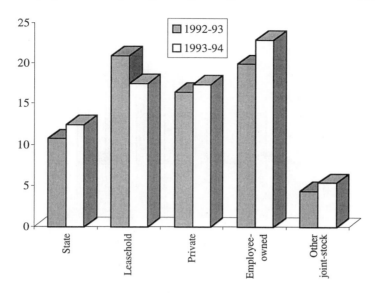

Figure 9.14 Productivity (sales/number of employees), by property form, Ukraine, 1992–94

Source: ULFS1.

Senior management were asked to identify the main sources of inefficiency in their enterprise. As with other enterprises, employee-owned enterprises suffered mainly from a shortage of materials, followed by lack of demand. Low wages also appeared to be a source of inefficiency in employee-owned, state-owned and leasehold enterprises, where the lowest wages were observed (*Figures 9.6a* and *9.6b*). As far as the main forms of inefficiency are concerned, employee-owned enterprises suffered mainly from periodical stops in production (42 per cent in 1994) and shortened working time (31 per cent), but did not seem to be affected by other forms of labour inefficiency, such as the low work intensity and high labour turnover observed in state-owned enterprises (20 per cent and 11 per cent). Low quality of work was also mentioned by 21 per cent of private enterprises. Leasehold and other joint-stock enterprises were also mainly affected by stops in production (55 per cent and 51 per cent).

Employee-owned enterprises tried to increase efficiency mainly through higher wages (39 per cent of employee-owned enterprises, compared to 17 per cent of other joint-stock enterprises); 27 per cent of employee-owned enterprises also tried to introduce new products to avoid shortages of materials and lack of demand. Changes in work organization were also mentioned by 11 per cent of enterprises, this percentage being the highest (13

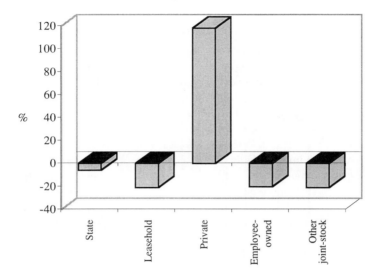

Figure 9.15   Output growth/fall (in constant prices), by property form, Ukraine, 1993–95

Source: ULFS2.

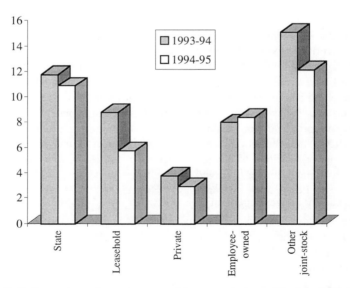

Figure 9.16   Percentage of output exported, by property form, Ukraine, 1993–95

Source: ULFS1, ULFS2.

per cent) among employee-owned enterprises which were also found to develop incentive programmes.

The fall in sales from 1993 to 1995 was not less likely to affect employee-owned enterprises (–20 per cent on average), which are also severely hurt by the economic crisis, than all other enterprises, with the probable exception of private enterprises, for which sales growth was artificially high in *Figure 9.15* due to the start-up of new small private enterprises.[7]

As shown in *Figure 9.16*, there is also a tendency for employee-owned enterprises to be less export-oriented, a feature which probably contributes to their difficulties in improving their sales performance. Joint-stock enterprises are the most dynamic in this regard. Surprisingly, state-owned enterprises are also exporting a substantial part of their production. In contrast, small private enterprises had problems exporting, and the propensity to export was not higher in joint ventures. Employee-owned enterprises, as predicted by the theory, have problems in shifting from the domestic market and finding new markets abroad. As observed in the enterprise example in Lviv (Western Ukraine) examined in the next section, partnership with foreign capital might be successfully implemented in those enterprises.

5 ENTERPRISE VESNA: COMBINING EMPLOYEE SHARE-OWNERSHIP WITH FOREIGN CAPITAL

The company produces clothes for women. In March 1994 it employed 640 workers, 90 per cent of whom were women. In 1990 the workers' collective bought all the enterprise's equipment from the state. In February 1993, pilot privatization projects were launched in the region of Lviv as part of the large-scale national privatization programme. The enterprise Vesna was transformed into a joint-stock company in November 1993. Since the Ministry of Industry did not succeed in attracting domestic capital to buy the company, it decided to go for a foreign partnership: 20 per cent of the capital was bought by a Swiss company, Interplastic; 80 per cent by the employees. The workers agreed with the management not to increase wages for two years, so that the corresponding amounts could be placed in a fund to buy the capital. Accordingly, wages remained frozen for two years regardless of inflation, so that the workers' purchasing power sharply declined. The company tried to compensate this decline by multiplying social services and fringe benefits to

---

[7] Similar results in Russia showed that falls in sales in 1993 were most widespread in open joint-stock and state enterprises while closed joint-stock enterprises – most of them being majority-owned by the workers – were the best property form to lead to sales growth (Standing, 1994a).

cover basic workers' needs, such as food and housing. The state helped Vesna in its restructuring process by providing funds for equipment and retraining. The capital to buy the company came entirely from the workers' savings.

When they acquired the enterprise workers received shares equivalent to two months' wages. A monthly wage of Krbs 40,000, the minimum salary at that time, yielded 20 shares; higher categories of workers received more. New employees who did not take part in the initial acquisition were not entitled to enterprise shares, although they could buy shares from previous employees. The enterprise rejected the option of organizing a second wave in order to keep the enterprise a closed joint-stock company. The management was aware of the risk of conflict between senior workers owning shares and new recruits temporarily not allowed to obtain shares.

Voting rights were distributed in accordance with a 'one share-one vote' system. There is an annual meeting of the workers' collective at which the strategic policy of the enterprise is defined. Workers are also involved in weekly meetings with managers. The employee share-ownership system, which was proposed by the previous managers, who were also previous employees and were not replaced after the property change, was immediately accepted by the collective. Trade unions were also very supportive of this economic democracy solution, and played an active part in informing workers and elaborating various scenarios with the workers' collective.

This association with a foreign partner did not generate any worries about the future management of the enterprise since the Swiss enterprise was already a partner of Vesna and involved in industrial operations in Ukraine. The workers' collective was cautious not to sell more than 20 per cent of the capital to the Swiss, however, in order to keep full control of decision-making. This percentage of foreign capital was entirely provided in the form of new technology from Switzerland and Italy. The management had to introduce changes in work organization in order to adapt its productive process to this new technology: some jobs were replaced by machines and some workers were shifted to other positions. New dresses were designed by computers, which also started to control the different garment pieces which were pro-duced and sewn together by the workers at the different production phases. The number of computers per employee rapidly increased, from 1 to 5 in 1989 to 1 to 3 in 1994. Training sessions were also organized to help the workers to understand the production process and to adapt their behaviour to their new tasks and the new technology requirements. Special educational spots were also shown on computers in the different establishments. A solid training programme was implemented, with 20 per cent of main production specialists being trained in Italy, and some engineers following special training courses in Switzerland. The management would like to go further in work reorganization, but this will be difficult to achieve in a short period of time.

The enterprise managed to maintain its labour force, so confirming our previous survey result on the employment stabilization policies implemented by employee-owned enterprises. The enterprise had to slightly modify its structure, however, mainly by reducing the number of managers. For other categories of employee, a normal turnover rate was followed, with new recruits replacing retirees.

Average wages at Vesna (Krbs 620,000 in March 1994) were found to be slightly below the industrial average in the region of Lviv (Krbs 694,000) and the industrial national average (Krbs 763,396). Although this average wage was ten times the national minimum wage (Krbs 60,000 at that time), it was well below the official subsistence minimum (Krbs 1,307,000 in January 1994). Since it was now a private enterprise, Vesna did not have to follow central wage regulations. In 1993 nominal wages increased by 7 times in order to reflect hyperinflation, the growth of which was much higher, however – more than 12,000 per cent in 1993. Although on several occasions in 1994 and 1995 there were problems with paying wages, the fact that the enterprise belongs to the workers' collective, and that these financial problems were discussed between management and employees helped to avoid the worker demotivation and strikes which were frequent in other textile enterprises. This enterprise example seems to confirm our survey results, which showed lower wages and greater difficulties in paying wages in employee-owned enterprises.

Workers are not paid according to a tariff system, but according to the number of pieces produced in a day. To complement this piece-rate system the enterprise has also promoted fringe benefits. Free meals are offered to the workers, doctors are paid by the enterprise, and two buildings have been provided by the enterprise, with cheap apartments for workers and their families; a variety of other services – from holiday facilities to hair-dressing – have also been financed by the enterprise social fund. Workers also receive a thirteenth month bonus.

The management, which was directly appointed by the workers' collective, tried to limit wage differentials within the enterprise. Unskilled workers in January 1994 were paid Krbs 440,000, while top managers were paid Krbs 880,000. This example confirms another finding of the survey, that wage differentials were smaller in employee-owned enterprises due to the wage solidarity principle which seems to prevail in such firms.

In contrast with other survey results, the enterprise Vesna did not introduce any profit-sharing or other payment system related to collective performance. Workers do get an annual bonus related to their shares, however. The shares yielded some dividends in 1993–94 and provided an additional source of income to complement falling real wages.

This privatization through a combination of worker share-ownership and foreign capital has clearly been successful. New technology provided by the

Swiss partner has made it possible to improve product quality and to modernize equipment, so improving international competitiveness. The Ukrainian firm is now using the most developed Western production techniques. Association with a foreign partner has also helped in developing contacts with foreign enterprises. High quality products are being directly exported to the German market or for German enterprises. Only 20 per cent of output is produced for the Ukrainian market, the rest being exported – in 1994, in order to meet particularly high demand from abroad, 95 per cent of production was exported. One of the main markets is the Czech Republic, but the enterprise is looking for others.

According to the Director of the Economics Department, the workers' collective was enthusiastic about this employee share-ownership system, aimed at involving employees in the management process, helping the company to increase its profitability and to avoid lay-offs in the privatization process. It has increased workers' motivation and helped the enterprise to produce more clothes. It has also contributed to a better adaptation of the labour force to the new technology provided by the foreign partner. The workers' collective started in 1995 to diversify production by building apartments and developing trading activities.

It must be stressed that this company was profitable even before privatization, but this does not detract from their successes in maintaining the labour force while increasing production despite the general fall in demand on both the domestic market and traditional foreign markets. This is a significant achievement at a time when all other enterprises are producing at less than 50 per cent of capacity and have had to lay off part of their labour force.

Although the enterprise had temporary problems paying wages it did not in the end have to resort to bank loans, a policy which contributed to keep prices low. Most other companies in the textile sector had to increase prices in order to repay the very high interest on borrowings. This phenomenon was an important source of inflation between 1993 and 1995, before a very restrictive monetary policy was implemented by the government early in 1996.

Because of its successful performance, Vesna was called by regional authorities the 'oasis in the desert'. The company's assets have been revalued by nearly 3.5 times in the course of two years.

This example is also important because most foreign companies do not place much confidence in Ukrainian firms. Foreign capital provided the new technology needed to modernize equipment, while employee share-ownership has brought employee support and motivation, leading to high productivity. The example of Vesna also shows that the combination of foreign investment and workers' shares is feasible. It is important to note that the decision to have a joint venture with a Swiss company was made by the workers' collective, so contradicting the first theoretical expectation that workers would be averse to foreign investment, and the second, that employee ownership would be too risky and therefore not advisable for a foreign firm.

It may be suggested that the enterprise would have performed well even if it had been offered to domestic or foreign investors in its entirety. This solution would probably have led to a different management approach: lay-offs might have occurred, so increasing unemployment and leading to conflict situations between management and workers or trade unions. In this difficult period social consensus was crucial. Moreover, a substantial sacrifice was needed from the workers, who decided to accept a wage freeze for two years despite rocketing inflation and increasing financial problems. The employees would probably not have accepted this policy from an external foreign or Ukrainian owner. The fact that they have been continuously involved in the strategic decisions of the enterprise has also been crucial for building social consensus and high worker motivation.

This example also shows that workers have not been too short-termist in their decision-making. They decided to invest substantially in new technology, even when it involved removing employees from one job to another. We would also like to emphasize that workers' share-ownership made it possible for the company to remain in Ukrainian hands. In the absence of domestic capital – one of major problems in Ukraine today – the company would probably have been totally (or at least largely) privatized on the basis of foreign investment. Alternatively, capital could have come from the conversion of citizens' vouchers into enterprise shares, a solution which leads to capital dispersion, one important consequence of which is that the owners cannot become involved in enterprise decision-making. In this context, the new managers might well have implemented lay-off programmes to increase profitability. Even more importantly, this would have done little to ensure worker support for the new management strategy or to establish solidarity between workers and management.

6 CONCLUSION

Although the development of employee share-ownership schemes is still in its infancy in Ukraine the Government has decided to encourage such schemes, and some enterprises have already successfully implemented employee share-ownership in the privatization process. Our survey results and enterprise example have emphasized the potential efficiency of employee ownership. First, the distribution of shares to the workers is a way of involving them in privatization and – in the long term – of providing them with a complementary source of income, which is particularly important in the context of falling real wages. Second, employee ownership experiences in Ukraine show that these schemes, by motivating workers to accept temporary wage cuts, might help avoid lay-offs, despite general mass unemployment. This greater employment stability could increase human capital and enhance worker motivation. Third, elements of economic democracy in employee-owned enterprises – such as shares, profit-sharing, participatory practices, changes in work organization – combined with a policy of maintaining employment seem to have a positive effect on worker motivation and productivity, much higher than in other enterprises. The willingness to keep their labour force through intensive product rationalization, worker mobility and training programmes does not, however, mean that these enterprises will not implement lay-offs when necessary, as our enterprise survey results show. Finally, the example of Vesna shows that an entrepreneur who shares the risks with the workers might be in a better position to promote innovation and investment while stabilizing employment. Contrary to theoretical expectations, these enterprises were found to invest in equipment and new technology. Fears of capital consumption by employees and excessively high wages were proved groundless. Private enterprises were also found to introduce new technology, but to neglect industrial relations, as shown by the lower number of collective agreements at the enterprise level. They were also characterized by low unionization, less training and fewer changes in work organization.

Employee-owned enterprises seem to have problems paying wages, however, which also appeared to be lower than at other enterprises, especially private and other joint-stock enterprises. They are also confronted by material shortages and a lack of demand, leading to a fall in sales and periodical stops in production. Although our survey results underlined that these enterprises are investing in high technology as much, if not more, than other enterprises, interviews with managers at a series of employee-owned enterprises in Kiev and Lviv in 1994, 1995 and 1996 emphasized their lack of capital and their difficulties in investing in new equipment and technology.

It is for this reason that we emphasize the value of combining workers' share-ownership with other property forms. For purposes of social equity and redistribution, it might be a good idea to combine worker share-ownership with privatization certificates or vouchers, which lead to a more general redistribution of capital among all citizens. Moreover, in regions, such as Lviv, that face a lack of local as well as foreign capital, this is probably also the only way in which privatization can be achieved. The workers, who are sometimes not paid for several months, may not have the money to buy shares, however, so that the state would need to develop a range of instruments for helping them. Coupon privatization might be one such instrument.

The combination of workers' shares with foreign capital seems to be particularly effective in increasing investment, providing new technology and finding new export opportunities, particularly important in a context of falling sales. Foreign capital might also help employee-owned enterprises to solve their problems paying wages and also raising them to levels more consistent with the current need for a better motivated and highly skilled labour force. This combination would also limit the possibility for foreign investors to avoid developing industrial relations and collective agreements and induce them to promote alternatives to lay-offs whenever possible.

Trade unions and employers have an important role in the development of worker share-ownership schemes and the promotion of property combinations able simultaneously to respond to redistributional and efficiency requirements. More empirical studies are also needed, including enterprise surveys but also specific enterprise case studies, in order to identify and provide solutions to the current drawbacks of this property form more precisely, making it easier to clear away the obstacles which presently impede full recognition of the success of this type of enterprise in the privatization process.

REFERENCES

Bartlett, W. and M. Uvalic (1986), 'Labour-managed firms, employee participation and profit-sharing – Theoretical perspectives and European experience', EUI Working Paper No. 86/236, European University Institute, Florence.

Earle, J. and S. Estrin (1996), 'Employee Ownership in Transition', in R. Frydman, C. Gray, A. Rapaczynski (eds), *Corporate Governance in Central Europe and Russia: Insiders and the State*, World Bank–CEU Press.

ILO–CEET/UNDP (1995), *The Ukrainian Challenge: Reforming Labour Market and Social Policy*, ILO–UNDP–CEU Press.

Khulikov, G. (1995), 'Wage Decentralization in Ukraine', in Vaughan-Whitehead (1995b).

OECD (1995), *Trends and Policies in Privatization*, OECD Centre for Co-operation with the Economies in Transition (CCET), Vol. 2, No. 2, Paris.

Standing, G. (1994a), 'Labour Market Dynamics in Russian Industry: Results of the Third Round of the RLFS,' ILO–CEET Policy Paper No. 2, Budapest.

Standing, G. (1994b), 'Labour Market Dynamics in Ukrainian Industry in 1992–94: Results from the ULFS', ILO–CEET, Report No. 11, Budapest.

Standing, G. and L. Zsoldos (1995), 'Labour Market Crisis in Ukrainian Industry: The 1995 ULFS,' Labour Market Paper No. 12, ILO, Employment Department, Geneva.

UNDP (1996), *1996 Ukraine Human Development Report – Looking Beyond the Triple Transition*, UNDP, Kiev, June.

Vaughan-Whitehead, D. et al. (1995a), *Workers' Financial Participation: East-West Experiences*, ILO Labour-Management Series, No. 30.

Vaughan-Whitehead, D. (ed.) (1995b), *Reforming Wage Policy in Central and Eastern Europe*, ILO/European Commission, ILO–CEET Budapest.

10. Privatization in the Yugoslav Successor States: Converting Self-management into Property Rights

Milica Uvalic

1 INTRODUCTION

When the transition to a mixed market economy started in Central and Eastern Europe in the late 1980s, in the former Yugoslavia the government chose the sale of enterprise assets on extremely favourable conditions to 'insiders' – workers and managers – as the main method of privatization. Because of the country's long tradition of worker self-management, it was believed that employees ought to be the main beneficiaries of privatization. For the same reason, after the disintegration of the Socialist Federal Republic of Yugoslavia (hereafter, SFR Yugoslavia) in 1991,[1] in the new privatization laws adopted by the governments of its successor states, preferential conditions have been maintained primarily for employees.

The present paper explores the role and the diffusion of employee ownership in four successor states of the former Yugoslavia: Croatia, the Federal Republic of Yugoslavia (hereafter FR Yugoslavia), the former Yugoslav Republic of Macedonia (hereafter FYR Macedonia), and Slovenia.[2] First, privatization legislation is briefly described, with particular emphasis on the conditions for sales to insiders (Section 2). Empirical evidence on property changes in the last five years in each of the four economies is then presented, in order to evaluate the relative importance of preferential sales to employees with respect to other privatization methods; where available, existing evidence on the effects of employee ownership on enterprise performance is also reported (Section 3).

---

[1] The following states were created on the territory of former Yugoslavia: Croatia, Slovenia, the Federal Republic of Yugoslavia (Serbia with its two regions Kosovo and Voivodina, and Montenegro), Macedonia (recognized under the name 'The Former Yugoslav Republic of Macedonia'), and Bosnia Herzegovina.

[2] Bosnia Herzegovina is not considered since the three-year war has halted the economic reforms in course, including privatization.

2 PRIVATIZATION LEGISLATION

Privatization in the former Yugoslavia got under way before the country disintegrated on the basis of legislation adopted by the federal government in 1988–90. However, from as early as autumn 1990, property reforms were substantially delayed by the general political, economic and institutional crisis which eventually led to the break-up of the Yugoslav federation. With the gradual disintegration of the economic and political system, each republic of the former Yugoslavia decided to elaborate its own privatization law; the discussion, drafting, and approval of these laws took a long time, especially in Slovenia and FYR Macedonia, where the new political environment of multi-party democracy did not make the task any easier. Moreover, in countries which in the meantime had become involved in the war – Bosnia Herzegovina, Croatia and FR Yugoslavia – the economic situation rapidly deteriorated immediately after the break-up of the former Yugoslavia, rendering property (and other) economic reforms more difficult to implement.

Both before and after the disintegration of the former Yugoslavia, the chosen privatization options were mainly determined by the existing economic system. The former Yugoslavia was distinguished among the socialist economies for its system of worker self-management, high degree of decentralization, and 'social' property (Uvalic, 1992). Under the system of social property, no one in particular had property rights over enterprises; firms could use only socially-owned capital and appropriate its product. Nevertheless, because of ample self-management rights and the ambiguous property regime, many workers in Yugoslavia felt that they were the real 'owners' of their firm, at least in respect of that part of income invested in the enterprise over the years. This is why both the federal legislation and the more recent privatization laws envisaged as the main privatization method the sale of assets on preferential terms primarily to employees. The obtaining of widespread support for privatization among the working class was regarded as an essential element in its successful implementation.

The preparation and adoption of new privatization laws by the governments of the single republics began before the former Yugoslavia disintegrated, in parallel with the suspension of some or all of the provisions of federal law (this took place as early as October 1990 in Slovenia and Croatia). Croatia was the first to adopt a new privatization law (April 1991, subsequently amended several times), followed by Serbia (August 1991, amended in mid-1994), Montenegro (January 1992, amended in 1994), Slovenia (November 1992, amended in June 1993) and FYR Macedonia (June 1993, amended in 1995). In all countries, the privatizations undertaken according to federal legislation were subject to formal verification in order to determine their regularity, and enterprises had to adjust their programmes to the new legislation.

In order to provide a comparative overview of the general terms envisaged for purchases by employees, we shall briefly describe each of the laws separately, including the legislation of the former Yugoslavia, given that initially many enterprises transformed their ownership status on that basis.

2.1 Privatization Legislation in the former SFR Yugoslavia

Property reforms in the former Yugoslavia started in 1988, well before the country disintegrated. The 1988 *Act on Enterprise* diversified existing types of property and forms of enterprise,[3] so enabling their commercialization, while the 1989–90 *Act on Social Capital* laid out the framework for the privatization of enterprises in the dominant (social) sector of the economy.[4]

The 1989–90 Federal Act on Social Capital envisaged the sale of enterprise shares at a discount of 30% to present and former employees, other citizens, and pension funds, on the basis of the book value of assets; employees (both present and former) were given a further 1% discount for each year of employment, up to a maximum of 70% of the nominal value of the shares. However, several limits on share issues at a discount had to be respected: their total value could not be greater than six times the firm's annual wage bill, while the value of shares sold to present and former employees could not exceed the annual wage bill by more than three times; the value of shares sold to an individual employee could not exceed his annual wage by more than three times. Shares sold at a discount could be paid for in instalments over a period of ten years, but they could not be traded on the stock exchange until fully paid. The part of social capital not subscribed on preferential terms was to be offered at public auctions to domestic and foreign enterprises or individuals. Since the law did not specify the destination of the remaining (unsold) social capital, it implicitly did not prohibit its continued existence.

In addition to these provisions, employee ownership was also promoted through the 1990 Federal *Act on Personal Incomes*,[5] which introduced the possibility for firms to distribute shares to workers in lieu of part of their regular incomes. These provisions were meant to compensate workers for the limits on wage increases introduced by the December 1989 stabilization programme, at the same time stimulating employee shareholding.

The federal legislation therefore offered extremely favourable conditions for

[3] See *Act on Enterprise, Official Gazette of the Socialist Federal Republic of Yugoslavia* (SFRY) No. 77, 1988.

[4] The *Act on the Circulation and Disposal of Social Capital* was adopted in December 1989 (see Official Gazette of SFRY No. 84), but due to insufficiently stimulative provisions it was applied by very few enterprises. The law was therefore amended in August 1990 (see Official Gazette of SFRY No. 46), when its name was changed to 'Act on Social Capital'.

[5] See *Official Gazette of SFRY* No. 37, 30 June 1990.

the diffusion of employee ownership: within the prescribed limits, employees could buy enterprise shares by paying only 30–70% of their price, and could repay shares over a ten-year period; in addition, they were to get some shares free as part of their regular earnings.

2.2 Privatization Legislation in Croatia

The *Act on the Transformation of Social Enterprises*, adopted by the Croatian government in April 1991,[6] envisaged the sale of shares of enterprises to be privatized to employed or retired workers, employees in enterprises not subject to privatization,[7] and other citizens or legal entities. Employees in firms to be privatized had priority in subscription, but privileged conditions were offered to all employees (in privatizing firms and those not undergoing privatization): a 20% discount and another 1% for each year of employment, and payment by instalments over a five-year period. The maximum value that could be subscribed by a single employee was DM 20,000, and only 50% of the firm's equity could be bought on preferential terms. After 30 June 1992, which was the deadline for enterprises to submit their privatization programmes,[8] all unsold capital was to be automatically transferred to three government funds: 70% went to the Development Fund,[9] which is obliged to offer transferred shares on sale on the stock exchange; the remaining 30% was distributed equally between two pension funds, for industrial workers and for farmers.

Several amendments to the law have in the meantime introduced additional incentives for acquisitions by 'small' shareholders, meaning those subscribing shares on privileged terms to a value not exceeding DM 20,000. Since by 1993 the substantial drop in real wages had rendered the repayment burden for most shareholders rather heavy, in October 1993 a further 35% discount on full payment of shares in the first year was introduced, and the trading of shares before they were fully paid was permitted. In January 1994, the possibility was introduced for shareholders to become owners of the discounted part of subscribed shares after having paid only the first annual instalment of 5%. Another important provision was adopted in March 1994: citizens were permitted to buy shares of privatizing enterprises using their foreign currency savings deposits, which had been frozen in banks since

---

[6] See *Official Gazette of Croatia* No. 19, 23 April 1991.

[7] Public enterprises in sectors such as health, education, public utilities, and government institutions; some of these firms will be privatized in a second stage according to a separate law.

[8] The deadline was postponed to the end of 1992 for a small group of enterprises located in war-affected territories.

[9] The Development Fund was later merged with the Privatization Agency, thus becoming the Croatian Privatization Fund.

1991.[10] In addition to these measures, which were meant to stimulate sales to small shareholders, during 1993 some shares were also freely distributed to disabled war veterans and the families of war victims, to a value ranging from DM 5,000 to DM 20,000; a similar distribution scheme will be applied for refugees (Cuckovic, 1995).

At the end of 1994, the preparation of a new privatization law began which, among other changes, envisages the prolongation of the repayment period for subscribed shares to 20 years, an additional discount for payment before maturity, and a grace period for socially disadvantaged citizens (see Ostovic and Gracanin, 1994, p. 25). However, as of mid-1995 the law had not yet been adopted.

2.3 Privatization Legislation in FR Yugoslavia

In the republics of FR Yugoslavia, Serbia and Montenegro two separate privatization laws have been adopted, in August 1991 and in January 1992; both were subsequently amended in 1994. Because of the constitutional obligation to adopt a privatization law applicable to the whole Yugoslav Federation a new Federal Law was adopted in mid-1996.

2.3.1 Privatization legislation in Serbia

The 1991 Serbian *Act on the Conditions and Procedure for Transforming Social into other Forms of Property* is similar to the Federal Act on Social Capital, although generally more restrictive.[11] Serbia, unlike the other former Yugoslav republics, has maintained social property as one of the possible property forms; and the methods envisaged for property transformation are similar to those in the Federal Law, all based on the sale of shares or assets. The three main methods are sale of social capital, new share issues, and sale of part or of the whole enterprise on preferential or other terms.

For a period of two years (until August 1993), employees had the right to subscribe to shares on preferential terms, receiving a 20% basic discount and an additional 1% for each year of employment (up to a maximum of 60%), the repayment period being five years. In order for an enterprise to transform itself into a shareholding company, subscriptions by employees have to amount to at least 10% of social capital. The maximum value of capital that can be

---

[10] In 1991, around DM 4 billion savings deposits in foreign currency of Croatian citizens was converted into public debt; initially it was planned that the frozen savings would be repaid to citizens in 20 biannual rates, starting from June 1995.

[11] See *Official Gazette of Serbia* No.48, 1991, and No. 75, 1991 (which included some revisions).

bought at a discount by a single worker is DM 20,000, and by a single director or manager to a value corresponding to his net salary in the previous two years, though not exceeding DM 30,000; the overall value of shares bought on privileged terms cannot exceed one-third of the value of the social capital. However, after the expiry of the deadline for preferential sales, the enterprise could again offer employees the remaining capital (on the same preferential terms), but this time up to 50% of the value of enterprise social capital, and up to DM 30,000 per person.

New regulations adopted in mid-1994 have substantially worsened the conditions regarding subscribed capital. Because of a highly inadequate provision of the law – that the revaluation of the unpaid portion of shares be undertaken only once a year – under hyper-inflationary conditions such as those in 1993, many individuals were able to pay for subscribed shares with ridiculously small amounts of money. Changes in the legislation were therefore proposed on the revaluation of the value of capital in all enterprises privatized in 1993, which led to the adoption of amendments to the privatization law (1 August 1994), and other legislation specifying the procedure for capital revaluation (October and November 1994).[12] Contrary to the initial proposal, however, the law has introduced the obligatory revaluation of capital in practically *all* enterprises privatized since 1990 (Vujacic, 1995). These provisions will entail a substantial increase of the value of non-privatized capital, and it is very likely that many shareholders will have to renounce their subscribed shares since their price after revaluation will be too high.

Because of these regulations, at present there is an urgent need to adopt new legislation in Serbia, which would possibly speed up the privatization process.[13]

2.3.2 Privatization legislation in Montenegro

In Montenegro, the *Act on the Transformation of Property and Management*, adopted in January 1992,[14] envisages a number of privatization methods: sale of social capital or new share issues to employees and citizens on preferential terms; sales to other domestic or foreign legal or natural persons; sales to individuals (insiders or outsiders) taking over the management of an

[12] See *Official Gazette of Serbia* No. 51, 1994, No. 62, 1994 and No. 65, 1994.

[13] Privatization proposals have been elaborated by Prof. Bozovic, member of the Socialist Party and former Prime Minister; by the Democratic Party; by the Institute of Economics; by the official Trade Unions; by the Institute of Social Sciences, by the Governor of the National Bank of Yugoslavia Professor Avramovic (to mention just the most important). These proposals are all very different and it is yet unclear which one (if any) will be adopted by the present government.

[14] See *Official Gazette of Montenegro* No. 2, 10 January 1992.

enterprise, if they subscribe at least 35% of the estimated value of the firm; debt–equity swaps; transfer of shares to government funds or direct nationalization; and the free distribution of vouchers, of a maximum value corresponding to ECU 5,000 per person, to workers who have remained unemployed due to privatization. Shares could be subscribed on preferential terms by present or former employees and by citizens up to the global limit of 30% of the value of social capital, but employees have priority. The general discount is 30%, but employees have the right to another 1% discount for each year of employment, and to payment by instalments within a period of five years; citizens are entitled to another 10% discount if shares are paid in cash. The maximum value of subscribed shares per person, including the discount, is set to the equivalent of ECU 10,000. All social capital not subscribed or sold should be transferred to government funds, and then sold to interested buyers.

Since little progress has been achieved with the privatization of Montenegran firms, amendments to the law adopted at the end of 1994 have introduced several new provisions,[15] primarily in order to improve the terms for employees. The general provisions regarding sales to employees on preferential terms have been maintained, but the repayment period has been prolonged to ten years. Moreover, in addition to sales, an enterprise can also decide to distribute shares freely – up to 10% of the value of social capital and up to ECU 3,000 per person – to all employees with a minimum three-years' service. The right of employees to receive free shares, or to subscribe shares on preferential terms, expires one year after the adoption of these provisions in small and medium-sized firms, and after two years in large firms. Government funds, to which enterprise shares are transferred, are obliged annually to offer at least 20% of these shares for sale; priority is given, for a period of three years, to employees of the enterprise concerned.

2.3.3 The new federal legislation

The delays in implementing privatization in Yugoslavia, together with the constitutional obligation to adopt a new federal privatization law by the end of 1996, have recently led to the elaboration of a number of privatization models by government officials, all the major political parties, several research institutes, trade unions, employers' associations, and individual experts. The proposal that probably attracted most attention was the privatization programme of Dragoslav Avramovic, Governor of the National Bank of Yugoslavia. The programme, elaborated in April–May 1996, was based on a broad political and social consensus, as it took into account all

---

[15] See *Official Gazette of Montenegro* No. 27, 1994.

existing models, as well as the opinions of members of a special Working Group for Privatization.[16] Avramovic's privatization programme envisaged obligatory privatization within a precise deadline, the complete elimination of social property, and highly preferential treatment of employees, which were the main features which distinguished it from the official proposal of the Yugoslav federal government, elaborated at the same time.

Avramovic's privatization programme was to be presented to the Yugoslav Parliament on 14 May 1996. On that occasion, however, Avramovic failed to win a vote of confidence and so ceased to be Governor. Consequently, his privatization programme was not put on the agenda of the parliamentary session, while the alternative law prepared by the Yugoslav government (*Act on the property transformation of social capital*) was adopted. The new federal law essentially leaves it to the enterprise to decide whether, when and to what extent it will implement privatization. It also leaves the regime of social property intact, since it does not envisage the obligatory elimination of social property (as has been done in all the other successor states of former Yugoslavia). It is highly unlikely that the new legislation will facilitate any fundamental changes in the property structure of the Yugoslav economy.

2.4 Privatization Legislation in FYR Macedonia

The *Act on the Transformation of Enterprises with Social Capital* was adopted by the Macedonian government only in June 1993,[17] after a very long debate. The law envisages that, in general, social capital can be sold at privileged conditions to presently or previously employed workers, up to the equivalent of DM 25,000 per person, and within the global limit of 30% of the appraised value of the enterprise. Employees have the right to a 30% discount and an additional 1% for each year of employment (or more in some cases),[18] but they are not offered the possibility of payment by instalments (this provision was changed in mid-1995; see below).

At the outset, 15% of social capital is transferred to the Pension Fund, while the remaining capital is privatized using different methods, which depend on enterprise size. Small enterprises can be sold either to employees, or through

---

[16] The members of the Working Group were representatives of all political parties, trade unions, employers' associations, and individual experts. The Chairman and Secretary of the Working Group were Dragoslav Avramovic and Milica Uvalic respectively.

[17] See *Official Gazette of Macedonia* No. 38, 21 June 1993.

[18] For employees of hotels, restaurants, leisure centres and the like, the basic discount is 50% of the nominal value of shares, increased by 1% for each year of employment, and thus the discount can reach 90% of the share price. The motivation for this provision was that most of these business units were built through enterprise investment, out of resources allocated for general consumption.

commercial sales to outsiders at public auction or by direct agreement. The employee buy-out option is available, however, only if employees purchase at least 51% of the appraised value of the firm; the remaining non-purchased part of capital is temporarily transferred to the Privatization Agency and should be bought by the employee-shareholders within five years, during which time dividends can be used only for this purpose.

Medium-sized enterprises can be privatized through commercial sales, buy-outs, buy-ins (sales to future managers), issue of shares for additional investment, and debt–equity swaps. In the case of buy-outs, priority is given to employees: a buy-out is considered successful if at least 51% of the appraised value of social capital is sold. Persons who wish to assume the management of the enterprise must propose a development programme and immediately buy at least 20%, and over the next five years, 51% of the value of the firm, using dividends solely for this purpose. In case shares are issued for the purpose of additional investment, if the nominal value of issued shares is at least 30% of the value of the firm, all unprivatized capital is transferred to the Agency, but the new shareholders are expected to buy at least 51% of the capital within the next five years.

The same applies to large enterprises, with some modifications: prospective future managers must initially buy 10% of the appraised value of the enterprise; and in case of share issues for the purpose of additional investment, it is sufficient that the value of purchased shares amount to 15% of the appraised value of the firm (the remaining part is transferred to the Agency).

In the meantime, the trade unions have on several occasions strongly criticized the privatization law: in their view, the terms for sales to employees were not sufficiently attractive. The negotiations between the government and the trade unions finally led in mid-1995 to an important modification to the advantage of employees: in addition to previous provisions on sales at a discount, employees may now pay for shares in five instalments, with a grace period of two years. Furthermore, trade unions will henceforth have a representative on the Management Board of the Privatization Agency and in the Government Commission for Privatization (Vukotic and Sukovic, 1996, p. 83).

2.5 Privatization Legislation in Slovenia

Also in Slovenia, a very long privatization debate delayed the final adoption of a new privatization law, in this case for over two years (see Mencinger, 1995; Bojnec, 1995). The *Act on the Transformation of Enterprises* was finally adopted in November 1992, and amended in June 1993.[19] According to Slovenian legislation, privatization is to be undertaken with a combination

---

[19] See *Official Gazette of Slovenia* No. 55, 20 November 1992, and No. 31, 11 June 1993.

of three main methods: sales, transfers to funds, and free distribution to Slovenian citizens. All Slovenians have received ownership certificates of various values – depending on age – which can be used in exchange for shares in either enterprises or authorized investment companies.

The standard model envisages the following allocation of the shares of privatizing enterprises. At the outset, 40% of the shares are transferred to three government funds: 10% to the Pension Fund, 10% to the Compensation (Restitution) Fund, and 20% to the Development Fund; these shares are to be sold to investment companies for cash, or in exchange for ownership certificates they have collected from citizens. Another 20% of the shares can be distributed to current, former or retired employees in exchange for their ownership certificates. The remaining 40% can be purchased by current and former employees through a buy-out on preferential terms, or offered for sale under normal conditions using various methods (public tender, public sale, public auction). Employees have priority in subscription, the right to a 50% discount and to deferred payment for a period of five years, but more than one-third of the employees should participate in the buy-out. The firm can also benefit from the proceeds obtained from a buy-out paid to the Development Fund, in the form of a five-year loan at a very favourable interest rate, but on condition that purchased shares are paid out of the company's profits; in this case, the profit used for buying shares for employees is tax free (Rop, 1995).

2.6 An Overview of Employee Ownership Legislation

All six privatization laws – SFR Yugoslavia, Croatia, FYR Macedonia, Montenegro, Serbia, and Slovenia – have some common general features, although they differ on a number of points. A comparative overview of the main features of these laws, including the terms for the sale or free distribution of shares to employees, is presented in *Table 10.1*.

The main feature which these privatization laws have in common is that they all offer very favourable general conditions for the diffusion of employee ownership. In all countries, the sale of enterprise shares to employees is stimulated through:

1) substantial discounts, in most cases consisting of a basic discount of 20-30% increased for each year of employment by an additional 1%, but up to a maximum of 60-70%, except in Slovenia,[20] where there is a general discount of 50% irrespective of length of employment;

---

[20] As already mentioned, in Slovenia an enterprise can receive a loan for the acquisition of shares for its employees at very favourable terms. In the other countries, although the privatization

Table 10.1 Conditions for employees in the privatization laws of the former Yugoslavia and its successor states, 1989–95

	SFR of Yugoslavia	Croatia	FYR of Macedonia	Monte-negro	Serbia	Slovenia
Date of adoption	Dec 1989	Apr 1991	Jun 1993	Jan 1992	Aug 1991	Nov 1992
Amendments	Aug 1990	Several	1995	1994	1994	1993
Main methods	Sale	Sale	Sale	Sale & distrib.	Sale	Sale & distrib.
Discounts for employees (%)						
– basic	30	20	30 (can be 50)	30	20	50
– per year of employment	1	1	1	1	1	NO
– maximum	70	60	70–90	70	60	50
Repayment period (yrs)	10	below 5 (now 20)	NO (now 5)	10	5	5
Limits on sales at a discount						
– total (%)	Up to 6 times the wage bill	50	30	30	30–50	40
– per employee	Up to 3 times the wage bill	DM 20,000	DM 25,000	ECU 10,000	DM 20,000 30,000	NO
Free distribution of shares	NO	Exceptional	NO	Up to 10% of of capital & ECU 3,000	NO	Up to 20% of capital

2)   priority subscription;
3)   payment by instalments for subscribed shares, over five or ten years; and sometimes,
4)   credit facilities (explicitly envisaged only in Slovenia). In addition to such favourable conditions for sales to employees, in two countries employee ownership is further facilitated through provisions concerning the free distribution of a certain portion of shares to enterprise employees: in Montenegro, employees can freely receive up to 10%, and in Slovenia up to 20% of enterprise capital, in exchange for their ownership certificates.

However, there are also a number of specific provisions which impose precise limits on employee ownership, whether directly or indirectly. First, in all the laws a time limit is set within which employees can purchase shares on preferential terms. Second, although the enterprise can choose which privatization method it will implement, in most laws some portion of capital is transferred to different agencies or funds, controlled (if not officially owned) by the government, either after the expiry of the deadline for preferential sales, or at the moment of property transformation; the only exceptions are the Federal and the Serbian law, both of which envisage that unsubscribed capital can remain within enterprises as social capital. Finally, in all the laws specific limits are set on sales to employees on preferential terms, both as to the total amount of enterprise capital (ranging from 30% to 50%), and as to the value of shares that can be purchased by a single employee (except in Slovenia).

Therefore, while all the privatization laws greatly favour employee ownership, they impose specific limits on preferential sales to employees, which are likely to determine the proportion of enterprise capital which may end up in their hands. Indeed, these ceilings will be crucial in determining whether, in each of these countries, majority or minority employee ownership will be more common among privatizing enterprises; the distinction between the two cases is important because of their very different implications for firm efficiency.[21] Although the imposed limits on preferential sales to employees do not, in principle, prevent employees from buying additional shares at their market price, in most cases this is unlikely to happen because of their very limited purchasing power.

(*continued from p. 275*) laws did not envisage any specific credit facilities, commercial banks usually offered special credits for buying shares of privatizing firms.

[21] It is usually considered that majority employee ownership will have a number of negative effects, including the reluctance of such firms to fire workers and undertake restructuring, the tendency to distribute excessive wages and underinvest, and the inability to attract foreign investment. By contrast, minority employee ownership is expected to lead to a number of positive effects, primarily improved incentives and higher labour productivity (see Nuti, 1995).

Majority employee ownership (over 51%) is explicitly envisaged only in Slovenia and in FYR Macedonia. In Slovenia, through share subscriptions on preferential terms (40%) and the free distribution of shares (20%), employees can effectively acquire 60% of enterprise capital. In FYR Macedonia, although sales to employees on preferential terms are restricted to 30% of enterprise capital, the law nevertheless encourages, or even obliges, insiders to become the dominant owners in a number of cases.[22]

By contrast, in Croatia, although the limit on employee purchases on preferential terms is higher than in the previous two cases (50%), it was introduced precisely in order to prevent dominant employee ownership.[23] Similarly in Montenegro, employees can end up owning 40% of enterprise capital (30% through purchases on preferential terms and 10% through free distribution), and may become dominant owners only if they decide to buy additional shares at their full price on the stock exchange.

In Serbia, finally, the situation is rather anomalous. Employee purchases on preferential terms in the first round of share offers are limited to 30%, and in the second round to 50% of enterprise capital, which suggests that employees, as in Croatia, are unlikely to become the dominant shareholders. Nevertheless, full control of the firm is still bound to remain, in many cases, in the hands of its employees. This is because unprivatized capital can remain in the form of social property, and so assure workers' self-management rights. Indeed, according to the Enterprise Law,[24] in mixed property firms decisions are taken jointly by the new (private) shareholders, and current employees, where employees have decision-making rights proportional to the share of social capital.[25]

Despite the general promotion of employee ownership in all the reviewed privatization laws, it is clear that the intentions of individual governments regarding its desirable extent were very different. We shall now turn to the

---

[22] As already mentioned, in small firms undertaking an employee buy-out, employees ought to subscribe at least 51% of capital, and the remainder over the next five years; in medium-sized enterprises, a buy-out is considered to be successful if at least 51% of shares have been sold; and in case of leveraged management buy-outs or buy-ins, the management group can control the firm as if it had a 51% holding by making a downpayment of only 20%, and is obliged to purchase 51% of the shares in the next five years.

[23] Again, the limit does not prevent employees to buy additional shares at their market price, thus becoming dominant owners, but in most cases this is unlikely to happen because of limited purchasing power of employees in Croatia.

[24] The present Enterprise Law in Serbia is based on some of the provisions of the original federal Enterprise Law (see *Official Gazette of the SFR of Yugoslavia* No. 77/88, No. 40/89, No. 46/90, and No. 61/90), but it has been amended in 1994 (see *Official Gazette of Serbia* No. 24/94) and further revisions are presently under discussion.

[25] This dual criterion for decision-making is likely to create serious conflicts of interest between the labour force, participating in the decision-making process on the basis of social (non-private) capital, and employee-shareholders, participating on the basis of private capital.

implementation of these privatization laws, in order to determine the actual extent of employee ownership in each of the countries.

3 THE DIFFUSION OF EMPLOYEE OWNERSHIP THROUGH PRIVATIZATION

The implementation of property reforms in the former Yugoslavia and in its successor states over the last five years has taken place in the context of a changing ownership structure, through both the privatization of enterprises in the social sector and the entry of new private firms. We will restrict our analysis to social sector privatization, since this was the main channel, in all countries, for the gradual diffusion of employee ownership.

Initially, preferential sales to employees were undertaken on the basis of federal legislation, through the privatization, usually only partial, of enterprises in the social sector, and their transformation from social into mixed property firms.[26] Thereafter, once implementation of the new privatization got under way, employee ownership remained the main method of privatization of social sector firms, but there was a notable differentiation in the dynamics of privatization. This is due primarily to the fact that the new laws were adopted, and so came into force, at very different times, between 1991 and as late as 1994. In each of these countries privatization, and so also employee ownership, has reached a very different stage.

3.1 Privatization in Croatia

In Croatia, the early adoption of a new privatization law, and the short time limit for the submission of privatization programmes by enterprises, have facilitated a relatively rapid process of property transformation.[27] By the end of 1994, out of some 3,000 social sector enterprises planned for privatization, 2,900 had submitted their privatization programmes, of which 2,601 had received approval from the Croatian Privatization Fund (CPF),[28] and 2,452 had completed their property transformation.

Basic information on these 2,452 enterprises is presented in *Table 10.2*, where enterprises are grouped according to the degree of effective privatization, that is, the portion of their unprivatized capital which has been

---

[26] Further details on the privatization results until the end of 1992, can be found in Uvalic (1994) and (1995).

[27] Property transformation of enterprises essentially means the elimination of capital in social property through its transformation into either private or state property.

[28] The remaining programmes were either in the final phase of elaboration, or had been rejected.

Table 10.2 Information on the 2,452 firms which had completed property transformation by 31 December 1994, Croatia

	No transfers to funds	Min. share transferred to funds	Maj. share transferred to funds	Total average
Firms				
Number	1 145	921	386	2,452
% of total	46.7	37.6	15.7	100.00
Estimated value				
DM million	2 024	12 242	9 394	23 660
% of total	8.6	51.7	39.7	100.00
Method of capital transformation (% of total)				
Sales	87.68	49.04	16.70	39.50
Transfers to:				
– CPF	0	22.15	50.73	31.60
– pension funds	0	11.07	25.37	15.80
Number of shareholders	98 524	360 324	103 674	562 522
of which 'small' shareholders				
– number	–	–	–	550 000
– capital share (%)	58.4	38.6	7.0	34.7
Average number of buyers/firm	86	391	269	229

Sources: Hrvatski Fond za Privatizaciju (1995), Table 2, and p. 2; and Ostovic and Gracanin (1994), p. 22.

transferred to government funds: (1) enterprises privatized with no capital transfers to funds; (2) enterprises privatized with a minority capital share transferred to funds (less than 50%); and (3) enterprises only partially privatized, with a majority capital share transferred to funds (more than 50%). In these 2,452 enterprises, almost 40% of capital has been privatized through the sale of shares or assets, where employee subscription at a discount has been the prevalent method. However, since according to the Croatian law all unsold (unsubscribed) capital was to be transferred to government funds, an even more substantial share – 47.4% of total capital – was transferred to the Croatian Privatization Fund and to the two pension funds (31.6% and 15.8% respectively).

Enterprises belonging to the first group – those privatized without any transfers of capital to funds – represent almost half (46.7%) of the firms that have completed property transformation; yet they account for less than 9% of the total capital of these firms, suggesting that it is mainly small, labour-intensive enterprises that have been completely privatized so far. Large and medium-sized, capital-intensive firms, on the other hand, are lagging behind, as insufficient demand for shares on the part of employees and other potential investors has led to the automatic transfer of an important part of their capital to government funds: on average, 33% in firms with a minority share, and as much as 76% of total capital in firms with a majority share.

At the end of 1994, these privatizing firms had some 562,000 shareholders of whom almost all (550,000 or 98%) were small shareholders – those who subscribed shares at a discount, to a value not exceeding DM 20,000. Initially, most shareholders were present and former employees,[29] although in the meantime some of these shares have been sold. Following the legalization in 1993 of the trading of contracts for subscribed shares, by the end of 1994 some 14,428 contracts (around 2.4% of the total) had been sold. In many cases, shares were sold primarily to enterprise managers and directors. Press articles have reported some malpractice in this regard: directors and managers interested in obtaining control over a given firm often tried to persuade workers to sell their shares, or to persuade pensioners to subscribe shares on their behalf in the first place; they also received highly preferential credits from banks for this purpose, in exchange for the bank obtaining a share in enterprise equity. These practices suggest that in quite a few cases, firms actually ended up being owned primarily by their managers and/or directors (although there are no statistics to confirm this hypothesis).

Small shareholders have subscribed shares worth approximately DM 7.5 billion (or around 80% of total capital sold). Due to the high discounts, these sales effectively involved a substantial element of free distribution: since the average discount was 40%, around DM 3 billion in shares has in this way been freely transferred to employees (Ostovic and Gracanin, 1994, p. 16).

Despite these generous provisions, the capital stake of small shareholders remains modest, as they have on average subscribed less than 35% of total capital of these privatizing enterprises (see *Table 10.2*). Only in the first group of firms (those with no transfers of capital to funds) will small shareholders become the dominant owners once the shares are fully repaid: they will hold, on average, 58.4% of total capital. In the other two groups, employees have

---

[29] Although the possibility of subscriptions at privileged terms was offered not only to present and former employees of privatizing firms, but also to employees in enterprises not planned for privatization, the first category had priority and thus the largest part of shares has indeed been subscribed by employees of privatizing enterprises.

Table 10.3 Contracts concluded with shareholders by the end of December 1994, Croatia

	Number	Value (DM million)
All contracts	610 513	9 793
of which:		
Sold at a discount		
number	560 985	8 488
percentage	91.9	86.7
Completely paid (by 31.12.94)		
number	69 642	1 276
percentage	11.4	13.0

Source: Hrvatski fond za privatizaciju (1995), p. 7.

subscribed a minority capital holding. In enterprises with less than 50% of capital transferred to funds, small shareholders will become owners of, on average, 38.6% of capital; while in enterprises with a majority share transferred to funds, of only 7%. Whereas in the first group of firms, the average number of buyers per firm was 86, in the other two groups their number has been much higher – 391 and 269 respectively – again confirming that enterprises belonging to these two groups are mainly large, capital-intensive firms (*Table 10.2*). By the end of 1994, 610,513 share contracts had been concluded with new shareholders, to a total nominal value of DM 9.8 billion (*Table 10.3*).

Of the total number of contracts, as much as 91.9% represent discount share subscriptions to a nominal value of DM 8.5 billion (or 86.7% of the total value). Most subscribers used the possibility of deferred payment, but even so many small shareholders could not cope with their repayment schedule and began selling their shares on the black market, or simply giving up the subscribed shares, which led to a continuous decline in the number of shareholders (Cuckovic, 1994, p. 3). This is the main reason why the government offered further discounts, legalized the trading of shares before they were fully paid up, and in 1994 made it possible to draw on frozen foreign exchange deposits to pay for enterprise shares.[30] While these measures have gone some way towards facilitating the more rapid repayment of shares, by

[30] As already mentioned, around DM 4 billion of citizens' foreign currency deposits frozen in banks, were converted into public debt in 1991. Although the possibility for swapping frozen savings deposits for enterprise shares existed until 1992, it was thereafter abolished and reintroduced only in February 1994 in order to decrease the public debt.

the end of 1994 only 69,642 contracts (11% of the total), had been fully paid. Moreover, small shareholders have used their frozen foreign exchange deposits primarily for paying their instalments (see below).

The Croatian Privatization Fund has been offering shares from its portfolio on the Zagreb stock exchange twice a week, but only a very small percentage have been sold. At the end of October 1994, the CPF still had in its portfolio capital worth some DM 6.5 billion, or 89% of the value of transferred shares; of the remaining 11%, less than 1% was sold for cash, 5% was sold in exchange for frozen foreign exchange deposits, 2% was distributed to war invalids, while the rest was transferred to the main petrochemical company (INA) or used for the regeneration of the health care system (Ostovic and Gracanin, 1994, p. 35). Frozen foreign currency savings deposits have been the main means of payment for shares: by the end of 1994, they had accounted for almost 75% of all payments for shares, in comparison with only 25% in cash (in Croatian Kunas, in foreign currency, or in bonds) (see Croatian Privatization Fund, 1995, p. 8).[31]

As we said at the beginning, the process of enterprise property transformation has been completed rather quickly in Croatia, but since almost half the capital of privatizing firms has become state property through transfers to government funds, the privatization process as a whole is far from completed. Such an outcome has frequently given rise to the criticism that, through the replacement of social property by state property, the Croatian economy, rather than having been privatized, has in fact been renationalized. Nevertheless, this privatization strategy has achieved the main objective of the Act on Property Transformation: the complete elimination of social property from enterprise balance sheets.

The Croatian government, disappointed with the results of CPF sales on the stock exchange, prepared a new privatization law which was finally adopted on 1 March 1996 (see Cuckovic, 1996). Among the main novelties of the law is the implementation of a 'mini' mass privatization scheme (namely, the free distribution of vouchers convertible into enterprise shares) to the most disadvantaged groups of the population (displaced persons, the disabled, families of war victims) in which about 300,000 people are eligible to participate; the setting up of privatization investment funds; the privatization of some large state-owned enterprises; allowing the sale of shares from the Croatian Privatization Fund's portfolio below their face value; and further

---

[31] Until the beginning of November 1994, the proceeds of the CPF from the sale of shares (both for cash and for frozen foreign exchange deposits) have been some DM 416 million, although the total proceeds from privatization (including initial sales to private shareholders) have been much higher, around DM 1.65 billion (but here again, only around 26% was paid in cash, and 74% in citizens' foreign exchange deposits) (Ostovic and Gracanin, 1994, pp. 23, 36).

incentives for small shareholders through the extension of the repayment period from five to twenty years (Cuckovic, 1996).

One case study of an employee buy-out suggests that the transformation of the enterprise has been rather successful (see Ostovic and Gracanin, 1994, pp. 19-20). The employees of a hotel company on the Adriatic coast, together with a few private individuals, each subscribed up to DM 20,000 worth of shares and up to 50% of the enterprise's total estimated value (and therefore the maximum permitted by law), while the other half was offered for sale through public tender. Since no bids came in, the unsold capital was transferred to the three government funds. The company then prepared a restructuring programme, and the management, in concert with members of the supervisory board which represents the owners, decided to sell two restaurants and one hotel immediately, as these were not part of the company's core business. Several night-clubs were leased out and four hotels were offered to joint ventures, two of which had a foreign interest of above 50%, the other two one of below 50%. The company retained the proceeds of these transactions for revitalizing other units and subsidiaries.

3.2 Privatization in FR Yugoslavia

In the two republics of the FR Yugoslavia, Serbia and Montenegro, the same federal legislation was used in the first year of privatization. With the adoption of the new republican laws, different privatization procedures began to be applied, and privatization statistics are now being collected separately by the two government agencies in charge of privatization. The two republics must therefore be examined separately.

3.2.1 Privatization in Serbia

In Serbia, privatization proceeded most quickly during the initial period, while the Federal Act on Social Capital was still in force. In only one year, from August 1990 to August 1991, a total of 1,210 enterprises commenced property transformation, around one-third of all enterprises in the social sector (*Table 10.4*).

The more restrictive Serbian privatization law has led to a general slowing down of property transformation: in the first four months (until the end of 1991) only 34 enterprises started property transformation, and only another 139 firms during the whole of 1992. The process speeded up slightly in 1993, primarily because of provisions ill-adapted to hyper-inflationary conditions – the revaluation of the unpaid portion of subscribed shares only once a year – which rendered the subscription of shares extremely favourable; thus in 1993, another 465 enterprises started property transformation. In 1994, there was

Table 10.4 Property transformation of enterprises, Serbia, August 1990–April 1994

	Federal Law		Serbian Law		TOTAL		
	Aug.– Dec. 1990	Jan.– Aug. 1991	Aug.– Dec. 1991	1992	1993	Jan.– April 1994	1990– April 1994
1) Transformed enterprises							
Total	169	1 051	34	139	469	46	1 904
– Central Serbia	63	617	19	76	255	21	1 051
– Voivodina	106	431	15	59	200	23	834
– Kosovo	0	3	0	4	10	2	19
Total		1 220			684		1 904
As % of social sector firms		33.17		27.8			60.97
2) Repeated transformations*							253
3) Transformations still in progress							921
TOTAL covered by transformation (1+2+3)							2 572
As % of social sector firms							69.93

* Enterprises transformed according to the federal law, which because of irregularities then had to repeat transformation according to the Serbian law. These repeated transformations must be deducted from the total as they appear twice.
Source: Zec (1994a), pp. 228–9, 233–4, 239–40.

again a drastic slow-down, primarily because the right to buy shares at a discount had expired in August 1993: in the first four months of 1994, only 46 enterprises undertook property transformation. During the entire period, from August 1990 until April 1994, 1,904 enterprises completed transformation, and another 921 were waiting for the approval of their transformation programmes by the Republican Agency.[32] Altogether, firms undergoing property transformation represent around 70% of the social sector firms which existed in 1990.

The privatization process is very unevenly distributed between the various regions of Serbia. Voivodina is ahead of other parts of Serbia, with almost

[32] The Republican Agency for the Evaluation of the Value of Social Capital, as the main institution in charge of privatization in Serbia.

Table 10.5 Enterprises undergoing property transformation by sector, Serbia, August 1990–April 1994

	SERBIA TOTAL	Central Serbia	Voivo- dina	Kosovo	As % of all social firms in the sector
TOTAL	2 572	1 469	811	253	69.93
Industry	1 187	672	367	121	79.77
Agriculture	204	103	88	13	48.92
Construction	227	145	39	32	53.92
Transport	122	69	41	12	68.54
Trade	388	233	81	36	65.43
Services	155	99	46	10	72.43
Other	289	148	149	29	78.75

Source: Zec (1994a), pp. 239–40.

82% of its enterprises involved in the transformation process, in comparison with 62% in Central Serbia. In Kosovo, although formally 83% of all social sector firms are involved in property transformation, only 19 enterprises have completed the process, 18 on the basis of autonomous programmes. The majority of enterprises (235) are being transformed directly by the government through the transfer of their capital, either to other enterprises or to the Republican Development Fund (Zec, 1994a, p. 236). As to the sectoral distribution of privatization, agriculture has the lowest percentage of enterprises involved in property transformation, with 49%, while the highest percentage is in industry, with almost 80% (*Table 10.5*).

Property transformation of a social sector firm has most frequently entailed the sale of some shares to private shareholders (employees) and the modification of its status to joint-stock (shareholding) company in mixed ownership (combination of social and private capital). This has led only to very partial privatizations, although some of these firms have also been completely privatized. On average, the capital structure in transformed enterprises was 80% private and 20% social capital (Zec, 1994a, p. 241). However, as already mentioned, the 1994 measures on capital revaluation are likely to reverse these proportions.

Given the provisions of both the federal and the Serbian privatization laws favouring employee ownership, these firms have been transformed almost exclusively through share sales to insiders on preferential terms, most frequently by way of a new share issue. By mid-1994, there were around

525,000 shareholders in privatizing firms in Serbia, mostly their own workers, managers and directors. The transformed enterprises represent 42% of total capital, and employ around 38% of all workers in the social sector of the Serbian economy. Around 80% of workers employed in these privatizing firms have subscribed shares (Zec, 1994a, p. 241), indicating substantial interest on the part of insiders in becoming shareholders.

A number of Serbian enterprises, partly or fully privatized through sales to employees, have performed rather well in the post-privatization period (for example, Galenika, Hemofarma, Metalac). The company Metalac from Gornji Milanovac has undertaken a number of measures which have improved its economic performance, including substantial investment (only recently, it has invested some DM 40 million), product diversification, the establishment of a quality control system, and worker retraining (see Djuricin, 1994).

Several empirical studies have been undertaken in order to compare the performance of enterprises in mixed ownership with those in social ownership. One of these studies, based on a sample of 1,137 industrial enterprises in social and 731 in mixed ownership in 1992, uses factor analysis to determine the relative importance of various indicators for the two groups of firms (see Labus and Kovacevic, 1994, pp. 250–7). The main findings were that for enterprises in mixed ownership, property ownership was the most important factor, followed by profitability; while for social sector enterprises, very different factors were given priority. Moreover, the mixed firms were two and a half times more profitable than the social sector firms (20% higher than the average).[33]

In the meantime, the obligatory capital revaluation procedure introduced in mid-1994 has blocked the further implementation of property transformation (see Mijatovic, 1995). Capital revaluation will also have very negative consequences, as it will lead to a drastic reduction of the share of private capital in privatizing firms, and the transformation of social into private capital will, in many cases, simply be cancelled (Vujacic, 1995).[34] Moreover, given the requirement that, for the organizational transformation of an

[33] For similar findings, see Bukvic (1995).

[34] Around 1,774 enterprises are covered by the process of revaluation: 876 which used the Federal law, 302 which used both the Federal and the Serbian law, and 566 which only used the Serbian law. By mid-1995, most of them had prepared the revaluation forms; according to a preliminary evaluation of one third of enterprise revaluation forms, the following results could be expected: in the first group (firms using only the Federal law), the proportions between social and share capital will on average be 62 to 38; in the second group (combination of Federal and Serbian law), the ratio will be 64 to 36; and in the third group (only Serbian law), 51 to 49. However, according to an alternative estimate (Vujacic, 1995), only 20–40% of capital will remain private in the first group of firms; 10% in the second group; and in the third, firms which started transformation in 1991 or 1992 will be left with a maximum of 5–10%, while those which started the process in 1993, with no more than 1-2% of share capital (Vujacic, 1995, p. 10).

enterprise to take place, a minimum 10% of social capital must be subscribed, capital revaluation will also mean that many enterprises which have already gone from social to mixed ownership, will be forced back into the social sector.

These are the main reasons why, by the end of 1995, privatization had again become the subject of widespread debate. It was hoped that a new privatization law would open new possibilities for accelerating the process, but the federal privatization law adopted in May 1996 does not provide the necessary framework.

3.2.2 Privatization in Montenegro

Initially, the transformation of social sector firms in Montenegro proceeded at a much slower pace than in Serbia. From August 1990 until July 1993, only 54 enterprises were transformed (less than 12% of all social sector enterprises), 26 according to the Federal Act on Social Capital and 28 according to the Montenegran law. In another 92 enterprises, property transformation was in process, and so by July 1993 a total of 146 firms (or only 31% of all social sector enterprises) were involved in the property transformation process. As to the sectoral distribution of these firms, services accounted for almost 47%, closely followed by industry (45%), with the construction sector (18%) bringing up the rear (*Table 10.6*).

Table 10.6 Enterprise property transformation by sector, Montenegro, August 1990–July 1993

| | Federal law | Monte-negran law | Trans-formed firms | Trans-form-ation in progress firms | Covered by transformation | |
					No. of firms	As % of social sector firms
TOTAL	26	28	54	92	146	31.53
Industry	6	10	16	28	44	44.90
Agriculture	1	2	3	10	13	36.11
Construction	1	2	3	3	6	17.65
Transport	3	0	3	5	8	30.77
Trade	5	9	14	18	32	35.96
Services	3	2	5	16	21	46.67
Other	7	3	10	12	22	16.30

Source: Zec (1994b), p. 306.

Table 10.7 Property transformation of enterprises, Montenegro, by September 1995

Enterprises	Number of firms	% of total	% of firms planned for privatization
Total number	365	100.0	–
Excluded from transformation*	42	11.5	–
Planned for transformation	323	88.5	100.0
Completely transformed	136	37.3	42.1
Almost completely transformed	112	30.7	34.7
In the initial phase of transformation	75	20.5	23.2

* Mainly public utilities (railways, electricity, the port of Bar, post, telecommunications), which will be transformed in a special privatization programme. The figures do not include social services (the so-called non-economic sectors such as education, culture, health).
Source: Agency of Montenegro for Economic Restructuring and Foreign Investment, Podgorica, October 1995.

One of the main reasons for such poor initial results was that the complex procedure incorporated in the 1992 Montenegran law for the appraisal of enterprise capital value, to be expressed in Deutschmarks. In most cases, capital value was set too high, reportedly by more than four times its book value on average (Zec, 1994b, p. 307). Moreover, since capital to be privatized was expressed in a foreign currency, the offer price remained relatively stable, with the result that no inflationary gains were to be had from share subscription under the hyper-inflationary conditions prevailing in 1992–93 (unlike in Serbia, where capital value was expressed in dinars and revalued only once a year). These provisions of the Montenegran law strongly discouraged potential buyers: inflationary gains had, in fact, been the main factor which had pushed Serbian firms into privatization during this period.

The process of property transformation has greatly accelerated over the last two years, after amendments to the privatization law were adopted in late 1994. The amendments introduced a number of new provisions meant to speed up privatization and offered more generous provisions to insiders, primarily the possibility for the firm to distribute freely up to 10% of its capital to its employees. By the end of September 1995, 136 firms (or 42% of enterprises planned for privatization) had completed property transformation, while all the remaining firms were in the process of being transformed (*Table 10.7*).

However, as in Serbia (and elsewhere), property transformation has in most cases not meant effective privatization. By mid-1993, only about 20% of the estimated value of capital in privatizing enterprises had been subscribed, some capital had been transferred to banks through debt–equity swaps, while the largest part of enterprise property had been transferred to the three government funds (Zec 1994b, p. 307). The main purchasers of enterprise shares were employees and, to a lesser extent, private individuals, within the global limit of 30% on sales on preferential terms. However, due to the economic crisis, in many cases the new shareholders had to postpone repayment (Zec 1994b, p. 307). The principal owners of enterprises in mid-1993 were the three funds, the government, and the banks, for which reason the law was revised in 1994, since when the situation has improved. It is reported that by late 1995 an average of 35% of shares in transformed enterprises had been subscribed or sold.

Because of the unattractiveness of the terms for employee share sales and the overcentralisation of the whole transformation process – which led to the transfer of the largest part of enterprise capital to government funds – employees appear to be extremely disillusioned. In common with other parts of the former Yugoslavia, workers in Montenegro felt that they were already part-owners of their firms and so expected to be offered more favourable conditions. This is probably the main reason why, today, many employees in Montenegro oppose privatization.

Strong employee resistance to privatization is suggested by a recent sociological survey, based on a questionnaire given to 500 employees, two-thirds of whom work in privatizing enterprises (see Agencija za prestruktuiranje privrede i strana ulaganja Vlade Crne Gore, 1995). The respondents were asked a number of questions directly related to privatization. To the question whether they were in favour of privatization, 45% gave a positive answer, 39% a negative answer, while 14% were undecided. Only 22% of the respondents preferred rapid privatization, 28% were in favour of a more gradual approach, 20% were undecided, while 24% were against any form of privatization. As to which property form should be dominant in Montenegro, only 24% of respondents chose private property in contrast with the 48% who favoured mixed property; 17% preferred social property and 9% state property. Resistance to privatization is strongest among unskilled workers, decreasing according to level of qualifications, the main reason being the fear of job losses. Among the respondents in favour of privatization, the most preferred method was sales to insiders (40%); other methods were favoured by a much smaller percentage of respondents: 11% were for external sales to private individuals and 10% for free distribution of vouchers.

3.3 Privatization in FYR Macedonia

More enterprises initiated privatization on the basis of federal legislation in Macedonia than in any other former Yugoslav republic. Between August 1990 and August 1991, around 450 social sector enterprises (41%) commenced privatization, through either the free distribution or the sale on preferential terms of shares to employees.[35] The first method was most frequent, the largest part of shares being freely distributed to workers as part of their regular wages (as envisaged by the Federal Act on Personal Incomes). Moreover, most of these firms were only very partially privatized and the dominant part of their capital remained social.[36] Nevertheless, these early privatizations through employee ownership effectively led to a much more rapid expansion of the mixed sector in Macedonia than elsewhere (Uvalic, 1994).

After the Federal Act on Social Capital was suspended in September 1991, the privatization process was practically blocked for three years. The new privatization law was adopted only in June 1993, the effective implementation of which was further delayed by some preliminary operations, including the setting up of the necessary institutions. The Agency for the Transformation of Enterprises with Social Property was set up in October 1993, and a special commission was assigned to investigate all privatizations undertaken according to the federal legislation. Once the commission had completed its reports, small and medium-sized firms were given one year, large firms two years, to prepare and submit their privatization programmes.

Because of this preparatory phase, the first privatization programmes were submitted only at the end of 1994, and property transformation effectively started only in 1995. The results achieved so far are quite impressive. Although at the beginning of 1995, the privatization process proceeded rather slowly, it speeded up substantially in the second half of the year. By the end of 1995, 82% of the enterprises planned for privatization (82% of their capital value and 96% of their employees) had already begun the process (*Table 10.8*). A possible explanation for such rapid results is that a number of these firms had started privatization in 1990–91 and were able to adjust their programmes to the provisions of the new Macedonian law quite quickly. Nevertheless, only around half (49.7%) of the total number of firms planned for privatization have been completely privatized, representing only 26% of employees and 28% of capital value (*Table 10.8*).

It is interesting to note that, contrary to the experience of many other countries, large firms were the first to submit privatization programmes. The limited interest of small and medium-sized enterprises led the Agency to offer to pay the asset valuation costs of the first 100 small enterprises that expressed an interest, an initiative which proved successful. In fact, the small enterprises are now the most numerous among those that have started property

---

[35] In a sample of 198 firms which had started privatization by 30 June 1991, the method of shares issued to insiders was used in almost 88% of cases, and 98.8% of shares was subscribed by present employees (see Uvalic, 1994).

[36] In a sample of 198 firms which had started privatization by 30 June 1991, social capital still represented, on average, 69% of total enterprise capital (see Uvalic, 1994).

Table 10.8 Enterprises planned for privatization and results so far, FYR of Macedonia, December 1995

	Number of firms	Number of employees	Value of capital (DM million)
Planned for privatization	1 216	228 850	3.299
Privatized	604	59 966	932
As % of those planned	49.7	26.2	28.3
Privatizations in progress	396	158 775	1.805
As % of those planned	32.6	69.4	54.7
Total (privatized and in course of privatization)	1 000	218 741	2.737
As % of those planned	82.3	95.6	83.0

Source: Agency for the Transformation of Enterprises with Social Property of the Republic of Macedonia, as reported in Vukotic and Sukovic (1996), pp. 86–7; and author's own calculations.

transformation. Already by April 1995, out of a total of 163 approved privatization programmes, 71% were from small, and another 16% from medium-sized enterprises. Most small enterprises have been privatized by employee buy-out, although some small and medium-sized firms have been bought by external owners, mainly domestic private enterprises and entrepreneurs (Fiti and Hadzi Vasileva-Markovska, 1995). A special restructuring programme is being implemented for 25 large loss-making firms, with the collaboration of World Bank experts (Fiti, 1995).

Analysis of the sectoral distribution of privatized and privatizing enterprises shows that the best results so far have been obtained in trade, followed by construction and crafts; in these three sectors the majority of enterprises planned for privatization have already been privatized (*Table 10.9*). The transformation process has been much slower in industry, where only 37% of the total number of firms has completed the process. The situation is similar in other sectors.

The end of 1995 should have marked the beginning of the direct involvement of the Agency in the privatization of large companies, as the deadline for submitting privatization programmes for these firms had expired. The Agency is also directly involved in the privatization of the remaining small and medium-sized firms that have failed to start privatization. Thus all remaining firms planned for privatization should be privatized during 1996.

According to the March 1995 Report of the Macedonian Transformation Agency, the main problem encountered so far in the privatization process is the resistance of firms – that is, employees – to commencing transformation. As in Montenegro, part of this resistance derives from objections in principle, primarily because privatization has in many countries actually led to the transfer of large parts of social capital to the state. There are also

Table 10.9 Sectoral distribution of privatized and privatizing enterprises, FYR of Macedonia, December 1995

Sector	Already privatized enterprises		Enterprises in process of being privatized	
	Number of firms	% of planned	Number of firms	% of planned
Industry	149	37.0	223	55.3
Construction	65	55.6	31	26.5
Trade	251	65.2	62	16.1
Transport	25	39.7	19	30.2
Financial & other services	56	46.7	31	25.8
Crafts	33	56.9	11	19.0
Catering & tourism	25	35.7	19	27.1
TOTAL	604	49.7	396	32.6

Source: Agency for Transformation of the Republic of Macedonia, as reported in Vukotic and Sukovic (1996), pp. 86–7; and author's own calculations.

organizational problems, including the lack of adequate legislation and institutions, and fully functioning capital markets. Some surveys also suggest resistance to privatization by the general public. According to one of these surveys, full support for privatization was given only by 15.5% respondents, whereas one-third considered that state property ought to be the dominant form of property in Macedonia (Institut ekonomskih nauka, *MAP*, 1995, no. 11, p. 16).

3.4 Privatization in Slovenia

In 1990, only 17 Slovenian firms initiated privatization through preferential share issues to insiders (Korze, 1992): the federal law provision on discount sales to insiders was suspended as early as October 1990. Nevertheless, the federal legislation was used for commercial sales and for forms of self-privatization through transfers of social capital from one legal entity to another, usually a newly established private firm. Although all cases of self-privatization were later re-examined, they initially led to a substantial reduction of the share of social capital, from 97% of the total in 1989, to 76% in 1992 (Bojnec, 1995, p. 14).

Due to the long privatization debate, the new privatization law was not adopted until November 1992. Since the law was again amended in summer 1993, privatization was effectively launched only in the second half of that

Table 10.10 Enterprises undergoing privatization under the Act on Ownership Transformation, Slovenia (1993 balance sheets)

	Whole economy	Enterprises planned for privatization	Privatization programmes received by end of 1994	
			Number	% of those planned
Number of enterprises	27 902*	1 345	1 211	90.04
Number of employees	480 625	231 750	206 848	89.25
Social capital (DM million)	27 168 185	10 168 864	8 971 488	88.23
Total revenues (DM million)	44 651 344	17 423 523	15 646 590	89.80
Export revenues (DM million)	9 431 342	4 265 567	3 951 329	92.63

Source: Rop (1995), p. 29, except for * which is from Bojnec (1995), p. 27.

year, when enterprises started preparing and submitting their privatization programmes. By the end of 1994, privatization programmes had been prepared and submitted to the Privatization Agency for approval by some 1,211 firms, over 90% of the enterprises planned for privatization (*Table 10.10*).

It should be noted, however, that a number of enterprises have been excluded from privatization, and will be subject to specific privatization programmes at a later stage.[37] As can be seen from *Table 10.10*, firms planned for privatization in the 1992 privatization law represent less than half of the total number of employees, value of social capital, revenues, and export revenues of the whole Slovenian economy.

Out of the 1,211 submitted privatization programmes, the Agency had approved 428 by the end of 1994, of which 233 commenced implementation. In these 233 enterprises, around 50% of social capital was privatized through the internal distribution of shares and the internal buy-out method, only 11.2% through the public sale of shares, while the rest was transferred to the three funds (*Table 10.11*).

---

[37] Banks and insurance companies, public service and economic infrastructure enterprises, cooperatives and a part of the food processing industry, gambling activities, companies in bankruptcy proceedings (Bojnec, 1995, p. 24).

Table 10.11 Enterprise privatization programmes, Slovenia, (end of 1994)

	Programmes approved	Programmes already processed
Number of programmes	428	233
Privatization method (% of value of social capital)		
Internal buy-outs	22.58	30.83
Internal distribution	16.23	19.39
Public sale of shares	18.10	11.21
Transfers to:		
Development Fund	18.96	19.99
Compensation Fund	9.48	9.24
Pension Fund	9.46	9.34
Voluntary transfers to		
Development Fund	2.73	0.00
Former owners	2.03	0.00
Sale of all assets	0.43	0.00
TOTAL	100.00	100.00

Source: Rop (1995), p. 30.

The 428 privatization programmes approved by the end of 1994 show that in the majority of enterprises, the majority shareholding will be held by internal owners (*Table 10.12*): in over 81% of enterprises, internal owners will jointly own 60%, and in another 4%, more than 50% of enterprise capital. Dominant employee ownership will be present in 85% of these enterprises, while external owners – financial institutions and dispersed owners – will have a majority ownership in 15% (*Table 10.12*).

If we consider the value of capital owned by insiders, the largest part (44%) will be concentrated in those firms where employees have a 60% shareholding, relatively little (6%) in firms holding 50–60%; the remaining 50% will be in firms with minority employee ownership (*Table 10.12*). Nevertheless, insiders will not own the dominant share of the overall capital of the enterprises involved; internally-owned capital will represent only 43.8% of the total capital value of the 428 privatizing enterprises. Insiders will be the dominant owners primarily in small and medium-sized firms, while in capital-intensive firms external owners, including funds, will dominate (see Rop, 1995, p. 21).

By April 1995, almost all the Slovenian firms concerned had prepared their privatization programmes, 647 of which had been approved by the Agency.

Table 10.12 Internal ownership in 428 enterprises whose privatization programmes were approved by the end of 1994, Slovenia

Share of internal ownership (%)	Number	Enterprises (%)	Value of capital owned by insiders (%)
60	349	81.62	43.71
50–60	17	3.94	6.33
25–50	48	11.16	23.94
Up to 25	14	3.28	26.02
TOTAL	428	100.00	100.00

Source: Rop (1995), p. 32.

Some 100 firms which have not submitted a programme will be privatized according to programmes to be designed by the Agency (SKLAD, 1995). The programmes approved by April 1995 again confirm the key role of employee ownership in Slovenia: more than 90% of these enterprises will use internal distribution of shares and internal buy-outs as one of the privatization methods. Only about 120 companies will use the method of public offers to domestic and foreign investors; by April 1995, 28 enterprises had already been partly privatized through public share offers (SKLAD, 1995).[38] Surprisingly, in only three of the submitted privatization programmes was the involvement of foreign investors anticipated (SKLAD, 1995).[39]

By March 1995, 82% of the issued ownership certificates had been invested by private individuals: 42% in the shares of privatizing enterprises and 40% in Privatization Investment Funds. Forty privatization investment funds have been set up – usually by state-owned banks – which are managed by a number of privatization management companies (23 such companies were set up in 1994). Since then, there has been a substantial concentration of shares in a limited number of privatization investment funds, particularly those owned by banks and insurance companies.[40]

[38] Enterprise shares through public offers were mostly paid with citizens' ownership certificates, rather than in cash (Bojnec, 1995, p. 23).

[39] However, it should be noted that in 1991–93, some 15 Slovenian firms sold part of their capital to foreign partners, establishing equity joint-ventures; the foreign partner's share in three large companies, among the first sold to foreigners, was between 76% and 80% (see Bojnec, 1995, p. 16).

[40] Privatization Investment Funds of the four largest Privatization Management Companies succeeded in collecting 54% of all ownership certificates, while the 12 largest Privatization Management Companies have collected more than 90% of all ownership certificates (Rop, 1995, p. 22).

The Development Fund has also started to sell shares from its portfolio. Out of some 98 loss-making enterprises, which were taken over by the Development Fund already in 1992, 38 enterprises were sold in 1993 (Bojnec, 1995).[41] In addition, the Development Fund started to sell the capital of all privatizing enterprises – usually 20% of enterprise capital had to be transferred to the Fund. At the first auction in December 1994, the Fund sold shares in 60 firms, and at the second, in March 1995, in 108, to a total value of US$ 126 million (SKLAD, 1995; Bojnec, 1995). In both cases privatization investment funds were the major purchasers.

In conclusion, employee shareholding is likely to be very diffused in Slovenia once the privatization process is completed. Employees will probably end up being the dominant owners in 90% of all enterprises planned for privatization, primarily in labour-intensive firms. In capital-intensive firms, the dominant share will be in the hands of external agents, mainly institutional owners.

A case study of a Slovenian firm suggests that employee ownership can very well be combined with foreign investment (see Smith, 1994). IBP Zalec, the Coca-Cola bottler for Slovenia, was privatized in 1994 as a fifty-fifty joint venture between Coca-Cola Co. and the Slovenians (with 40% of the shares on the domestic side being held by government funds and 60% by employees). The agreement was that, in the long run, employees would continue to hold at most 25% of the shares, and that the foreign partner would purchase all the shares the employees wished to sell. Coca-Cola representatives favoured employee ownership primarily because of its likely motivation effects, but also as a tactic to terminate the state presence as quickly as possible. It was anticipated that the foreign partner would provide a significant amount of financing in order to shorten the buy-out period for the shares subscribed by employees (Smith, 1994).

4 CONCLUSION

When the transition to a market economy started in the successor states of the former Yugoslavia, the institutional setting in all of them was quite similar. These countries had inherited a system of self-management which entailed two principal forms of economic democracy: the workers' right to participate in decision-making and to share in enterprise profits. At the same time, the

---

[41] These loss-making enterprises were sold mostly to private entrepreneurs and enterprises (12 firms), to managers (8 firms), managers and workers (8 firms), to banks and financial institutions (3 firms), to foreigners (3 firms), to non-privatized enterprises (3 firms) and to a mixed foreign and domestic company (1 firm) (see Bojnec, 1995).

third main form of economic democracy – employee ownership – was completely absent, since the bulk of enterprises, contributing over 90% of gross domestic product, were in the form of non-private (so-called 'social') property (see Uvalic, 1995).

Five years later, the situation is very different, if not completely reversed. The general tendency has been to replace the system of self-management with standard company laws, envisaging organizational and decision-making structures similar to those in the West. Although in some countries, such as Slovenia, employees have also been given some say in decision-making; while in others, such as Serbia, self-management has been partly preserved,[42] the extent of employee participation is in both cases more limited than under the previous system. Similarly, profit-sharing has generally been of limited importance in recent years in most of these countries, largely because many enterprises are unprofitable, although it continues to be applied by some firms on a voluntary basis. By contrast, employee ownership, which previously had no role whatsoever, has been spreading thanks to privatization in all countries, so replacing the system of self-management as the most important form of economic democracy.

Empirical evidence on privatization in the countries of the former Yugoslavia has shown that preferential sale of shares to employees has been the most frequently used method of privatization (apart from the obligatory transfer of some capital to government funds). This is not surprising, given the highly attractive provisions for employee purchase in all the privatization laws. The actual extent of employee ownership is, however, rather different, since some privatization laws encourage, while others indirectly prevent, dominant employee ownership. In this regard, Slovenia has probably been most pragmatic, offering the most favourable conditions for the spread of employee ownership, even if this means that most Slovenian firms will have a majority employee shareholding. Although the privatization strategy based on substantial employee ownership may have shortcomings, it is certainly a better solution than the maintenance of the status quo, or the transfer of a large portion of shares to government funds which subsequently cannot be sold.

Generally speaking, the highly advantageous terms on which shares were sold to employees in these countries were crucial to the success of the process, not only because of the heritage of the self-management system, but also because of the shortage of domestic capital and the very difficult economic conditions of employees in most countries. In the countries of the former Yugoslavia, employee ownership was not only the most politically feasible

---

[42] Slovenia has adopted a co-determination law providing for employee representatives on company boards, while Serbia has maintained workers' decisional rights in those enterprises which still have social property, proportional to the share of social property.

privatization method, it was also the one most likely to lead to rapid results. Had the conditions for employee purchases been less advantageous, the privatization process would certainly have been delayed even further.

REFERENCES

Agencija za prestruktuiranje privrede i strana ulaganja Vlade Crne Gore (1995), 'Otpori privatizaciji u Republici Crnoj Gori', Agencija Partner, Belgrade, May.

Bojnec, S. (1995), 'Company management and privatization in Slovenia', The Leuven Institute for Central and East European Studies, *Working Paper* no. 42/95.

Bukvic, R. (1995), 'Efikasnost drustvenog, privatnog i mesovitog sektora industrije Srbije u 1994', *Ekonomika*, vol. XXXI, No. 9–10, September.

Croatian Privatization Fund (1995), 'Izvjesce o tijeku i rezultatima pretvorbe drustvenih poduzeca', Zagreb, January.

Cuckovic, N. (1994), 'Privatization process in Croatia: the new legislative solutions and the old problems?', *Reform Round Table Working Paper* No. 14, IRMO, Zagreb, September.

Cuckovic, N. (1995), 'Privatization process and its consequences for distribution of welfare: The case of Croatia', Paper prepared for the *EACES Workshop on Privatization and Distribution*, Trento, March.

Cuckovic, N. (1996), 'Institutional change, privatization and restructuring: how far has Croatia gone?', paper presented at the conference on Economic Reconstruction and Developmental Policies in the Yugoslav Successor States, Bristol, 27–28 June.

Djuricin, N.D. (1994), *Economies in Transition: Privatization and Related Issues*, Cornji Milanovac, Decje Novine.

Fiti, T. (1995), 'Problemi privatizacije i uloga drzave u periodu tranzicije', Paper prepared for the Conference *Economic prospects of the Balkans and South East Europe*, Peace and Crises Management Foundation, Paris, June.

Fiti, T. and V. Hadzi Vasileva-Markovska (1995), 'Small business development and the privatization process in the Republic of Macedonia', Paper prepared for the conference *SME Development Policy in Transition Economies*, University of Wolverhampton.

Institut ekonomskih nauka, *Mesecne analize i prognoze (MAP)*, various issues.

Korze, U. (1992), 'Decentralized privatization strategy: pitfalls and benefits – Slovenia', in M. Simoneti and A. Bohm (eds) (1992), *Privatization in Central & Eastern Europe 1991*, Central & Eastern European Privatization Network, Annual Conference Series no. 2, Ljubljana.

Labus, M. and Kovacevic, M. (1994), 'Privatizacija i porast efikasnosti', in M. Zec. B. Mijatovic, D. Djuricin, i N. Savic (eds) (1994).

Madzar, Lj. (ed.) (1995), *Projekat privatizacije u Srbiji – Osnov moderne trzisne privrede*, Belgrade, Unija poslodavaca Srbije.

Mencinger, J. (1995), 'The creation of capitalism in Slovenia', mimeo, Ljubljana.

Mijatovic, B. (1995), 'Privatizacija u Srbiji tokom 1994', Belgrade, mimeo.

Nuti, D.M. (1995), 'Employeeism: Corporate governance and employee share ownership in transitional economies', Paper prepared for the *Conference on Workers' Co-operatives*, Reggio Emilia, May 5.

Ostovic, D. and Gracanin, B. (1994), 'Privatization Report – 1994', Zagreb, Republic of Croatia, Croatian Privatization Fund, November.

Rop, A. (1995), 'Privatization in Slovenia: General framework for privatization in Slovenia', Ljubljana, CEEPN Academy, February, mimeo.

SKLAD (1995), 'Privatization in Slovenia', Ljubljana, Development Fund and Agency of the Republic of Slovenia.

Smith, Stephen C. (1994), 'On the law and economics of employee ownership in privatization in developing and transition economies', *Annals of Public and Co-operative Economy*, Vol. 64, No. 3.

Stojanova, V. (1995), 'Wrong therapy – influence of the privatization in creating the market economy and restructuring enterprises production and management', Paper presented at the conference *Economic prospects of the Balkans and South East Europe*, Peace and Crises Management Foundation, Paris, June.

Uvalic, M. (1992), *Investment and Property Rights in Yugoslavia – The Long Transition to a Market Economy*, Cambridge, Cambridge University Press.

Uvalic, M. (1994), 'Privatization in disintegrating East European States: The case of former Yugoslavia', Florence, European University Institute *Working Paper RSC* no. 94/11.

Uvalic, M. (1995), 'The former Yugoslavia: Workers' share-ownership in the self-management tradition', in D. Vaughan-Whitehead et al., *Workers' Financial Participation – East–West Experiences*, Geneva, International Labour Office, Labour–Management Relations Series no. 80.

Vujacic, I. (1995), 'Zaustavljena privatizacija: slucaj Srbije', Paper prepared for the Conference *Economic prospects of the Balkans and South East Europe*, Peace and Crises Management Foundation, Paris, June.

Vukotic, V. and Sukovic, D. (1996), *Privatizacija*, Institut drustvenih nauka, Beograd.

Zec, M. (1994a), 'Obuhvat, modeli i efekti privatizacije', in M. Zec. B. Mijatovic, D. Djuricin, i N. Savic (eds) (1994).

Zec, M. (1994b), 'Crna Gora', in M. Zec. B. Mijatovic, D. Djuricin, i N. Savic (eds.) (1994).

Zec, M., B. Mijatovic, D. Djuricin, i N. Savic (eds.) (1994), *Privatizacija – Nuznost ili sloboda izbora*, Belgrade, Jugoslovenska knjiga and Ekonomski institut.

Index